Date Due

THE
Seven Signs
of Ethical Collapse

Also by Marianne M. Jennings, J. D.

Nobody Fixes Real Carrot Sticks Anymore

Business Ethics: Cases and Readings

Board of Directors

*A Business Tale: A Story of Ethics, Choices, Success
(and a Very Large Rabbit)*

THE

Seven Signs
of Ethical Collapse

How to Spot Moral Meltdowns
in Companies . . . Before It's Too Late

Marianne M. Jennings, J.D.

St. Martin's Press
New York

www.stmartins.com

Library of Congress Cataloging-in-Publication Data

Jennings, Marianne.
The seven signs of ethical collapse : how to spot moral meltdowns in companies . . . before it's too late / Marianne M. Jennings. — 1st ed.
p. cm.
Includes index.
ISBN-13: 978-0-312-35430-5
ISBN-10: 0-312-35430-4
1. Business ethics. 2. Organizational effectiveness. I. Title.
HF5387. J47 2006
174' .4—dc22   2006041094

First Edition: August 2006

10 9 8 7 6 5 4 3 2 1

To those who fight
the good fight

Contents

Author's Note

Both guilty. Today as this book goes to press, Ken Lay was found guilty of all six charges of conspiracy and fraud, and Jeffrey Skilling was convicted of nineteen of twenty-eight charges of conspiracy, fraud, false statements, and insider trading. Mr. Lay was also found guilty on all four charges of bank fraud and false statements in a separate bench trial. The convictions covered everything from misrepresentations to auditors to falsehoods in discussions with analysts. In other words, the factual bases for the charges consisted of behavior that occurred while they were doing the day-to-day activities of CEOs. Both men now face maximum sentences at levels I cannot compute without the aid of a calculator.

Their own testimony was perhaps their undoing. Hubris, as this book discusses, is the stuff that comes before a fall. Skilling and Lay, like so many executives who reach stellar performance levels for their companies and experience the resulting iconic status, honestly believe that they can pull a rabbit out of a hat and defy reality and truth to save themselves. Mr. Lay was a piece of work on the witness stand. He even took his own lawyer to task in front of the jury! This classic and dangerous imperial CEO could not be persuaded to, just this once, listen to someone else's advice. Mr. Lay went so far as to allege that it was that diabolical band of socialists at *The Wall Street Journal* who brought down his otherwise thriving company. Even Oliver Stone got a chuckle out of that one from his perch on a nearby grassy knoll. Mr. Skilling was better on the stand but still showed a profound detachment from ethical reality. He didn't think that investing in an ex-girlfriend's company that just happened to do business with Enron was a big deal. Conflict? What conflict?

Mr. Skilling had a tin ear on perception and a blind eye for writing on the wall. When Daniel Petrocelli, Mr. Skilling's lawyer for the trial, first met with Mr. Skilling to discuss serving as his defense lawyer, Mr. Petrocelli owned to him that he was not a criminal lawyer. Mr. Skilling's response was, "That's okay. I'm not a criminal." Wrong again, this time wrong for a lifetime.

These verdicts, coupled with the convictions of Bernie Ebbers, former CEO of WorldCom, Dennis Kozlowski, former CEO of Tyco, and John Rigas, former CEO of Adelphia, surely put the fear into executives. Dear executives, have no fear. Do something to be sure that you do not become one of these bright and capable but detached-from-reality CEOs.

To me, the news of the Skilling and Lay guilty verdicts is not as important as some other business news. Even as their trial progressed, UnitedHealth Group announced the following: (1) It was conducting an internal investigation from 1994 forward on its stock options awards; (2) its earnings might have to be restated because of questions related to its accounting for those options; (3) the SEC had launched an informal investigation into the stock options issues; (4) it had received a subpoena from the U.S. attorney for the Southern District of New York related to its stock options during the period from 1999 forward; and (5) it had received a request from the IRS for information on its stock options from 2003 forward. That's just one company!

Here we are nearly five years out from Enron's fall and four years from Sarbanes-Oxley's mandates on financial reporting and the same business ethical missteps keep cropping up. Franklin Raines, the former CEO of Fannie Mae, testified in favor of Sarbanes-Oxley but was ousted as its CEO two years later even as the company made a $1.1 billion financial restatement. Nearly every day another company's pension woes or some other accounting issue bring more ethical (and sometimes legal) lapses that are inevitably followed by financial bad news. Heck, even the lawyers are now being indicted for kickbacks.

How can we be this far out from the huge scandals with so many convictions and still experience almost daily, as Yogi Berra would say, déjà vu all over again? Did these post-Enron problem companies and their leaders not take the lessons to heart? Did they fancy themselves different from Enron? Did they think they were immune from the rules? It's worse than we realize. I can take you back through decades and show you that the anatomy and activities of scandalous companies are all alike. The reason we are still at it is because the factors that lead to ethical collapse are still with us. The failure to recognize them and put antidotes in place ensures that the scandals will continue. The Skilling and Lay guilty verdicts sober us and give us pause. But do we fancy ourselves different from these companies and the now-convicts who led them, or do we work to be sure we don't fall into the same traps? We need some new ideas and a different road. Herein, the tools for the journey to propriety and ethics. Appropriately, and with great reassurance, the path for our journey is far, far away from criminal convictions.

—Marianne Jennings, May 25, 2006

Preface

"How could you not see this coming?" That's my standard response when another industry giant falls into ethical collapse. But the answer to my repetitive question is not obvious or simple. Not everyone has connected the dots on the patterns in ethical collapse. Ethical collapse is a state of moral malaise. Ethical collapse happens when organizations are unable to see that bright line between right and wrong. Or perhaps those within the organization see that bright line, but the culture is so fearful, wild, or obsessed with numbers and goals that no one wants to hear about the bright line anymore. Some organizations pull themselves back from ethical collapse. Others continue right on into legal and financial collapse. While most people are enamored of continuous double-digit growth in earnings, I have always seen it as a warning sign. While most people feel terrific when the CEO of the company in which they own stock becomes an iconic media darling, I worry. And while most people see corporate philanthropy as evidence of an ethical commitment, I know different. Not every philanthropist is headed toward ethical collapse. But not every philanthropist is ethical. They couldn't see the ethical, and possibly financial, collapse coming because the traditional tools used for evaluating companies and their potential are too rote, mechanical, and numerical. The tests for company viability and financial performance are too facile. A good analysis of where a company is headed demands a look at qualitative factors, those touchy-feely, squishy, from-the-gut factors that are ignored despite the fact that they often determine the company's fate. In my views on companies and their future, I follow Jeffersonian wisdom: "In matters of style, swim with the current; in matters of principle, stand like a rock." There has been too much falling for style and too little substantive analysis. Principle dictates digging a little deeper to find the soul and potential of a company—and too often these days, the lack thereof.

I had seen what I suspected was a pattern in companies that collapse because of ethical issues and the resulting legal problems in the savings and loan debacles and also during the Boesky and Milken junk-bond era. But when we hit the dot-coms turning into dot-bombs and rolled right on into Enron, Adelphia, WorldCom, HealthSouth, and more recently Nortel, Fannie Mae, and—Refco, and, well, this time the list is too long to catch them all—I knew I had found something. The third time is the charm, and I concluded that it was time to share the evaluation tools I have been using to determine the ethical culture of companies. That ethical culture, its absence or its presence, controls all the other quantitative factors. In early 2005 I listened to Abby Joseph Cohen, one of Wall Street's top analysts, explain how those in her profession could have been so wrong in their evaluations from 1999 to 2003. Her explanation was that the companies gave analysts incorrect numbers. Don't blame it on us, she proffered, because the analysts were also victims of these gargantuan frauds. My response was "How could you not know that the numbers were incorrect?" Yet she was not alone in that thinking. Everyone relied on company numbers. But assuming that the numbers are correct ignores critical issues in qualitative analyses of companies, issues that can influence the numbers as well as the eventual fate of those companies. With the best of the best overlooking these key qualitative factors in analysis, I realized that my seven signs of ethical collapse might help.

The question "What are the seven signs?" is compelling, but another question stares us boldly in the face: "What the heck is ethical collapse?" Ethical collapse does not mean an organization joins the ranks of Enron, WorldCom, Adelphia, the Baptist Foundation of Arizona, or Arthur Andersen in financial collapse. Indeed, the whole purpose of this undertaking is to bring ethically troubled company souls back from the brink before that occurs. Ethical collapse occurs when any organization has drifted from the basic principles of right and wrong. Some drift in the area of financial reporting standards and accounting rules. Others drift with safety issues surrounding their products. In government many drift when it comes to working with and accepting gifts from lobbyists. Not all the companies that drift ethically have violated any laws. There are many pleas, settlements, and agreements that companies discussed and studied in these pages have reached for the sake of expediency and/or not because of any legal violations. The majority of the reports on settlements indicate that the company involved does not admit any wrongdoing. Indeed, I would be the first to state unequivocally that hung juries and acquittals in these cases are reassurance that the jury system works. The "common man," when presented with the tasks of finding intent and guilt beyond a reasonable doubt, cannot always conclude that either was present in the complex transactions that often do carry the protection of technical compliance with the law. However, the law was never intended to be the maximum for standards of behavior. The law represents the minimum standard of behavior required. We are permitted to do more than the law requires and less than the law allows. A company can be teetering ethically without crossing legal lines.

When an organization collapses ethically, it means that those in the organization have drifted into rationalizations and legalisms, and all for the purpose of getting the results they want and need at almost any cost. This drift into "Everybody does this" and "It's not a question of 'Should we do it?' it's 'Can we do it legally?'" mentality occurs because of the combination of the seven factors working together to cloud judgment. False impressions or even concealment seem to offer perfect candor to those ethically collapsed organizations. Indeed, their conduct may be perfectly legal, but that standard is one of the problems in ethically collapsed organizations. They meet legal standards without really considering the long-term implications of technicalities, taking advantage of loopholes, and the resulting impact on the individual and organizational soul. They are concentrating so much on the "Gotcha strategy" of finding the loophole or the easier way around the tough slog of diligent competition that they are no longer managing as effectively, creatively, or successfully as they could.

It's the complacency that kills companies and individuals. We all drift in the day-to-day pressures and decisions. The key is pulling back, putting checks and balances on the complacency, and recognizing parallels between the decisions and practices you have chosen that, while legal, look very much like the beginnings of a dangerous journey. When we buy a new car we are attuned to its pristine feel and smell. We are also keenly aware of its cost. The result is that we only allow bottled water as our sole means of auto refreshment. The months go by and we let our absolute standard down and move into the brown beverages. By the end of the first year, food has crept into the refreshment standard. If we don't pull back, ketchup, Hawaiian Punch, hot fudge, and all manner of permanent-stain food become regulars in our auto life. The purpose in understanding ethical collapse is to pull back before we get to Hawaiian Punch, to catch ourselves before there is permanent damage to company and career. Companies in ethical collapse or headed toward ethical collapse always have the option of reform, of going back to the heightened sensitivity of the pristine conditions they once had in their autos. To avoid the permanent consequences of ethical collapse, we have to once again sensitize our desensitized selves and companies to those bright lines between right and wrong that have gradually eroded. Managers in companies in ethical collapse have lost the ability to stop and take a hard look at whether their practices are in the best long-term interest of themselves and their shareholders. If they can take the route of painful introspection and its demand for changes, they may be able to turn things around. If they can't see the damage they are doing with their shortcuts, they will find trouble lies ahead. If they can change and reinvigorate their ethical cultures, they can go forward with strategic moves grounded in solid business principles, not slippery gotchas.

Since the passage of Sarbanes-Oxley, there is reason to hope that the introspection is happening. Companies are pausing for a "Wait a minute!" They are looking at their numbers, their products, their marketing practices, and asking, "While this may be legal, is it really ethical? Are we following the spirit of the law here?" The number of earnings restatements set a record in 2005—slightly more than 1,200—but the number of investor lawsuits against companies is down, with only five cases filed in 2005. What we have with this attention to numbers is evidence of companies taking that difficult and introspective look at their own accounting and financial reporting and making better decisions. To use a Seinfeldism, "Not that there was anything wrong with that," the companies are taking the accounting high road on many issues to avoid the consequences of flying too close to the treetops. Many of the earnings restatements by companies are over issues upon which those within the company, and even outside experts, disagree. That these issues percolated into the public eye and were raised within these companies when there was plenty of the so-called and infamous "gray area" in many of these restatements is a tip of the hat to the checks and balances, presented in Chapters 2 through 8, to prevent, curb, or come back from ethical collapse.

A simple illustration and challenge I give to my students provides a micro look at what ethical collapse is and what it does. I caution my students about the use of "stuff" to win friends, contracts, and influence. "Stuff" consists of lunches, dinners, rounds of golf, cookie platters, golf clubs, tickets, a place in a private box at a concert or sports event. Stuff is everywhere in the business world and, I am assured, absolutely necessary for the so-called "face time" with those with whom you are trying to curry favor. Stuff always starts small and continues to grow until we are all in there slugging with more and more stuff until we turn into a Jack Abramoff. When we look back at the stuff that was generously bestowed, we find it all very embarrassing, to giver and givee. We read about this embarrassment of increasing stuff and wonder, What was *he* thinking? Worse, we look at all the stuff and realize that despite our best hopes and pride in gifting stuff, the impact and results from stuff were marginal. Ethical collapse in this micro example of stuff occurs when we can no longer evaluate objectively whether the stuff is necessary, whether it is effective, and whether we have crossed some lines in our use of it.

In organizations, ethical collapse occurs when they can no longer evaluate their position, conduct, goals, numbers, and performance with an objective eye. They may not have crossed any legal lines but they have lost their edge because they cannot see the risks in their choices, conduct, and strategies. What the rest of the world will look at as pushing the envelope makes ethically collapsed organizations issue a type of George Costanza (of *Seinfeld*) response, "What? You mean there's something wrong with this?" This Costanza syndrome is a one-sentence summary of ethical collapse. There is a problem, or two or more, but those inside the organizations either do not see it or would prefer to continue along a path that will prove to be damaging, if not destructive. The seven signs are here to head these organizations off at the path to damage and destruction.

My hope is that by using these seven tools, analysts will be able to look more deeply at those who furnish the numbers and thereby be able to detect when those numbers seem suspicious or should be subjected to greater scrutiny. These seven factors detect risk for numbers being wrong. I also hope that investors can spot failing cultures, that regulators can stop the train wrecks of fraud, and that every other type of organization, from government agency to nonprofit, can benefit from the organizational lessons that are universally applicable. An ethical culture nurtures growth and success. An ethically risky culture harms investors in public companies.

However, ethically risky cultures are everywhere, alive even in government agencies and nonprofits. When these nonbusiness organizations collapse, there is enormous fallout, in everything from the breach of public trust to the loss of support for noble causes. A poor ethical culture breeds ethical breaches. Ethical breaches then often lead to legal violations. Too often accompanying both is financial collapse. NASA had its ethical and cultural issues, and the results were the deadly accidents involving the space shuttles in 1986 and again in 2003 and the embarrassing debacle of the nonfunctioning Hubble telescope. Ethical collapse permitted the sexual-abuse scandals of the Catholic Church to parboil for decades. When the truth finally percolated to the surface, the fallout for the Church was financial and ecclesiastical. In the United States, payouts to victims of sexual abuse by priests was $1 billion as of June 2006. The criminal prosecution of priests and the daily press coverage found members and nonmembers alike wondering, "How could it have gone this far? Why did no one see this happening or take action?" The United Way experienced years of declining donations and great dissent following the wild ride of William Aramony's tenure as its free-spending CEO. That sore spot still surfaces as the United Way recovers its reputation from the damage of ethical collapse.

With each company, agency, and nonprofit collapse, we look at the long ride there and wonder how those involved could not have seen it coming. We learn of the transfers of employees, even priests, so that the truth did not emerge. We note the pacts of silence among employees and others. The pattern is the same, but we missed seeing all the crises coming because we did not yet understand the pattern or have the skills for spotting the evolving signs of ethical collapse. Now, having the rich experience of reviewing such collapse across decades and all forms of organizations, we have the pattern.

More important, and happily, we also have the antidotes for ethical collapse. This book is not just a forecasting tool for investors and analysts. This is a book written to provide prevention tools for all types of organizations. For every sign of ethical collapse, there are antidotes, checks and balances that can be put into place to thwart the march to the ethical cliff.

It's a tall order to take over twenty years of research, observations, and work and plunk them into three hundred or so pages. I continue to be grateful to my agent, Greg Dinkin, and his partner, Frank Scatoni. They have believed in me and my work since the time Greg was a student in my MBA class. He urged me to put my work into a book so that others could benefit. I am grateful to both of them for their ethics in everything from negotiations with publishers to advice on content, direction, and decisions. In a competitive and cutthroat business, they have eloquent and ethical restraint.

My students are in this book because with each case study they have offered insights and refinements on my theories of ethical collapse. They continue to teach me as they write to me with more examples and illustrations of ethical collapse. "You probably already saw this but . . ." is the way their e-mails to me begin. More often than not I have missed the information they are sending along, and I am grateful for their keen eyes and powers of observation. I am honored that they have remembered what they learned.

I am grateful for the wisdom of my parents, whose solid advice of "if it sounds too good to be true, it is too good to be true" led me to this exploration of ethical collapse. The seven signs of ethical collapse represent more details on this notion of "too good to be true," their general theory on investments and life.

I owe my husband and children for their sacrifice of time and for their help as I write and research. I owe them for grounding me. Their presence and needs allow me the daily opportunity to step back from work and ponder. In that reflection, those times of Little League games and carpools, my best insights come. Without them I would not have the luxury of reflection that comes only when the mind is distracted. If *A Beautiful Mind* is an accurate portrayal, game theory was born because scientists were trying to pick up girls in a bar. *The Seven Signs of Ethical Collapse* took flight because I was at one of my children's Little League games and a four-foot, eight-inch batter didn't have the legs to steal second. He was out, in a series of events that was not even a close call for the ump. His team lost the game. The season was over and done. The short-legged batter should have stuck with solid hits and sprint training. Stealing was not the secret to success. So it is with companies that try unethical shortcuts to success. They may get ahead in the game for a while, but they collapse. In finding the signs of ethical collapse, I also found the antidotes; and all of this arrived courtesy of a Little League season for the B players and unsuccessful base snatchers. That kind of inspiration and insight doesn't come without serendipity. Thank you, dear family, for all your interruptions. Without them and you, life would be dull and my work devoid of serendipitous inspiration.

THE

Seven Signs
of Ethical Collapse

CHAPTER ONE

What Are the Seven Signs?
Where Did They Come From?
Why Should Anyone Care?

Predicting rain doesn't count; building arks does.

—Warren Buffett, from his 2001 letter to
Berkshire Hathaway shareholders

It was just after the collapse of Lincoln Savings and Loan and Charles Keating's criminal trial that I began to notice a pattern. Tolstoy wrote that all happy families are alike and all unhappy families are unhappy in their own ways. The inverse appears to be true when it comes to ethics in organizations. All unethical organizations are alike; their cultures are identical, and their collapses become predictable. More than once I have been interrupted with a correction as I have told the story of General Motors, its redesign of the Malibu, and the memo from the young engineer who expressed concern that the car's gas tank was too close to the rear bumper and not insulated sufficiently in the event of rear-end collisions.

As I explain the young engineer's fears that the cars would explode too readily and upon the slightest rear-end impact, someone usually raises a hand and says, "Excuse me, but don't you mean Ford and the Pinto?" I gracefully assure them that I am aware of the Ford Pinto case and how its gas tank was also positioned too close to the rear bumper, but that I really do mean GM and its Malibu. History repeats itself when it comes to ethical lapses and collapses.

The pattern is the same. Pressure to design a new car and get it out on the market to meet the competition. A flaw in the design. A young engineer who sees the flaw. A supervisor who doesn't want bad news. A management team counting on no bad news. A shortsighted decision to skip the expense of the fix to the flawed design. Then the cars are in flames, the lawsuits begin, and those involved have the nerve to act surprised that all this is happening to them. The Malibu and Pinto stories include ethical-culture issues that are common to companies that endeavor to postpone or hide the truth about their products. As the problems with the gas tanks and explosions in the Ford Crown Victoria police cars (the Crown Vics, as they are called) emerge, the same story is likely to be repeated in the company that brought us the Pinto thirty-five years ago. You could substitute Johns-Manville and asbestos, Merck and Vioxx, or any other product-liability case and find a similar pattern. New-product problem arises, employee spots the issue, company hides the problem, press releases equivocate, and officers postpone public disclosure as they try to control the truth about that problem and continue to hope for the best. The strategy never works, but these companies have created a culture destined to follow this failing strategy.

Almost daily there is a breaking story about another company or individual who has fallen off the ethical cliff. In 2006 Nortel had to postpone the release of its 2005 earnings because of questions about its accounting that arose while it was still in the process of restating its earnings for 2001 through 2004. In 2005 the company announced earnings restatements for 2004, which followed a 2004 announcement of earnings restatements for 2003 that would cut half of the company's $732 million in profits. For those of you still keeping score, that's three restatements in three years. As one analyst noted, these kinds of accounting issues make it difficult for investors to trust the company. Further, the fallout for employees and company size is significant. A company that had 95,000 workers in 2001 will have 30,000 workers once it completes its latest 10 percent downsizing. Somewhere during the humiliation of the restatement activity there must have been one or two employees who thought that perhaps correcting the problems of the past required that they not be making the same mistakes presently.

In this Nortel story and so many others about companies and executives, we find ourselves shaking our heads in wonder. Martha Stewart and her broker tried to use Knicks tickets to persuade her broker's assistant to join ranks and stick with their story about a stop-loss order as the reason for their sudden sale of her ImClone shares one day before the company announced that FDA approval would not be forthcoming for its anticancer drug and star product, Erbitux. Add to this amateur tool of persuasion the altered phone logs, changed stop-loss-order date, and inconsistent stories among these three musketeers of manipulation, and the whole scenario has all the sophistication of elementary-school children caught lifting cookies from the cafeteria line. The conduct, whether over shares of stock or Toll House cookies, is wrong. When the SEC or school principal steps in, the fallout is always the same. One of the amateur conspirators breaks ranks on the concocted, unimaginative story.

This behavior is not exactly the stuff of the so-called gray area. Nor are any of the activities of the companies and their officers we will look at be nuanced. Former Tyco CEO Dennis Kozlowski and his $6,000 shower curtain for his highfalutin apartment, all at Tyco expense, is not the kind of story that causes us to ponder, "Wow, that was really a subtle ethical issue. I never would have seen that." Maurice "Hank" Greenberg, the former CEO of AIG, found a board waiting with his walking papers when revelations about creative insurance policies and even more creative accounting for such became public. The board had no difficulty in spotting the ethical lapses there. Nor should those in the company—or Greenberg, for that matter—have had any great mental or philosophical strain in spotting the issue. Somehow, however, the issue trotted right by very bright and capable employees and executives who are well trained in accounting, insurance, and where the two meet.

What we have seen and continue to witness is ethically "dumb" behavior. There was no discussion of gray areas as these stories unfolded. When World-Com was forced to reveal that its officers had capitalized $11 billion in ordinary expenses, no one slapped his forehead and said, "Gosh, I never would have seen that ethical issue coming!"

When Enron collapsed because it had created more than three thousand off-the-books entities in order to make its debt burden look better and its financial picture seem brighter, no one looked at the Caribbean infrastructure of deceit and muttered, "Wow—that was really a nuanced ethical issue."

There have been so many of these not-so-subtle corporate ethical missteps: HealthSouth's fabricated numbers that had it meeting its earnings goals for a phenomenal forty-seven quarters in a row; Royal Dutch's overstatement of reserves; Adelphia officers' personal use of company funds for family and personal projects; and Marsh & McLennan's illegal fee arrangements in exchange for insurance bids. No one looked at Frank Quattrone and Arthur Andersen and their document shredding and wondered, "Would I have been able to see that coming?" Even when there is no criminal behavior, the magnitude of the ethical lapses finds us shaking our heads as companies and careers crash and burn. Smart and talented people make career-ending decisions as they lead their companies and organizations to ethical collapse. Quattrone's and Andersen's verdict reversals tell us their conduct was legal. Why, however, take the risk of document destruction when your company faces regulatory scrutiny? Finding the solution to this seemingly inexplicable march to self-destruction should be the focus of all ethics programs.

These ethical missteps are not the stuff of complexity or even debate. They were downright gross ethical breaches. Indeed, in many of the cases there were blatant violations of laws and basic accounting. But if the problems and missteps were so obvious, how come those involved—bright and with years of business experience—let them slip by or joined in on the fraud festivities? Why didn't someone in the company step up and correct the behavior? And how come no one in the company told the board? Perhaps mentioned it to a regulator? Was there not a lawyer in the house? Why does it take so long before the charade of solvency is dropped? What makes people with graduate degrees in law and business come to work and shred documents or forge bank statements? Why do good, smart people do ethically dumb things?

When Martha Stewart was indicted—and her indictment followed on the heels of the Enron, WorldCom, Adelphia, HealthSouth, and Kozlowski indictments—a reporter asked me, "What is the difference between you and me and a Martha Stewart or a Jeffrey Skilling of Enron or a John Rigas of Adelphia?"

My reply was "Not much."

The reporter was taken aback, outraged that I would not portray these icons of greed as one-eyed Cyclopes with radically different, mutantly unethical DNA.

Sure, Martha and her obstruction, Andrew Fastow and his spinning off debt, and Dennis Kozlowski and his chutzpah with the corporate kitty are the end of the line for ethical collapse. Yes, yes, they descended quite far into the depths of ethical missteps, but no one should assume a perch detached and above this type of behavior. No one wakes up one day and decides, "You know what would be good? A gigantic fraud! I think I'll perpetuate a myth through accounting fraud and make money that way." Nor does anyone suddenly wake up and exclaim, "Forgery! Forging bank documents to show lots of assets. There's the key to business success."

These icons of ethical collapse did not descend into the depths of misdeeds overnight. Nor did they descend alone. To be able to forge bank documents, one needs a fairly large staff and a great many averted eyes. To drain the corporate treasury for personal use requires many pacts of silence among staff and even board members. Overstating the company's reserves requires more than one signature. Those who are indicted may have made the accounting entries, approved the defective product launch, ordered the shredding, or skirted the law. But they were not alone. They had to have help, or at least benign neglect from others in the organization.

Which leads to these questions: How does an organization allow individuals to engage in such behavior? What goes wrong in a company that permits executives to profit and pilfer as sullen but mute employees stand idle?

The latest federal reforms on accounting, corporate governance, and financial reporting, in the form of the Sarbanes-Oxley Act of 2002 (SOX, as it is fondly known among executives), have lawyers and accountants scrambling to meet requirements for ethics programs and other statutory mandates. The demands of SOX represent the third great regulatory reform I have witnessed in my nearly three decades of detached academic observation and research. When Boesky, Milken, and junk bonds stormed Wall Street and then collapsed, we passed massive reforms and we all swore, in Edgar Allan Poe fashion, "Nevermore."

But then came the savings and loans, real estate investments, appraisers with conflicts of interest, Charles Keating, and the inevitable collapse that follows self-dealing and enrichment, as well as the accompanying damage to the retail investors in these enterprises. So we passed more massive federal reforms on S&Ls, accounting, and appraisal, swearing and quoting, once again, "Nevermore!"

Yet here we are, five years after Enron's collapse, still debating all the rules and regulations that should be applied and grappling with the complexities and demands of Sarbanes-Oxley, and this time we swear that we really mean it when we say, "Nevermore!"

But it will all happen again as the cycle continues, because we keep trying to legislate ethical behavior. There are not enough lawyers, legislators, sessions, or votes to close every possible loophole that can be found as we continue to regulate business behavior. Professor Richard Leftwich has offered this description of the relationship between accounting rules and standards and business practice: "It takes FASB [The Financial Accounting Standards Board] two years to issue a ruling and the investment bankers two weeks to figure out a way around it."

The penalties increase with each massive regulatory reform, but so also does the size of the frauds and collapses. This latest go-round of ethical collapses has brought us several of the top ten corporate bankruptcies of all time. Although that list is a tough call. I am reluctant to name these companies to the list because I have to rely on their numbers for that ranking. Who could say how big their bankruptcies really are?

These massive legislative and regulatory reforms cannot solve the underlying problems. They are not the cure for the disease of fraud. The audits, the corporate governance, and the accounting focus on getting good numbers are superficial fixes. Legal changes create artificial hope that massive regulations will stop ethical lapses. But these facile solutions of how to count, when to count, and even how many board members count as independent and which ones qualify as experts in finance have not worked in the past and will not work to prevent similar collapses in the future. The focus on detailed rules makes us overlook the qualitative factors that have more control over the ethical culture of organizations.

Prevention is the key. Stopping the inexorable march to that ethical cliff demands something more than a look at ROE (return on equity) and other financial measures and promised deliverables that are so easily quantified. There are qualitative characteristics to look for in companies that can provide insight into the organizations that produce the external facade of financial reports, fund-raising, and shuttles launched. There are marking points in that descent from financial reports with integrity to the shredding and forgery. In fact, after performing decades of research and studying three great ethical collapses, I've identified seven of them.

An Overview of the Seven Signs

The seven signs became clear as I prepared to participate in a 2003 symposium on corporate governance and ethics. My presentation there was published in the more formal format of a seminal law review article titled "Restoring Ethical Gumption in the Corporation: A Federalist Paper on Corporate Governance—Restoration of Active Virtue in the Corporate Structure to Curb the 'Yeehaw Culture' in Organizations" in the *Wyoming Law Review*. The title describes the culture and nature of companies that ethically collapse. These companies have a culture best reflected by the Wild West battle cry when things in the town got a bit out of the local sheriff's control, "Yeehaw!" "Yeehaw!" was also the battle cry of Billy Crystal's cohorts, actually the citified dentists, when they headed out to their first cattle drive in the film *City Slickers*. Either source of the term "yeehaw" connotes trouble ahead.

Building on that work, I can now answer the following questions: What do you look for in a company or organization that can provide insight into whether it is at risk for ethical lapses? And what happens to us that allows us to descend to these bizarre forms of conduct? Finally, what can be done to curb these problems and flaws?

Through the three great collapses and reforms over the past twenty years, I have had both the luxury of detached perspective of an academic and the time for studying common traits. Are there similarities between Charles Keating and his Lincoln Savings and Loan and John Rigas and his Adelphia? Are there common factors between junk bonds and the telecoms and dot-coms? What happens in a company that allows a CEO to loot the organization? How does a company persuade bright and capable individuals to stand at the shredding machine?

There is a pattern to ethical collapse—that descent into truly obvious missteps that make us all wonder, "Where were their minds and what were they thinking when they decided to behave this way?" The simple answer is that they failed to see and heed the seven warning signs of ethical collapse:

1. Pressure to maintain those numbers

2. Fear and silence

3. Young 'uns and a bigger-than-life CEO

4. Weak board

5. Conflicts

6. Innovation like no other

7. Goodness in some areas atoning for evil in others

These seven signs are easily observable from the outside, and almost always discernible even without one-on-one interviews with employees. But give me a one-on-one with an employee and I can tap a vein. I always offer companies: "After I do my outside research, using the signs listed above as the focus, give me just five minutes alone with a frontline employee and I can tell you the culture of your organization and whether it is at risk."

While it is true that every company has one or more of the seven signs, not every company is at risk of ethical collapse. The difference between a company at risk and one that collapses lies in curbing the culture and controlling the worst of the seven signs. A little fear of the CEO is not a bad thing. The fear of telling the CEO the truth is. Antidotes for curbing the seven "yeehaw" factors abound. Managers, executives, and boards just need to learn the signs and work to counterbalance their overpowering influence in an organization.

The signs can also be seen in government agencies and nonprofits. The Yeehaw Culture has invaded churches, the United Way, and newspapers. The signs are universally applicable and offer a checklist for managers, trustees, shareholders, donors, and anyone else who wants to prevent or curb the Yeehaw Culture. Analysts who seek to get their arms around those qualitative and often controlling factors in a company can find insight here. Investors who want to know if their investment is at risk because of potential ethical collapse can look for these signs. The seven signs can help employees who want to preserve an ethical culture in their companies and can offer insight and suggestions to employees at companies that are at risk for the Yeehaw Culture.

The chapters that follow detail the seven signs, as well as give examples of the companies, agencies, and nonprofits that have had them all and their resulting fates. Along the way you find the tools for curbing the behaviors that give rise to the seven signs and for preventing ethical collapse.

By studying the qualitative factors that lead to obviously wrong behaviors, individuals learn when they are unwitting, or perhaps even witting, accomplices to the collapse. They learn when to be agents of change in an ethically risky culture, or when to hold 'em and when to fold 'em. Very bright people are now serving sentences as a result of guilty pleas. They made the accounting entries their executives asked them to. An understanding of the seven signs offers individuals guidance on how to choose among companies and when they have hit an ethical wall.

My former students often call me to find out what company will be the focus of seven-sign analysis by my current students on the midterm and final. They call because they want to position themselves short on the companies. Applying the seven signs and finding them missing in a company means a good investment. Applying the seven signs and finding them all present and accounted for means the company is headed for a drop. In the fall of 2004, the students focused on Krispy Kreme. Any company that tries to attribute a downturn in its revenues to the pervasiveness of the Atkins low-carb diet has a problem. "We hit a low-carb wall" was the explanation of former CEO Scott Livengood. By January 4, 2005, Krispy Kreme had announced that it would be restating its earnings.

At the start of the work on this proposal in the summer of 2004, Greg Dinkin, my agent, asked me if there was any company I would point to at that time that had seven-sign risk. I responded that it was Coca-Cola. Following our discussion, Coke had a series of legal and ethical issues. But Coke may now be a company to study for its ability to pull back and, with tough introspection, make the changes needed to reform a culture that led them down the path of trying to dupe both its shareholders and even one of its own customers. The channel-stuffing charges it settled in April 2005 resulted, according to the SEC, from the pressure at Coke to meet earnings expectations and continue that long streak of phenomenal earnings that hit a wall in 1998 via an economic downturn, particularly in foreign markets. The Burger King debacle discussed in Chapter 4 may have saved the company from worse. From management to policies to products, Coke has been changing, thinking, and working to avoid the damage that comes if companies don't use the checks and balances on the signs of ethical collapse. When Neville Isdell took over as CEO, he spoke bluntly to employees about "personal accountability" and challenged them to rise above the personal politics and get back to developing what it takes to succeed. The charge to employees was a classic one designed to send the message of hard work and innovation, not manipulation or deception. Coke settled its accounting issues with the SEC in April 2005 even as the Justice Department dropped its investigation into the Burger King incident (see Chapter 9 for more information). And it paid its former employee Matthew Whitley, who questioned the reimbursement of the marketing consultant for the Burger King test market, a total of $540,000 to settle his wrongful termination suit. Coke also shifted to focusing on long-term goals over quarterly earnings targets. The pulling back is neither cheap nor easy, but it does avoid the financial fallout of continuing to operate with an ethically challenged culture. Coke's Burger King division even had the guts to have me and my bluntness in to help them analyze what went wrong with the slip into "adjusted" market studies.

Study a company with the seven signs and you spot risks that analysts have not begun to understand. The analysts were describing Tyco as a phenomenon and crowning its then-CEO, Dennis Kozlowski, as the next Jack Welch. In fact, *Business Week* named now-convicted CEO Dennis Kozlowski one of its top managers for three years running. I said, "Run away! Run away!" You will learn why. An isolated look at one company or one collapse does not provide tools for application and prevention. A study of three eras of ethical collapse provides signs and principles for curbing the atmosphere that leads to ethical collapse. And ethical collapse is not just applicable in hindsight. I can see it coming.

In a speech at AstraZeneca, the international pharmaceutical company, in the fall of 2004, an employee, during the Q&A, asked me what I thought of the Merck and Vioxx situation. The timing of my speech was just days after Merck had announced it was halting sales of its arthritic pain medication, Vioxx, because of increased risk of heart attacks and strokes. I responded that I had no thoughts on whether the statements about the drug and its effect on heart patients were true or false, but I did predict how the case would unfold: there would be hints of a problem early on and internal e-mails or memos would reflect concern on the part of some scientists and employees; as the concerns began to increase and those outside the company began to discover the same problems with Vioxx, there would be evidence of the living-in-denial phase along with the usual instructions to employees and others to hold firm and fast on a drug that generated $2.5 billion in sales in 2003. I explained that the pattern, so evident in other companies that face such a public crisis, would hold true: Merck would hope for the best to come if they could just hold the issue back from scrutiny long enough. The irony is that a great product suffers from the postponement of full-blown disclosure.

There is no best to come because concealment never works and is a strategy chosen by those bound and consumed by a culture of ethical collapse. Within one month following that speech, *The Wall Street Journal* reported on page A1 that the e-mails I predicted did exist, that some of those within the company were hopeful that scientists challenging Vioxx would "flame out," and that instructions for new trainees on questions about Vioxx included, in capital letters, this instruction: "DODGE!" The pattern holds true because all companies travel the same road down the slippery slope of ethical collapse.

Why Read This Book? What's Different?

This is a book for everyone who has looked at these fallen executives and their crashing-and-burning companies and wondered, "Why did they do it?" or

"How does someone sink so low?" Some observers conclude that bad people (think "rogues") ran the ethically collapsed companies. They assume, with a great sense of calm and comfort, that such a monumental collapse could never happen to them because they are, of course, not rogues. There is a tendency in human nature to take away immunity from any analyses of ethically collapsed companies and conclude, "Well, it was greed," or "They were just awful people." We fancy ourselves to be different from these rogues and hence not susceptible to monumental ethical collapse. Perhaps we are nothing like any one individual rogue, but the better analysis and questions are "What do companies with rogues have in common?" and "How do rogues obtain such a grip on a company or organization?" This book will teach us not to dismiss these "bad seeds" so readily as being different from us. Given enough pressure and culturally induced myopia, we are all vulnerable. The checks and balances come from being able to recognize when you are at risk. This book helps us spot the slippery slope, the ethical cliff, and any other physical and philosophical metaphors for doom. We need to be able to recognize the danger signs before we come too close to that slope, edge, cliff, precipice. . . .

Because the focus of this book is on preventing ethical collapse, it charts new territory. A quick glance down the extensive list of books on business ethics finds a plethora on two themes: (1) Ethics is important in business and (2) the story of individuals and companies that collapsed. We are at a point where we know that ethics is important. In this post-Sarbanes-Oxley world, everyone from executives who sign off on financial statements to employees who must sign off on ethics codes and attend ethics training is inundated with ethics programs and training. Every publicly traded company must have ethics codes, ethics training, and all ethics all the time. Sometimes I worry that the zeal for compliance with federal law will blind us to really working on a solid ethical culture. Would we really know if we were headed down the same path as those companies whose stories dominate the business bestseller lists?

Most companies and their ethics programs fall short of taking the steps necessary to create a culture in which employees come forward with concerns and feel comfortable making ethical choices and in which ethics is paramount in decision making. There are magnets, pens, pads, and even Slinky toys and Rubik Cubes with the ethics hotline information on them, and everyone talks a good game. There are help lines, hotlines, always-tell lines, honesty-first lines, and all manner of what employees often perceive to be the career-ending rat-fink telephone lines to report a legal or ethical issue. But more executives, boards, and ethics officers themselves are asking, "We know what we're supposed to do and what the law requires, but how do we do it?" This book represents the next generation of business ethics book—this is the action and prevention book. This book takes ethics from philosophy and being simply a remote goal to making it a critical part of a culture and, ultimately, successful. The principles on ethical culture and ethical collapse are, like management books' discussions about service, greatness, and quality, universally applicable—for companies, nonprofits, and government agencies. This book is a how-to: how a business should create and sustain an ethical culture.

Most books on ethics in business tell businesspeople to be ethical. This book presumes that we understand that part of the equation and moves on to the next phase: How do we do it? Therein lies the key question; and once we do it, how do we sustain it? There are traits, habits, and cultural factors that actually get in the way of ethical decisions. There are also ethical checks and balances that can serve as stop signs when unethical conduct is proposed.

This book also provides the tools for addressing the rising need in corporations for evidence that they and their employees are focusing on ethics. The real issue in all the hand-wringing over ethics and Sarbanes-Oxley is how to ensure not only that we have core values but that they survive and thrive once we have them. Enron had core values. Arthur Andersen had core values, as did WorldCom, Adelphia, and Tyco—they all touted them. The problem was in implementation and maintenance: creating and sustaining a culture in which those values could survive and thrive. How do we know when we are drifting? How do we curb the drift? What allows us to drift? Enron did not have "push the envelope on accounting rules" as a core value. How did it get to a point where that value consumed its executives and staff? In the chapters that follow you will learn how to determine if you are on course and whether your culture allows you to practice and live the ethical standards we now know are a critical factor in a company's financial success. In a 2004 study from the *Journal of Business Ethics,* employees stunned most academics by saying that the code of ethics for their company had very little influence on whether they made ethically correct choices. It was the culture of their companies and the examples set by their leaders that influenced their conduct. We understand that ethics is important; we have not yet taken the time to nurture it and create an atmosphere of ethical leaders and influences. This is a positive "How do we prevent it?" tome, not a negative "I can't believe they did this!"

It is tragic when we witness these stunning organizational collapses. These collapses are pervasive, and the passage of Sarbanes-Oxley has not halted them. Refco's creative accounting came four years after the legislation despite its resemblance to the Enron approach to financial reporting—get that debt off the books. Royal Shell's reserves overstatements were revealed two years after the harsh warnings on financial statements. Even religious organizations, such as the Baptist Foundation of Arizona, have fallen victim to ethical collapse, taking down their faithful investors who had given their life savings to an organization they trusted. Initially, the Baptist Foundation of Arizona was an organization that had values and could be trusted, but its initial great success, a weak board, and investors equating social good with accounting honesty allowed it to slip until eventually the accounting practices consumed even its outside auditor. CBS was once the Tiffany network, the standard for television journalism. Yet during the 2004 presidential campaign it was reduced to issuing press releases explaining Dan Rather's *60 Minutes II* stories on President George W. Bush's National Guard service as follows: "This story is true. The questions we raised about then-Lieutenant Bush's National Guard service are serious and legitimate." The documents on which we based the story may have come from a questionable source, but the underlying story is true? *The New York Times* used this incredulous headline on the same story: MEMOS ON BUSH ARE FAKE, BUT ACCURATE. And *The New York Times* itself found that one of its important reporters, Jayson Blair, was fabricating and plagiarizing stories. The nature of the leadership in these news organizations, the pressures, and the structure all demonstrate that the Yeehaw Culture can be found even in the media as they pursue the idealistic goal of uncovering and reporting the truth. Even the *Times* itself noted "a rich supply of scandals at news organizations, including the New York Times."

What happens to reduce a company, an agency, a foundation, or a news organization to such defiance of ethics—indeed, of logic? There is a pattern of devolution, and warning signs that tell us when we are headed toward the slippery slope of ethical collapse.

When we look at many of the scandals and the backdrop of the decisions of companies that hit ethical road bumps—such as Ford and Firestone and the Explorer tires, Al Dunlap and Sunbeam's accounting, price-fixing at Archer Daniels Midland (ADM) and Marsh & McLennan—we know that those decisions were flawed and the fallout from those decisions destructive. Bad decisions and ethical missteps will continue as long as human beings run companies. The ethical issues at Ford and Firestone existed long before executives faced the questions of what to do about the tires or the Ford Explorer, to recall or not to recall, to litigate or not to litigate, to report accidents in other countries to the Consumer Product Safety Commission or not. The questions that should have been answered long before the stories in *USA Today* appeared were: How on earth did the data on both the Explorer and the tires go unheeded for so long in these companies? What made good engineers dismiss the data on peeling tires for so long? Why didn't lawyers report the overseas incidents of rollovers and tire problems to the Consumer Product Safety Commission? The price-fixing at ADM and the decision of executives there to involve themselves in this activity were just plain wrong. What makes bright, capable people think they can get away with such behavior? But the better questions are: What went wrong and what happens in a company that allows employees to even think about engaging in price-fixing? This book teaches individuals how to avoid the ethical issues, problems, and collapse by studying when, where, and how the managers went wrong and why they did what they did. Assume that the managers and employees in these companies realized then, as we do now in hindsight, that what they were doing was wrong. Where were the checks and balances to help them make the obviously correct choices instead of the damaging, wrong choices? What kinds of conditions exist in organizations that allow the employees and officers to devolve from a point of being decent people to becoming diabolical? Presuppose human nature and learn to avoid the pitfalls even as you create gates and gatekeepers to save us from our natural selves.

This is not a book for the ethically fainthearted. Too few books have offered moral judgment and, as a result, have fallen short in giving guidance on the difference between right and wrong. For example, a classic dilemma in business ethics books and discussions is whether an executive should launch a questionable product. The ethical dilemma is not whether to launch; the ethical dilemma is why does a debate on launching a questionable product ever gain traction? More relevant, what is in your company's culture that encourages you to even think about launching a questionable product? By portraying everything in shades of gray, we create an ethical culture that leads to a constantly moving line of propriety that takes executives from shades of gray in accounting right into fraud. In other words, this method of analysis, in which there is no right or wrong, is part of the problem with corporate cultures and contributes to collapse.

There are also those who want to posture all business ethical dilemmas as a right vs. right context. "Do I take a vacation, or save the money for my children's college tuition?" "Do I log, or do I preserve the spotted owl?" These types of decisions are complex ones and require an examination of values, intentions, and alternatives. They are not, however, the issues that affected Enron, WorldCom, Adelphia, AIG, Fannie Mae, and Tyco. Indeed, WorldCom and Adelphia always saved the spotted owls; they just had a great deal of difficulty with their accounting, executive loans, and that fluctuating line (as they saw it) between company and personal property. Altruistic salve for the executive conscience—there is no right or wrong, just good analysis. Creating a culture that prevents ethical collapse means looking beyond whether we are good citizens, in our corporate and organizational worlds as well as in our communities. We have to determine whether we have raised difficult obstacles and pressures and created an atmosphere in which employees and executives reflect in the company accounting that orders have been filled so as to meet their quarterly numbers when they know that the orders cannot physically be filled by the end of the day. What makes employees trot down this path of fudging numbers, a practice that leads to outright cooking of the books? Why was no one comfortable reflecting on this decision and questioning whether it was ethical? And why wasn't anyone in the company available to listen to employee concerns about the decision? To whom do they turn for help? Were there systems in place for voicing their concerns? What if they experience resistance? What makes it difficult for executives to do the right thing in this accounting dilemma? We work and live among groupthink, incentive plans, pressure from supervisors, and a host of other environmental factors that must first be controlled before we have the personal luxury of right vs. right.

Some have argued that all we need is moral courage, people who stand up to accept responsibility and take the consequences. It's tough to argue against moral courage. But reality and my studies of organizations show that moral courage doesn't face nearly as many hurdles and is exercised more frequently when employees are not in an environment of fear, retaliation, and incentives for doing the wrong thing. Getting sacked for raising ethical issues does not build moral courage. Yet, in the companies that experienced ethical collapse, the terminations were fast and furious for those who pointed to the naked emperors, whether in accounting and financial reporting or product flaws. We do indeed need more individuals with moral courage. Putting checks and balances in place to curb the seven signs can help with the systemic problems that inhibit the exercise of moral courage. The realistic issue is whether an organization has created barriers to entry into the magnificent field of the morally courageous. Even the stoutest of heart falter when the consequences of exercising moral courage are too great.

One must never presume that we have created an atmosphere appropriate for moral courage. That assumption is wrong. Too few organizations foster forthrightness and moral courage. However, an ethical culture that allows and then nurtures moral courage can be created and fostered. We can work at the other end, curbing the seven bad habits, to provide and sustain an ethical culture. Further, identifying the seven signs allows those who are seeking employment or a change in positions to examine the company's culture and decide if they really want to work in an environment that will not permit ethical dissent. Investors can examine companies and decide if they want to own part of something that has a culture ripe for moral compromise. We know companies need moral courage, and the seven signs measure whether it exists or even can exist in the organization and whether management's tolerance allows its exercise.

How do you find companies that nurture moral courage? How could so few people see the cultural problems at Enron, WorldCom, Adelphia, and Tyco?

Are there warnings signs? Prospectively, how do we put into place the checks and balances that prevent us from labeling everything gray and crossing over those fine lines into unethical behavior? Can we spot trouble before it is too late? The answer is unequivocally yes. I want people, including managers, employees, and investors, to be able to spot the risk before the company takes the step to front-page news. Using the tools presented in the chapters as the signs are explained, prevention is possible. With these tools, we can examine companies for the qualitative signs that often determine success or failure. When all the ratios are calculated and the economic forecasts completed, we are left with the question of whether we can trust companies to exercise their stewardship with investor funds in an ethical manner. A close look at the factors common to those who have not exercised that stewardship yields new insight and foresight.

The pattern that we discover carries with it a list of prevention tools. Relying on the rich business history presented by looking across these scandals of nearly three decades, anyone can make the case for change in his or her own organization. Showing the collapse of organizations that did not self-correct makes the case for any organization to change. Now we have the red flags to look for. Think how many people were aware of what was happening in these organizations! Tapping into that resource provides a means for halting the march to collapse. Long before companies collapse, with the accompanying front-page embarrassment, there are definitive cultural factors to watch and the areas in which self-correction can curb ethical decline that leads to the well-publicized and financially devastating collapse.

In this post-Sarbanes-Oxley world, with all of its focus on ethics training, companies must be able to demonstrate to government regulators that they have produced an ethical culture. Such proof offers insight into the creation and maintenance of an ethical culture by avoiding the pitfalls that destroy such an environment. CEOs and CFOs must certify that their firms' financial statements are accurate, but more important, they must certify that their companies have the right checks and balances and culture to ensure that the numbers and reports were prepared according to high ethical standards. Those certifications can be offered without as much anxiety when there is a comfort level with the culture that produced the numbers in those reports.

The patterns for good ethical cultures as well as bad are out there, and studying and understanding both gives companies a chance to keep the organization away from that slippery slope. By the time the company hits the slope, it is too late. The goal is to eliminate the slippery slope altogether by creating a culture that fosters and nurtures ethical choices. The only variation is the type of ethical or legal issue. For some companies, like so many of the Enron era, their ethical collapse comes over financial reports. For others, such as

Sotheby's, Christie's, and ADM, it is price-fixing. For still others, such as Boeing and Marsh & McLennan, there are collapses that come from unlawful means to circumvent the bid processes. The underlying pressure that causes the descent down the slippery slope and collapse may be different, but the cultures in the company or organization that allowed an issue to get to the point of "Where were their minds? What were they thinking?" are the same. This book helps us avoid that precipice through the use of a checklist of factors. Now we can all point to tangible organizational and individual signs and determine whether ethical risk exists, and if it does, make the changes necessary to halt the conduct and end the grip of the rogues who will take their organizations to ethical collapse without the intervention of those who understand and are willing to manage the Yeehaw Culture.

CHAPTER TWO

Sign #

1

Pressure to Maintain Those Numbers

The weak, the meek, and the ignorant.

—Charles Keating's instructions to his bond sales force
on whom they should target for selling bonds
in Lincoln Savings and Loan

All companies experience pressure to maintain solid performance. The tension between ethics and the bottom line will always be present. Indeed, such pressure motivates us and keeps us working and striving. But in this first sign of a culture at risk for ethical collapse, there is not just a focus on numbers and results but an unreasonable and unrealistic *obsession* with meeting quantitative goals. "Meet those numbers!" is the mantra. A survey taken as this third round of scandals began found that 17 percent of all CFOs of public companies felt pressure from their CEOs to misrepresent financial results. Not just pressure to meet numbers, but pressure so great that they made up numbers. These companies, through their officers, pledge precisely quantified growth in income, sales, and ROI. Sometimes they even make promises about the price of their stock. Nor is numbers pressure peculiar to business. Nonprofit managers make promises to raise a given amount of money and then put pressure on their staff that is so great that judgment is impaired and schemes to defraud are born even in nonprofits of noble origins and divine causes. Universities have felt the pressure to achieve certain rankings or ratings by academic and business publications. Even the ivory tower has been caught manipulating numbers such as job-placement percentages for graduates and GMATs for admits in order to boost rankings by business and popular magazines. Government agencies, from DNA labs to NASA, also feel the need to produce results for the public and their form of customer: the other government entities that use their services or have a say in their funding levels and programs. The nature of the numerical goal may be different in that universities seek a high placement ranking, corporations need a good bond rating, agencies need their budgets, and nonprofits need funds, but the pressures in all types of organizations are identical.

What happens when companies, individuals, agencies, and nonprofits can no longer deliver on stellar performances-to-date? What happens when a business with no competition suddenly has competition and cannot earn as much? A declining stock price can cause bizarre accounting behavior. The drive for numbers, numbers, numbers can take us right to the slippery slope and into ethical collapse. When the SEC released its 2004 report on the areas of financial reporting that are most susceptible to fraud, it concluded that revenue-recognition issues were the most common form of numbers manipulation, with postponement or misclassification of expenses beings the second. Of the 227 investigations by the SEC related to revenue recognition between 1997 and 2002, the SEC undertook 126 enforcement actions and charged at least one senior officer in 104 of them. The drive for numbers is not isolated to the lower ranks of the company; there are signals to which employees respond. Many of those enforcement actions involved companies like MicroStrategy, a firm that experienced phenomenal growth and returns (as so many others of the dot-com era did) that became difficult to carry on for more than a few quarters and certainly not longer than a few years. Founded in 1990, MicroStrategy's initial public offering was in 1998, and its shares sold for $20 each. It was selling at $333 per share at the start of 2000, its ten-year anniversary. By March of 2000 MicroStrategy had announced that it was restating its earnings for the past two years. The stock price dropped from $140 per share to $86.75, a drop of 61.7 percent in one day. By December of 2000 the company and some officers had settled charges brought by the SEC. Too late for rebuilding trust, because the share price was at $15.19 by then. Part of the settlement was a promise for the company to be under supervision for its accounting practices. The experience allowed MicroStrategy to change its culture and accounting practices and recover to a share price of over $90 by 2006.

Every organization that experiences a double-digit ride to the top, whether in revenue, funds raised, or rankings, is at risk of developing this odd obsession with numbers that then translates into pressure on employees, which then manifests itself in questionable judgment. Every organization faced with expected results, whether launching a rocket or meeting a fund-raising goal, has the potential for obsession with numbers and the resulting ride to ethical collapse. A look at several of these cultures, across years, industries, and types of organizations, shows us how pervasive sign #1 is. The chilling message from these experiences is that none of us is immune.

MiniScribe, Pressure, Evaluations, and Those Numbers Goals

One of the most common responses I get when I discuss sign #1 and the obsession with numbers is "It's not us. It's Wall Street and their demands for results. It wasn't always like this." Actually, yes, there has always been the pressure to meet the numbers, and the tension that comes with the need for results. For example, in the 1980s case of the Colorado-based disk drive manufacturer MiniScribe, the company rode the wave of the computer revolution to unprecedented success. When IBM parted ways with the company, MiniScribe seemed doomed. But with Q. T. Wiles leading it in the recovery back from the loss of its largest customer, MiniScribe flourished. Sales went from $113.9 million in 1985 to nearly $600 million in 1988. Doubling and tripling sales is not a result that comes without pressure. By the end of 1986 the only criterion for performance evaluations and bonuses at MiniScribe was whether the individuals, units, and divisions had met their financial goals, be it in sales or budget. Then, in the last quarter of 1988, there was another slowdown in the computer industry. Still, Wiles was relentless on those "meet the numbers" demands. He held weekly "dash meetings" during which the numbers were visited and revisited. Indeed, other than motivational platitudes for meeting the numbers, there was not another topic of discussion. The message to everyone was clear: meet your numbers, or you are out of a job. Rather than face a downturn in sales, managers began smoothing the books, hoping sales would return. The managers shipped twice as many disk drives as they had orders for, hoping to make up the declining numbers in the next quarter. Sales were booked without shipment. Managers and executives even falsified inventory to justify the sales numbers. Employees went to work each day and wrapped bricks (the equivalent weight of the disk drives) in disk drive boxes in order to dupe the auditors. College-educated and graduate-degree managers were breaking into the trunks of the auditors at night to alter their work. All those years of study so that they could be deft with the Wite-Out in the wee hours of the morning. I always counsel my students on this case, "Never mind the ethical issues. What of human dignity?" Numbers pressure impairs judgment and robs dignity.

Finova Group Inc. and Capturing the Secondary Loan Market

Finova was formed in 1992 as a spin-off from the Greyhound Corporation with a target market of making loans to small businesses and dabbling in those markets higher in risk than the banks and major financial players such as GE Capital. Finova took the loans on time-share properties and small businesses no one else wanted. The risk was higher, but the growth potential tremendous. By 1993 Finova's loan portfolio was over $1 billion through its own aggressive growth as well as its acquisition of U.S. Bancorp, Ambassador Factors, and Tri-Con Capital. Its margins were phenomenal because with customers who could not qualify with other lenders, Finova was in a position to charge high rates for its loans. And the drive to keep those margins rolling and the portfolio increasing was tremendous. An excerpt from Finova's 1997 annual report includes the following performance recap and pledges from its then-CEO, Sam Eichenfield:

> *The goals we set forth in our first Annual Report were to:*
>
> - *Grow our income by no less than 10% per year*
> - *Provide our shareholders with an overall greater return than that of the S&P 500*
> - *Preserve and enhance the quality of our loan portfolios*
> - *Continue enjoying improved credit ratings.*
>
> *We have met those goals and, because they remain equally valid today, we intend to continue meeting or surpassing them in the future. Many observers comment on FINOVA's thoughtfulness and discipline and, indeed, FINOVA prides itself on its focus.*

Thoughtfulness and discipline had less to do with the results than did the pressure placed on executives, managers, and employees at all levels to meet the income and portfolio-growth goals of the company. There was even the unwritten but well-understood goal of getting the share price of Finova to $60. Compensation packages were tied to achievement of that share price.

Now, it is a basic principle of Accounting 101 that bad loans and their write-downs get in the way of loan-portfolio growth. Finova employees who knew the extraordinary numbers goals and that their compensation packages were tied to those goals soon discovered that the downside to this principle of portfolio growth could be no bonuses at all. The result was that Finova divisions were carrying loans that should have been written down, and in some cases, Finova capitalized expenses related to repossessed property so that the portfolio value would go up despite the clear uncollectibility of the loan. A bad loan is not an asset, but in this world of promises of continued double-digit growth, employees do rationalize. For example, Finova had one loan to finance a time-share RV golf resort in Arkansas. The loan of $800,000 for this tempting Garden of Eden, complete with wheels and sewerage hookups, was made in 1992.

By 1995 the loan was in default and the property was worth only $500,000. However, no one wanted to take the hit to the portfolio, so the loan was carried as an asset and then some as the managers capitalized expenses for the golf course and its restaurant. By the time this accounting impropriety was uncovered, the loan was being carried as a $5.5 million asset. As one of the managers I interviewed said, "All of Arkansas isn't worth $5.5 million."

By 1999 the auditors began to ask questions, and there were other loans, of significantly higher amounts, that had questions, baggage, and problems. Ernst & Young refused to certify the company's financial statements until it wrote down a $70 million loan to a California computer manufacturer that had gone bad months and possibly years earlier. Shareholder lawsuits filed against the company alleged that the write-down was postponed because bonus and compensation packages that were tied to the share price would have suffered. The result was a 38 percent drop in share price and a loss of analyst confidence and investor trust. Finova would roll into bankruptcy with its shares hovering around 68 cents each, a far cry from its numbers goal of $60.

Bausch & Lomb: Cannibalizing Itself to Meet the Numbers

Bausch & Lomb was on a roll from 1982 to 1994: it had experienced double-digit growth for twelve years in a row. That kind of growth does not come without two things: pressure and accounting chicanery. Employees who would eventually testify at hearings and during litigation indicated that they were given target numbers for sales and operations and that there were never any excuses accepted for not meeting their numbers. One manager noted that he was told to meet the numbers but not to do anything "stupid." The manager concluded, "I'd walk away saying, 'I'd be stupid not to make the numbers.'"

To meet those numbers in any way, managers shipped products, including Ray-Ban sunglasses and contact lenses, to distributors so that the sales could be booked. Some distributors were holding up to two years of inventory as a result. Doctors received shipments of contact lenses that they had not ordered. In 1993 the Bausch & Lomb Hong Kong division even cannibalized the company itself by falsely booking sales to customers and then turning around and dumping merchandise onto the gray market.

When the SEC moved in to investigate overstatement of earnings, senior management protested that it had no idea what was going on with the falsified sales. The response of the SEC official indicates that he understood some ten years ago what a numbers culture can do: "That's precisely the point. Here is a company where there is tremendous pressure down the line to meet the numbers. The commission's view is that senior management has to be especially vigilant where the pressure to make the numbers creates the risk of improper revenue recognition."

Bausch & Lomb would settle with the SEC, hire a new CEO, and work to regain its market share as well as the trust of regulators and customers. Reestablishing trust after such a fall off the ethical cliff is a tall order. Bausch & Lomb had still not recovered in sales, revenues, earnings, or market trust through 2001. Live by the numbers pressure, die by the numbers pressure. In 2005, Bausch & Lomb announced an earnings restatement and internal control investigations in its Brazilian and Korean subsidiaries. Rapid action, candid public disclosures, and internal investigations show Bausch & Lomb has learned from its prior experience. Checking the cultures in foreign subsidiaries is now critical and done to prevent ethical lapses.

Chainsaw Al Dunlap and Sunbeam

Hiring a CEO who is nicknamed "Chainsaw" perhaps foreshadows that numbers pressure and book cooking cannot be far behind. Al Dunlap had been brought in as CEO at a number of troubled companies and he had always managed to turn them around. His moniker on Wall Street was "Mr. Fix-It." His strategy was one of slashing costs—including substantial reductions in payroll, something that comes from downsizing. After he had turned around Scott Paper using his slashing strategies, with the resulting payoff in terms of increased share value, the directors at Sunbeam hired Dunlap to do the same thing. Just the announcement of Dunlap's appointment as CEO brought a significant market rally and a resulting positive impact on Sunbeam's share price.

Mr. Dunlap took over, closed plants, and promised analysts in 1996 that "we are winning in every aspect of our business." Shareholders loved him. Employees despised him, for the fearful culture he grew via pink slips and intimidation. In fact, because he was known as a master of layoffs (they didn't call him "Chainsaw" for nothing), Dunlap created a culture in which employees would do anything to meet the numbers goals he had established for the company. The result was that the SEC would investigate and conclude that $62 million of the $189 million reported as Sunbeam's income for 1997 was spun out of whole cloth in the following ways:

- Fake sales were transacted with "agreements to agree" that were later voided once the company had met its sales numbers for the quarter or year.

- The value of company inventory was reduced so that profits looked very high.

- So many write-downs had been taken in 1996 during the layoffs that the company had substantial reserves, which it then borrowed from during 1997 to boost results.

- Channel stuffing was common, a practice Bausch & Lomb also used, in which products are shipped prematurely or, in some cases, even before they are requested or purchased, so as to make the sales numbers look better. Sunbeam even rewarded distributors who took product and kept it by giving them a portion of the eventual profits.

Using those tactics, Sunbeam employees met the numbers, but at all costs, one of which was the bankruptcy of the company. Sunbeam filled for chapter 11 bankruptcy in 2001 and emerged newly organized at the end of November 2002.

WorldCom and Double-Digit Growth Regardless of How We Keep the Roll Going

Moving to the third round of ethical collapses, we find all of the poster children of corporate ethical collapse to be victims of numbers pressure. WorldCom provides a classic example of a numbers culture. Mr. Ebbers described his business strategy for WorldCom quite succinctly in 1997: "Our goal is not to capture market share or be global. Our goal is to be the No. 1 stock on Wall Street." In fact, Bernie was right, for a time. WorldCom's revenues went from $950 million in 1992 to $4.5 billion by 1996, at least as far as we know.

WorldCom had relied on an acquisition strategy to fuel its growth and stock market status. But the downside was the need to keep going with bigger and better mergers. If the mergers stopped, so did the fancy accounting WorldCom used in booking the mergers. Here's how an expert described the merger/accounting drive: "The acquirer uses its high stock price—and often heaps of debt—to make a purchase that automatically boosts dollar earnings. But it also dilutes the stock of the buyer's shareholders. Serial acquirers [and WorldCom was a serial acquirer] typically pay large premiums, and the bigger the premium, the more shares or debt they must issue. To overcome the dilution of their shares or rising interest payments, the combined company must rapidly grow earnings by creating huge synergies. That seldom happens, and when the synergies don't materialize, the stock price drops. The company can no longer trade highflying shares for acquisitions. The game is over." One former WorldCom executive phrased it this way: "The boost from post-acquisition accounting was like a drug. But it meant bigger deals had to come along to keep the ball rolling."

WorldCom's numbers strategy had several components, one of which was utter confusion. The pace of the mergers was so frenetic and the accounting and financials so different because of interim mergers that even the most so-phisticated analysts had trouble keeping up with the books. Analysts were of-ten at a loss to explain earnings growth, P/E ratios, cash sources, and all the gravity-defying growth of WorldCom. WorldCom's stock reached $64.50 per share in June 1999 but sank to $.83 on June 26, 2002, following the announce-ment of the application of real accounting and the resulting impact of, initially, about $3 billion, which would grow to $11 billion.

WorldCom's fancy merger accounting also gave its officers flexibility in numbers. Such accounting goes like this: a company acquires another (as WorldCom did sixty-five times) and is permitted to take a restructuring charge against earnings, the infamous "one-time charge." The restructuring charge is a management determination, and both reasonable and unreason-able minds differ on what the charges for restructuring following a merger should be. The tendency for managers is to overstate the restructuring charges and toss these extra charges, over and above actual charges, into reserves, sometimes referred to as the "cookie jar." So, if, for example, a company made an acquisition and booked $2 billion for restructuring charges, its earnings picture for that year would look quite awful. However, the actual costs of the restructuring are spread out over the time it takes for the company to restruc-ture, which is actually two to three years, and some of the charges booked may not actually occur. The hit to earnings has already been taken all at once with this factor by itself opening the door for upwards and rosier earnings growth in subsequent years. By making the restructuring costs high in the year of ac-quisition, even flat earnings the following year will seem to be a real and sub-stantial uptick because expenses are so diminished with no restructuring costs. Further, when the restructuring costs are lower, that lump sum of excess comes back in from reserves. Then, one mustn't forget that there is the cookie jar into which management can dip to use reserves should a subsequent year prove to be truly awful, thereby boosting earnings, or at least smoothing them out for investors. Indeed, the reserves can then be used to meet targets so that investors, Wall Street, and everyone else is happy because the company is sail-ing along as promised. Herein rests the concept of managing earnings, another wonderful numbers term that infiltrates the numbers-pressure culture that leads to ethical collapse. It's not cooking the books, it is managing earnings. A numbers obsession finds employees and officers not managing strategically but manipulating numbers for results.

Scott Sullivan, the CFO of WorldCom, was able to employ reserves to keep WorldCom going for two years after WorldCom's final merger attempt with Sprint failed in 2000. Because there were no further mergers, the serial Ponzi scheme built on acquisitions had to end and would have ended in 2000 had it not been for WorldCom's rather sizable reserves. Again, management discretion allows the reserves to be fed back into earnings as desired. Earnings can appear to be growing, but they are not doing so as a result of product sales; they are growing because of reserves being fed into the earnings picture.

WorldCom also faced another change beyond the loss of the acquisitions accounting flexibility, owing largely to the loss of acquisitions. As the telecommunications industry was deregulated, WorldCom was one of a few players in a field with tremendous growth potential, whether through customers or acquisitions. Its operating income in those noncompete years rose 132 percent from 1997 to 1998, its sales increased to $800 billion, and the price of WorldCom's stock rose 137 percent, all of which were mentioned in Mr. Ebbers's opening letter in the annual report. The language of WorldCom's annual reports shows what a company obsessed with numbers looks, sounds, and reads like before it hits the slope. The report pledges "the effective deployment of capital," something that sounds as if it involves the use of anti-aircraft missiles and rations. What follows is an excerpt from Bernie's 1997 letter to shareholders, which demonstrates the level of numbers obsession and the pressure that results:

> On a pro forma basis, total revenues increased over 30 percent on volume gains of 35 percent. WorldCom's efficiency in SG&A [selling, general and administrative expenses—a combination of salaries, advertising, commissions, and travel expenses] per revenue dollar is not at the expense of effectiveness, as the Company once again outstripped its major competitors with its ability to add incremental year-over-year internal revenue growth of $1.7 billion for the year. WorldCom continues to lead with the productivity of its employees. On average, each employee generates over $500,000 of revenue per year, based on 1997 results.

Therein Mr. Ebbers offers us a new performance ratio: income generated "per employee" as a basis for measuring earnings—but no pressure here! In hindsight, this numbers obsession reaches Monty Python satirical skit levels. By 1999 Mr. Ebbers had little but numbers in his annual-report letter: Internet business for WorldCom was up 57 percent, its data business was up 27 percent, its international business was up 53 percent, and its increase in net income was 217 percent. Competition forced WorldCom into a mode beyond those initial easy pickings for earnings. The time eventually came when numbers growth wouldn't come without some business strategy.

Still, Bernie always promised more and better with each annual report, which placed enormous pressure on officers and employees whose pensions, compensation, and bonuses were tied to continuing growth. When the dot-com bubble burst in 2000, Bernie had no numbers in his annual-report letter to the shareholders. Things were grim that year, but he still promised that the company had learned from this temporary setback, and he proceeded with another promise on earnings, albeit one with no numbers: He would deliver a "strong, solid performance in 2001." By 2002 Mr. Ebbers would leave the company and WorldCom would announce, in agonizing increments, that its numbers for the past three years would have to be restated, by $11 billion. That's not cooking the books. That's London broiling the books, and employees throughout this culture of amorality knew what was happening but could not find their way through the heavy atmosphere of meeting numbers and the path to ethical collapse to turn around their company culture. In the following excerpt from the criminal complaint against David Myers, who was WorldCom's controller, the drive to meet numbers controlled judgment, even to the point of crossing over into felony territory: "Sullivan and Myers decided to work backward, picking the earnings numbers that they knew the analysts expected to see, and then forcing WorldCom's financials to match those numbers." Mr. Sullivan's mantra was that the company had to keep line costs at 42 percent; anything that went beyond that was just shifted to capital expenditures. Once they developed the correct numbers, they simply relied on employees to make "journal entries" so that the miraculous accounting changes would appear. Their conduct was akin to us deciding that we wanted a certain amount for a tax refund and then working our way backward to develop the deductions to reach that goal. In WorldCom's case, employees were reduced to simply making the journal entries to achieve the pie-in-the-sky numbers. So, there really was not pressure at WorldCom to meet the numbers. There was, however, pressure to make them up.

Enron: A Billion or So, Here and There, in Accounting Mumbo Jumbo

In 2001, when Enron announced that it would have to restate a billion dollars or so in earnings, we were gasping for air over the shock of such a massive accounting fraud. But it's all relative. Now that we know about WorldCom's $11 billion, the $1 billion seems like chump change. But the actors got there in the same fashion. Enron also had a culture in which the pressure to meet the numbers was extraordinary. Granted, the executives and managers at Enron were a bit more clever about their accounting practices. They didn't make stuff up; they pushed the envelope on accounting rules to get their results.

Like WorldCom, Enron enjoyed the advantage of the first-mover position in a market just beginning deregulation. WorldCom enjoyed growth because it was buying long distance wholesale and selling it retail, but more cheaply than its competitors, at a time when telecommunications deregulation was just taking hold. Enron entered the wholesale power markets at a time when they were just opening up, and it was the first to realize the local, national, and international benefits of power trading. Enron not only experienced double-digit growth, it found that there was room for much interpretation in booking revenues for energy trading, an accounting practice referred to as mark-to-market accounting. Under FASB 133, for example, energy traders, like Enron, were permitted to include in current earnings those profits they expected to earn on energy contracts and related derivative estimates. Because of FASB 133, many energy companies were posting noncash earnings that they expected to realize sometime in the future. Enron was not alone in this practice, although it was the king of the hill for these types of earnings, boasting 80 percent of its earnings from the elusive and nonexistent mark-to-market accounting. Most utilities and energy companies disclosed what percentage of their reported earnings was attributable to noncash mark-to-market contracts, with most hovering around the 25–50 percent range.

That flexibility in accounting, coupled with internal pressure to meet earnings goals, meant that Enron was booking revenues for energy contracts that would not be performed for decades, and in some cases the sales were in regulated states that did not allow such contracts and power trades. Counting revenues from contracts that would be illegal perhaps pushes the envelope on even aggressive accounting just a bit. "Pick, pick, pick" was the attitude of the financial wizards at Enron whose goal was simply to meet the numbers each quarter. ABN Amro analyst Paul Patterson, a specialist in energy-trading firms, phrased the problem in diplomatic, perhaps even charitable, fashion: "Whenever there's a considerable amount of discretion that companies have in reporting their earnings, one gets concerned that some companies may overstate those earnings in certain situations where they feel pressure to make earnings goals."

Meeting those numbers became a tall order because between mid-1998 and the end of 1999, Enron's stock price tripled, from $20 to over $60 per share. By 2001 it had $100 billion in annual revenues, it was number seven on both the Fortune 500 and the Forbes 500. Enron was ranked above IBM and AT&T, as far as we knew at that time, which would be when we believed the numbers companies released as earnings and balance sheet statements. We now know rankings are all relative, relative to the fabrications of officers and doting auditors. Before its bubble burst, Enron's stock would climb to over $90 per share in 2000. Chairman Ken Lay continued to promise more. In a conference call with analysts, on July 13, 2001, a call he had to handle alone because his CEO, Jeffrey Skilling, had announced he was leaving the company to "spend more time with his family," Lay promised, "We've been doubling revenue and doubling income quarter on quarter, year on year for now about the last three years. We expect that to continue to grow very, very strong. . . ."

The goal of Enron's senior management was to meet or exceed the pledges of earnings growth of 15–20 percent per year. To meet those goals, the senior executives at the company imposed "budget targets" on all of the company's business units. Following the formula that seems to permeate ethically collapsed companies, the budget targets were derived by working backward from the EPS (earnings per share) numbers the executives had promised in their forecasts. So, once again, we had the "I want this much for a refund" strategy at work. However, the stiff earnings goals could not be met with mark-to-market accounting alone. The Enron executives would have to delve more deeply into accounting sleights-of-hands to meet those aggressive EPS goals. As a result, Andrew Fastow, then the CFO of Enron, found FASB 125 and a liberal interpretation that would take them right to the EPS they needed. The GAAP (Generally Accepted Accounting Principles) and FASB standards for disclosure of a company's transactions with related entities (FASB 125), or those entities in which the company holds an interest, apply only when the company owns at least 50 percent of the related entity. If a company owns 49 percent or less, any debt obligations of the related entity need not be carried as debt on the company's balance sheet. Consolidation is not required until the company owns 50 percent or more of its subsidiaries and other business ventures. So, owing mostly to auditors who were worried but silent, Fastow *et al.* would over time create about three thousand off-the-books entities in which they would dump Enron's debt and consequently keep the share price up—all while earning commissions for themselves in the transfer of the debt. Finder's fees are frequently paid for these sorts of transactions. But, truly, how hard do officers of a company have to look to find a taker for the company debt when they are creating the taker and then own the taken and even agree to stand responsible for the taker's debt?

From late 1999 on, creative business strategies, diversification, product development, and competition were not the focus of Enron activities. Rather, the character of the business was that of folks reporting to work each day to manipulate numbers via FASB loopholes such as FASB 125. So consumed were these folks with numbers and loopholes that they even named some of their off-the-books entities after the FASB rule they were manipulating. Hence, we had Raptor 125, a limited-liability partnership owned by Enron personnel who were funded by Enron. Such a brilliant loophole must offer credit to its source in FASB 125 as the genesis of the authorization for spinning Enron debt off the books. Still, despite this public thumbing of the executive nose at accounting principles (indeed, even this clue as to what was happening), the belief in the magic of double-digit growth allowed the facade to continue for years. Enron was a culture of numbers pressure writ large, pushing even geographic boundaries right on into the Cayman Islands and other offshore havens for SPEs (special purpose entities). "Figures lie, liars figure" was the motto of one Enron accountant who also believed that numbers varied depending upon who requested them. Performance evaluations, through the semiannual performance review committee, were dominated by Andrew Fastow, who saw to it that those who brought in the numbers were given the greatest rewards. Their loyalty and increasing devotion to meeting the numbers stemmed from those rewards.

Arthur Andersen: Handmaiden to Enron, Sunbeam, Waste Management, and a Goodly Number of Other Companies Involved in Ethical Collapse, Fraud, and Mighty SEC Problems

There was really numbers pressure to the second power in many of these ethically collapsed companies because those working there were not the only ones laboring mightily to meet the numbers. Their external auditors, more often than not Arthur Andersen, also had their own internal pressures to meet the numbers, particularly to retain audit clients as consulting clients as well. Some of Andersen's biggest hits of all time for accounting missteps include Global Crossing (in bankruptcy with questions about its accounting practices), WorldCom, Qwest Communications (the subject of an SEC inquiry that was settled by Qwest in 2004 for $250 million), Level 3 Communications (issues with restatements of financial information in August 2002 pursuant to SEC accounting interpretations that the company labeled "immaterial"), Waste Management (just now recovering from issues surrounding its financial reports), Baptist Foundation of Arizona (in liquidation bankruptcy, with Andersen recently settling a suit with investors for $100 million), and Sunbeam (in litigation over accounting and restatement issues).

All of these ethically collapsed companies were must-keep clients for Andersen. Andersen was paid $25 million for its audit work for Enron and $27 million for nonaudit work, including both tax and consulting services. Andersen, because of its focus on revenue figures for its own operations, could not see that the independence of its audits was compromised by its desire to please on the consulting work. Andersen joined the happy hoopla of all the other accounting firms in their assurances that consulting and auditing do mix. Congress saw otherwise, and Sarbanes-Oxley now prohibits the arrangements that created pressure to retain audit clients for the sake of the consulting dollars. Some companies halted the practice once Enron and Andersen collapsed, prior to the federal mandate.

It wasn't as if David Duncan, the audit partner who handled the Enron account for Andersen, did not see the accounting and auditing issues. He saw them quite clearly but couldn't bring himself to walk away from the $50 million in fees for his office, a contract that translated to $1 million in annual compensation for him. But he felt the pressure, and after Duncan entered his guilty plea to obstruction of justice (a plea he withdrew in 2006 following the U.S. Supreme Court's reversal of Andersen's conviction) following the Enron and Andersen collapses, his pastor offered the following explanation, "He basically said it was unrelenting. It was a constant fight. Wherever he drew that line, Enron pushed that line—he was under constant pressure from year to year to push that line."

But it wasn't just Andersen's Houston office, Enron, or Duncan feeling the pressure. There were other organizations using Andersen, and audit partners around the world were pushing the envelope in terms of financial-statement certification for clients because Andersen's own culture was a numbers culture. In her book about the fall of Andersen, *Final Accounting*, Barbara Ley Toffler, ironically the head of Andersen's ethics consulting division, describes the culture there: "The brutally competitive atmosphere within the Firm made a mockery of its principles and culture. . . . People were under tremendous pressure to bring in money, and instead of collaborators or colleagues, they now saw rivals and fee suckers." She describes their billing practices as "Billing Our Brains Out." Andersen head Joe Berardino praised the million-dollar teams, those who billed $1 million or more, as if they were rock stars, without ever mentioning what work they had done or what had been accomplished for the clients who paid the $1 million.

The so-called partner purge at Andersen in 1992 changed the character of this onetime gold-standard audit firm into a sales firm. Generating sales by consulting became the sole measure of success for the partners who remained. Compensation was tied to sales dollars, and they came through consulting, not auditing. Training shifted from the traditional Andersen integrity mantra to the how-to's of revenue generation. Getting close to clients for purposes of sales meant compromising audit independence. Audit partners felt pressure from consulting partners to please the clients. The numbers Andersen needed to make in-house controlled the auditors' take on the clients' numbers. When the problems with Sunbeam, Waste Management, Enron, and the Baptist Foundation of Arizona percolated to the surface, Andersen was quick to revoke its imprimatur in the public eye. But in the years leading up to the eventual revelations of fraud, Andersen remained quietly complicit. For the continuation of the consulting relationship that was nearly always worth more than the revenue the client's audit work brought in, Andersen auditors would sign off on everything from channel stuffing to thousands of off-the-books entities.

Nor was it a matter of Andersen's being duped by the clients. David Duncan saw the issue with Enron SPEs immediately upon their proposal by Andrew Fastow and even e-mailed Andersen's Chicago headquarters, seeking advice and counsel. In a May 28, 1999, e-mail to David Duncan, Benjamin Neuhausen, a member of Andersen's Professional Standards Group, wrote back, "Setting aside the accounting, idea of a venture entity managed by CFO is terrible from a business point of view. Conflicts galore. Why would any director in his or her right mind ever approve such a scheme?" So why did an audit firm and one of its senior partners sign off on such a proposal? Numbers pressure makes good, smart people do ethically dumb things and takes them closer toward ethical collapse.

HealthSouth: Just Get Those Numbers Where I Want Them to Be

HealthSouth, a chain of hospitals and rehabilitation centers, was one of those companies whose stodgy competitors dreamed of becoming during the pinnacle of its inexplicable success and earnings. As with Enron and WorldCom, its competitors sat on the sidelines for a time, dismayed by the performance of a superstar company that they could not replicate. Shaquille O'Neal, Michael Jordan, and Roger Clemens used HealthSouth facilities on a regular basis. HealthSouth issued press releases when sports figures such as Lucio, the Brazilian World Cup soccer star, had surgery at one of its facilities. Its model for new hospitals it was building was supposed to be the hospital of the future, something others would emulate.

Richard M. Scrushy, HealthSouth's CEO, began the company in 1984 with just $55,000 in capital gathered from three friends. The company's stock climbed from its first public offering as an obscure stock in late 1986 for about $1 per share to a darling of Wall Street, selling at nearly $31 per share in 1998.

In September 1998 Scrushy and other executives, including the company's CFO, began selling off their shares of HealthSouth. While there were suggestions of fraud, no charges were brought against Scrushy or the executives for their stock sales. Following these large sales, the company announced a reduction in forecasted earnings because, as Scrushy explained, there had been a change in Medicare rules. There was indeed a change in Medicare rules, but the reduction in forecasted earnings should have been $20–$30 million, not the $175 million HealthSouth announced.

HealthSouth enjoyed some recovery from the 1998 setback, with the stock climbing back from $5 to nearly $16 by May 2002. However, during this period the company was involved in a whistle-blower lawsuit that alleged Medicare fraud as well as a defamation suit brought against a former employee who had accused HealthSouth of admitting Medicare patients its facilities were not equipped to handle. Kimberly Landry, the former employee, had posted her concerns on the Internet and fought the defamation suit until the company recently withdrew the suit. HealthSouth settled Medicare fraud charges in 2004 by agreeing to pay $325 million to resolve a range of issues.

In August 2002 HealthSouth issued another restatement of forecasted earnings because it was discontinuing its practice of billing Medicare for individual therapies for patients who were receiving group therapy. The announcement caused the stock price to plunge 50 percent, to below $4 per share. HealthSouth profits were restated in 2002 and 2003 to reflect $2.5 billion less in earnings for periods dating back to 1994, with $1.1 billion coming from 1997 and 1998. The stock was trading on pink sheets at $0.165 per share in mid-April 2003, from, as noted earlier, a $31 high in 1998. HealthSouth settled SEC charges on the restatements with payment of a $100 penalty in 2005.

There were again allegations by investigators of insider trading by Scrushy, but the company hired an outside law firm to investigate and was cleared of any wrongdoing, and then-Chairman Scrushy issued the following statement in a press release in August 2002:

> *I have spent the past twenty years building the most profitable healthcare company in the business. Any challenges we face are here with or without me. As I have told the media and regulators, I am committed to getting all the facts out about the concerns expressed through a policy of complete transparency. I have done this because I know there has been absolutely no impropriety in anything I have done. I have complete confidence in our new Chief Executive Officer, Bill Owens.*

That new CEO, Owens, the former CFO, issued the following accompanying statement:

> *As the new Chief Executive Officer of HealthSouth, I want to make it clear that Richard M. Scrushy had absolutely no knowledge about any change in Medicare reimbursement rules until August 6, 2002, and none of us had any knowledge whatsoever that a possible rule change would have a material, financial impact on our company until August 15, 2002. This was two weeks after he repaid a stock loan and $4 million in interest, and three months after he sold company stock as a result of the pending expiration of stock options. Richard and the Board of Directors have entrusted me with the position of CEO, and I am fully executing my duties and running the day to day operations; however, the company is still faced with the challenges of overcoming the CMS [Centers for Medicare and Medicaid Services (federal agency)] rule change and getting the truth out regardless if Richard Scrushy is chairman or not. I, and the Board of Directors, have full confidence in, and more importantly completely depend on, Richard Scrushy's continued leadership and vision. The personal attacks on Richard are wrong, and those making the attacks obviously don't have the facts. You must understand this is not about Richard Scrushy, myself, or HealthSouth. This is about a government issued rule change. Those are the facts, and anything else is nonsense. We have a highly profitable company with operating margins in the mid-20s, and all our*

lines of business are doing well. We are 110% committed to working through these issues and getting all this behind us.

It was 1998 when Scrushy announced with great fanfare that HealthSouth had matched or beat earnings estimates for forty-seven quarters in a row. What is perhaps most revealing are the statements Scrushy made to Owens, who was aiding both the FBI and SEC investigators in exchange for leniency in the charges against him. Owens wore a wire in his meetings with Scrushy, thereby allowing law enforcement officials to record Scrushy's statements. At the time, Scrushy was unaware of the investigations of Owens and the other officers. Below are some excerpts from the recordings that were played in federal district court in Alabama as Scrushy attempted to have some of his assets (his request was for $70 million) released for his defense:

"[If you] fixed [financial statements] immediately, you'll get killed. But if you fix it over time, if you go quarter to quarter, you can fix it."

"Engineer your way out of what you engineered your way into."

"I don't know what to say. You need to do what you need to do."

"We just need to get those numbers where we want them to be. You're my guy. You've got the technology and the know-how."

Scrushy's lawyers did play other excerpts from the tapes in court to bolster their argument that Scrushy did not know until the end that there were problems with the company's financial statements. At one point in the 4.5 hours of tape, Scrushy is heard to say, "What are you talking about, Bill?" The company's auditor during the period from 1994 to 2002, Ernst & Young (the HealthSouth board has since replaced the firm with PricewaterhouseCoopers), has indicated that it was duped by executives who created false documents and journal entries. One of the Ernst & Young auditors produced three sets of fraudulent documents in court and noted, "The level of fraud and financial deceptions that took place at HealthSouth is a blatant violation of investor trust, and Ernst & Young is as outraged as the investing public." Ernst & Young also noted in a press release that "when individuals are determined to commit a crime, as was the case with certain executives at HealthSouth, a financial audit cannot be expected to detect that crime."

Scrushy was masterful at applying numbers pressure. Again, in the recordings with Mr. Owens, Scrushy noted to his subordinates, "Look at how profitable this company is. Do we really want to trash all of this?" When the company was not meeting the numbers and analysts' expectations, Scrushy's instructions to the officers were "Go figure it out." One of five former Health-South CFOs indicted by the Justice Department upon HealthSouth's restatement of earnings testified that HealthSouth had overstated revenues by $2.5 billion, a figure 2,500 percent higher than what was reported, with accounting employees inflating assets and revenues from 1997 to 2001. One officer noted, "The corporate culture created the fraud, and the fraud created the corporate culture." In an interview in the fall of 2002, Scrushy explained his management technique: "Shine a light on someone—it's funny how numbers improve." Even at the last officer meeting, recordings indicate that Scrushy was trying to make it all work. "I want each one of the [divisional] presidents to e-mail all of their people who miss their budgets. I don't care whether it's by a dollar." Nonetheless, while 13 of 15 HealthSouth employees who were charged would enter pleas, Scrushy was acquitted of all charges.

HealthSouth employees kept up a feverish pace because of the work required to meet the numbers. Testimony at Scrushy's trial offered a chilling picture of a culture consumed not with running a business but with finding ways to make the numbers play out so that they showed continuing high growth and returns. One of the many financial officers of the company testified at Scrushy's trial how he and another officer explained to Scrushy how they were able to get rid of $300 million in expenses through some highfalutin acquisition accounting. Scrushy screamed at those who did not come through, but he loved those who did meet the numbers, and he told then-CFO Michael Martin in that meeting, "Damn, you guys are good."

Only one officer, former treasurer Leif Murphy, would leave the company when he discovered what was happening with the accounting. At his farewell party, the cake read, "Eat s——and die." Rebecca Kay Morgan, the vice president of accounting, said that she had an epiphany when she read the Sarbanes-Oxley legislation after it was passed and realized that she had been cooking the books. She refused to go forward with the financials, and HealthSouth began to unravel. Her guilty plea netted her house arrest and probation.

Marsh & McLennan (MMC): An Insurer Whose Income Defied Claims

It all began innocently enough, as all New York Attorney General Eliot Spitzer investigations do, with the culling of e-mails. In so culling, Spitzer's office uncovered at Marsh & McLennan (MMC) some gravity-defying moral relativism in action. MMC was (until this debacle and it was damaging with just the first quarter of 2005 bringing a 70 percent drop in MMC's revenue) a huge insurance broker with 43,000 employees in its global operations. MMC's revenues were $2 billion more than its closest competitor, Aon Corporation. Those revenues are really the result of MMC's conglomerate structure, which consists of Marsh, its risk and insurance division; Putnam Investments, a mutual-fund and investment-management company; and Mercer Inc., a human-resources consulting company. For those of you schooled in business scandals from 2001 to 2005, you may already realize that MMC, hit by rumblings from Enron, commenced a cleansing period in 2002 and 2003 in which all manner of earnings management, earnings restatements, off-the-books debts, and your general creative accounting and IPO allocations were revealed in layers of state and federal investigations. Following that regulatory assault, MMC's Putnam Investments was investigated by the SEC, sued by its mutual-fund customers, and required to pay fines to one and damages to the other. In 2003 Putnam earned the ignominious honor of becoming the first mutual-fund company to be charged with showing favoritism to certain customers by allowing them to buy and sell shares that resulted in losses to less-favored customers. But MMC would soon be 0 for 3. Within the same time frame, Mercer, its consulting arm that specializes in executive compensation, was hit along with 15 other companies with an SEC request for information on conflicts of interest that arose as it tried to retain clients as well as for its role in not disclosing the full terms of the compensation package for NYSE chairman Dick Grasso. Mercer settled with Eliot Spitzer on the Grasso issue. The SEC formal investigation of Mercer, begun in August 2005, is pending. MMC was clearly an ethically troubled company long before Eliot Spitzer rooted through insurance brokers' e-mails.

Facing these setbacks and concluding that seeking bids and making recommendations on insurers was too tough a slog, MMC developed a "pay to play" format for obtaining bids that allowed the insurers and MMC to profit. Not only did MMC receive its commissions, it also received payments from insurers in exchange for renewals, or bonuses paid to MMC when its corporate customers renewed their policies. To be sure that (a) the policies were renewed and (b) the renewal bonus was a given, MMC had all of its insurers agree to roll over on renewals. For example, if Insurer A was up for renewal, Insurers B and C would submit fake and higher bids that MMC would then take to the corporate client and, of course, recommend renewal at the lower rate. In some cases, as alleged in the suit filed by Spitzer, MMC did not even have official bids from the competing insurers. MMC sent bids forward that had not even been signed by the patsy insurers who were playing along in order to receive the same treatment when their renewals came along. This type of an arrangement cuts way back on the rigors of competition. There was no competitive bidding, and the payments inflated the prices.

Perhaps MMC's difficulties could be summarized in one word: "cartel." That same word was used in the civil suit filed by Spitzer against MMC. For example, in the MMC investigation, Spitzer quotes this e-mail from an ACE assistant vice president to ACE's vice president of underwriting (ACE is the third-largest insurance broker in the industry after MMC and American International): "Original quote $990,000. . . . We were more competitive than AIG in price and terms. MMGB [Marsh McLennan Global Broking] requested we increase the premium to $1.1M to be less competitive, so AIG does not loose [sic] the business." The rich veins of e-mail Spitzer tapped into during the MMC investigation show that he has found the Achilles' heel of many a Goliath. Mixed metaphors aside, Spitzer uses the words of businesspeople themselves to condemn and try them and their companies.

Cartels are not the kind of thing that bring a great deal of price competition—or any competition, for that matter. But cartel activity surely does roll in the revenues and profits. Once the "pay to play" system was implemented at MCC, its insurance revenue became 67.1 percent of its revenue. Commissions from these arrangements represented half of MMC's 2003 income of $1.5 billion. Marsh reported a 94 percent drop in its third-quarter profit for 2004 from 2003 because it agreed to drop the commission system. Its income for 2003 was $357 million, but for 2004 it was just $21 million.

Once again, multinational antitrust violations are hardly a close call. There are e-mails between and among companies and employees indicating their understanding that they were violating antitrust laws. In one e-mail quoted in the Spitzer suit, an MMC executive (whose name is redacted) even jokes about the practice of sending a fake emissary to a meeting for taking bids on insurance policies. 'Tis all but a facade because the bid price is fixed. "This month's recipient of our Coordinator of the Month Award requests a body at the rescheduled April 23 meeting. He just needs a live body. Anyone from New York office would do. Given recent activities, perhaps you can send someone from your janitorial staff—preferably a recent hire from the U.S. Postal Service." The executive from the other company was not interested in the bid-rigging and responded, in all capital letters: "WE DON'T HAVE THE STAFF TO ATTEND MEETING JUST FOR THE SAKE OF BEING A 'BODY.' WHILE YOU MAY NEED 'A LIVE BODY,' WE NEED A 'LIVE OPPORTUNITY.' WE'LL TAKE A PASS."

An executive at Munich Re, an insurer that worked with MMC, indicated in another e-mail, as in all situations in which ethical collapse is imminent, full knowledge that what was going on was wrong, if not illegal: "I am not some Goody Two Shoes who believes that truth is absolute, but I do feel I have a pretty strict ethical code about being truthful and honest. This idea of 'throwing the quote' by quoting artificially high numbers in some predetermined arrangement for us to lose is repugnant to me, not so much because I hate to lose, but because it is basically dishonest. And I basically agree with the comments of others that it comes awfully close to collusion and price-fixing." Apparently he was not alone in spotting the antitrust issues.

But the numbers pressure was everywhere. As MMC's profitability increased, it became more and more difficult to meet the past numbers, let alone increase them. One branch manager explained, "We had to do our very best to hit our numbers. Each year our goals were more aggressive." Jeff Greenberg, the CEO, was a tyrant when it came to the numbers. Roger Egan, the president and COO of MMC, explained the culture and the fear in this statement to his direct reports: "Each time I see Jeff [Greenberg] I feel like I have a bull's eye on my forehead." That quote was one kept by an accounting employee who agreed to testify for Mr. Spitzer if needed. With MMC's settlement, the pressure on these brokers has ended, along with the obligation to serve as witnesses.

Tyco and the Acquisition Accounting Flexibility

Tyco International had its humble beginnings as a research laboratory in 1960. When it was founded by Arthur Rosenburg, his unassuming idea was that the company would do contract research work for the government. By 1962 Rosenburg had incorporated and created two divisions of Tyco: the holding company called Tyco Semiconductor, and Materials Research Laboratory. By 1964 the company had gone public and its focus had become one of manufacturing products for commercial use. Under the leadership of Dennis Kozlowski, Tyco would grow into a conglomerate with a presence in more than a hundred countries and over 250,000 employees. Between 1991 and 2001, Kozlowski took Tyco from $3 billion in annual sales to $36 billion, mostly through acquisitions totaling $60 billion. Tyco's share price at its high point would reach $62. Tyco became the parent company of Grinnell Security Systems, health-care-products companies, and just about anything else it could acquire—because buying companies was its strategy for growth.

Along with Kozlowski's acquisition strategy came an obsession with numbers. Employees responded to his public statements and private demands for results and double-digit increases, and Tyco's performance, at least as far as we knew back then, was nothing less than phenomenal. From 1992, when Kozlowski took over as CEO, to 1999, the stock price had jumped fifteenfold. In January 2002 *Business Week*, in praising Kozlowski's performance, wrote, "Kozlowski vows Tyco's earnings will once again grow by more than 20% a year. That would bring him closer to his ultimate goal: inheriting the mantle once worn by Jack Welch."

The numbers culture made it all the way down to even the factory workers. One employee noted, "Tyco is so big, they don't even know where Rock Hill is. They just know the numbers. All we hear is, 'If we don't hit these numbers, we're in trouble.'"

Tyco had an additional issue beyond the numbers pressure. Tyco had the flexibility of acquisitions accounting in which to mask any shortfalls in the double-digit achievements demanded by Kozlowski. Where there are acquisitions aplenty, there is room for creative accounting.

Tyco's financials were odd in that it seemed to be heavily in debt but was still reporting oodles of cash flow. Therein lies the beauty, flexibility, and numbers-goal savior: goodwill. When one company acquires another, it must include the assets acquired on its balance sheet. The acquirer, who we now know was really interested in making its numbers, is, in an odd conflict-of-interest irony, in charge of establishing the value of the assets acquired. From 1998 to 2001 Tyco spent $30 billion on acquisitions and attributed $30 billion to goodwill. Those of you unschooled in the ways of debit and credit accounting may be thinking, "But the numbers still match; whatever could be the problem?"

The problem lies in the fact that the assets acquired are not carried on Tyco's books with any significant value. Assets, under accounting rules, lose their value over time. Goodwill stays the same in perpetuity. However, if Tyco turns around and sells the assets it has acquired and booked at virtually zero value, the profit is a big chunk of change and is reflected in the income of the company. The only way an investor in Tyco would be able to tell what has really happened would be to have access to the balance sheets of the acquired companies so that he or she could see the value of the assets as they were carried on the books of the acquired company. The bump to earnings from the sale of the assets is lovely, but the bump to profits, with no offsetting costs, is tremendous. By September 2002 Tyco would be forced to announce a $2.5 billion charge to correct past misdeeds on these types of understatements of assets in its acquisitions.

Tyco employed all of the "iffy" additional accounting practices when it completed its acquisitions, the practices that the then-chairman of the SEC, Arthur Levitt, was decrying as problematic. Tyco's goal was always to make the acquired company look as much like a dog as possible. Referred to as spring-loading, this process pumps up the bad numbers to make the acquired company look worse than it really is. The next year, following the Tyco acquisition, if the company just continues along as normal, it looks terrific compared with the dog of a company Tyco had reported as part of the acquisition. Tyco enjoys not just a boost in terms of revenue; it gets respect for its management acumen. Spring-loading is easily accomplished by having the acquired company pay everything for which it has a bill, whether that bill is due or not. For example, when Tyco acquired Raychem, its treasurer sent out the following e-mail:

At Tyco's request, all major Raychem sites will pay all pending payables, whether they are due or not. . . . I understand from Ray [Raychem's CFO] that we have agreed to do this, even though we will be spending the money for no tangible benefit either to Raychem or Tyco.

Lars Larsen, the Raychem treasurer at the time of the acquisition wrote in a follow-up memo, "The purpose of this effort is, at Tyco's request, to cause cash flows to be negative in the 'old' Raychem, and more positive in the new company." For those of you keeping score, we have hit company number four that found its numbers by working backward from the desired result. When working with a company to be acquired, Tyco employees would also pump up the reserves, with one employee of Tyco asking an employee of an acquired firm, "How high can we get these things? How can we justify getting this higher?" The final report on the Tyco collapse, commissioned by the new Tyco board of directors and written by a team led by attorney David Boies, concluded that Tyco used both incentives and pressure on executives to get them to push the envelope on accounting rules in order to maximize results. The language from the report reads, "Tyco pursued a pattern of aggressive accounting that was intended, within the range of accounting permitted by GAAP, to increase current earnings above what they would have been if a more conservative approach had been followed."

The SEC began investigating the settlement of a lawsuit between Tyco and U.S. Surgical, a company it took over in 1998. Documents that emerged in the case included memoranda between Tyco financial executives in which they discuss methods whereby U.S. Surgical could slow growth in between the time Tyco announced its acquisition and when the actual transfers were made. Just prior to the closure of the deal, U.S. Surgical took a onetime hit of $322 million in miscellaneous charges. Interestingly, the memos refer to the practice as "financial engineering," thus creating a comfort level with the ethical questions. If we call what we are doing something lovely, it cannot be an ethical issue. Downloading music without paying is not copyright infringement; it's peer-to-peer file sharing. Earnings management. Smoothing earnings. Terms of art and science that avoid drawing bright lines between right and wrong. Pursuant to recommendations in the Boies report, Tyco filed an 8-K report in December 2002 in which it disclosed the "financial engineering" issues and restated the earnings for U.S. Surgical for that time frame. Nonetheless, a standout line in the quasi-remorse of Tyco's corrective 8-K is "Aggressive accounting is not necessarily improper accounting."

Perhaps the numbers pressure at this company was most evident when Tyco acquired ADT Security Services. A burglar-alarm dealer who worked for ADT prior to the Tyco acquisition summarized the change in culture post-acquisition as one of wanting salespeople to target "the scummiest neighborhoods possible . . . neighborhoods where there were problems, where Mookie was standing on a corner selling rock [crack cocaine]. Tyco kept pushing. They wanted numbers. They didn't give a crap if the accounts fell off the books later." About 20 percent of the contracts signed during the initial Tyco era were with customers who had very poor credit. The sales staff was in on the pressure to such an extent that the scripts for the ADT salespeople read like a bad *Saturday Night Live* skit. For example, if when selling in a high-crime area, the potential customers said, "The Lord will protect me," the ADT salesperson was to say, "Yes, I know. That's why He sent me here today." The sales force also used the attacks of September 11, 2001, on New York City and Washington as a selling point, shamelessly hitting the streets of those cities afterward to capitalize on rampant fear. The company pushed so hard for expansion and continuing sales that it was even reduced to giving dealerships to convicted felons, a practice that was specifically prohibited by company policy. The intense numbers focus and the pressure blinded them to long-term issues and robbed them of continued growth and success. ADT had truly alarming, as it were, cancellation rates because of the low-credit quality of customers, with cancellation rates reaching 50 percent in many areas.

The numbers pressure became apparent even to outside legal counsel for Tyco during the 1999 SEC investigation of the company. In a May 25, 2000, e-mail from William McLucas of Wilmer Cutler to Mr. Mark Belnick, general counsel for Tyco, is the following admonition on the accounting practices of Tyco and what pressure the managers were experiencing: "We have found issues that will likely interest the SEC. . . . Creativeness is employed in hitting the forecasts. . . . There is also a bad letter from the Sigma people just before the acquisition confirming that they were asked to hold product shipment just before the closing." The e-mail goes on to state that, overall, Tyco's financial reports suggest "something funny which is likely apparent if any decent accountant looks at this."

Meeting numbers was everything. But those executives who exceeded goals enjoyed rewards that sent an even more intense focus on those numbers. The CEO of one of Tyco's subsidiaries had a salary of $625,000, but when he boosted sales by 62 percent his bonus was $13 million. Kozlowski's bonus for that same year was $125 million.

Oh, Ye of Little Faith in Ponzi Schemes: Numbers Pressure at the Baptist Foundation

Bennett M. Weiner, head of the Philanthropic Advisory Service of the Council of Better Business Bureaus, warns, "There's tremendous pressure on charities today to increase their revenues to meet expenses and growing public needs. Unfortunately, this can influence some organizations to take financial risks because of potential rewards." Nonprofits have the same risks of ethical collapse because of numbers pressure and other danger signs. Ethical collapse is not unique to Wall Street or for-profit firms.

The Baptist Foundation of Arizona (BFA) offers an example of a nonprofit led astray, all in the name of serving with faith its even more faithful investors who trusted that those of the cloth, and those working closely with them, would not fall victim to ethical collapse. The faithful investors learned that although the Lord giveth, He too is subject to the natural forces of the market and that even cultures dedicated to faith and other good causes can collapse ethically without the necessary checks and balances.

By the time the BFA collapsed in 1999, about eleven thousand investors would lose $590 million in a faith-based Ponzi scheme permitted to march onward despite its defiance of all natural market forces. The foundation had the added credibility of ministers encouraging members of their flocks to invest in the foundation that was created for the noble causes of building retirement nest eggs even as it constructed retirement and nursing homes for the aging and infirm, paid the salaries of pastors, and generally provided funds for Baptist ministries. However, noble causes are not immune from paying bills and the pressures of showing ROI. In other words, even portfolios of the cloth are accountable in a numbers sense.

The numbers braggadocio of the BFA annual reports gave new meaning to the New Testament adage of the lilies of the field neither toiling nor spinning but doing just fine nonetheless. The BFA was represented as a miraculous investment fund that was yielding double-digit returns as no one in nonprofits or Wall Street had ever seen before. But the annual reports did not do justice to the numbers obsession of this miraculous fund. The BFA distributed to "messengers" at its annual convention, along with the usual doctrinal advice and inspiration, the "Book of Reports," which was a compendium filled with statistics on BFA performance. However, the "Book of Reports" was available to others upon request because it was the key tool for bringing money into the fold, a practice critical to all Ponzi schemes. And all the numbers were encased in a philosophy called "stewardship investment," a term that had a multitude, as it were, of interpretations but was winkingly known by the faithful as a practice that most assuredly would bring higher-than-market and greater-than-any-index returns to those who invested.

However, the BFA, begun in 1984, was heavily invested in real estate, and in 1988 the real estate market was tanking. Rather than disclose those difficulties and face the buffetings of the marketplace and economic cycles, something that should have been obvious to even the least astute economist among us, the BFA opted not to write down properties. The management team, with its compensation and reputation on the line, chose not to disclose the devaluation issues to the board, and instead decided to engage in complex layers of transactions involving sales, accounts receivable, overvalued collateral, and re-lated parties in order to maintain the appearance of having both assets and income. Along the lines of the Finova syndrome, the BFA carried on its books the properties at their full original value, not their true market value, figures that would have been significantly less and were driving many other real es-tate investment firms into bankruptcy. The BFA, convinced of the virtue of its ends, used means even beyond the Finova "let's not write it down just yet" theory of financial reporting. Indeed, its income doubled between 1996 and 1997 and had grown from $350,000 in 1988 to $2.5 million in 1997, all dur-ing a downturn in the real estate market. Employing a quasi-Enron approach, BFA also began a program of selling its assets to related parties (including some board members and companies of board members) at their book value or slightly more in order to show income for the BFA. The difficulty was that the sales were simply sham transactions among related parties. No money ever changed hands. Some of the twenty-one individuals who sat on the BFA board and were involved in the decisions to carry properties at their original value were also involved in the sales transactions for these properties. Five officers and board members were charged with fraud. Former directors Lawrence Dwain Hoover, Harold Dewayne Friend, and Richard Lee Rolfes were indicted. They entered not-guilty pleas (along with William Pierre Crotts, former CEO, and Thomas Dale Grabinski, former general counsel, who were also charged), but these initial indictments were dismissed when a judge determined that some of the evidence presented to the grand jury was improper and prejudicial.

When new thirty-two-count indictments were re-issued, Friend entered a guilty plea to one count of attempting to assist a crime syndicate. As part of his plea, he agreed to testify in the trials of other BFA defendants, including Crotts and Grabinski. Friend is expected to testify that BFA was inflating the numbers for the financial statements as early as 1989 and creating transactions in order to present a solvent and high-performing portfolio.

Donald Dale Deardoff, Jalma W. Hunsinger, and Edgar Alan Kuhn entered guilty pleas to fraud schemes, facilitation of fraud schemes, and facilitation of conducting illegal schemes. Crotts and Grabinski again entered not-guilty pleas. After years of preparation, the trial for Crotts's and Grabinski's charges of three counts of fraud, twenty-seven counts of theft, and two counts of con-ducting an illegal enterprise each began in the fall of 2005, with an estimate that it would run six months. As of May 2006, the trial, like an Energizer bunny, was still going strong.

However, the air concept for showing good financial results never made its way onto the balance sheet. As a result, BFA looked great, more investors joined in, and the Ponzi scheme continued. Amazingly, the fraud lasted until 1999, when state officials issued a cease and desist order to stop the BFA from its financial proselytizing. In 1998 Andersen had identified "earnings management" as a significant problem at the BFA but still continued its certification of the foundation's financial reports. Andersen also noted that management had specific revenue targets and that it undertook whatever means necessary to achieve those numbers. There it is again, that deciding on a number for revenue and then working backward.

The web of subsidiaries, such as Christian Financial Partners, EVIG, ALO, Select Trading Group, and Arizona Southern Baptist New Church Ventures, made the complexities difficult for newcomers to the Ponzi scheme to unravel. To an outsider, the complexities translated into sophistication, and those increasing income numbers were persuasive. When the criminal indictments were issued Arizona officials called the BFA the largest "affinity fraud" in U.S. history. Affinity fraud is one that targets true believers. Given the magnitude of the WorldCom fraud and the loyalty of its investors and employees, it almost seems like an affinity fraud as well. True believers also exist in telecom and on Wall Street.

A Government Agency: NASA and Budget and Performance Pressure Over Safety

Following three different accidents that revealed safety compromises, NASA, an agency of the U.S. government, concluded from its own reflective study that internal pressure to meet deadlines and budget constraints caused its lapses in judgment on safety. The types of numbers that government employees were expected to meet were different, but they felt the same pressure to meet them nonetheless, and at the expense of safety. Unreasonable numbers pressure interferes with ethics and good judgment, whether related to financial statements or safety issues. The third report, issued in late 2003, concluded that pressure to meet budget constraints and complete a launch on time were the contributing causes of the accident that cost the lives of all seven who were aboard the *Columbia* shuttle that crashed upon reentry in the summer of 2003: "The past decisions of national leaders—the White House, Congress, and NASA Headquarters—set the *Columbia* accident in motion by creating resource and schedule strains that compromised the principles of a high-risk technology organization. . . . The measure of NASA's success became how much costs were reduced and how efficiently the schedule was met. But the space shuttle is not now, nor has it ever been, an operational vehicle. We cannot explore space on a fixed-cost basis."

The report describes a culture that minimized safety because of the pressures related to time and money. The pressures were different, but the impact was the same—employees' judgment was clouded when they were faced with critical decision points. Interviews with NASA employees showed that they felt the budget and schedule pressures as they made decisions about postponing launches, proposing changes, and suggesting additional costs to ensure safety.

> *I don't know what Congress communicated to O'Keefe [head of NASA at the time]. I don't really understand the criticality of February 19th, that if we didn't make that date, did that mean the end of NASA? I don't know. . . . I would like to think that the technical issues and safety resolving technical issues can take priority over any budget or scheduling issue.*

Another employee noted, "And I have to think that subconsciously that even though you don't want it to affect decision-making, it probably does."

E-mails throughout the analysis report of what went wrong and why no one fixed the problem that caused the fatal crash show that employees were concerned about various structural issues on the space shuttle, including the tiles on the wings, something that would eventually be a contributing cause of the fatal crash. Nonetheless, the pressure to meet budgets and deadlines impaired their judgment, and none were vocal enough in their concerns to halt the launch or even suggest repairs and alternatives as the flight progressed.

The Antidotes for Pressure to Maintain Those Numbers

Not every company doing well and seeing its sales numbers increase is headed for ethical collapse. Not every company that has numbers goals and compensation tied to reaching those goals will wind up in the annals of financial history as a "gigantic fraud." So, what is the difference between an achiever and a manipulator? Where is that fine line between quantitative targets and diabolical obsession? There are checks and balances—antidotes, if you will—to the numbers culture. Putting them into place does not curb employee or company achievement. These antidotes curb only achievement at any cost. These fixes are designed to prevent a "meeting numbers" type of ethical culture in which numbers trump ethics.

Antidote #1 for Pressure to Maintain Those Numbers: Surround Goal Achievement in a Square Box of Values

If you tell employees nine times a day to "meet those numbers" and then remind them once a year in a superficial training session on ethics to "never do anything unethical," which direction will they follow? I have helped many companies and organizations with their once-each-year ethical training, and I am pleased to help. But a once-a-year reminder session on ethics does not provide a sufficient antidote to numbers-pressure culture. One annual session on ethics does not an ethical culture make! Employees can be encouraged to strive, work extra hours, follow up with customer service, and deliver orders themselves if necessary in order to meet their sales numbers. But they should also be told that shipments made without orders, channel stuffing, sham transactions, and just about everything you read that was done in the companies just highlighted are all just plain wrong. Managers should state without equivocation what company values are and that those values are honored, always. Employees should have specific examples of right and wrong, particularly examples within their industry. Explaining the lines employees should not cross in meeting sales goals and then providing examples of conduct that does and does not cross those lines gives employees a straight baseline. When all values and examples have been given on all the possible means of pumping numbers, we find that employees have been encased in a box of straight lines that form the company values. The box of values surrounds and dictates the activities and decisions of employees. The values give the means to the end: the financial and other goals of the organization. Meeting numbers does not define the values. Values determine what we will and will not do to get to the numbers. Communicating that values are first and numbers second is a tall order, but there are several steps that can help managers communicate what the lines are, where those lines meet to form the four corners of the values box, and that numbers, achieved using illegal or unethical means, just don't count.

Just Because It's Legal Doesn't Mean It's Ethical

One of the stunning realities of companies with a numbers culture is the high comfort level employees feel with their questionable accounting practices. Ironically, they are justified in many cases in that comfort level. Andrew Fastow, the CFO of Enron, found the noted former accounting rule, FASB 125 (thankfully no longer with us) to be the rationalization for his conduct. Once named CFO of the year, Fastow used creative booking that did not violate any accounting rules, yet he still managed to perpetuate a gigantic fraud. In fact, Fastow's comfort level was so high that he bragged about his acumen in interpreting accounting rules in a 1999 interview with *CFO Magazine* (which did give him the honor of CFO of the year). His candid answer when asked how Enron looked so good financially was that he spun the debt off the books. He even went so far, with pride in having uncovered a loophole, as to name some of these off-the-books entities Raptor 125 and Hawaii 125-0. Much as we name streets and buildings after our leaders and benefactors, Fastow named his creations in honor of the FASB rule that he found so helpful in meeting his numbers and that brought him millions in personal gain. Could he legally operate such a scheme? Sure, and this example illustrates why there are so many hung juries in these cases and such great difficulty in making the case for criminal intent. However, answering the "should" question is more difficult because his use of the rule meant that he presented a financial picture of Enron that was completely deceptive. Oddly, compliance with accounting rules is not compliance with the law. "One can violate SEC laws and still comply with generally accepted accounting principles." That challenge remains today and should be a matter of concern and focus for boards, officers, and employees. Understanding the accounting rules and the law is only the beginning of compliance. Boards and officers have to establish the "should" constraints of the laws and rules.

Establishing the "should vs. could" standard helps curb the Yeehaw Culture because mere compliance with the law and accounting rules may actually create disincentives for an ethical culture. The result of such a letter-of-the-law atmosphere is an abuse of form over substance. The antidote for this problem of rules, rules, rules is for managers to emphasize that false impressions are an ethical violation even when those false impressions are created in complete compliance with accounting rules. Avoiding ethical collapse requires flying a bit above the treetops on the accounting rules and the law. A legendary story from Hank Greenberg's life offers some insight into how AIG could have devolved under his leadership into accounting shenanigans and his ouster as CEO. When he was in the army and stationed in London, the commanding officers gave their men an extra day of leave if they would use it for culture, such as attending the theater, rather than the usual activities—drinking and chasing and, often, catching women. The soldiers only had to bring back the program from whatever play, concert, or event they attended. Greenberg would purchase a ticket to a play, go into the theater and pick up a copy of the playbill, and then exit through a side door for a day of fun, passion, and everything else the commanders were trying to rein in. Ah, blessed loopholes that allow the clever to circumvent the rules, standards of proof, and requirements put into place for a program that benefits them. What fascinating parallels can be drawn between the "could do it" habits of a young solider and the "could do it" circumvention of a CEO running a multinational insurer. Legal but not necessarily ethical. In compliance, but clearly violative of the intent of the commanding officers.

On the eve of his second trial for charges of looting Tyco for personal gain, Dennis Kozlowski granted an interview to *The New York Times* and assured the reporter that what he did, having Tyco pay the $20 million in expenses for remodeling his apartment, was not larceny (one of the charges against him) because the money he used for personal needs was funneled to him and his decorators through a board-approved key-employee loan program. "I firmly believe that I never did nor intended to do anything wrong." From a legal standpoint, there is some merit to his "technically speaking, I didn't embezzle because I authorized it and the board never objected." The jury in the second trial didn't buy the theory that an embezzler is not an embezzler if he authorized himself to embezzle. During their eleven days of deliberation, Kozlowski's and Mark Swartz's (CFO under Kozlowski) jurors found that technicalities do not a meaningful authorization make. But from an ethical perspective, the money was used in ways never imagined when the loan program was put into place. He had found a loophole. Indeed, the jury in the trial of Tyco's former general counsel, Mark Belnick, also accused of unauthorized use of corporate funds, concluded as much. He was found not guilty despite his extensive use of the same loan program for the purchase of a New York City apartment and a Park City, Utah, residence, with all of the loans eventually forgiven. Even the jurors, who deliberated for five days, were troubled by the judge's instruction that so long as Mr. Belnick believed he had the right to the money, he could not be found guilty of larceny. The money was there for the taking under the company's lax controls. Legally, the jury was correct in its conclusions about Belnick. Belnick did nothing legally wrong. However, it was unethical for him to use corporate funds for such extensive personal expenses. And how does someone explain to a shareholder that this use of funds was perfectly proper, using only this legal standard? The full sentence with that phrase "perfectly proper" would not leave one's lips before the shareholder exploded with the outrage that should accompany such ethical lapses. Reminding employees, managers, and officers of the distinction between what is legal and what is ethical is key to countering the numbers culture. One benefit of this standard for decision making is that employees are forced to think more and more regularly about ethics, decisions, and values. The exercise of this mental and philosophical debate keeps ethics at the forefront. Ethics out in the open and part of discussions is itself an antidote to the Yeehaw Culture generally.

Know Thy Industry: Be Familiar with Accounting Peculiarities and What "Everybody Else Is Doing" and Address Those Peculiarities with Employees

Mark-to-market accounting was not dreamed up by Enron officers. This accounting issue was a common topic of discussion in the energy industry, as well as in other industries with long-term futures contracts or valuation issues for multiyear contracts. The issues of flexibility in valuation, compensation tied to those valuation figures, and their resulting impact on the financials were on everyone's mind. In fact, abuses that were already surfacing (such as in hedging) should have been red flags for analysts, investors, and managers in Enron and other companies with similar operations and structure. This notion of spinning debt off the books had been gaining some traction since the Marriott Corporation began with what was a novel approach to debt reduction when it brought in Stephen Bollenbach as its CFO in 1992. Bollenbach had a history of innovative restructuring in the hotel industry. Bollenbach came up with a brilliant plan that enabled Marriott to raise money but also skirted legal issues and obligations. The Bollenbach plan split the Marriott Corporation into two divisions and was thereby able to spin debt off as a result. The result would be two entities of Host Marriott and Marriott International, with Host Marriott owning all the properties and carrying all the debt. Bondholders who had purchased Marriott bonds with the assumption that they were buying Marriott gold would suddenly find themselves holding bonds in a company that was about 90 percent leveraged. But Marriott' share price would climb, the company would be relatively debt-free, and the resulting capital would allow the gobbling up of some of the real estate bargains that were there for the taking at that time. When the first debt spin-off discussions occurred, Walter S. Miller—a Marriott director since 1982, a former CEO, and a renowned philanthropist—was clearly troubled by the plan. To avoid dissent on the board and that much-avoided nonunanimous board vote, Miller resigned before the decision on the split was made. His letter of resignation is a remarkable one in its demonstration of integrity, respect, and concern for all parties affected by the decision to split the company. Miller's actions reveal the type of strength we wish all board members had.

These types of movements in financial practices and accounting, while perfectly legal and within accounting rules, are the very areas that managers, audit committees, and boards should scrutinize and debate as their industries and financial practices change and evolve (not always for the better). Evolving accounting issues, coupled with room for interpretation by officers whose compensation is tied to performance, yield aggressive—indeed, often questionable—accounting choices on valuation. Understanding industry developments, nuances, and, yeah, the newest frauds in accounting is now a critical function of boards. Drawing parallels between your company and other industries that face similar accounting issues is mandatory. For example, the valuation of long-term contracts for purposes of booking revenues was not just an Enron issue. Any company with multiyear contracts faces the same issues. Xerox and many others have faced the wrath of the SEC and shareholders for officers' decisions on booking revenues. Valuation of contracts left to those whose compensation is determined by those valuations leaves the fox to guard the henhouse. In 2002 Xerox settled with the SEC on booking prematurely the revenues from lease agreements. By the time all was said and done, Xerox would restate $1.4 billion in revenues and six officers would pay fines totaling $22 million. Every industry and company has accounting issues in which temptation and pressure collide. Address those issues before pressure, analysts' expectations, and incentive plans cloud managers' and employees' judgment as they are making revenue and expense decisions and the accounting journal entries. Develop the lines for employees so that they are not left without guidance in those murky areas of "could" when they need a signal of "should not." Being at the forefront on accounting issues becomes a critical part of the antidote for the numbers pressure in the Yeehaw Culture. For example, Warren Buffett has been saying since 1996 that options should be expensed. The law has evolved to that point, but he had resolved the issue long before the law on accounting dictated treatment of options. Given the hits to companies that are just now expensing options, it would have been best to 'fess up much earlier on because the companies that 'fessed up early look great in comparison to the options-expensing-come-latelys.

Chainsaw Al did not invent cookie-jar reserves or channel stuffing. Bausch & Lomb did it long before Al did it at Sunbeam. The lessons of Bausch & Lomb should have been heeded at every company that had inventory, warehouses, and sales. Policies on accounting as well as incentives and bonuses tied to meeting numbers should have influenced every board and officer in every company that sells inventory. Practices such as reserves and channel stuffing were out there in reams. Sunbeam was ripe for both issues because of its extensive acquisitions and the ability to gin up those reserves. Its warehousing system made stuffing orders into the system quite an easy task. Sunbeam's lessons have been available to every company since its collapse. Tyco and WorldCom also had flexibility through their acquisition frenzies and the resulting reserves available for the taking and, frankly, the confusion that comes from rapid-fire purchases. It is tough for experienced analysts and auditors to get their arms around the numbers of fluid conglomerates. However, boards, officers, and managers of those companies can be given absolutes on accounting practices for acquisitions. As noted earlier, the language from the special report done for the Tyco board after it discovered it had to make billions in restatements concluded that Tyco had been using aggressive accounting practices in its acquisition accounting. Acquisition accounting is an area that has some leeway for interpretation, and that leeway largely rests with managers who have a financial interest in the results that come from those accounting decisions. Every company engaged in acquisitions now has examples for employees. Directors can study standards in accounting to set clear values in their companies and establish rules and policies for their acquisition accounting. Lessons from these companies somehow don't infiltrate the psyches of companies similarly situated. This gap in historical knowledge and ethical application allows the Yeehaw Culture to thrive in yet another organization. With each new company crisis, we wonder if others are processing the lessons. Refco entered bankruptcy as its CEO repaid a loan of nearly one-half billion dollars. AIG had offshore activities. Krispy Kreme shipped equipment prematurely. These are 2005 examples. Conduct continued despite the lessons unfolding in companies in the news.

As much as we love to cite "it's a gray area" as a rationalization for our conduct, it really is not as prevalent as our conversations lead us to believe. There is not much gray area when the line in acquisitions accounting is defined as "Close the books as they are; no stuffing in as much in expenses as you can to make us look better later." No technical rules. Just a clearly stated value, with the intentions of accuracy and honesty paramount in the general guideline. There are new accounting issues evolving within industries, across industries, and even over cross-connecting industries. Every company, board member, officer, and employee should be studying these issues and examples in order to draw parallels and develop policies before employees, concerned about meeting goals and earning bonuses, get creative under pressure because they don't have clear guidance.

An issue that has been evolving for some time but has been ignored by those most affected by it is the chargeback process of retailers. I wrote about this issue in 1999 as "the Squeeze," and included it in a special text box in one of my books because there were so many contractual and ethical issues surrounding these chargebacks that affected payments, accounting, and even the performance of both supplier and vendor. Kmart was one of the companies whose accounting was affected by these issues, and in 2002 there were FBI criminal investigations into the conduct of Kmart officers with respect to vendors. The SEC filed fraud charges against Kmart's former CFO and CEO in 2005. The issue of vendor chargebacks in the retail industry is not unique to Kmart and presents some murky accounting issues. The result of this discretion is that numbers are controlled by those who stand to benefit from that murkiness. For example, markdowns in the retail industry have long been negotiated items between manufacturers and retailers, but who will absorb how much of the markdown is generally a verbal agreement. The intentions are good: manufacturer and retailer share the risk of selling the goods, and the retailer can afford to carry more items and brands when the risk is lower. However, markdown abuses have been growing as retailers demand more from manufacturers, and often more than their agreements allow. To the extent those chargebacks have been reflected in the revenues of the retailer, the earnings have been overstated. Saks Fifth Avenue recently announced that it was returning chargebacks to several of its vendors. The amount for the period between 1999 and 2003 is $20 million. Along with that announcement came the revelation that the SEC and U.S. Attorney's Office were investigating the issues surrounding the markdowns. Saks delayed its annual report in 2005 even as the investigation was pending. The report had not been filed by mid-2006.

It can hardly be a surprise that there would be tomfoolery related to chargebacks. You had an area with no written agreements for payments and those who were in charge of both those agreements and chargebacks were also in charge of the financial reports, all while their bonuses were determined by meeting the numbers goals for the company. These murky systems for charge-backs and slotting fees and other indefinite revenue arrangements have been well documented as critical accounting and ethical and legal-breach areas and were significantly controversial during the 1999 time frame when the questionable Saks chargebacks began. Know thy industry and its accounting issues.

Antidote #2 for Pressure to Maintain Those Numbers: Fire Those Who Cross the Lines You've Established

If you fire an employee who has crossed any of the lines you have established as absolute values, you will purchase five years of compliance by the rest of the employees. Rules without enforcement allow the ethical culture to slip, often to the point of collapse. Rules must be enforced swiftly, unequivocally, and in egalitarian fashion. Without this signal of termination or discipline for violations, employees will take risks and cross lines. They will also duly note, and with rapid-fire speed, when any officer, director, or stellar performer gets away with crossing those lines. The Saks board may have been asleep at the wheel in initially noticing the evolving markdown/chargeback issue, but they did exactly what had to be done once its investigation revealed misconduct by officers. The Saks board terminated three of its top executives: senior vice president Brian Martin, who was general counsel at the time of the 2002 chargeback investigation that netted the board little feedback and who is also the brother of Saks chief executive R. Brad Martin; chief accounting officer Donald Wright; and chief administrative officer Donald Watros. Mr. Watros has waived both his options and bonuses for the periods under review by the SEC and other federal officials. The Saks board and audit committee were also publicly critical of senior managers for their failure to follow up on the board's 2002 inquiry about chargebacks. The audit committee released a public statement to underscore that there had been improper conduct by these officers in handling the chargebacks. Other employees involved in the chargeback misconduct were also terminated, but their identity (because they were not officers) was not disclosed. The Saks board went even further to restructure reporting lines and responsibilities so that there would be more checks and balances on those numbers in the future. Not only will Saks have a new chief accounting officer, but that position will now report directly to the CEO. The board relieved numbers pressure and temptation by separating out the role of the CFO. The CFO will be involved in dealing with the capital markets but will no longer have responsibility for preparing financial reports. The person who must sell the investment community on the financials no longer has the conflicted interest of preparing those financials.

Having worked with Boeing for nearly two years, I have seen the company struggle to regain its ethical culture following several serious ethical lapses that resulted in banishment from government programs as well as criminal sanctions against its CFO. However, those in the company did not see that they had turned a corner recently when the board confronted then-CEO Harry Stonecipher and demanded his resignation for having an affair. Based upon an anonymous tip, the ethics office investigated the allegation that Stonecipher was having an affair with an executive in the company. The investigation confirmed the tip, the ethics officer took the matter to general counsel, general counsel took the matter to the board, the board confronted Stonecipher, and everyone agreed that Stonecipher's resignation was necessary because it is Boeing policy that employees cannot have affairs with their direct reports. Also, perhaps, not a bad management principle. The board took the same step any manager or officer would have to take for such a rules violation. Swift (it took only about forty-eight hours for the final decision), unequivocal (the company sent a message on its clear and definitive lines of propriety), and egalitarian—they sacked their own CEO for misconduct. Because Boeing had been through so many issues, with the Lockheed Martin document use and the termination of its CFO for recruiting a government official while she still had authority to award contracts, the conduct of the CEO who had been brought back to reinstill ethics into the culture might have been seen by many as a sign of ethical collapse. Even Mr. Stonecipher agreed he was no longer suited for his role because of his indiscretion. No one can prevent human folly, especially in the case of love and/or lust. As long as human beings run companies there will be mistakes. The key to preserving ethics in the company culture when these very visible ethical lapses occur is responding in an unequivocal manner. When I heard of Stonecipher's termination, I sent the following note to Boeing's ethics officer, Martha Ries, which was then widely circulated throughout the company:

> I read about the problems this morning, and I realize these are difficult times. But I still care very much about the wonderful employees of Boeing and to help with morale (I have seen this happen at other organizations and employees are crestfallen), please emphasize the following (and if it will help, you are welcome to quote me):
>
> a. It came from an anonymous tip (you want those and welcome those and everyone should embrace this procedure and use it).
>
> b. An investigation followed promptly.
>
> c. Action was taken in swift, unequivocal, and egalitarian fashion—same rules apply to everyone.

d. *The culture is on its way up despite this recent setback precisely because this happened. This is not a signal something is wrong, but a signal that something is right. Other issues will emerge, as they should, as the culture fights for and demands high ethical standards.*

My heart just ached when I read of the Stonecipher issues and actions, but I wrote only to say, "Take heart." You asked me once how do you know if the ethical culture is taking hold. You have your answer. You just sacked your CEO following an investigation based on an anonymous tip. It is working, It IS working.

Keep a salesperson around who does well but violates the code of ethics and employees dismiss the ethics code and company officers and managers as hypocrites. Credibility is a key component of an ethical culture, and hypocrisy is its death knell. At one company where I was working on the ethical culture, there was a provision in the code of ethics that prohibited employees from accepting gifts of excessive value. The employees held themselves to a $25 maximum. Imagine the employees' outrage when they learned that executives at the company took golf packages to Ireland (estimated value of about $15,000 per person) as gifts. Rules without consistent enforcement lead to more violations, dismissal of the rules, and ethical collapse.

Antidote #3 for Pressure to Maintain Those Numbers: Watch the Nonverbal and Nuanced Communication and Signals

Nuanced numbers pressure can come through the language used in company reports, the warnings or discussions in meetings, and in actions by leaders. These indirect signals through the nuance of language or perceived authority are perhaps not intended to be pressure, but employees feel it anyway. Even the language of the annual report, as evidenced by the HealthSouth, Finova, and WorldCom excerpts cited previously, sends a clear signal to employees—an annual report with a numbers obsession speaks volumes about what's important. The presence of numbers goals and promises of double-digit returns in that external document exacerbates the problem because now the outside world has expectations on performance, promised by a CEO who talks performance without necessarily offering the candor and vision necessary to get the company there.

One of my sons brought home a grade of 55 on his first Algebra II exam. For those of you far removed from the madding hoopla of grades, that is indeed a failing score. I told my son that the grade was "unacceptable" and then dabbled in the usual lecture of college, life, success, work, striving, and the general parental admonitions for these circumstances. My oldest daughter is away at graduate school but remains close to her siblings. With the luxury of unlimited cell-phone minutes, they talk nearly daily. A few days after my lecture to my son, my oldest daughter called me and said, "Mom, Sam says you're going to set his hair on fire if he doesn't get an A in Algebra II." I am a strict parent, but those words never left my lips. However, I had made the mistake many managers make when communicating with those who report to them. They discount the disparity in position and bargaining power. They address only the issue at hand, and not the value system that should control the solutions for the issue. Pressure to meet those numbers no matter what is something very few executives will own up to doing. Pressure to meet those numbers any way possible is something all employees feel despite their managers' denials. The nonverbal signals, the phraseology, the tone, the authority figure syndrome, and the implications of what is said count more than good intentions and assumed ethical parameters.

A company was losing every case that was brought before the Department of Labor administrative law judge (ALJ) assigned to its district. A director on the company's board was grappling with this stunning loss record and wondered whether the company's labor practices were flawed or whether there was a bias on the part of the ALJ. Trying to sort through the circumstances, costs, and cases, the board member asked that the company's internal and external legal counsel come to a board meeting to discuss what was wrong with either the company's practices or its litigation team. During the meeting the director wondered aloud to the lawyer guests of the board, "How is it possible that we lose every labor case? Are we flagrant violators of the law?"

He and the other directors understood that any perceived outrage in his tone and questions was a function of frustration with what had happened. In fact, the director was doing what more directors should be doing: following up on issues, drilling down deep to find cause and effect, and making sure the company's practices are legal and ethical. However, the message that the lawyer guests probably took away from the meeting was that their performance was subpar and that they had been brought before the board to offer what could only be an elusive explanation for their loss record. Perhaps it was similar to the circumstances in which Chief Justice John Roberts tried to explain to one of his clients why he lost a U.S. Supreme Court appeal on a 9–0 vote. His client also asked, "How is this possible?" and Justice Roberts responded, "Because there are only nine justices." Perhaps it was the company's practices that never gave it a shot in any labor department hearing. But two lawyers who have their jobs and livelihood hanging in the balance will not say so aloud. The justifiable signal they took from the board's expressed frustration was that a win was needed, and straight away. Often those in positions of authority fail to realize the unintentional interpretations of those who report to them. Fear does give birth to unintended interpretations and its consequences.

In the company's next labor case an issue of whether a document had been withheld by the company arose. Along with the surfacing of that damaging document came necessary questions such as whether employees had perjured themselves in the labor hearing to cover what was in the damaging document, and whether the lawyers knew about either the document and/or the perjury and when they knew it. Not only did the company lose the case, but it was investigated by several different agencies and sanctioned for the conduct of withholding the document after it had reached a settlement with the employee who had brought the action before the Department of Labor. Careers of some former employees were destroyed because of the hazy handling of the mysterious document. No one ever really concluded who among the legal team knew what and when they knew it, but perhaps the signals from the board perhaps inspired pressure, clouded their discernment, or made what was to them initially suspicious seem fine when a turnaround victory was possible. The company pointed to its lawyers and the lawyers pointed to the employees of the company and maintained that they, too, were duped. The company's already poor reputation with the Department of Labor suffered further.

The whole scenario was an unmitigated mess and the company demanded that the external lawyer self-report to the state bar. No action was taken by that body. Still, if there was a document withheld or even if the lawyer simply looked the other way in grilling the company employees, how could a lawyer possibly think that any misconduct or questionable judgment in order to get a win was what the board wanted? No one gave any lawyer that imperative. But the confrontation at a meeting where one side has authority and the other needs the job can breed strange and unintended responses. In organizations with ethical collapse, everyone sees the issues, but they are afraid to speak up because those who have authority over them and their livelihoods have made their desired outcome, at any cost, known. In this situation with the board and lawyers, both the verbal and nonverbal communication directed at the lawyers was: You need a win here, buddy. The board had created a numbers pressure. Unintentionally, but the numbers pressure was very real to those whose livelihood depended on board and company continuation of the legal representation contract.

When I talk with executives in companies that have had to restate their earnings because employees simply lied to meet their numbers goals, they ask similar questions: "How could they possibly think that I would want them to make stuff up?" The employees hear, day in and day out, what it costs the company when there are safety delays or what it will mean if a product is not released on time. The NASA employees heard about budget cuts if the agency did not deliver launches on time. Teachers know the salary penalties and budget cuts if test scores are not where they should be. Few executives actually instruct their employees to lie. At manufacturing and power plants, shop meetings devote the first few minutes to reminders about safety, but the remainder of the meeting is devoted to budget issues and production goals. Safety becomes a checked-off mandatory topic, but it is not a central theme. There's another indirect and perhaps unintentional signal to employees that with obligatory lip service given to safety, we can now return to the numbers, for numbers are everything.

Continually emphasizing to employees that getting "those numbers where they need to be" means that strategic vision has fallen by the wayside. Emphasizing strategic vision means explaining clearly where the company is headed, what its values are, and that with such a clarity of vision executed properly, the numbers will follow. This approach curbs the nonverbal numbers signals because employees learn that effort and strategy produce numbers, not manipulation. Organizations focused on numbers, whether universities seeking a ranking for their MBA programs or nonprofits stretching to meet fund-raising goals, are at ethical risk. But even if you don't buy the ethics part of this whole analysis, the focus on nothin' but numbers carries another weighty problem. Focusing on nothing but numbers detracts from the art of business, the strategic thinking of the next move, and addressing the real issues the organization faces. Recent accounting studies show that as the earnings numbers for companies become less predictable, the more optimistic and accurate analysts become because of their perceptions about candor on the part of the company. In other words, honesty and a grip on reality are the checks and balances for managing this ethical culture factor and also contribute to the overall better performance of the company. Honesty in numbers means that a company is facing up to its shortcomings in marketing because its sales are simply not there. Masking the reality does not allow a business to solve its problems. A hypothetical example on cio.com involved a chief information officer who knows that the marketing VP has turned in sales numbers that are inflated, but the numbers are not material in terms of accounting and financial-reporting disclosure. The ethical dilemma presented was whether the CIO should confront the VP and then, if necessary, let the CEO know of the problem. The most frequent response initially in the chat board was that it was a "gray area" and that it need not be disclosed. There is no gray area. In fact, there is not an ethical issue, but, rather, a business issue everyone needs to be aware of and help to solve. If the company wants to continue living in denial, conceal the real numbers. The problem of declining sales remains a secret, perhaps for so long that the lost market share becomes irretrievable. Behind the issue of honesty and candor in financials is the real business issue of grappling with the problems the real numbers show. We are not ethical for the sake of ethics; we are ethical for the sake of business survival.

Antidote #4 for Pressure to Maintain Those Numbers: Encourage Your Employees to Use a Time-Out

I listened to Cynthia Cooper, the former head of internal auditing for World-Com and the person who blew the whistle on all $11 billion in wrongly capitalized ordinary expenses, speak to a group of accounting students. She gave them some advice for their career. If something doesn't seem right, she explained, "trust your gut." She was encouraging them to raise issues, ask questions, and speak out when something strikes them as just not right. But giving employees the means for spilling their guts is no small task.

The "time-out" antidote is one that I have borrowed from the NASA evaluation report and recommendations on rebuilding a safety culture there. Give your employees "time-out cards." And follow-up experiences and reports indicate that NASA's culture is changing and that employees are raising issues. A time-out card can be literal or symbolic, but it is given to employees to use when they find themselves in an awkward situation on the job. A time-out card is for when employees' guts will simply not let them rest. They see an issue, problem, or a line crossed in the course of their work, but those around them seem to be stampeding toward results, numbers, end products, and good quarterlies. Time-out is a universal, diplomatic way for employees to go with their guts and ask for a pause in the march toward numbers and results. The beauty of time-out is that any employee can use it and need not be able to articulate exactly what the concern is. The goal is to get employees to raise issues and ask questions and point out when lines are crossed. But even if they are unable to explain exactly what is bothering them, those around them know to explore more deeply just by virtue of the fact that time-out has been called.

Certainly anonymous tip lines, hotlines, compliance lines, and any number of creatively named reporting systems are a form of time-out, but the time-out presents a form of universal language that can be used in meetings, in day-to-day interaction, and, most important, in face-to-face communication. Anonymous reporting avoids that face-to-face interaction. The issue is investigated and ethics officers take appropriate steps to correct the situation. However, with that anonymity and having others work through the problem, no one ever really gets any better about communicating, raising issues, or even self-correcting when there has been an ethical breach. The universal language and symbolism of holding up a time-out card breaks down the barriers that exist in our one-on-one communication about ethical concerns. One additional beauty of time-out is that it can stop the steamroller before further damage is done. Employees at MiniScribe could have used a time-out when they were asked to wrap bricks in disk drive boxes. Andersen partners could have used a time-out as they watched the billing practices and competition related to the consulting business. And a time-out anytime along the path from Enron's one off-the-books entity to three thousand might have curtailed the mighty financial and ethical collapse of that company. Those involved in the sham transactions at the BFA could have used a time-out card to halt the continuing damage of the Ponzi scheme.

Time-out can be a handheld stop sign or a verbal signal. The critical part of this tool is that it is available to every employee because it is not just those who make the financial-reporting and accounting decisions who are affected by numbers pressure. Clerical employees who do the accounting-journal entries also need time-out when they are asked to do something unethical, and perhaps illegal. Most employees will feel far more comfortable saying, "Time-out!" than they would launching into a tirade about ethics, morality, greed, and corruption. This pause is an easygoing approach that stops everyone and has them reflect. A little reflection can go a long way in preventing ethical collapse.

The following diagram outlines the antidotes for preventing the numbers culture and its probable result of ethical collapse.

Sign # 1

Pressure to Maintain Those Numbers

Antidotes

1. Surround goal achievement in a square box of values.

   a. Just because it's legal doesn't mean it's ethical.

   b. Be familiar with accounting peculiarities and what "everybody else is doing" and address those peculiarities with employees.

2. Fire those who cross the lines you've established.

Numbers Pressure

3. Watch the nonverbal and nuanced communication and signals.

4. Encourage your employees to use a time-out.

CHAPTER THREE

Sign

2

Fear and Silence

*People have an obligation to dissent in this company. . . . I mean,
I sit up there on the 50th floor, in the library. I have no idea what's
going on down there, so if you've got a problem with it, speak up.
And if you don't speak up, that's not good.*

—Jeffrey Skilling, former CEO of Enron, a man who withheld business
from companies whose analysts did not give Enron a "strong buy"

Moral meltdown cannot occur with objection in the air. Something wicked this way comes only when dissent has gone south. The culture of ethical collapse is one that does not encourage dissent, or even discussion. The classic "no one wants bad news" syndrome exists in these organizations to the point of paralysis and inaction. In every corporation that has collapsed ethically (and almost always as a result, financially), there were always employees struggling to get their questions answered or their concerns addressed. Sometimes the companies had no avenues for employees to raise concerns. Sometimes the employees were rebuffed by supervisors. In some companies employees who raised concerns were fired, demoted, or transferred. As my friend Steve Priest, the head of the Ethical Leadership Group, has heard in his interviews with employees in troubled companies, their reticence is metaphorically explained as "the first whale to the surface gets harpooned."

Fear, silence, and sycophancy are things you can feel in these companies that are teetering near ethical collapse as they flirt with invincibility. Fear hangs like Florida humidity in August as you sense that human dignity has fled and automaton-like employees numb themselves to the immorality around them because they feel helpless. Employees in these cultures not only know that their companies are engaged in simply awful behavior (a realization that your source of livelihood may well be criminal, harmful, or unethical conduct is depressing enough) but also realize their impending doom. I witnessed this gloom and doom in the halls of Finova in early 1999, when their officers asked me to take a look at their culture. Some employees knew the write-downs that needed to be made were being masked. Many employees knew the bubble would burst soon. All of them understood that they dare not speak of either. Those who did speak of the issues were transferred because Finova's multiple-division structure made it possible to use some of the accounting chicanery through a sort of shell game of transfers among those divisions. For example, Jeff Dangemond, who has served as a witness in many of the legal proceedings involving Finova, left the company prior to its collapse because he was transferred from division to division as he raised questions related to accounting issues. He also carried that horrific taint that employees who ask questions in a culture of fear and silence take on because they point out the elephant in the room. His career was very much flatlined because he dared raise the obvious questions.

I was asked to discuss Finova's ethical culture with former CEO Sam Eichenfield, along with company senior executives, at a retreat held in the Phoenix area. I warned them of their risk and discussed the importance of ethics, listening to employees, and owning up if they had made any mistakes. I believe the group fancied me loony, a conclusion the sycophantic officers and senior managers reached shortly after Mr. Eichenfield burst out laughing at some of my thoughts on the fate of companies that suppress dissent and discussion.

I never accepted any consulting fees or donations for the university from Finova for my efforts there because I knew what awaited the company and its Yeehaw Culture. By the beginning of 2000 Finova had to announce a delay in its annual report because of critical disagreements (some related to write-downs) with the company's external auditors. I felt embarrassment for the officers I had worked with because they were good people who sensed that their company had problems but were unable, perhaps because of the incredible compensation packages or maybe because of the fear that they would lose their jobs, to muster the courage to state the obvious. They reminded me of the conquistador-booted wimpy Joey who is part of John Travolta's *Saturday Night Fever* foursome of friends. Joey is not a logical fit with the other three macho men, but they embrace him as one of them because, well, they need his car, 1965 Chevy Impala though it is. When Joey, who doesn't quite have the Brooklyn *je ne sais quoi* of his cohorts, learns that his girlfriend is pregnant, he seeks reassurance from anyone who will listen. He even resorts to asking Father Frank, a man leaving the priesthood, for advice and an imprimatur. He just wants someone with some small connection to morality to offer assurance that he has done nothing wrong. Like Joey, employees in these Yeehaw Cultures, often feeling as insecure and fearful as Joey, know there are problems. They understand the ethical and even financial implications (once the information becomes public) of that problem. But they will let the problem march onward as they rationalize, "Hey, it's not big deal!" They continue to hope against hope that someone else will solve the problem or that, given enough time, the problem will simply go away. But silence never solves the problem, and hard truth concealed over time, like a pregnancy, only becomes more obvious. When the baby is born or the truth comes out, metaphorically speaking, significant changes result in the lives of the parents and everyone around the blessed, albeit somewhat traumatic, event.

This phenomenon of employee silence attributable to the fear of no longer "fitting in" is well documented in workplace surveys. A 1999 survey by the Society for Human Resource Management found that of those employees who saw something illegal or unethical at work, only 66 percent would say something about it. In company surveys done in 2005 and 2006, we find that about 50 percent of employees will report illegal or unethical conduct. Of those who would say nothing, nearly all of them (96 percent) indicated that the reason for their inaction was that they did not want to be called "not a team player." Cultures of fear and silence nurture the team-player concept, borrowing the buy-in and strong hold that comes from groupthink and the inability, as Solomon Asch's studies on social conformity pressure concluded, of most of us to speak up when we see something wrong if those around us either do not see the problem or have chosen to remain silent. Even the most honorable people are submissive and subdued in a culture of fear and silence.

There are subtle and not-so-subtle means used by executives who are running a culture of numbers to ensure that those in their organizations remain quiet about any questionable activities, whether those activities relate to accounting and financial reporting, the unfavorable science on a product or prescription drug, or the use of price-fixing to stifle competition. Suppressing those employee concerns sets the tone and culture for moral meltdown. As noted earlier, CFOs report pressure from their CEOs to misrepresent financial results. The CEO pushes for results, but others in the company push the pencils to make the results happen. Sycophants are the enablers of ethical collapse. Fear and silence are the enemies of an ethical culture.

Enron: Sycophants Galore, Even as Their Pensions Languished

Even for an experienced corporate-culture watcher such as I, Enron was a vision to behold because of the unabashed obsequiousness of its employees.

They all seemed fully aware that they were cruising on the *Titanic,* but fear trumped reason and they wouldn't even venture to rearrange the deck chairs. They stayed silently aboard, hoping against all odds that the iceberg they all duly noted would melt in a miraculous tsunami of sunshine. They wanted to believe that no one would catch on to their Ponzi scheme of off-the-books entities or their darn creative accounting for energy contracts and broadband operations. Even their infamous whistle-blower was gutless. I quite enjoy the accolades that have come Sherron Watkins's way as *Time*'s Person of the Year for 2001 and the resulting speaker fees and book. By Enron standards, and under the medieval levels of fear at this house of cards, an officer such as Watkins who, with her résumé already firmly planted at other companies, speaks out on accounting fraud about a month before the company collapses is indeed *Braveheart* material. But her story says more about the culture of fear and silence that dooms a company than it does about her bravery and role as a whistle-blower.

Ms. Watkins, now co-author of *Power Failure: The Inside Story of the Collapse of Enron* ($2.79 on Amazon), was a vice president of corporate development at Enron. Ms. Watkins, a former Andersen employee, had been hired away by Enron and was possessed of some fairly good accounting instincts. She realized very quickly after assuming her position as a vice president and gaining access to the company's complete financials that something was amiss with Enron's books and financial reporting. Fearful about what she called the "fuzzy" accounting of the off-the-books entities, she was in the process of looking for another job as she planned to write a memo objecting to the company's accounting. There was no rush on Ms. Watkins's part to speak up despite sleuthing that revealed what she called "a smoking gun."

However, then came the abrupt departure of CEO Jeffrey Skilling. The sudden departure of a CEO who has a Harvard MBA and came through the McKinsey consulting ranks to spend more time with his family is a sure-fire signal that things may not be quite right at the OK Corral. Harvard McKinsey types are much like the British. They breed, but they don't embrace children. Ms. Watkins finally felt that the time had come to raise questions about fraud, securities-law violations, conflicts of interest, and a host of other activities generally correlating with double-digit earnings and lots of MBAs. Ms. Watkins went out on a limb by sending an anonymous memo to Ken Lay, Enron's new CEO. The memo itself offers a glimpse of the Enron culture with "arrogance" and "intimidating" being its themes. Her description is of textbook fear and silence that was consuming a company already in ethical collapse. The pattern is chillingly similar across companies, decades, and collapses. A former student of mine who had become a CPA and who was concerned about accounting practices wrote a similar letter to Charles Keating when he was the chairman of American Continental, the parent organization to Lincoln Savings and Loan, describing her questions about its practices and her inability to make any headway in communicating her concerns to folks such as the CFO. Charles Keating wrote her a combination thank-you note and pink slip.

The August Watkins 2001 memo reveals that Enron had that humid atmosphere of fear hanging heavy at Enron headquarters. As in all cultures of fear and silence, the employees seemed fully aware of their problems and eventual fate. Ms. Watkins described that she was not alone in her fears or dismay: "I am incredibly nervous that we will implode in a wave of accounting scandals. I have heard one manager-level employee from the principal investments group say, 'I know it would be devastating to all of us, but I wish we would get caught. We're such a crooked company.'" In papers she reviewed to prepare the memo, Ms. Watkins had written in the margins, "There it is! That is the smoking gun. You cannot do this! My understanding as an accountant is that a company can never use its own stock to generate a gain or avoid a loss on its income statement." Ms. Watkins advised Mr. Lay in that first anonymous memo that because of the accounting improprieties, "it sure looks to the layman on the street that we are hiding losses in a related company."

By August 22, 2001, after discussing the issues with former colleagues at Andersen, Ms. Watkins confessed to Mr. Lay in a face-to-face meeting that she was the one who had written the memo. She testified before Congress that she did not discuss her concerns or confess to writing the memo to Mr. Skilling or Mr. Fastow, because, she said, "it would have been a job-terminating move." In fact, we learned from other sources following the congressional hearings that in his demented view of the world, Fastow was livid with Watkins when he learned of the memo, not because he saw his world crumbling but because he felt she was after his job. With this kind of "passing Andy a note in study hall" maturity ruling the executive suite, one wonders why climbing the corporate ladder at Enron was viewed as a good thing. Fastow was the soulless heart of Enron's culture of fear and silence. Fastow was graced with a hair-trigger temper as well as Machiavellian ruthlessness. This charming combination created a "fear factor" between Fastow and anybody, from employees to investment bankers to mechanics who serviced the motorcycles and cars at the officers' retreats, who had to deal with him.

It wasn't that employees, well beyond Watkins, didn't see Enron's ethical and legal missteps. Knowledge about problems with Enron's true financial picture and its accounting practices were well known among employees. But that fear factor got in the way. Enron employees were circulating via e-mail a top ten list called "Top Ten Reasons Enron Restructures So Frequently"; number seven on the list was "Because the basic business model is to keep the outside investment analysts so confused that they will not be able to figure out that we don't know what we're doing," and number one was "Forget all the hype about Fortune's #1—congratulations to Enron for having broken a Guinness Book of World Record with 942 organizations in one year." In 1997, as a videotape bears out, Enron executives had a farewell dinner and roast for Rich Kinder, president of Enron prior to Skilling's assuming the reins. In a skit that was part of the roast, Kinder's executive assistant played Kinder and Jeffrey Skilling played himself and a third Enron employee played an accountant. Skilling has a line in which he suggests that Enron move from "mark-to-market" accounting to "hypothetical future value accounting" because, as he follows up, such a move will "add a ka-zillion dollars to the bottom line." The accountant in the skit does object, but Skilling calls him a "spoilsport." They saw the ethical issues they were living with and even made sport of them, but fear kept employees oppressed in silence. Skilling created such fear even in those outside the company. James Chanos, a shortseller, found himself being called an "a——h——" by Jeffrey Skilling in April 2001 in response to a simple question: "Why is your earnings rate below your cost of capital?"

There were many employees throughout Enron who voiced concerns, and not anonymously as Sherron Watkins did initially, about the accounting and viability of the company. Margaret Ceconi, an eight-month employee with Enron Energy Services, wrote a five-page memo to HR that she asked them to deliver to Kenneth Lay and the board on August 28, 2001. Ceconi stated that losses from Enron Energy Services were being moved to another sector in Enron in order to make the Energy Services arm look profitable. Mr. Lay referred her to HR for counseling on employee morale. One line from her memo read, "Some would say the house of cards are [sic] falling." While famous whistleblower Sherron Watkins hid, Ceconi came forward. Ceconi went to Congress when she got no response. Employee Clayton Vernon was fired after he posted a question on the company's internal online chat board about whether Enron's accounting was too aggressive and used to overstate its profits. Another employee was fired for commenting on $55 million paid to officers as retention bonuses in early December 2001. Note that Mr. Vernon was fired after the public disclosure of problems, as Enron was headed into bankruptcy. Cultures of fear and silence die hard. Mr. Vernon remained deferential to the end. The report of his termination in the *The New York Times* included the following excerpt:

> Mr. Vernon acknowledges that he got carried away with his language in the note and says he will not litigate. "I was using their equipment. I was in their building, and it was a flagrant violation of company policy to do what I did. I'm not going to litigate it. I don't think it was unfair." He indicated that the cancellation of the company Christmas party, coupled with the loss of value in

his stock and the lack of any work to do at the office were the contributing factors for his messages and use of vulgarity therein.

In 1995, fully six years before Enron collapsed, James Alexander, an executive at Enron's Global Power subsidiary, spoke with Mr. Lay about his concerns that there were accounting irregularities within the company and that deal makers within Enron were enriching themselves through the complex accounting transactions. Referring to himself as the "dead canary in the coal mine" (yet another dead-animal metaphor that employees in cultures of fear have coined), Mr. Alexander spoke directly to Mr. Lay about his concerns. Mr. Alexander's assertions were dismissed when Mr. Lay asked others about the issues and was assured that Mr. Alexander was just "overanxious." No changes were made, but Mr. Alexander was often referred to as a "thorn" in CEO Jeffrey Skilling's side. Interestingly, Andrew Fastow was brought in as CFO when Mr. Alexander refused to sign off on the financials because he was not convinced about the integrity of the numbers and was not given control over determinations about their authenticity or the internal controls designed to provide such assurance. Even when those who raise issues in cultures of fear and silence are not terminated, they are flatlined. They become like the crazy cousin at family reunions. Everyone tolerates them, no one takes them seriously, and when their backs are turned we engage in knowing, understanding, and compassionate glances at one another about these less fortunate among us.

At the time of the Alexander protestations, Brent Scowcroft, the former presidential adviser and a retired general, was on the outside board of Enron Global Power and did confront Ken Lay about Alexander's concerns. Lay employed classic groupthink psychology in his response to Scowcroft: "How could you be right and men of this caliber be wrong?" pointing to Fastow and Skilling. Mr. Alexander was thereby dismissed out of hand, and board member Scowcroft was brought back into the line of silence that consumed the culture, even extending to outsiders.

Scowcroft was not the only board member who would see the issues at Enron. Fear and silence also takes in board members, thereby eliminating that potential for the checks and balances of corporate governance. The board's management of Fastow's compensation and its resulting failure to really get at the heart of what Fastow was doing to meet financial goals shows the vulnerability of Enron's board. It was one enormously deferential board.

At one point, the board started to see that creating about three thousand off-the-books entities might raise a regulatory or market eyebrow or two. Thinking it should probably look into the thousands of deals, the Enron board put its foot down, but only as the slightest tap to the floor, so as not to alert the hucksters. The board required a one-time review of Fastow's compensation as a precondition for approval of yet another off-the-books transaction. Dr. Charles A. LeMaistre, head of the Enron board's compensation committee, requested information on Fastow's compensation from Mary Joyce, Enron's senior compensation officer. His expanded request applied to all 16(b) officers. One year would pass and the head of the compensation committee would still not have the information from Ms. Joyce. At this point the board directed Dr. LeMaistre and John Duncan, another board member, to approach Mr. Fastow himself to obtain the information. The two Billy Goats Gruff, cognizant of their fearful task ahead, confronting the mean troll, asked Enron's legal counsel to draft a set of questions that they could take with them to meet Mr. Fastow. The board, with the power to hire and fire officers and set the direction of the company, was afraid of its own CFO. The film *Oliver!* comes to mind as the two board orphans approach Mr. Bumble with the unmitigated gall to say, "Please, sir, could we have some more?" For those of you still keeping score, a board was forced to send a delegation with a script from legal counsel to get information from the company's chief financial officer about how much money he was making from deals with the company and whether his family members might also be profiting from these deals. We return once again to the theme of "Never mind the ethics. What of human dignity?"

It is difficult to understand in hindsight why such accomplished and experienced professionals would allow an officer to dismiss them out of hand. However, this scenario serves to emphasize the impact that fear and silence can have on an organization. We also learn why employees are reticent. If bright and credentialed board members feared confronting an officer over whom they had authority in terms of compensation and continuing employment, imagine how an employee who works at that individual's behest feels about raising similar concerns. This story gives us new empathy and greater understanding for the huge obstacle fear presents in organizations. This is a tall order, this task of convincing employees to speak up and raise concerns. Daily reassurance of protection for raising good-faith concerns still may not be enough for curbing fear and silence.

MiniScribe: Intimidation and Fear, but No Loathing

MiniScribe, noted in the previous chapter for its numbers drive, hit its slump in sales in the mid-1980s because it had lost its largest customer, IBM. The board of directors brought in Q. T. Wiles. Called the "Mr. Fix-It" of high-technology industries, Wiles had turned around Adobe Systems, Granger Associates, and Silicon General Inc. For a time Mr. Wiles turned around MiniScribe, but then the double-digit growth became harder to meet and impossible to top. Managers had difficulty meeting Mr. Wiles's tough sales goals. He responded as an autocratic manager who wanted only fear in the hearts of his employees. At the "dash meetings," mentioned in Chapter 1, in which Wiles spouted his management philosophies. In one such meeting Wiles had two controllers stand as he fired them, saying, "That's just to show everyone I'm in control of the company." That kind of behavior instills in employees the desire to do whatever it takes to meet the numbers and remain silent about their modus operandi because hopelessness sets in and finds them living in denial on their *Titanic* cruise.

WorldCom: Mississippi Fear

Enron's accounting issues at least had some nuance to them. WorldCom's cooking the books was not as clever. With the merger reserves quickly eaten away and no future mergers pending, WorldCom's CFO, Scott Sullivan, had to find a means for keeping those earnings singing. While the precise timing for a new accounting strategy remains unclear, most experts agree that at least by the first quarter of 2001, Mr. Sullivan and his cohorts embarked on a not-so-fancy accounting strategy that would keep WorldCom afloat but was not exactly in compliance with GAAP. In fact, the not-so-fancy accounting strategy was not even in compliance with common sense. Mr. Sullivan convinced his merry band of accountants to take ordinary expenses and book them as capital expenditures so as to boost earnings.

However, one does have to come up with such capital-expenditure entries for the books. And making stuff up does not always leave time for creating an accompanying paper trail that auditors always get so testy about having. If you are going to book $11 billion or so in capital expenses, GAAP demands some invoices for the property that you are capitalizing. This rather novice lapse in accounting judgment began unwinding when Gene Morse, a member of WorldCom's internal audit group, found $500 million in computer expenses but could not find any documentation or invoices.

The less clever the fraud, the more oppressive the culture must be because executives are asking employees to go above and beyond the call of duty in playing dumb. Given the obvious nature of WorldCom's not-so-creative accounting, many WorldCom employees realized that fraud was in the air. But WorldCom's culture reeked of fear and silence. Fraud smells better than unemployment, and those who spoke up and stated the obvious were chastised mightily. For example, Steven Brabbs, the WorldCom director of international finance and control who was based in London, raised questions about accounting changes that were being made at headquarters but affected the reported results for his division. Brabbs discovered, after his division's books had been closed, that $33.6 million in line costs had been dropped from his books through a journal entry. Unable to find support or explanation for the entry, Mr. Brabbs raised the question of documentation to David Myers, WorldCom's controller. When he got no response, he suggested that perhaps Arthur Andersen should be consulted to determine the propriety of the changes. Brabbs also raised his concerns in a meeting with other internal financial executives at WorldCom. Following the meeting, Myers let Brabbs know that there would be no more Andersen involvement in internal accounting issues, a fascinating perspective on the role of one's audit firm and a great irony, given Andersen's detached presence at WorldCom. If Andersen had been any more hands-off, it would have certified WorldCom's financials without even seeing the numbers first.

When the next quarter's financials were due, Brabbs received instructions to make these transfers at his level rather than having them done by journal entry at the corporate level. Because he was still uncomfortable with the process but could get no response from headquarters, he established an entity and placed the costs there. He felt his solution at least kept his books for the international division clean. He continued to raise the question about the accounting propriety, but the only response he ever got was that it was being done as a "Scott Sullivan directive."

Congressional documents verify that many WorldCom employees approached Myers, as far back as July 2000, to voice concern about the accounting changes, but he went forward with them anyway. Myers, sycophant extraordinaire, was described by his coworkers as a "cheerleader" when it came to WorldCom and its numbers performance. Congressman Billy Tauzin described the congressional findings related to the culture of fear and pressure as follows: "The bottomline [sic] is people inside this company were trying to tell its leaders you can't do what you want to do, and these leaders were telling them they had to." When Steven Brabbs continued to raise concerns about the accounting practices at WorldCom, even with Arthur Andersen, he received an e-mail from Myers ordering him to "not have any more meetings with AA for any reason."

There was a well-documented clarity among WorldCom employees that what they were doing with the company's financials clearly violated accounting principles. Buford "Buddy" Yates, the director of general accounting for WorldCom, sent an e-mail on July 25, 2000, to Myers that indicated his doubts about changing the operating expense of purchased wire capacity to a capital expense: "I might be narrow-minded, but I can't see a logical path for capitalizing excess capacity." The two of them then went via e-mail to Scott Sullivan, with Yates's e-mail reading, "David and I have reviewed and discussed your logic of capitalizing excess capacity and can find no support within the current accounting guidelines that would allow for this accounting treatment." The change from operating expenses to capitalization went forward nevertheless, with Betty Vinson and Troy Normand, employees in accounting, making the adjustments in the books per orders from Myers. Incredibly, Sullivan was able to convince these three bright professionals that silence was indeed golden. He explained that they should think of the company as an aircraft carrier that has planes still in the air. He told them that they needed to get planes landed before he could let them worry about GAAP, GAAS, FASB, and other testy accounting principles. None of the three consulted with Andersen about these issues. It's not entirely clear that such consultation would have made much of a difference. Shredding acquittals aside, Andersen was not really into crackerjack audits during this phase of its strategic evolution into an expert consulting firm and an audit firm with the motto of "Whatever."

Many employees were not as lucky as Betty Vinson and Troy Normand; they were fired for raising the accounting issues. Mark Abide, an employee in charge of accounting at WorldCom's Richardson, Texas, office, sent the internal audit staff at company headquarters a newspaper article about an employee in his office who had been fired after the employee had raised questions about the accounting related to capital expenditures. The termination of the employee for raising questions was typical, but Abide sent the article with the hope that the internal audit staff would look into the issue that had been raised.

Employees at WorldCom knew that they too were on the corporate *Titanic,* but they stayed the course because the rest of the world was ignoring the writing on the wall. For example, when the loans by the board to Ebbers began, employees began calling their company "WorldRon" because the share prices, the cash concerns, and the too-good-to-be-true financials bore an eerie resemblance to Enron's inexplicability and final fall. They saw the companies as similar, but no one within WorldCom dared discuss the similarities except with wry humor spoken softly behind closed doors and never within earshot of an officer.

When WorldCom's internal audit staff began to raise questions about the reserves and the capitalization of ordinary expenses, they were forbidden from doing further work. As a result of these internal roadblocks as well as the capitulation of Andersen, the WorldCom internal audit group began its own audit and inquiry. Their fear of discovery was so great that their work was done after hours and on weekends. A member of the internal audit staff personally purchased a CD burner for their late and after-hours work because they feared storing papers and data on-site at the company. Believing that their work would be destroyed if found, they burned it all onto CDs as they finished it and then stored the CDs outside the company.

During the internal audit team's stealth audit, Scott Sullivan ran into Gene

Morse, the audit team member who first discovered the receipt problem with capitalization, in the WorldCom headquarters cafeteria. Sullivan had spoken to Morse only twice in his five years with the internal audit staff. Sullivan sat with Morse and inquired about his current projects. When Morse responded that he was working on "international capital expenditures," Mr. Sullivan left. Sullivan then asked the audit staff to wait at least another quarter before continuing with their investigation. The internal audit staff could find no ethical gumption or support from Andersen. In fact, Andersen auditors reported any questions raised by the WorldCom internal audit staff to Sullivan and would not follow through on any staff questions and concerns. WorldCom's new board, established in 2003, commissioned a report that concluded that dozens of employees knew about the accounting fraud but were afraid to tell anyone. The atmosphere was thick and soupy, and they were not on an aircraft carrier waiting for planes to land. They were on a sinking ship, and they knew it.

Tyco: Purchasing Silence and the Fear of Having to Repay Loans

Tyco had the usual autocratic CEO/sycophant atmosphere of a failed ethical culture. When he was CEO of Tyco's Grinnell Fire Protection Systems Co., Dennis Kozlowski held an annual banquet at which he presented awards to the best warehouse manager as well as to the worst. The worst manager would have to walk to the front of the room in what other managers described as a "death sentence." One wonders why these managers made the walk, for shortly after this public humiliation came termination. That human-dignity issue rises again.

But Tyco introduces us to a different type of fear and silence, one not uncommon in failed ethical cultures. This fear and silence comes from a more sophisticated approach than bullying tyrants and the swords of termination they yield. Dennis Kozlowski used the tactic of getting his executives inextricably intertwined to him and Tyco as a means of ensuring their complicity in Tyco's wild accounting. Tyco had the Key Employee Loan Program (KELP), which was originally established to encourage employees to own Tyco shares by offering them loans to be used to pay taxes due when their ownership of shares granted to them under Tyco's restricted plan vested. There was no way for these key employees (executives and officers) to pay the taxes except to sell some of the shares for cash, and the loan program permitted the officers to pledge their shares in exchange for cash that was then used to pay the income tax. Kozlowski made it clear that the loan program was available to all of his new hires, including CFO Mark Swartz and Mark Belnick, Tyco's general counsel and executive vice president. All three were tried for larceny related to

KELP. Belnick was acquitted, but Kozlowski and Swartz were convicted in a second trial that followed a mistrial. To a jury, the loans had more in common with looting the company than borrowing.

The second loan program provided low-interest loans to employees who had to move from Tyco headquarters in New Hampshire to company offices in New York or Florida. The purpose of the 6.24 percent relocation loans was to lessen the impact of their moves to more expensive housing markets. One of the requirements of the program was the employee's certification that he or she was indeed moving from New Hampshire to New York or, in some cases, to Boca Raton.

Employees were simply not capable of repaying the loans under either program, and indeed most did not. So the loans became a secret fetter used by Kozlowski to keep executives close to the vest. Mark Belnick, as noted earlier, was one of the loan beneficiaries and was, by all publicized accounts, a respected lawyer who played by the rules. From the time that he began his work with Tyco, he had told friends that he was uncomfortable because he was not in the info loop with Kozlowski or the board. Former U.S. Senator Warren Rudman said, when told of Belnick's fall from grace, "I don't understand. Ethical, straight, cross the t's, dot the i's—that's my experience with Mark Belnick." However, Kozlowski offered Belnick more and more lucrative compensation plans and bonuses and additional loans, and Belnick stayed the silent course. It is stunning to realize that as general counsel for Tyco, the lawyer responsible for signing off on every SEC document the company filed, a man with Belnick's credentials and position would allow himself to remain silent. But a culture of fear and silence ropes in even the bright and capable, and often with the simple fear of losing compensation or, in this case, the greater fear of having all the loans called in. Belnick saw the red flags and was aware of the evolving issues but took no action. There is an e-mail from Tyco's outside counsel, Lewis Liman, of the Wilmer Cutler law firm, to Belnick on March 23, 2000, that reads, "There are payments to a woman whom the folks in finance describe as Dennis's girlfriend. I do not know Dennis's situation, but this is an embarrassing fact." "Embarrassing" is a charitable description. Embezzlement captures the conduct and the moment. Not only were outside counsel and general counsel aware of company payments to the girlfriend of a married CEO, but they received that information in e-mail that was being culled to respond to an SEC request for information in an investigation of the company. Liman suggested that the e-mail documentation on the payments be sent along to the SEC. Belnick declined to do so because the SEC had not asked specifically for documents of this nature.

CFO Mark Swartz was also fettered with the financial-entanglement strategy of fear and silence, but to a larger extent, to the tune of $85 million in

KELP loans. Swartz paid $13 million in taxes on the share-related income and spent the remaining $72 million for personal investments, business ventures, real estate holdings, and trusts. Swartz took more than $32 million in interest-free relocation loans and, according to SEC documents, used almost $9 million of it for purposes not authorized under the program, including purchasing a yacht and investing in real estate.

The issue of prior board approval of the loans remained a question through the trials of Swartz and Kozlowski, largely because Kozlowski insisted that he had approval from a board member who had died prior to the trial. The comedic richness of "But the dead guy said okay!" was apparently not lost on the second jury. However, the loans were not disclosed in any SEC filings until after the 2002 collapse of Tyco because the KELP loans were not available to just the SEC reporting officers, such as Belnick and Swartz, but to a total of fifty-one employees. Widespread availability of the loans not only opened up the group silence to a broader cross-section of employees, it also let the loans fly beneath the SEC radar.

The loans were disclosed to the auditors, and board minutes show that they were revealed to the board, but not until February 2002, just months before Kozlowski's art-sales tax-evasion scam hit the fan and the spool began unwinding. Disclosure of the loans made the prosecution of Kozwloski and Swartz for embezzlement difficult (one mistrial and a second trial that required eleven days of jury deliberations). Their "it's technically not embezzlement if we have paperwork for it" defense worked for Belnick, who was acquitted of any charges related to the loans, but not for Kozlowski and Swartz. Tyco's compensation committee minutes from the February 21, 2002, board meeting show that the committee was given a list of loans to officers along with the details of a new compensation package for Belnick, which they approved. Board members disagree on whether they knew about use of the loans for unauthorized purposes.

The employees understood what was happening and were uneasy about it, and that uneasiness had crossed over to a board that was acquiescent. (See Chapter 5 for more details on the Tyco board.) In grand jury testimony given in exchange for immunity, Patricia Prue, the Tyco officer responsible for administering KELP, testified that, in her view, she had been pressured by board member Joshua Berman. In June 2002 Ms. Prue testified that she felt that he asked her to change the minutes from that February compensation committee meeting. While Berman denies the Prue allegations of pressure, there is a contemporaneous June 7, 2002, memo from Ms. Prue to John Fort (the former CEO of Tyco pre-Kozlowski and Tyco's lead director), Mr. Swartz, and the board's governance committee that includes following: "As a result of the fact that I was recently pressured by Josh Berman to engage in conduct which I regarded as dishonest—and which I have refused to do—I will decline to have any personal contact with him in the future. In addition, I ask that Josh not go to my staff with any requests for information or directions." She made it far enough to protect herself and her staff with an internal memo but could not muster the courage to disclose her concerns at that time to those who would be affected, shareholders and employees, by what was really being done with company funds. Ms. Prue may have seen the issue, but it did lie flat despite its dynamic character.

HealthSouth: Parking Lot Raids in the Wee Hours and Monday-Morning Beatings

Richard Scrushy, former HealthSouth CEO, was the classic autocratic CEO, and he had succeeded in creating a culture of sycophants who responded to whatever demands he made. Employees referred to their Monday morning meetings with Scrushy on the numbers as the "Monday-morning beatings." In these meetings, Scrushy would question employees about everything from hospital performance to cell phone bills. A popular response from Scrushy when employees were asked to explain their numbers, decisions, or actions: "That was the stupidest thing I ever heard." One reporter's conclusion about the culture: "Interviews with associates of Mr. Scrushy, government officials and former employees, as well as a review of the litigation history of Health-South, paint a picture of an executive who ruled by top-down fear, threatened critics with reprisals and paid his loyal subordinates well." When Scrushy was indicted, there was rejoicing among employees at HealthSouth headquarters because they saw themselves as "survivors of an abusive relationship." Some said they were quite nearly singing, "Ding, dong, the wicked witch is dead."

In 1998 employees began posting notices on Yahoo message board about HealthSouth, along with derogatory comments about Scrushy, using pseudonyms. Scrushy hired security to determine who was responsible for the postings and eventually shut down employee computer access to the message boards.

Scrushy was known to place calls to his facility administrators from parking lots of HealthSouth facilities at one A.M. to notify them that he was standing in their parking lots and that he had found litter there. They were then forced to go there immediately to clean up. Ah, the human-dignity problem again. Employees referred to Scrushy as "the king," and Scrushy, according to employee folklore, made every decision in the company. He had the trappings of an aloof ruler. He had a ubiquitous security force with him everywhere he went, even when he was in his office at the HealthSouth headquarters. Somehow an open-door policy doesn't carry credibility when there are guards posted outside the CEO's door at all times.

Fear and silence often come from the simple root cause of a mean boss. Scrushy fit the bill. He was a boss with a temper and used it to bully employees, even to the point of getting them to certify false financial statements. Leif Murphy, a former HealthSouth vice president who testified at Mr. Scrushy's trial, detailed how Scrushy had stormed into his office, screaming because the financial reports Murphy had developed put HealthSouth's earnings at 72 cents below what had been announced previously. Scrushy told Murphy to change the numbers because Murphy had not been running the business for fourteen years. Murphy, who was never charged with a crime, did change the numbers and then certified the false financial statements. Murphy would resign following an August 1999 phone conference with analysts in which he said he intentionally gave false financial information. Murphy testified for the government, indicating that he left behind $1 million on the table, an amount offered to him by then-CFO Martin if he would not leave the company.

The executive team at HealthSouth also used the more subtle fear factor of flatlining employees who did not go along with the numbers game. Diana Henze, who was a vice president for finance at HealthSouth, refused to certify financial statements in 1999 because the numbers had been changed so many times and she suspected fraud. While the executives were able to get other employees to sign off, Ms. Henze's punishment was that she was passed over for a promotion that had been hers. When a less-qualified person got the job, she confronted CFO Owens and he responded, "You have made it clear that you won't do what we ask."

Royal Dutch/Shell Group—Skits, Memos, and Unbelievable Oil Reserves

As the wicked truth about Royal Dutch/Shell Group's misrepresentations have emerged, we learned that an executive who voiced concerns about the overstatement of reserves was given a negative performance evaluation. Chairman Sir Philip Watts placed tremendous numbers pressure on Walter van de Vijver, the company's exploration chief, to get the company's reserves where they needed to be for purposes of ensuring a AAA rating. His instructions were to "leave no stone unturned" in making sure that for every barrel of oil sold, there was another barrel added to the reported reserves. Van de Vijver first raised the issue with Watts in early 2002 and then later documented his concerns with a memo to his files. Watts gave van de Vijver a negative evaluation because of increasing tension between the two over the reserves, and van de Vijver fired off an angry e-mail in November 2003 with the following complaint: "I am becoming sick and tired of lying about the extent of our reserves issues and the downward revisions that need to be done because of far too aggressive/optimistic bookings." Despite the increasing tension and concern, it would be months before the reserves issue would be tackled and write-downs taken. Further, the 2 percent bonuses for 2003 and 2004 were tied to increases in reserves. Those bonuses would be booked before any action was taken on correcting the reserves. Memos and e-mails during this time period are disturbing because of the cloud of questions about reserves that encased the inaction. The company's chief financial officer, Judy Boynton, had received a memo on the reserves, but she did not pursue the issue. Through her lawyer she has indicated that she relied on the representations of others as she raised questions. She, too, believes she was misled. Following an SEC inquiry in February 2004, Royal Dutch would go public with the problem and announce a reduction of 22 percent in its reserves. Earnings for the period from 2000 to 2003 were revised downward by $100 million. Boynton, Watts, and Van de Vijver have left the company. The board concluded that they did not know enough to be culpable. No one ever does in these massive restatements. They are amorphous creatures that appear suddenly with no accountability or culpability on the part of those running the company. Legal accountability, unfortunately, does not include the generic responsibility theory of "It happened on your watch!"

In what appears to be a situation of an elephant in the room, the company, consumed with aggressive numbers targets for reserves and fears related to not meeting those numbers, suppressed its ethics and its courage. In what also had to be the worst of the human-dignity tales of this era's scandals, a new culture at Royal Dutch replaced the staid geologists' control and scientific approach to reserves with motivational skits on finding new reserves. Managers were required to write and appear in skits to impress the officers and chairman with creative ways of finding reserves. One manager ran onstage naked to draw attention to his aggressiveness. Another staged a Jerry Springer skit, and still another pledged to return to the Dutch oil fields and bring more from those declining wells. Managers were forced to hold hands and share one another's intimate secrets. They were also asked to raise their arms in the air in an exercise whose purpose no one is quite sure about—perhaps a barrel dance to bring the fertile oil fields to their door, something about as realistic as the company's reserves statements. How can adults be persuaded to engage in such humiliation? And all for the privilege of earnings restatements, a tanked share price, and fines of $150 million to securities officials in Britain and the United States.

Nonprofits Also Have Fear and Silence: New Era Philanthropy

New Era Philanthropy provides insight into how silence and fear can be purchased with subtle social ordering within an organization. The Foundation for New Era Philanthropy was founded in 1989 by John G. Bennett Jr. and became a phenomenon in the world of nonprofits and institutions of higher learning. New Era was their key to effective endowment and fund management, and they all flocked to deposit their funds in exchange for high rates of return. Indeed, the promise was that anonymous donors would double nonprofits participants' funds in six months. Among the individual investors in New Era were Laurance Rockefeller, Pat Boone, then-president of Procter & Gamble John Pepper, and former treasury secretary William Simon. The institutional investors looking for the high returns included the University of Pennsylvania, the Nature Conservancy, and the National Museum of American Jewish History. New Era took in more than $200 million between 1989 and May 1995, when the SEC brought suit against New Era and it went into bankruptcy. New Era was not technically a foundation, but, then again, it was not remotely a for-profit venture either. It was a scam with a minimal paper trail.

In 1991 Melenie and Albert Meyer moved from their native South Africa to Michigan, where Mr. Meyer took a tenure-track position as an accounting professor at Spring Arbor College. Because there were only three accounting majors at the time he was hired, Mr. Meyer was also required to work part-time in the college business office.

During his first month of work in the office, Mr. Meyer was concerned about the direction of $294,000 of college funds to Heritage of Values Foundation Inc. At that time Reverend Jim Bakker had been indicted for fraud and the term *Heritage* USA had been used for his religious theme park and had become associated with the PTL ministry, Bakker's organization. Meyer was reassured when he found no connection between Jim Bakker and New Era. But his comfort was short-lived. He could find no other information on this organization to which so much of the college's endowment had been entrusted. Meyer could not find a nonprofit registration for New Era in Pennsylvania, its headquarters. Further, New Era had not filed a tax return until 1993. Meyer went to his supervisor, the vice president for business affairs, Ms. Janet M. Tjepkema, and asked about Heritage of Values. She told Meyer that Heritage was the consultant that had founded the New Era Foundation and that she was proud of having discovered this "double your investment" fund and recommended it to the college.

Meyer still suspected fraud, as should anyone who witnesses a "double your money" fund with no government agency records, but Meyer remained silent because he was the target of another tactic that creates fear and silence in an organization—supervisors who seem annoyed. Each time Meyer raised concerns about the "double your money" promises and the dead-end trails on information about Heritage or New Era, he got the administrative cold shoulder. By April 1994 he and his wife were no longer attending any social functions held by the college. College administrators scolded Meyer, reminding him that raising funds was tough enough without his meddling. Meyer's efforts to persuade administrators not to put any more money into New Era went unheeded. Spring Arbor invested an additional $1.5 million in 1994, placing one-fourth of its total endowment of $6 million into this questionable basket. Spring Arbor would lose all of that money when New Era went into bankruptcy. Fear of losing his job, being unable to support his family, and having his visa revoked as a result of his unemployment were frightening thoughts. Virtue is its own reward, but like most employees, Meyer didn't want to be foolish about rent and food as rewards for silence. While he continued to collect information about New Era, Meyer would say little about what he had found because he knew his great personal risk and the clear disdain with which his supervisors met his findings and concerns. He was an untenured faculty member in the country on a temporary work visa and he had a wife and three children to support.

Nevertheless, the evidence of New Era problems was overwhelming. So, Meyer continued to collect information on the fund in a file he had marked "Ponzi File." For example, he discovered that New Era's reportable tax income was only $34,000. That income, just to pay the interest due the clients, should have been at least $1 million. Some major disconnect existed between the hype and the reality. But with no audience to hear his concern and administrators who determined his fate wanting New Era to succeed, Meyer opted for silence on what he uncovered.

In March 1995, when Mr. Meyer received tenure, that magical assurance that the cold shoulder is benign in terms of employment continuation, he wrote to the SEC to turn over his "Ponzi File" information and voice his concerns. The SEC then notified Prudential Securities, which was holding $73 million in New Era stock. Prudential began its own investigation and found that the New Era officers were as resistant to it as they had been to Meyer. Thus began the unraveling and collapse of New Era. By June 1995 it was in bankruptcy. New Era had more than three hundred creditors named and net losses of $107 million. New Era was, as Meyer had determined years earlier, nothing but a Ponzi scheme. Bennett was indicted on eighty-two counts of fraud, money laundering, and tax code violations in March 1997. Bennett entered a no-contest plea and was released after posting his daughter's $115,000 house to cover his bond. Mr. Bennett was sentenced to twelve years in prison following six days of testimony during his sentencing hearing, including his emotional pleas.

No man is a prophet in his own land, and Meyer was still shunned at that time at his school for his efforts. Many true believers there still maintain (and it is also a common trait of ethically collapsed companies for the rogue officers to recite, "If the government had let us alone, we could have pulled it all out!") that if Meyer had remained quiet, New Era would have survived. However, those outside the school recognize his worth, and Meyer was named a Michiganian of the Year for 1995.

NASA: A Government Agency Still Generates Fear in the Heart of Employees

The investigation into the disintegration of the *Columbia* space shuttle upon its reentry to Earth reveals a culture at NASA in which fear silenced employees. One of the conclusions of the report on the accident states:

> *The organizational structure and hierarchy blocked effective communication of technical problems. Signals were overlooked, people were silenced, and useful information and dissenting views on technical issues did not surface at higher levels.*

The report discusses intimidation of engineers and the classic statement from an earlier NASA investigation of "take your engineer hats off and put on your management hats." In some cases mockery was used as a means of intimidation, with one manager asking, "When do you want me to launch? Next April?" "Faster, better, cheaper" was the NASA motto of the 1990s, and those who performed according to that mantra were rewarded. Those who raised safety issues, technical concerns, and different solutions were flatlined in the organization. The "can-do" atmosphere of the agency made yes-men a valued commodity, and the naysayers were looked down upon and passed over for promotions and key projects.

NASA also had a unique and additional means of ensuring silence within the organization. It implemented a hierarchy for decisions that dictated that once engineers had signed off on something as an "acceptable risk," it was irrelevant whether anyone else saw a problem. NASA, in effect, concentrated all issues and possible dissent into one section of the organization. Anyone outside that area who raised issues was dismissed easily because the hierarchy dictated that, for example, even when there was a design flaw, as long as engineering had signed off as the flaw being an acceptable risk, there could be no further discussion.

This government-agency phenomenon on silence translates across into corporations because too often employees outside accounting, finance, or product development saw issues and concerns, but their questions were dismissed because they were outside the line of authority for dealing with possible safety, disclosure, or other issues. In perhaps what can be the most innocent form of creating a culture of silence, the organization actually prevents dissent through a structure that may have been created with all good intentions of efficiency and expertise. The lesson of NASA is that dissent on company issues knows no boundaries when it comes to perspective on ethical and legal matters. Structure cannot be so rigid that those who are outside the lines of authority do not have an opportunity to dissent, voice concerns, or simply raise questions and issues.

Antidotes for Fear and Silence

The employees in these cultures of fear and silence didn't begin their downward slide into ethical collapse by wrapping bricks—there were signals along the way to that degradation, such as the CEO firing salespeople in public meetings when they did not meet their quotas. You have to engage in a little channel stuffing or earnings manipulation before you graduate to making up inventory, bank accounts, and oil reserves. Parmalat officers and lawyers didn't begin that company's $4.9 billion fraud by going to work each day forging and faxing documents to prove that they had that money in a nonexistent Bank of America account. They began with the fear of reporting that there had been a bad quarter in South America and that Parmalat would not meet its earnings numbers. They opted for silence on telling the real story about the earnings, believing they could make it up in the next quarter. The next quarter didn't prove to be much better, and now they had two quarters in the cover-up; and so it went for nine years of silence in an increasingly heavy atmosphere of fear that led them down a path of escalating ethical lapses and misconduct. Fausto Tonna, the chief financial officer of Parmalat, has admitted to cooking the books to buoy the company until it could get a capital infusion. When that infusion did not come, it was too late to stop the fraud and they just kept rolling with it, hoping it would all go away or never be uncovered. The internal fear and silence soon expanded to include the fear of disclosure and the disgrace they would experience in the world outside Parmalat's mighty fax machine of fraud. Think how pervasive the tentacles of unethical behavior had seeped into this company to allow Europe's largest-ever fraud to continue for so long.

To date, sixty-four people have been indicted in the Parmalat scam. An Italian court is reviewing whether the indictments will stand, and it is not clear who in the company has been indicted. Thus, because of a near decade of deception by those within the company, thousands of investors are left to recover from accounting firms, banks, and other third parties, if they can prove that these companies aided the fraud. Silence is really not golden in business.

First comes fear, then comes silence, and then comes ethical collapse. Everyone and every organization needs candid feedback from those who can see and report the issues. And when they do see and report issues, the company must have the infrastructure to respond. Being able to tell someone about ethical and legal problems and being guaranteed a response other than termination or a downgraded performance evaluation are the key antidotes to a culture of fear and silence. This trait of fear and silence in ethically collapsed companies tells us that the organizations most vulnerable are those that either silence their workers' feedback or fail to heed their expressions of concern. This signal of silence is the most frequent cultural issue I encounter in companies as they try to find ways to overcome employees' fear in coming forward with problems, violations, and concerns.

There are companies that have done things a different way. When the electric utility industry was hit with a study that concluded its overhead transmission wires caused leukemia in children, concealment, denial, and hope that it would all go away could have turned the industry into another asbestos debacle, with years of litigation and a loss of 25 percent of their profits to a trust for compensating the victims. However, members of the electric utility industry went public with the electromagnetic field (EMF) and cancer issue, began research, placed lines farther away from residences and residential areas, and even reconfigured the wires on the lines to reduce the EMF. The result was eventual vindication through follow-up studies that showed the leukemia was caused by other factors. More important, the result was the electric utilities' great credibility with the public for their forthright handling of the issue and their great savings to shareholders for not succumbing to the pattern of ethical collapse. Eliminating fear and silence is also not a bad business strategy. Openness, disclosure, and finding and proposing solutions are the antidotes to fear and silence.

Antidote #1 for Fear and Silence: Tell Employees to Speak Up and Provide the Means for Them to Do So

I heard a frustrated executive in a meeting with employees who were justifiably irate about the conduct of their supervisors that had gone on for far too long without anyone speaking up: "How can I fix something when you don't let me know about it?" As I listened, my observation was "When did you let them know to tell you? How were they supposed to tell you?" While the incident was pre-Sarbanes-Oxley, when hotlines were not common except in the defense and nuclear industries, my question still remains relevant in this era of every company with a hotline. Employees must be told, reminded, and reassured that you really do want to hear from them. Get some form of anonymous reporting system because even in the most open cultures, there is a natural reticence among employees. There is tension in the supervisor-employee relationship. Anonymity brings employees forward with some confidence.

Once a reporting system is in place, the follow-up signal for employees comes from what is done with the information reported. This post-Sarbanes-Oxley world has dictated much of the response, but beyond the legal-compliance issues are the perception concerns. Are employees aware that someone looks at and into, when necessary, every complaint? Do employees understand that board members also examine the information that comes in through the reporting systems? Have employees seen that someone responds to them (if they asked for a response) and to the information or situation reported? A reporting system is but a step in curbing fear and silence because employees gauge their willingness to come forward from the quality of the response to what is placed in the reporting hopper. Over time, as each allegation is handled and appropriate actions are taken, employees develop confidence in reporting legal and ethical concerns. A culture of trust in the reporting system builds over time. It is in the execution of this reporting/feedback function that most companies falter terribly.

One thing that enhances anonymous reporting and trust is getting back to employees on the types of reports, action taken, and changes made. This information can be included in company e-mails, newsletters, and any other vehicle that makes its way into employee hands. For example, if a purchasing manager is caught taking kickbacks because of a tip from the company hotline and a follow-up investigation confirms it, employees need to know that. That information can be disclosed generically without violating any of the 2,587 laws protecting the graft-laden purchasing manager. But disclosure is everything. When employees feel their efforts fall into a management black hole, they (a) make stuff up about what really happened (and Hollywood should purchase some of the corporate legends that circulate about what happens when employees use the anonymous reporting line), (b) sit and wait to be fired, or worst of all, (c) continue to assume that management talks a good game but does little else. The result of disclosure is that employees are reminded that kickbacks are unethical and illegal, that the company really does investigate hotline tips, and that the company takes action based on conduct revealed through the hotline.

Many companies have tablets, desk trinkets, pens, and other items with the company hotline number on them so that employees have reminders. While such items seem superficial, they are the first step: reminding employees that they can speak up. The trinkets do not create a culture or ensure ethical conduct. Enron had clever trinkets galore scattered everywhere about the employees' desks and offices. But these small symbols are one step in the process of getting employees to speak up about ethical and legal issues. The remaining antidotes cover the issues that arise once the first hurdle of reporting (where and to whom) is conquered.

Antidote #2 for Fear and Silence: Avoid the Signals of Silence: Don't Fire Employees for Speaking Up; Don't Flatline Employees for Speaking Up; Don't Transfer, Reassign, Trample, Muck Up or Malign Employees for Speaking Up

With apologies to Simon and Garfunkel, the signals of silence are a death knell to employees' willingness to raise their concerns. I have never heard a chairman or CEO stand before employees and say, "Really don't want to hear about any legal or ethical issues. They are a pain. Keep them to yourselves, or else." Yet, somehow, in companies headed toward ethical collapse and those that have arrived, employees' almost universal perception is that they will be sacked, demoted, or flatlined for raising concerns. They also feel very much as if that message is communicated to them on a daily basis. They feel it in their bones. They feel it because actions and responses have become the substitute for the clear message. If there have been past instances of employees being disciplined for raising concerns, the perception of retaliation will have control over any promised present-day protection. Until employees see a "tattletale" promoted, the retaliatory perception controls. As delineated in the case studies earlier, employees were demoted, humiliated, fired, and sent to Siberia when they spoke up about the very issues that proved to be the company's demise. Speaking of Siberia, the Center for Business Ethics and Corporate Governance, based in St. Petersburg, Russia, has developed a set of questions that employees seem to have on their minds when they are told to behave ethically:

Will the boss back me up if I am ethical? What happens to me if I behave ethically and, as a result, make less profit for my company in the short term?

What's in it for me to be ethical? Why should I be the first one in the organization to try and do things differently? All I can see is hard times and less money in the short run.

What will ensure that my coworkers are ethical? If they meet their quotas without being ethical and my performance goes flat because I do behave ethically, how will that reflect upon me?

These are the issues managers must address and the barriers that must be broken down if antidote #1 to the culture of fear and silence is to work. The barriers come from the signals of silence that arise, perhaps unintentionally, by how employees who raise issues are treated.

State Clearly What Should Be Reported

Companies must state clearly their expectations for employees' reporting legal and ethical issues and violations. Perhaps more important, companies should state clearly their obligations to those employees who do raise legal and ethical concerns. The two policies together mean that companies must face off squarely with cranks. Cranks are best described by one ethics officer I worked with, who said, "Could you somehow make clear to employees that just because they disagree with a decision does not mean that the company is unethical or has done something illegal?" In short, cranks report, report, report and just generally cry wolf. They can be conspiracy theorists who see plotting behind the order of the beverages in the cafeteria pop machines. Some cranks even use the hotline for their own retaliatory purposes, that is, they report pseudoviolations in order to get back at someone. Companies should address with clarity, by giving examples, the difference between ethical and legal issues and disagreement with supervisors over decisions, evaluations, and other matters that plague manager-employee relationships. Just because a manager does not give a good performance evaluation does not mean there has been an ethical violation. However, if a manager is conducting performance evaluations differently for different employees, there is an issue. If a manager is using different standards for employees performing the same job, there is also a problem. Helping employees understand these distinctions cuts down on the noise that comes from employees saying, "I called the hotline with a problem and they did nothing." Even when the complaint they made or the concern they raised is baseless, other employees adopt this employee's experience with the reporting line and launch their corporate folklore. The anonymous reporting line becomes a perfunctory service, placed there by managers to comply with the law. In some cases doing nothing is the correct response. However, the culture evolves around reporting and responsiveness. Employees clam up when the perception, rightly or wrongly, is that there is a lack of response. Silence results from perceived indifference. Clarifying action vs. nonaction items helps reduce the company myths that hamper reporting.

Once companies establish the difference between legal and ethical violations and disgruntlement, the next step is to provide employees with information on protecting them for raising issues. The parameters of Sarbanes-Oxley are a beginning here, but companies should go beyond stating statutory protections. That the law will help them if they are sacked is not the positive message or encouragement that prevents a culture of silence and fear. Give employees the assurance that anyone who raises a legal or ethical issue or concern in good faith will not experience retaliation. Tell them that someone will investigate the problem and protect their identity as much as possible. Tell them they need not fear when issues are raised in good faith. However, just as employees require definitional parameters on what is and is not a legal or ethical issue, they also require examples of what is and is not good faith. An employee who reports his or her own misconduct cannot be protected. George Couto was a marketing manager with Bayer Corporation, the U.S. subsidiary of Bayer A.G., a German-based company. In 1995 Kaiser Permanente, the largest HMO in the United States, demanded a discount from Bayer for its bulk purchases of Cipro, one of Bayer's antibiotics. Kaiser indicated that it would turn to Johnson & Johnson for an alternative drug if it was not given a deep enough discount. Bayer could grant the discount to Kaiser; however, if it granted that discount to Kaiser, federal regulations required that it sell Cipro at the same price to the federal government (under Medicaid regulations).

In order to avoid having to give the federal government the discount, Couto oversaw the development and sale of a private-label Cipro for Kaiser. The drug was manufactured in Connecticut and sold to Kaiser under a private label at a 40 percent discount. However, after attending an ethics class at Bayer during which Bayer's CEO appeared on a videotape and urged employees to follow not just the letter of the law but also the spirit of the law, Couto was consumed by pangs of conscience and wrote a letter to the Medicaid administration that outlined his private-label plan. He had used the plan to Kaiser's benefit for almost five years. There is no indication that Kaiser was aware of any violations of the law. Interestingly, Couto, despite his misgivings about the private-label plan, did seek to obtain a President's Achievement Award from the CEO of Bayer for his retention of the Kaiser account.

Bayer agreed to pay $257 million to the federal government, the largest Medicaid fraud settlement to date. Under federal law, Couto was entitled to as much as 30 percent of the amount of the penalty recovered by the government. Couto admitted his role in the case but was still awarded 24 percent ($34 million) of the fine the federal government collected just three months after his deposition and just five months before Bayer settled the case. Couto (thirty-nine) died of pancreatic cancer, and the award was granted posthumously. The case is on appeal, and if the award to Couto is upheld, it will be shared by his three children. Bayer had terminated Couto after he notified the Medicaid administration, and for good reason. The legal doctrine of unclean hands prevents those who mastermind wrongdoing from benefiting from the wrongdoing. Such was the case here. Couto gave chutzpah new meaning. Had Bayer not terminated him, it would have sent the signal to its employees to find loopholes, use them, and then collect from the feds for reporting the company.

Less clear to employees and infinitely more difficult to explain are situations in which marginal employees report legal or ethical violations. Company myths from the rumor mill regarding terminated whistle-blowers are legion. Sometimes "iffy" employees see wrongdoing. A psychological component kicks in with managers and supervisors when an employee who reports misconduct has long been a thorn in their side. Perhaps they have failed to take disciplinary action, choosing instead that great managerial alternative of avoiding confrontation. The employee, who has now reported misconduct, hurls the last straw in a long history of problematic performance. In some cases the employee who has raised the issue draws attention to the employee's work. Ward Churchill, the University of Colorado professor who created a political firestorm with his comments about the 9/11 victims, is in trouble for his alleged plagiarism, not his controversial writing and speeches. But few who share his views are convinced that the speech simply drew attention to his somewhat checkered academic career.

Wal-Mart is grappling with such a situation and the resulting perception in an embarrassing case that involves its former second-in-command officer. Jared Bowen, a former vice president for operations at the company whose blood ran Wal-Mart blue and who had worked his way up from the Flagstaff, Arizona, Wal-Mart as a $4.50-per-hour clerk, to vice president at Arkansas headquarters, raised concerns about signing off on the invoices for personal items for vice chairman and senior officer Thomas Coughlin. Coughlin, a brilliant manager, is credited with the development of Wal-Mart's incredible supply chain system. Some of the invoices Coughlin asked his subordinates to sign off on included a pair of $1,359 custom-made cowboy boots (in Mr. Coughlin's size, of course), $2,500 in fencing for Coughlin's hunting dog pens, a rump roast, and some Celine Dion CDs. Really, embezzlement mandates something more along the lines of Aerosmith. Now, to be fair, Mr. Coughlin's lawyer has stated unequivocally that Mr. Coughlin, whose salary and bonuses were between $4 and $6 million per year, did not take any Wal-Mart funds for personal use. He maintains that the invoices were phony and were a cover for getting cash to informants who were providing Wal-Mart with information about union activities, all part of what he alleges was a Wal-Mart anti-union program. If it's a choice between embezzlement and federal felonies, I am bamboozled as to which is the lesser of the two evils. Following a federal grand jury investigation, Coughlin entered a guilty plea to five counts of federal wire fraud and one count of tax evasion. Nonetheless, both Coughlin and Bowen were terminated. Coughlin's termination was necessary. Indeed, he resigned from the board and Wal-Mart rescinded Coughlin's multimillion-dollar retirement agreement. He and Wal-Mart have agreed not to sue each other, and a federal judge dismissed Wal-Mart's suit against Coughlin, noting that the parties had agreed not to sue each other over the events or the termination. Bowen's sacking, even if it was with justification, as Wal-Mart alleges, sends the wrong message to employees. Bowen's exit interview indicates that he was terminated because of "loss of confidence in associate as a company officer." Employees who raise flags are not always clean as a whistle. Wal-Mart has alleged that Bowen inflated both his college transcript GPA and credit hours as well as his travel expenses while at the company. Bowen's wrongful termination and Sarbanes-Oxley whistle-blower suit against Wal-Mart was in the discovery stages in early 2005. Bowen has asked federal officials to investigate his termination. Wrong signal. Bad timing. Both are bound to exacerbate the culture of fear and silence. Worse, we may never learn what really happened here. Too many companies have similar patterns and then wonder why employees are reticent about raising concerns.

Wal-Mart CEO Lee Scott offered the following to Wal-Mart employees after the Coughlin issues emerged and Bowen's termination and subsequent suit had occurred: "If someone asks you to do something that you know is wrong—whether that is a buddy or a supervisor or Lee Scott—you must have the courage to say no. We all have to do this, no matter our role or position within the company." The words may be sincere, but actions thunder so loudly that employees cannot hear what is said. The termination of even a marginal employee who has correctly raised an important ethical concern has a chilling effect on the ethical culture of an organization.

In a company I worked with, a similar series of events took place when an employee raised concerns about financial reporting. The company investigated and found that the employee was mistaken about the financial issues, but in the course of the investigation several concerns regarding both his performance and his loyalty to the company arose. While his supervisors had said nothing about his problems when his performance and loyalty issues first arose, they spilled their guts when this wild card suddenly turned on them and the company. Employees who provided information during the investigation of the employee's allegations were now more than willing to reveal the role this employee had played in nearly sabotaging negotiations in the purchase of another company. When he put them on the spot, they were offended and regretted that they had protected him for so long by saying nothing. He had drawn attention to himself and his conduct. The old adage of people who live in glass houses comes to mind. And there is another lesson for employees to encourage them to report misconduct when it happens. Also, never trust a saboteur! They turn on you eventually. While this employee was terminated, not for reporting a concern but for turning over proprietary information to another company, the real story was unknown in company folklore. The timing of the termination was not coincidental—he had drawn attention and scrutiny to himself. But the termination imposed more fear and silence on the culture.

He was clearly wrong in his conduct, and the company had grounds for termination. Nevertheless, the company ended up in litigation with the employee and settled the suit. Worse, the ethics officer and others were left to undo the damage from what flew around the company rumor mill: an employee was sacked for raising an ethical issue. It was difficult even in a legal sense to make the case that raising the issue was not the cause of his termination. The nuance of his misconduct never accompanied the rumors because, under privacy protections, the company could not tell its side of the story. The timing of the termination sent an unintended signal to employees who did not know the particulars. In companies with a "10 percent gone formula," known by the lovely label of "rank and yank," managers are required to weed out the worst 10 percent each year. GE still uses the formula, but other companies, such as Ford, have abandoned it. The formula often becomes a cover for termination of employees who have raised issues. If other employees see a pattern in which employees are part of the 10 percent who are yanked, they reach conclusions about raising issues. In order to avoid chilling the culture and inculcating fear in the hearts of good employees, timing is everything. You may just have to hang on to the marginal employee who has raised an issue in order to preserve the company culture. Sifting the wheat from the chaff, when the chaff have raised a legal issue or two, sends the signal that silence is the best policy.

Watch Other Signals of Silence

THE TRANSFER. Employees at Finova who raised issues about the company's loan portfolio and loans that were in default but were still being carried on the books were often transferred out of their divisions. Finova was structured with five separate divisions and a great deal of autonomy that opened the door for cross-subsidization, cross-cookie-jar reserve dipping, and other such financial engineering. There was one more benefit to the structure: employees could be transferred back and forth among the divisions with relative ease when they raised ethical issues. This approach to managing employees who raise concerns is more subtle than the swift chop to the knees because the employee still works for the company. However, the signal to other employees is no different. They interpret the change to mean "keep quiet for your own good." With the five divisions of Finova so autonomous, employees were often not sure what happened to their colleagues once their transfer was complete. They interpreted the transfer as the precursor to termination out of the full view of the employee's former coworkers. Often employees who were transferred to other divisions left the company for various reasons. That their departure was voluntary was lost in the company grapevine. Employee perception was still that those who raised concerns were treated as pariahs.

THE FLATLINERS. Another signal of silence is when an employee who has raised an issue, and has often been right, levels off in progress in the organization. I once helped an employee work through being flatlined in a company because of her reputation for honesty. Her story was similar to one of a vice president of a Fortune 100 company who left when his career stalled for the same reason. Both had been in meetings with their supervisors and senior management that were focused on a new and critical project, and one of the purposes of the meetings was to decide who would be in charge of the project, a plum assignment that would be a big stepping-stone for progress up the executive ranks. The CEOs in both companies were about to assign the plum jobs to employees with reputations for honesty and then quickly retracted with "Never mind. You're too honest. It won't work." Yet both CEOs had spoken to all employees about the importance of always being honest and ethical. They had also assured employees that it was important for them to speak up and let their concerns be known. However, the actions of the two CEOs spoke louder than all the platitudes. Their attitude and choice of employees for important jobs were signals of silence. Honest employees were being flatlined and were not trusted with the most important assignments. The sweet irony that being honest takes you down a dead end in a company is never lost on employees who must survive in that culture.

THE SILENCE-IS-GOLDEN HANDCUFFS. There is one more personnel action that should be monitored, revamped, and revisited so that it does not buy silence and fear. In Tyco, employees kept quiet because they had so much personal financial risk tied up with the company. They dared not rock the boat because they had vested interests. The KELP bought silence. Sometimes employees remain silent because so much of their incentive program and bonuses depend upon no revelations that change numbers. For example, in the Marsh & McLennan cartel scandal, now settled with New York Attorney General Eliot Spitzer, a former MMC branch executive who was aware of the price-fixing and bid-rigging but never spoke up, offered his explanation for his silence: "I got back my P&L [profit and loss statement], and nearly a million dollars was added to the bottom line. It was pure profit and it was on a new line called PSA [placement service agreement]. The money was like heroin. Once you got the taste of it, you were hooked." The incentive programs, bonuses, who is covered, and how much they get send direct signals of silence to those who are part of the compensation programs and indirect signals to employees who are not. They see the rewards for silence and also see that those who say nothing about ethical or legal issues or allow unethical or illegal conduct to continue enjoy personal benefits from bonuses or just an increasing stock price. These incentive programs, if not monitored and structured carefully with an ethics component, are often signals for silence.

Antidote #3 for Fear and Silence: Reward Employees Who Speak Up and Point Out Ethical and Legal Issues

Texas Instruments' former CEO Carl Skooglund once noted, "Employees learn very quickly what they really get stroked for, and if the rewards come solely from shipping product or making financial forecasts, then that's the drumbeat they're going to march to. And that's a tough problem for any company's ethics." Skoogland offered this insight fifteen years ago. Things don't change much when it comes to signals of silence and rewards. Rewarding employees for ethics is a tough slog because, as many have noted, "who wants to be known as 'Fink of the Month'?" Some CEOs have trouble embracing the notion of rewarding employees for doing the right thing because their position is that employees are supposed to do the right thing. Well, employees are supposed to perform to other standards as well, and they don't always make it there. So, to provide incentives, we reward those who do. Why should ethical behavior be any different from behavior that results in meeting sales goals? Further, organizational cultures must create a signal that speaking up is not a job-terminating move. The inherent fear and silence and the tension in the employer-employee relationship take some hefty antidotes and cultural changes. Rewarding employees for doing the right thing creates a darn good feeling in any organization. The news that an employee has been recognized for doing the right thing reaches employees in their senses before any verbal communication of its reality. Like animals before an earthquake, they can sense the vibrations. Except in this case, those vibrations are a good thing.

Annual Recognition of Employees for Ethical Choices and Behavior

Despite these compelling reasons for rewarding employees, the practice of recognizing employees who act ethically is rare. Only 60 percent of U.S. companies place notations in company newsletters (electronic or otherwise) about ethical choices and conduct by employees. There is much work to be done in this area of communicating to employees the positive side of ethical choices. Some of the practices companies have undertaken include annual breakfasts, luncheons, or dinners for employees who demonstrated a commitment to ethics during the past year. The awards presented include bonuses. The celebration can generate momentum. For example, one company with a large fleet of delivery trucks recognized its drivers for safety records, with bonuses presented at the annual shareholders meeting. The drivers and their families joined the officers and board members for lunch. In the first few years of the program, there were only a handful of drivers who had met the standard of driving accident-free for ten years. Now the company honors twenty to thirty each year. The additional benefit of the program is direct interaction among officers, board members, and frontline employees. The company also discovered the types of candid discussions that can emerge when officers and truck drivers break bread together. This access to employees beyond management has emerged in our post-Sarbanes-Oxley world as a key to good governance. (For more on boards and governance, see Chapter 5.) Companies that curbed fear and silence before always held that key.

Annual Performance Reviews Where Ethics Count

Some companies make ethics 10 percent of their employees' performance evaluation. Indeed, new changes in the federal sentencing guidelines now require a carrot for ethical behavior. One company requires all employees, from janitors to CEOs, to give a specific example in their performance reviews of one time during the past year when they were forthright with a customer, supplier, or fellow worker. The impact of the 10 percent evaluation tool is that employees compete with one another to offer the best example of ethical behavior. The examples of employees' ethical behavior are then circulated throughout the year in the company's electronic newsletter. The impact on the culture is positive, but there is a dual purpose. Employees are able to see concrete examples of ethical dilemmas and coworkers' doing the right thing in real situations. They don't just talk about the rewards; they discuss the behavior that led to the rewards. And there is a third accomplishment: employees are talking about ethics in a positive way.

Antidote #4 for Fear and Silence: Tell Employees Bad News Happens

I was once in a board meeting at a company when an officer pledged that one of her goals as the vice president of marketing was that she was not going to lose more than one customer during the coming year. The CEO, the chairman, and several board members joked for months about the nature of their marketing vice president's goal. Many felt it was the goal that cost her any further progress up the executive ranks. She had presented a harsh reality in the company's industry that they were losing customers. She intended to communicate that she and her team were going to pull out all the stops to defy that trend. She was a realist who was sent a very clear signal by the reaction of the senior executives and the board: no bad news at all. The failure to face the realities of competition, the company's pricing, and the marketplace realities creates a culture in which employees will do whatever it takes to avoid being the bearer of bad news, including crossing ethical lines. What the marketing VP should have discussed was that until the company reduced its prices, losing customers was inevitable. Reducing prices meant cutting costs, revisiting the company structure, and a host of other strategic issues that the board had not yet grappled with. A proposal on price or cost reduction should have accompanied the "we're losing customers" news. But the board had sent the signal that it wanted only good news, even to the point that officers were trying to manage the continuing bad news instead of trying to curb it! Further, when bad news happens, as it inevitably will (and it was ongoing in this particular company), employees resort to concealment and saying nothing (and there is that culture of silence) because they have been conditioned to believe that management doesn't want bad news (and therein lies their fear). "No bad news wanted here!" A nonverbal signal of silence.

The nature of capitalism means that there will always be bad news. For every bid won by one company, there are many others that lost it. Facing bad news is not an antidote intended to condition employees to believe that failure is an option. But it is one intended to communicate to employees that if a business does not face its current market conditions, aggressive competition, and shortfalls, it cannot succeed. Harsh reality concealed from management does not get better over time. Problems in business are not like fine wine; they don't get better with age. Parmalat is a great entrepreneurial story of an Italian company founded with four or five dairy cows and the sale of milk. From those humble beginnings came a good international company with 36,000 employees, the pride of Italy. However, as noted earlier, there was that bad quarter in its South American operations. Rather than disclose some unstable performance in an often unstable region, some Parmalat officers began the task of covering up the real numbers with cooked ones. Nine years later the cover-up had evolved to the point made earlier: that officers and employees were forging and faxing documents to prove that Parmalat had almost $5 billion in a Bank of America account that did not exist. Parmalat concealment of a bad quarter over nine years certainly did not help the bottom line.

Parmalat's story is not unique. Bad news concealed over time does not improve. Johns-Manville's hiding the truth about asbestos and workers' health problems over three decades certainly did not make the company a better one.

Its board was aware of the health problems workers were experiencing because of exposure to asbestos dust. There were respiratory ailments, and later we would find a cancer that also afflicted the lungs of those exposed to asbestos. Board minutes of the 1930s reveal knowledge of the issue, which was buried through pacts of silence with lawyers for workers, scientists who knew of the problems, and doctors who treated the debilitated workers. Johns-Manville would end up in bankruptcy and its cost for the concealment would be the assignment of 25 percent of its profits in perpetuity. Oh, and a living hell on earth: unending class-action litigation and the resulting daily exposure to product-liability plaintiffs' lawyers. No one was well served by the postponement of bad news.

Bad news concealed over time doesn't get any better. See those studies again: companies with the most candid disclosures in their financial statements perform better over the long term and have higher share prices. Companies that put their current positions and performance right out there for investors and analysts to study are the companies to put your money in. The same studies also show that 87 percent of companies are not really being candid in those reports.

How can companies face and solve problems they don't know exist? Helping employees understand that bad news happens is a critical component in combating the culture of fear and silence. However, the message that bad news happens should be coupled with this admonition: accompany the report of bad news with a strategy for making it better, and that strategy can't be numbers manipulation. The message to employees should be not so much that bad news happens as that the company cannot survive unless it faces its challenges head-on. And no one can face the challenges head-on if they are concealed. Coke provides an example of a company not willing to face bad news, and the consequences and fallout were more costly than simply facing the bad news and fixing it with solid business strategy. Tom Moore, president of Coca-Cola's Foodservice and Hospitality Division, found that sales in the fountain division were responsible for one-third of all of Coke's revenues but that sales had been flat, as it were, Pepsi was aggressive in fountain sales and was targeting Coke customers. At the time, Coke held about 66 percent of the fountain-drink business and 44.3 percent of the soda market overall. Pepsi held 22 percent of the fountain market and 31.4 percent of the overall market.

Thinking strategically, Moore felt there was potential for Frozen Coke as a fountain product beyond the current convenience-store presence. Moore's team at Coke pitched the idea of having Frozen Coke at Burger King. Before Burger King would commit to the new product and a big ad campaign, it asked for some numbers from a test market. Richmond, Virginia, was chosen.

When promotions and sales for Frozen Coke began in 2000, the initial results were not good. The Coke team had had only thirty days to make the numbers look good. Perhaps the reason for the less-than-expected sales was seasonal; Frozen Coke sales are a function of temperature. And adjusting numbers for that seasonal advantage sounds logical, scientific, and statistically supportable. But you can't fool around with numbers unless you tell all affected that you are fooling around with numbers, and you should explain your rationale, in all its logical and statistical glory. When evaluating numbers and their meaning or accuracy, whether the numbers are related to sales or to product safety, as with Merck's and Guidant's justifiable and scientific evaluations of their products, there is always a statistical and scientifically supportable conclusion. However, science and logic must still be framed with the perception of the ordinary person, including emotions as well as hindsight bias. Outcome fuels perception even when science supported the conclusion at the time. Statistical science often gets in the way of gut reaction, and it should not. Robert Bader, the Coke marketing manager charged with the Richmond test market, hired marketing consultant Ronald Berryman to get more Frozen Coke purchases at Burger King. Mr. Berryman gave $9,000 cash to the directors of the Boys & Girls Clubs in the Richmond area for a homework-reward program: if the kids did their homework, they would get cash to use at Burger King. The only catch was that they had to buy Frozen Coke!

The sales growth from the Boys & Girls Clubs was triple what Burger King was used to when there were promotional items being touted in ads. According to *The Wall Street Journal*, Burger King signed on and spent $10 million to promote Frozen Coke and $37 million in equipment, training, and distribution. Others say the deal had already been struck and only the promotional tools were at issue.

Dreams turned to dust when those realists with numbers, internal auditors, found the $9,000 payment to the marketing consultant from the dark side. During some routine audit work at Coke, Matthew Whitley questioned who Berryman was and why there were large expenses with odd explanations. Coke fired Whitley. Fear, silence, termination, and bad news—all wrapped in a culture pressured to meet numbers. Oh, the signals of silence! Whitley filed suit for wrongful termination. The story of his suit, and the facts in his complaint about Frozen Coke and Richmond, appeared in *The Wall Street Journal*, p. A1, right-hand side of that august business publication, for Burger King's CEO to read. Bad news concealed does not look better when revealed on the front page of America's premier business newspaper.

Coke's president and chief operating officer, Steve Heyer, sent an apology to Burger King CEO Bradley Blum: "These actions were wrong and inconsistent with values of the Coca-Cola Co. Our relationships with Burger King and all our customers are of the utmost importance to us and should be firmly grounded in only the highest-integrity actions." Coke negotiated a settlement with Burger King that required a payment of $10 million up front and up to $21.2 million to franchisees who were left to decide for themselves whether to carry Frozen Coke.

What is interesting is Mr. Whitley's observation when he settled his suit with Coke for $540,000. "Over the past several weeks I have reflected on my relationship with Coca-Cola, a company I still respect and love. It's become increasingly clear to me that the company has taken seriously the issues I raised. That's all I ever wanted."

Deval Patrick, executive vice president and Coke's general counsel, responded with the following statement when Whitley's suit was settled: "Mr. Whitley was a diligent employee with a solid record. It is disappointing that he felt he needed to file a lawsuit in order to be heard. We want everyone in this company to bring their issues to the attention of management through appropriate channels, and every manager to take them seriously, investigate them, and make necessary changes." Federal prosecutors began an investigation of the Frozen Coke marketing tests for possible fraud charges in 2003. In April 2005 Coke announced a settlement with the SEC on financial reporting issues and the Justice Department ended its two-year investigation with no action taken.

The fear of bad news that no one wanted to face all around: fountain sales flat, Frozen Coke possibly not panning out. However, concealing that bad news served no one well. Face numbers. Don't manipulate them. Think strategically, not about doctoring numbers. The story of Frozen Coke is one every company should tell its employees with the backdrop of "If it isn't working, we want to know. Just bring along your plan for change." Coke did the right thing in settling the matter and removing it all from the headlines. It has also recommitted the company to its basic values and acknowledged the issue with Whitley's raising concerns.

Antidote #5 for Fear and Silence: Tell Employees You Trust Their Wisdom and That You Are Counting on Them

In a recent e-mail from an employee at one of the companies I have been working with, there was the following thought: "In short, madam, tell them [the officers], not us." Once I got beyond the notion of being called "madam," I realized there was something most revealing in the employee's thought. His perception, rightly or wrongly, was that he and his coworkers in the trenches were not the problem. Rather, he felt that the officers of the company were the problem. My correspondent had missed the point of my discussions with employees. Talking with them about ethics was not undertaken with just the idea of keeping them on the straight and narrow. We were conveying the idea of enlisting them in the battle against fear and silence. We were not just teaching them to be honest on their expense accounts. We were asking them to tell us when they saw anyone else who was not honest on his or her expense accounts, including the officers. We thought we were reaching out to employees to ask them to tell us when they were asked to do things that made them uncomfortable, but the message had not gotten through. All the employees were taking away from the ethics training was that they had to sit through hours of thoughts on ethics when it was the officers who needed it more. If the officers did need it more, then we needed specifics from them on what those officers were doing that caused this perception of a disconnect between their ethics and the ethics of management.

I have learned through my work that employees often take offense at ethics training and slip into silence-and-fear mode because they believe that it is the leadership in their companies that is unethical, not them. Statistics from the Society for Human Resource Management bear this out. In 1999, 99 percent of employees believed that their ethical standards were higher than those of the folks they worked with. Everyone believes that he or she is the most ethical person in the room. That attitude makes employees resent training, see only the mote in others' eyes, and fail to engage in the serious introspection of questioning their behavior and what their organizations are doing. They even develop resentment that they have to be trained in ethics when they have seen those who lead them involved in ethically questionable conduct. One of the primary goals of ethics training and a critical message managers need to get out to employees to curb fear and silence is "We are telling you all of this because we are counting on you to see the difference between right and wrong in the conduct of all of those around you and let us know when that conduct falls short of the standards you have learned."

One of my favorite sayings to executives and boards is "the collective wisdom of employees always exceeds the collective wisdom of management." The stories presented in the first part of this chapter highlight that there have been no situations in which the ethical or legal issues were so nuanced that no one saw them coming. *Au contraire*, employees at all levels saw the issues even as managers and officers continued to spin what was happening to avoid facing the consequences and fallout. The perspective of employees who are not involved in either the bonus pool or the decision process is critical in curbing the culture of fear and silence. Their input offers great moral clarity, and they need to be told that this is one of the reasons they are given training: use the moral clarity. Help them understand that their moral clarity is necessary to keep the company from becoming one with a Yeehaw Culture. Encourage them to let you know what they see and what concerns them.

Without their perspective, managers and executives develop blinders. Because managers and executives face so many pressures, and perhaps have already crossed one too many lines, they have been known to miss ethical issues altogether. Hank Greenberg has referred to AIG's reinsurance investigations, SEC problems, and earnings restatements as "foot faults." Actually, $1.7 billion in "improper" accounting, as AIG has admitted, is a tad worse than crossing the line in tennis. Mr. Greenberg has drifted so far that the moral clarity that what AIG has done is dishonest has been lost in the shuffle, as it were, of technicalities. AIG paid the largest fine in U.S. corporate history to settle state and federal fraud probes.

I was working with a company that had a culture of fear and silence. It had been pulled back from the brink of ethical collapse, and executives recognized that they needed to change. I encouraged managers, supervisors, and officers to talk with their employees regularly about ethical dilemmas their company, division, unit, shop, office faced. Each day, each meeting, every chance, iron out ethical issues. One high-level manager shared with me that he had been out to dinner with several customers and some suppliers. When the tab for the evening came, he realized that the waiter had forgotten to add in the two $75 bottles of wine the group had consumed. "So," he said, "I went right to the cashier and told her to add the wine back into the bill because I was a representative of the company and my company is an honest one with integrity." He said he shared this example with his employees in his unit. I suggested that it probably did not go well. He asked how I knew. He had lost sight of a simple provision in the company's code of ethics about excessive entertainment. Granted, there was a group of people and perhaps if we did the math, six people sharing two $75 bottles of wine works out to the company code of no more than $25 per person. However, the perception of employees was, first and foremost, "I've never even tasted $75 wine. Ten $7.50 bottles of wine, maybe," followed by "Does this guy not understand the code of ethics?"

Apparently not, but that's the point. Employees could see the issue when the executive did not. His years of displacement from the pure perceptions of employees had blinded him to his own conduct. Trust employees to see the issues and tell them that because of their skill, you are counting on them to speak up. Indeed, let them know that you are dependent upon them because you can't fix what you don't know about or, in some cases, don't even see. Wal-Mart CEO Lee Scott's admonition discussed earlier applies, when he spoke via video to all Wal-Mart employees following the Coughlin issues and said, basically, "Let us know what you see." Now, if the company just hadn't fired the guy who had the courage to report Coughlin. The antidotes have to work together to work!

Fear and Silence

Antidotes

1. Tell employees to speak and provide the means for them to do so.

2. Don't fire employees for speaking up! Don't flatline employees for speaking up! Don't transfer, reassign, or trample, muck up, or malign employees for speaking up.

   a. State clearly what should be reported.

   b. State clearly how and when employees are protected for reporting violations.

   c. Watch other signals of silence.

3. Reward employees who speak up.

   a. Annual recognition for ethical employees

   b. Annual performance reviews with an ethics component worth at least 10 percent of the evaluation

4. Tell employees that bad news happens.

5. Tell employees that you trust their wisdom and that you are counting on them.

Fear and Silence

CHAPTER FOUR

Sign #

3

Young 'Uns and a Bigger-than-Life CEO

I hire them just like me: smart, young, wants to be rich.

—Former Tyco CEO Dennis Kozlowski on
how he chose his executive team

O rganizations headed for ethical collapse have two structural components that enable a culture of fear and silence and create the pressure for numbers, the first two signs of ethical collapse. The structural component that fuels fear and silence and numbers pressure is the presence of an iconic CEO who is adored by the community, media, and just about anyone at a distance. Iconic CEOs are not necessarily adored by employees. In fact, quite the opposite may be true, but because of the adoration of an outside world and that ever-present fear factor, employees are hesitant to mention those little accounting problems like $11 billion in capitalized ordinary expenses. So enamored are the media of these larger-than-life CEOs that even they fall into the fear-and-silence trap. Those who cover business don't want to challenge the legendary CEO because of their fear that they might be wrong about the company, especially when so many others "see" the aura.

The second structural component is that the iconic CEO surrounds himself with a sycophantic management team. Most often the sycophantism stems from youth and inexperience. These young 'uns don't have enough experience or wisdom to challenge the CEO, and the CEO has roped them in with executive success. They are hooked on the cash and its trappings and cannot speak up about obvious ethical and legal issues because they might lose the homes, the boats, the cars, and, yes, the prestige that comes with astronomical financial success at a young age. They fail to realize that they play the role of "useful idiots" for a diabolical CEO. Young sycophants come in all forms and are found in all industries. Iconic CEOs are all alike, and the pattern runs across scandals. Charles Keating used $52 million in junk bonds, raised for him through junk-bond financier Michael Milken, to buy Lincoln Savings and Loan. When Lincoln collapsed after Keating and his sons and sons-in-law had served as its executives, he was defiant and autocratic to the end: "You got a bunch of know-nothings trying to tell business people how to invest money." Keating would go on, prior to his trial and conviction, to refer to regulators as "scum." His labels for government officials were no less charitable: "Finaciopath of obscene proportions" and "Blackbeard of finance." And he did it all with yet another similarity that runs across scandal eras: Arthur Andersen was the auditor for Keating's parent corporation, American Continental. Defiant to the end. Ego-centricity that cannot allow them to even hear dissent, let alone bring it in through a management team. The pattern is not limited to a rogue here and there. Archer Daniels Midland and its international price-fixing scandal also had the pattern of family icons in charge as the young 'uns of their loins direct the federal felonies. The son of the chairman of the board was an officer and vice chairman of the board. Not much room for dissenting opinions in such a company, but plenty of room for the Yeehaw Culture to take hold.

This latest round of ethical collapses had its bigger-than-life CEOs that fit the pattern to a T. Herein are the stories of the bigger-than-life CEOs and their direct reports who couldn't say no. Their concentration of power, coupled with their unwavering belief that their abilities required that they transcend the boundaries of law and ethics, found them leading many companies over the cliff to financial destruction.

AIG, Marsh & McLennan (MMC), and My Three Sons (MTS)

Boy, howdy, it is difficult to know where to start to describe the Yeehaw CEOs and sycophants in these companies that proved such fertile territory for investigations and the attention of Eliot Spitzer. Their cultures were all the more "Yeehaw!" because their misdeeds occurred post-Enron and post-Sarbanes-Oxley. This group of companies had the further challenges of the classic father and sons working together in one Fortune 500 corporate outing. Hank Greenberg, the father, was at the helm of AIG. Son Evan joined AIG in 1975 and left in 2000 to join ACE Ltd., a Bermuda-based insurer. Hank's other son, Jeffrey Greenberg, joined AIG in 1978 and left in 1995 to join MMC, where he became CEO in 2000. For those of you still with us and keeping score, father and sons were running two insurance companies and one insurance broker. Spitzer alleged in his civil suit that MMC obtained dummy bids to ensure that ACE and AIG got the insurance business. Spitzer did not file criminal charges against the companies or the Greenbergs. As one expert noted, it is difficult to imagine how they could not trot across antitrust lines when they sat down to dinner and talked business.

These family relationships interlocking across companies can be problematic. Charles Keating, with his Lincoln Savings and Loan, in one of the two previous reform eras, had a similar structure with his sons and sons-in-law working as officers and managers in his companies. Keating was thus a full generation older than his direct reports, and he had the added sycophantic bonus of having most of them being related to him by blood or marriage. So it was with AIG. Hank Greenberg ran AIG and his sons ran MMC, Putnam, ACE, and Mercer, and they were all inextricably intertwined. MMC settled with Eliot Spitzer and replaced its CEO. Spitzer has filed a civil suit against Mr. Greenberg and AIG former CFO Howard I. Smith, a suit Mr. Greenberg is fighting vigorously.

Here were companies and officers arrogant in manner and operations. As described previously, MMC had created an international cartel of price-fixing, but coupled with this initial misstep into antitrust law was an accounting twist that was eerily similar to Enron's off-the-books entities.

Mercer and Putnam had already been through the legal and regulatory wringer when MMC's cartel approach to insurance brokering came to light, courtesy of Spitzer. However, for purposes of understanding this larger-than-life-CEO factor in ethical collapse, it is important to see the executive structures of these companies because they truly fit the classic profile of larger-than-life CEOs and attending sycophants.

MMC was part of a family insurance dynasty, with a father and two sons running companies. Jeffrey Greenberg ran MMC (which he joined after serving as an executive under his father at AIG and from which he resigned as part of a settlement deal with Spitzer's office), Putnam, and Mercer. Father Maurice "Hank" Greenberg was the CEO of insurer American International Group (AIG), a company under all manner of investigation, including by the SEC, for failure to adequately disclose to investors the use of insurance policies to eliminate debt from the books in what the SEC has referred to as a sham transaction in which no risk was transferred. As noted, Howard Smith, a former CFO and Greenberg protégé, has been charged civilly by Eliot Spitzer. Son Evan Greenberg left AIG to run ACE Ltd., the third-largest insurance broker in the world, an event that took place after AIG's board indicated that Evan would not succeed his father at AIG. With so much concentrated family power, even concerned employees would find no outlet for their concerns. Add to that Hank Greenberg's legendary short fuse and the atmosphere is ripe for saying nothing.

But questions were necessary because the dynasty was engaged in creative insurance and creative accounting. AIG has admitted that it engaged in questionable accounting related to the issuance of insurance policies and initially announced a $1.7 billion downward restatement of its assets to reflect the problems with these policies. The amount would increase another $1 billion within the month following the initial restatement. AIG's admission was extraordinary in many ways but carried the additional oomph of a cavalier purpose of achieving accounting results using the questionable policies. One does have to give this crowd credit for creativity. AIG shifted $500 million in expected claims that would be made to General Re to itself as a reinsurance transaction. General Re is a subsidiary of Berkshire Hathaway (something that put these accounting shenanigans in Warren Buffett's lap), but upon pressure from the feds in the inquiry, Mr. Buffett cooperated. AIG booked $500 million as a premium for the transaction but also added $500 million to its reserves in expectation of payouts. There was no risk, so using the reserves was incorrect. And General Re did not book the transaction as a reinsurance deal but rather as a financing transaction. This scenario opened up AIG's books to other questions. Numerous changes in accounting practices for compensation, commissions, bad debts, and just about anything related to income and balance sheets are in the offing.

The end is typical for a CEO who was described as "imperial." AIG had the first structural component, an iconic CEO. Manhattan folklore has it that one day Greenberg emerged from a meeting and got into a limo and the driver asked where he wanted to go. Greenberg responded, "Take me anywhere—everybody needs me." Mr. Greenberg was a legend in his thirty-seven years at AIG. He had taken the company's earnings from $14 million per year in 1967 to $11 billion in 2003. Like any CEO in a numbers culture, he touted that growth for all to see. Of course, we may never know the real figures. Still, Greenberg had the world's attention and accolades for his stunning business acumen. When Greenberg spoke on any topic related to insurance, from tort reform to asbestos, everyone listened. He even defied legal advice and accounting convention long before the issues that led to his ouster arose. In 1992 he received a memo from the company's legal counsel that called AIG's accounting practices related to worker's compensation as "permeated with illegality" and "so serious it could threaten the existence of senior management if disclosed." Outside legal counsel confirmed the internal take on the accounting practices, but those in AIG continued with business (and accounting) as usual. Not until 1997, under regulatory pressure, were the necessary accounting changes made.

This behavior of employees' continuing to do things that are wrong parallels that of the subjects in Stanley Milgram's work on the administration of electric shock upon command. (See Chapter 7 for more information on Milgram, pressure, and the studies.) They knew that what they were doing was wrong and that it would cause pain, but they continued anyway because the person in charge told them to do so. Greenberg had complete control of his direct reports and employees, but his seemingly indisputable success at running the company meant no one was asking questions. Therein lies the risk of the iconic CEO coupled with the obsequious—that second structural component, sycophants.

Hank Greenberg ran the company, right down to calling low- and mid-level managers for clarifications. The numbers culture was clearly there. But as is always the case, those smooth earnings don't come easily. An internal report reached the hardly surprising conclusion that the AIG executive team ran the company without internal controls, always a risky factor when it comes to the SEC.

"Internal controls" takes on a new meaning for companies with an iconic CEO and young 'uns. The icon is surrounded by extraordinarily motivated sycophants. Greenberg may have varied slightly in his choice of an executive team, with many of them long-term and older associates. However, that may have been the problem. They lasted because they did exactly as Greenberg asked. Greenberg surrounded himself with officers who could be trusted to see things his way. For example, L. Michael Murphy, a tax expert for AIG who was terminated for his failure to cooperate with investigators in the reinsurance and SEC investigations, also served as a director, officer, and adviser in AIG's global operations, including Starr International, the offshore company that now faces questions about its role as a compensation vehicle for AIG executives (a sort of off-the-books, offshore bonus plan). Mr. Murphy has denied all allegations. Starr was owned by key executives of AIG, and its shares were awarded to AIG employees as part of incentive plans—all without costing AIG anything. "The program motivated people to be loyal to Hank," was one executive's take on the complex structure that was created in 1970. But their take from Starr depended upon the value of AIG's shares, so their decisions were guided, and clouded, by what would get the AIG share price up. Murphy, loyal to the end, has offered no information on Starr or his role in the reinsurance scandals. In fact, in its thirty-four years of existence, no one questioned the Starr plan. Once each year, key executives at AIG would travel to New York to meet in a small room and be handed a slip of paper that had on it two things: their name and how many preferred shares they would receive in Starr. No one dared ask questions in the meeting because Greenberg would upbraid them if they did. But they were tied to him with the "golden handcuffs" of Starr ownership. It meant that they, collectively, had a multibillion-dollar interest in AIG and that they weren't going anywhere and were even less likely to challenge Greenberg. Sycophants came via an offshore private compensation plan.

Few people dared confront either CEO Jeffrey Skilling or chairman Ken Lay, for both had become business legends. Lay had been able to put Houston on the map. He was generous, almost to a fault (well, actually, it would be because of a fault, or at least because of filthy lucre), and the community responded with a petard, complete with hoist.

Lay also had the same gift of other iconic CEOs: the ability to charm analysts in such a manner that they did not ask questions about how the stellar achievements of the company were possible. Indeed, when one analyst in the Houston area, John Olson, asked questions about the company's accounting, Lay protested mightily to Olson's boss. Lay wrote a letter to Olson's employer complaining about the caution Mr. Olson had issued to clients and noted that "John Olson has been wrong about Enron for over ten years and is still wrong. But he is consistant [sic]." Olson's concerns were dismissed out of hand and he was persona non grata until the collapse of Enron, when everyone realized that the iconic CEO had eclipsed the truth that Olson had offered. Later Olson would observe that too few analysts were kicking Enron's tires as they should have.

Even the media gave Lay a pass, apparently on the basis of financial glory. Only one reporter picked up on early questions about Enron, Bethany McLean of *Fortune*. Her story appeared and then vanished. *Fortune*'s managing editor, Rick Kirkland, called Bethany McLean's March 2001 story on Enron "prescient, but it kind of went out and sank." Peter Eavis of TheStreet.com also raised questions about Enron, including concerns about Fastow's dual roles in the many LCCs and partnerships, but no mainstream media picked up on his insights or writings. Only shortsellers seemed to see the issues.

Lay enjoyed much more immunity than what generally springs from the halo effect of the big spender he was and had caused Enron to be. He had surrounded himself with young 'uns trained in the ways of creative corporate finance who earned him the respect of Wall Street. He hired Harvard MBA Jeffrey Skilling as his second-in-command. Skilling, as noted earlier, was a pick from the McKinsey & Company consulting team that had been doing work for Enron on the energy-trading strategy. Lay had been grooming him and he had been grooming Lay with the company-consultant relationship for years before Skilling joined Enron as an employee.

Andrew Fastow, Enron's CFO, was young, eager to be rich, and consumed with maintaining the company's status and his station in life. At the time of Enron's collapse, Fastow and his wife, also an Enron executive, were building an 11,500-square-foot house in a tony Houston suburb. Fastow graduated from Tufts University and then the Kellogg School of Management at Northwestern University. Hired by Skilling, Fastow was only twenty-nine at the time and rose quickly through the Enron ranks to emerge as CFO at age thirty-six, after functioning as third-in-command, behind Skilling and Lay, from the time he was thirty-one. Skilling and Fastow were so well regarded in the business community that none dared question them or their methodologies. When Fastow was honored as CFO of the year by *CFO Magazine* for 1999 for his innovative financing structures he held nothing back. In his interview with the magazine editors, he unabashedly proclaimed that he kept Enron's credit rating high by keeping its debt off the balance sheet. Lack of transparency was not necessarily an issue with Enron's byzantine financial empire. The magazine noted its honor and that interview with this observation from a hindsight perch following Enron's collapse:

> *In an interview with CFO in mid-1999, Fastow asserted that he had helped keep almost $1 billion in debt off Enron's balance sheet through the use of a complex and innovative arrangement. "It's not consolidated and it's nonrecourse," he told CFO.*

Of course, the "nonrecourse" label was inaccurate. He might have been the best CFO in America, but he was a lyin' son of a gun from a Yeehaw Culture.

Sherron Watkins, the vice president for corporate development who sent that initially anonymous whistle-blowing memo, also gave us a sense of the Enron culture through her disclosures. Ms. Watkins used terms such as "arrogance" and "intimidating." She had a specific fear of Ken Lay, a CEO who fit the classic pattern of being a full generation older than his young direct reports. Further, he had the status of founder of the company, the respect of Wall Street and analysts, the worship of Houston residents, and the resulting status that Greek gods would have thrown lightning bolts to have. As they worked for this seemingly flawless CEO, these officers had the additional disadvantage of being unseasoned executives in positions of responsibility. They lacked proper regard for either market forces or the critical role of trust in markets and capitalism.

WorldCom's Bernie Ebbers: Coach, Sunday School Teacher, and Legendary CEO

Like Enron, WorldCom was run by an iconic CEO and a group of young executives. Mr. Ebbers was as flamboyant and iconic as Scott Sullivan, WorldCom's CFO, was sycophantic. And Ebbers fit the pattern of the CEOs at companies that have experienced ethical collapse, which includes the traits of being bigger-than-life and often quirky. Charles Keating and Lincoln Savings and Loan, Q. T. Wiles and MiniScribe, Al "Chainsaw" Dunlap and Sunbeam, John DeLorean and the DeLorean Corporation, Steve Madden and his shoe company, and John Bennett and New Era Philanthropy. Fraud keeps company with flamboyance. This combo could also go the other way, with the whole fraud-and-flamboyancy issue boiling down to a chicken-and-egg proposition. The investment community is enamored of the CEO; the CEO has profligate spending habits; and the CEO breeds sycophantism in employees by his demands, their compensation packages, and the deference to icons in the business press.

Even as the company was crumbling around them, few who lived in Mississippi who had invested in WorldCom could bring themselves to denounce Bernie. The same was true of Wall Street. Still posted on WorldCom's website on August 7, 2002, as the company was sinking further with each passing minute, was this accolade from Jack Grubman of Salomon Smith Barney:

> If one were to find comparables to WorldCom . . . the list would be very short and would include the likes of Merck, Home Depot, Wal-Mart, Coke, Microsoft, Gillette and Disney.

Mr. Ebbers was six-four, without his cowboy boots. All color, charm, and command, there was no question that he was charismatic, at home anywhere from Jackson, Mississippi, to Wall Street. Mr. Ebbers's story of a lanky kid from a Canadian high school winning a basketball scholarship to a small Mississippi college and then staying on as a hometown boy was endearing. He used his reputation in the community to start a successful business in a state that was hungry for economic development. He began with motels and then fronted most of the money for WorldCom. By 1999 Mr. Ebbers had a net worth of $1.4 billion, which put him at number 174 among the richest Americans. There were ranches, hockey teams (the Jackson Bandits, of all things), a fly-fishing resort, an ATC dealership, a lumberyard, one plantation, two farms, twenty thousand head of Hereford, and a great many loans tied up in tree-laden properties. Mr. Ebbers's personal life carried some indiscretions, something not unusual among the iconic CEOs. With WorldCom at its height of success, Ebbers divorced his wife of twenty-seven years and married a WorldCom executive who was nearly thirty years his junior. This pattern of adultery and remarriage runs across iconic CEOs as well, from Jack Welch to Dennis Kozlowski to Bill Clinton.

Surrounding Bernie was an officer team he could control. Scott Sullivan, WorldCom's CFO at the height of its acquisitions and, eventually, slide into accounting improprieties, turned forty on the day he was fired by the WorldCom board. He had assumed the helm of WorldCom's finances as CFO in 1994 at the ripe old age of thirty-two. By thirty-four, he was a member of the board and the secretary of the corporation. The joke around the WorldCom offices when Sullivan assumed the CFO slot was that he was "barely shaving." He had arrived at WorldCom only two years earlier, courtesy of the 1992 merger with Advanced Telecommunications, where he had been since 1987.

Sullivan and Ebbers would become the dynamic duo, joined at the hip at meetings with analysts as they put together the mergers and deals of World-Com over the next eight years. Ebbers would refer to Sullivan as "the whiz kid."

Sullivan wanted to please Ebbers, and in this mutual admiration society of future felons, Ebbers praised Sullivan publicly and saw to it that he was well compensated for his efforts. Like the executives at AIG and Enron, Sullivan soon enjoyed Bernie's benevolence, which took his compensation from a $500,000 salary and $3.5 million bonus in 1997 to a $700,000 salary and $10 million bonus in 2001, the last year before WorldCom would collapse under the sheer weight of admitting the need for $11 billion in earnings restatements for slightly over a two-year period. The stock options he was granted are not included in these figures. Sullivan was addicted to the trappings of power, and possibly other things, given his confession during cross-examination at Mr. Ebbers's trial that he had used cocaine while an officer of the company. Yeehaw—how did these people get any paperwork done? By the time World-Com collapsed, Sullivan was a true jet-setter, constructing a $10 million home on a $2.5 million lot in Boca Raton. He flew on the company jet from his home in Florida to WorldCom headquarters in a commuter arrangement. He made the most of the success and finances that came his way.

Ebbers was able to make his group of direct reports, who were, like his new wife, a full generation younger, beholden to him for their compensation. Because of the board compensation committee's abdication of its responsibilities to Ebbers, Bernie ended up with sole discretion in setting their salaries and bonuses. He made multimillionaires out of all the officers of the company. The balance of power in the executive team was such that there would be no internal challenges to Bernie. Ebbers was described as "intimidating and brusque." But he also took an intense personal interest in the members of his officer team. Not only were they beholden to Ebbers for their jobs, bonuses, and stock options, but Ebbers made personal loans to many of them. Ah, the power of personally owing the CEO. In the movie *Picture Perfect*, the head of an advertising agency describes to a young employee why he is not promoting her. He tells her that everyone he has promoted owes him because he has cosigned for their cars and houses, and he knows that they are not going anywhere. They cannot pick up and leave because they owe him personally. Ebbers purchased loyalty with low-interest loans.

When Ronald Beaumont, the chief operating officer of WorldCom, asked Mr. Ebbers for an advance on his bonus in 2001, Ebbers denied it. Beaumont had used his WorldCom stock to collateralize a loan on a ranch he had purchased. Facing margin calls on the loan, he wanted his bonus early. Instead,

Ebbers personally loaned the $650,000 to Beaumont. It's darn tough to say something bad about what your boss is doing. Even tougher when you're into the boss for over half a mil.

Tyco: An Iconic CEO with a $6,000 Shower Curtain

Dennis Kozlowski made no bones about it. He wanted to be the next Jack Welch and he wanted Tyco to be the new GE. In his infamous interview in 2001 when he was named CEO of the year by *Business Week,* he said that he wanted to be remembered as the world's greatest business executive, a "combination of what Jack Welch put together at GE and Warren Buffett's very practical ideas on how you go about creating return for shareholders." Run-on sentences aside, one gets the idea of the drive behind this ego. Indeed, there was little consideration of strategy, expertise, or fit in his acquisition drives. Kozlowski had Tyco purchase CIT Group, a finance company that specialized in loans to small and midsize businesses, for $9.2 billion in 2001. The acquisition was mystifying in terms of Tyco's core competencies but completely logical if one is trying to emulate GE and GE Capital. Even the market issued a big "huh?" upon the announcement of the acquisition, causing an 8 percent drop in Tyco's stock. Within months Tyco would have to sell CIT.

But the iconic CEO knows no limitations, and Mr. Kozlowski's derring-do in business acquisition carried over into his personal life, and vice versa. It seemed as if his humble beginnings (in Newark), a trait many iconic CEOs share, were a driving force behind the desire for more, more, more, by doing whatever it takes. "Koz," as he was known, grew up in an area that was eventually destroyed by race riots in the 1960s. Amazingly, Kozlowski is an accountant by training, but he morphed into a helicopter pilot, a Harley-Davidson rider (sporting $20,000 cycles), and a self-described risk-taker. The trappings of wealth were important to Mr. Kozlowski. In 2001 he held the number two spot for CEO compensation, raking in $411 million, finishing second only to Citigroup's Sanford Weill. And Kozlowksi had the lifestyle that comes with that level of compensation. Whether his own salary or company dollars paid the bills has become a contentious subject of two criminal trials. His Fifth Avenue apartment cost $16.8 million to buy, $3 million to renovate. He would then spend $11 million on furnishings—or the company would, depending upon jury findings. The hope of so much lavishness was more attraction for his business acumen. Ironically, the iconic CEO never sees the problem. Mr. Kozlowski bristled at the suggestion that CEOs were high rollers. In his May 2001 interview for its cover story, he told *Business Week,* "We've been made out to be freewheeling jet-setters, playboys reliving our adolescent years. . . . For me, and for most CEOs, that irresponsible image really rankles."

Kozlowski was partially correct. He was not reliving his adolescence. He instead went for the *Animal House* toga party. He was remarried in 2001, and for new wife Karen Mayo's fortieth birthday, Kozlowski flew in singer Jimmy Buffett and dozens of his wife's friends to a villa on Sardinia for a days-long celebration. The tab for the party, infamously described in the first of Kozlowski's criminal trials, was put at $2.1 million. For some fun reading, with some insight into the iconic CEO ego writ large, go to a Tyco internal memo on the party that is attached as an exhibit to Tyco's 8-K filed on September 17, 2002. The process for receiving guests and the party schedule are described in detail, right down to what type of music was playing and at what level. The memo includes a guest list and space for the crew of the yacht that the Kozlowskis sailed to Sardinia. The waiters were dressed in Roman togas, and there was an ice sculpture of David through which the vodka flowed. There are no details on the location of the spigot.

This lavish lifestyle found its financing partially through the KELP (Key Employee Loan Program) (see Chapter 3 for more details) and relocation loan programs. According to SEC documents, Mr. Kozlowski borrowed more than $270 million from the KELP "but us[ed] only about $29 million to cover taxes due as a result of the vesting of his restricted shares of the company. He used the remaining $242 million of KELP loans for personal expenses, including yachts, fine art, estate jewelry, luxury apartments and vacation estates, personal business ventures and investments, all unrelated to Tyco." The items, delineated in both the SEC documents and the press, that were charged to Tyco for Mr. Kozlowski's apartment included a $6,000 shower curtain, $15,000 dog umbrella stand, $6,300 sewing basket, $17,100 traveling toilette box, $2,200 gilt metal wastebasket, $2,900 coat hangers, $5,960 sheets (two sets), $1,650 notebook, and $445 pin cushion. Ironically, Mr. Kozlowski told a *Business Week* reporter in 2001 during a tour of the humble Exeter, New Hampshire, offices of Tyco, "We don't believe in perks, not even executive parking spots." Another one of the great ironies in the Kozlowski spending machine is that Tyco owned a company that manufactured plastic coat hangers, but buying in-house was apparently out of the question. The lawsuit filed by Tyco against Kozlowski seeking recovery of many of these expenses also asks for reimbursement for $52,334 for wine and $96,943 for flowers. One wonders how this man ever did a lick of work, what with all the spending, umbrella stands, and parties.

In an interview on the eve of his second trial on embezzlement and other charges, Kozlowski was outraged at the press coverage because he was not aware of how much was being spent and, he noted, they took a picture of the wrong house when explaining a party he had held. There was no denial of the fact that there were extensive parties, only displeasure that the wrong house was displayed and anger at the media for what appear to be only technical inaccuracies:

"The general public perception of me—a lot of it's been brought on by a lot of inaccurate reporting in the media," he said. He recounted how a tabloid newspaper ran a front-page article "saying I had this massive party on Nantucket when I wasn't even there. And then that just snowballed into a lot of other stories" like a television newsmagazine program "taking pictures of a big mansion in Boca Raton, Fla., and putting it on television."

"Well, they had the wrong house," he said. "So it's just one thing after another. I had no rebuttals to this whatsoever."

Horrors! These detached, defensive, and defiant statements (as well as the absence of logic) offer insight into the iconic CEO personality that leads a company into ethical collapse. These men are so insulated from criticism, feedback, and reality checks that they remain defiant to the end, bizarrely detached from the real issues and excesses of their conduct. Michael Milken, Charles Keating, and many of the partners at Arthur Andersen remained defiant through criminal litigation, trials, and convictions. Their conduct had gone unchecked for so long that they are incapable of introspection, and no one can rein them back into reality.

Without board approval (although in his mind and according to his testimony at his second trial, he believed he did have the board's imprimatur), Kozlowski made his senior staff beholden to him through the payment of $56 million in bonuses to executives who were eligible for KELP loans. He then gave them $39 million to pay the taxes on the bonuses, and followed up with forgiving the KELP loans (which were given to pay taxes on the shares of stock he had awarded them). It was almost as if Kozlowski and the other officers were involved in a gigantic game of chicken as the loans, payments, forgiveness, and other manipulations continued. Those involved in abuses of the KELP loan program knew too much about one another and their interactions with the company to bring a halt to the programs, but at the same time all knew that the financial shenanigans could not go on forever.

The relocation loan program was a source of $46 million for home-buying funds for Kozlowksi. SEC documents filed by the Tyco board after Kozlowski's departure include the statement that he "used at least $28 million of those relocation loans to purchase, among other things, luxury properties in New Hampshire, Nantucket and Connecticut as well as a $7 million Park Avenue apartment for his then (now former) wife," who, ironically, had to post Kozlowski's bail upon his arrest.

Kozlowski's officer team was small and obedient, owing largely to those bonuses and the uncalled loans. Only three members of the executive team had any contact with investors: Kozwloski, CFO Mark Swartz, and Brad McGee, an executive vice president. Tyco was fairly lean in terms of its corporate staff, with just four hundred employees at its central office. Kozlowksi interacted with only a few of his officers, which was a means of keeping information close to the vest. He also used intense personal involvement to keep officers playing the game of chicken. CFO Swartz served as trustee for one of Mr. Kozlowski's trusts for holding title to real property. As already noted, general counsel Mark Belnick was an extensive beneficiary of the KELP. Both men were also exploiting a loophole in securities law to sell millions of shares of Tyco stock even as they declared publicly that they were not selling their shares in the company.

Those within the small group who reported to Kozlowski were indeed young 'uns. Mark Swartz was only forty years old at the time of Tyco's fall and his indictment on thirty-eight counts of grand larceny, conspiracy, and falsifying business records. And now, at age forty-four, he faces fifteen to twenty-five years following the convictions in the second trial. Swartz was actually hired at the ground level at an earlier age than were Fastow and Skilling. Tyco hired Swartz away from Deloitte & Touche's due diligence team in 1991, when he was but thirty years old. By 1993 he was head of Tyco's acquisitions team and by 1995 he was Tyco's CFO, at age thirty-three. He also followed the Fastow pattern of being named CFO of the Year. Kozlowski nominated Mr. Swartz for a CFO award, and *CFO Magazine* honored Swartz with its 2000 Excellence Award. And like Fastow, Swartz talked to the press often. In an interview with CFO.com in October 2000, he exuded the same swagger that the Enron boys had. When the reporter questioned Swartz about Tyco's accounting practices and the ongoing investigations because of all the problems following the bubble and the exposure of the dot-coms, Swartz offered the following: "We were very, very confident of our accounting. Despite all that people were saying and what was happening to the stock price, we knew what the truth was." Safety tip to directors: when the CFO is very, very confident about the company's accounting, get a second opinion.

Patricia Prue—the vice president for HR at Tyco, another Kozlowski officer, and the one responsible for processing the paperwork for the forgiveness of the KELP officers' loans—had benefited from the loan-forgiveness program herself. Prue had a loan of $748,309, then had the loan forgiven, and finally was given $521,087 to pay the taxes on the loan forgiveness. She was also most beholden to Kozlowski for a heck of a salary for someone in HR. She was given bonuses of $13,534,523 and $9,424,815 to pay the taxes on the bonuses. Kozlowski was a big believer in the "gross-up," or the practice of making the amount paid greater in order to help the employee cover the taxes that will be due.

Prue's loyalty was true until the end. Indeed, she testified at the trials of Kozlowski and Swartz but was not charged with any crimes. Ms. Prue had, however, shown a streak of defiance or had finally noted her possible culpability in KELP. As a result, she approached Kozlowski in September 2000 and asked for documentation that the board had indeed approved all the loan forgiveness for which she was doing the paperwork. Kozlowski, without ever producing a board minute, wrote a memo to Ms. Prue: "A decision has been made to forgive the relocation loans for those individuals whose efforts were instrumental to successfully completing the TyCom I.P.O." Because she worked for an iconic CEO, she took him at his word, and so the loan program marched onward and upward, at least in total amount due. Whether Tyco will recoup the loan losses from the mighty borrowing officers remains an issue.

Adelphia: Like Father and Sons and a Lot Like Charles Keating and Sons

Adelphia, a cable company founded by John Rigas and then run by him and his sons, was like a corporate commune of sorts. There were twelve Rigas family/Adelphia officers and their families nestled in and around the small town of Coudersport, Pennsylvania, Adelphia's headquarters. Adelphia was also a classic numbers culture. The criminal complaint against three members of the Rigas family and two company officers alleged that they followed the old EBITDA (earnings before interest, taxes, depreciation, and amortization, which, roughly translated means "if it hadn't been for all these expenses, we would have had some terrific earnings") accounting popularized in the dotcom era in which the officers picked a number for a goal and then pretty much worked backward to make the accounting fit the desired result. But Adelphia had a numbers culture coupled with a Charles Keating management structure, making it a Yeehaw Culture extraordinaire.

John Rigas, head of the family and Adelphia, had put Coudersport on the map. He grew Adelphia from the local theater up. In 1952 he started his first business by opening a theater in the small Pennsylvania town, a theater he still owned through the collapse of Adelphia. He and his brother bought one of the first cable franchises in the country for $300 in 1952 and named their new company Adelphia, which is Greek for "brothers." By 1982 John had purchased his brother's interest in Adelphia and begun the process of succession planning by bringing his sons into the business. By 2002 Adelphia was doing business in thirty-two states and had 5.7 million subscribers. The Rigas family had built a huge company, but apparently not big enough to fuel their needs for cash. But before the fall, Adelphia and the Rigas family were revered.

Icons don't get much larger than John Rigas. The Coudersport locals referred to him as "a Greek god." But the downside of being a god is that one often behaves like one, in complete defiance of the principles of corporate governance as well as the laws against embezzlement. There is nothing clever in Adelphia's collapse nor is there any accounting mumbo jumbo. The story is really quite simple. Adelphia made a great deal of money because it capitalized on the early days of cable television, soon becoming the sixth-largest cable company in America. But iconic CEOs being what they are, and their sons more than willing to go along, the family together managed to "borrow" more than $3 billion from the corporation for personal investments in everything from hockey teams to golf courses to independent film companies for daughter Ellen Rigas Venetis (married to Peter Venetis, who had the good fortune of being officer material and was given a slot at Adelphia in the executive suite). John Rigas owned a furniture store that sold all of Adelphia's office furniture to it, but in exchange, Adelphia gave the furniture store free ads on its cable and Internet services. A federal investigator involved with the case said, "We've never seen anything like this. The level of self-dealing is quite serious." Cash flow was off by, oh, about $50 million per quarter, and all $3 billion or so was concealed from Deloitte & Touche, the company's auditor.

It was not difficult for the Rigas clan to loot the $3 billion-plus because although the Rigases owned only 20 percent of Adelphia stock, they held 60 percent of the votes and the board consisted of John Rigas, sons Michael, James, and Timothy, and son-in-law Peter Venetis. The family was not without scruples. Just as they took cash out of Adelphia for personal investments, they funneled it back in when those investments made money. However, the deals were not always, as the Fox News folks say and as corporate governance dictates, fair and balanced. For example, Adelphia paid $25 million for the timber rights to a piece of property. The Rigas family then purchased the same land from Adelphia for $500,000. All in all, not bad work if you can get it. No heavy lifting required, at least until the prison sentences. The outsiders on the board were kept out of the loop, perhaps a wise call on any embezzler's part. Even the outside board members were astonished at the level of self-dealing, both by how much or how much got by them. The loans to the Rigas family from the company were also problematic, especially when they went south and Adelphia headed into bankruptcy.

All this was going on under any number of noses inside and outside the company, but that Greek god status required great deference. A World War II vet, Rigas paid his employees well and brought the town great economic prosperity, something not seen often in the declining economies of coal and steel in Pennsylvania. John Rigas was to Coudersport, Pennsylvania, what Bernie Ebbers was to Jackson, Mississippi. Nearly everyone in the town had benefited directly or indirectly from the Rigas family, and the term *father figure* emerges in nearly all descriptions. When Rigas walked the streets of small downtown Coudersport, it would often take him an hour to walk one block along Main Street because people always stopped to greet him and talk. Generous to a fault with the locals, members of the Rigas family were known around Coudersport as big spenders. As many as twenty employees of the company worked directly for the Rigas family, including a chef. The townspeople referred to themselves as serfs, sharecroppers on the land holding the stately homes built by the Rigas clan/commune. Mrs. John Rigas, Doris, was particularly known as a profligate spender. When the local dry cleaner said to Mr. Rigas, "That woman is costing you millions," Mr. Rigas responded, "Well, sometimes it's worth it. Because when she's bothering [the contractors], she's not bothering me."

The executive team also fit the Keating pattern established over a decade earlier in the savings-and-loan series of ethical collapses. Adelphia's top team consisted of John Rigas (seventy-six) as CEO and chairman of the board, his son Michael (forty-seven) as secretary and executive vice president of operations, his son Timothy (forty-four) as treasurer and executive vice president, and his son James (forty-three) as executive vice president for strategic planning. They were Wharton, Stanford, and Harvard alums from their graduate work in business and law. Mr. Venetis rebelled and went to Columbia. They were also the only officers listed in the proxy. Timothy Rigas (note: an insider) was chair of the Adelphia audit committee.

The layer of executives just beneath the powerful Rigas family consisted of young 'uns in the twenty-eight-to-thirty-five age bracket, the one that seems most dangerous in the companies of this era of scandals. For example, one of these youthful executives, Timothy Werth, who served as Adelphia's director of accounting, entered a guilty plea to securities fraud, and conspiracy to commit securities, wire, and bank fraud, the other types of crimes that stem from taking EBITDA and working backward to get earnings right. He indicated that he conspired to falsify the books from the time he joined Adelphia when he was thirty years old.

Perhaps the officer who was most easily manipulated in the hierarchy just beneath the Rigases was James Brown, the vice president of finance. He had joined Adelphia in 1984, just two years into its existence. At age twenty-two and three months out of college, he became a management trainee who would climb to the top of the company and serve in the inner sanctum of the Rigas family. Despite Brown's lack of training in either accounting or finance, the centralized management team of Rigas, Rigas, and Rigas promoted him to handle the finances and financial reporting for the company. Michael Rigas served as the best man at Brown's wedding, but Brown would eventually be a key government witness at the Adelphia trial, at which he indicated that manipulating Adelphia's books began almost immediately when the company went public in 1986. Everything from subscriber numbers to earnings were manipulated. Mr. Brown testified that he "lied" to everyone from analysts to investors to the press, even keeping two sets of books, one of which was known as the "Jim Brown numbers." From age thirty-one forward, or from 1992 to the collapse, he had the two sets of books. Interestingly, the highest compensation he ever received was $175,000 per year.

A different fate awaited those on the executive team who dared disagree with the family. In 1993, just after joining Adelphia, LeMoyne Zacherl, who served as vice president of financial operations, warned John Rigas about using corporate funds for personal expenses. Mr. Rigas promised Mr. Zacherl that he would stop, but he found another way to get his money. Mr. Zacherl was demoted, but he continued to find what he called "backdoor means" that Mr. Rigas used to get funds. In his testimony at the Rigas trial he indicated that the Rigases used the company as a checkbook. Mr. Zacherl left Adelphia in 1995 after a confrontation with Mr. Rigas over a wire transfer that was clearly for personal use of corporate funds. Mr. Rigas told him that it would be best if they "part ways."

Mr. Rigas and his sons rarely returned calls to analysts because with their status and the reported performance of the company, they felt no need to do so. Yet there were questions as to how Adelphia was financing its acquisitions, maintaining its large margins, and still managing to continue its double-digit growth. Oren Cohen, an analyst who was in Merrill Lynch's fixed income division, called frequently to ask how purchases were being financed. The response from the Rigases was "we're not telling you." Mr. Cohen examined the various off-the-books entities owned by the Rigas family members, concluded that they were at least $900 million to $1 billion in debt, and asked how the debt was being carried. He got the brush-off until March 27, 2002, when Adelphia filed an 8-K indicating that it could be liable for up to $2.3 billion in Rigas family debt. Ironically, the information was part of a footnote that described the relationship as "co-borrowing." By the beginning of June 2002, Adelphia's stock would be delisted by NASDAQ; and before June ended, the company would be in bankruptcy.

To the end, John Rigas was defiantly iconic. "We did nothing wrong. My conscience is clear about that." And he added that the criminal case and litigation by shareholders was "a big P.R. effort on the part of the outside directors and their lawyers to shift responsibility." And his status found him not alone in that defiance. Even as the indictments against Rigas, two of his sons, and corporate officers were handed down, the locals continued their unwavering support. John Rigas and his son Timothy were convicted of bank fraud, securities fraud, and conspiracy. Michael Rigas was acquitted of conspiracy and wire fraud, but the jury deadlocked on securities and bank fraud and the judge declared a mistrial. The former assistant treasurer, Michael Mulcahey, was acquitted. John Rigas was sentenced to fifteen years at age eighty, and his life will end as he serves his stint.

Those who looked up to the Rigas family still do, despite the verdict. "I know the man. I just can't believe he would do something like that" was the take of a Coudersportian who has known John Rigas since she was a child and who has worked for Adelphia most of her adult life as a housekeeper. Icons die hard, especially in small towns beholden to them.

Scrushy, HealthSouth, and King Richard

HealthSouth presents a perfect portrait of the Yeehaw bigger-than-life CEO and the young 'uns. Of all the companies, the officers in HealthSouth were the youngest with the least amount of experience. For example, the vice president of reimbursements (a critical position, given the Medicare rules and the company's ongoing issues with submissions and how it reflected the resulting revenues) was just twenty-seven years old when she wielded that authority. William T. Owens, the man who served as CFO and wore the wire for the government in order to record Mr. Scrushy in those infamous "meet the numbers" statements, was groomed in various executive and officer positions from the age of twenty-eight until he climbed to the top position, next in line to Mr. Scrushy, a climb that took only fifteen years.

The HealthSouth executive team also had a tremendous level of turnover, particularly among those executives who were fifty and older. These executives disappeared rapidly from the slate of officers, and that age group was no longer represented after 1998. Those officers who were experienced were replaced by younger and younger officers brought in by Mr. Scrushy. There was little continuity in the officer team from year to year, but the salaries and bonuses of those who actually were retained grew at exponential rates. Tragically, the photo of four of HealthSouth's former executives in *The New York Times*, shown leaving court after they were spared prison terms and given probation and fines, is striking because their youth glares at you. Their lawyers argued that they made the accounting entries because they "feared" they would lose their jobs and that there was no one to whom they could turn in the company to address their concerns about the accounting practices. Eleven would enter guilty pleas within a seven-week period in 2003, and all five of the CFOs (and isn't five CFOs in five years some indication of trouble?) would plead guilty to federal felonies related to fraudulent accounting. The officers and employees at HealthSouth had nowhere to turn because the composition, turnover, and obsequiousness of the top executive team existed on account of the persona of one person, King Richard, as he was often called both within and without the company. In fact, when Joel Gordon took over as CEO of HealthSouth following Scrushy's ouster, he said, "The imperial master is gone. We want people to feel that we are running the company for the benefit of the patients and the employees, not for one individual who lived a very broad-based, costly lifestyle."

Like Bernie Ebbers, Dennis Kozlowski, and John Rigas, Marin Richard Scrushy (Marin was dropped sometime after he went to community college and became a respiratory therapist) was a larger-than-life figure in the company as well as in the Birmingham, Alabama, area, headquarters for Health-South. Richard Scrushy was described by Kenneth Livesay, one of the company's financial officers (assistant controller and CIO) who testified against him, and who also entered a guilty plea, as follows: "He is an incredibly intelligent and gifted man. It was like he could achieve anything he put his mind to." *Fortune* magazine's profile of Scrushy following HealthSouth's tailspin summarized Scrushy in the following caricature language: Scrushy didn't want to be treated like a rock star; he wanted to be a rock star. And he did reform an old band into a rock group that performed around the South, flying his private jet to their various gigs. Another profligate spender, Scrushy's living expenses were estimated by the court to be $233,000 per month. He hired Bo Jackson to accompany him to company events, and Jason Hervey, the teenager from the TV series *The Wonder Years,* became nearly a permanent fixture at Mr. Scrushy's side. The two had a weekly radio show that was sponsored by HealthSouth. Mr. Scrushy's personal assets, estimated to total $175 million, included:

- a mansion in Birmingham

- a mansion in Palm Beach

- a $3 million lakefront home in Lake Martin, Alabama

- a $135,000 bulletproof BMW

- thirty-four other cars

- a $7.5 million helicopter

- a private jet

- a ninety-two-foot yacht

- three dozen cars, including two Rolls-Royces and one Lamborghini

- eleven businesses controlled through an operating company that also included a clothing company (Upseedaisees) owned and operated by his wife, Leslie.

The personal staff was nothing to sneeze at either: four housekeepers, two nannies, a ship captain, a boat crew, two ex-wives, one current wife, nine children, and security personnel at all assets and formerly at the office. He had even created a rock group, 3rd Faze, an all-female band that once had risen to the point of being Britney Spears's opening act (if that is, indeed, considered a climb upward).

Also, much as with Bernie Ebbers, the locals seem to refuse to believe that Scrushy was involved in the gigantic fraud at HealthSouth. He is an active and respected member of a local Pentecostal church where Leslie speaks in tongues at the pulpit. Still, that's better than speaking in accounting tongues, with various sets of books.

Nonprofits Are Not Exempt from Larger-than-Life CEOs: the United Way and a Charitable Profligate Spender

Iconic CEOs are not limited to public companies. They are everywhere, even in nonprofits. The United Way fell victim to the charismatic CEO and suffered for years as a result of his conduct. William Aramony served as president of the United Way from 1970 to 1992. He was a heck of a CEO for the organization. Like his for-profit counterparts, Aramony grew the organization and brought in the bucks, and he used no accounting mumbo jumbo to show growth. Mr. Aramony was a capable and talented fund-raiser for the United Way. During his tenure, United Way receipts grew from $787 million in 1970 to $3 billion in 1990. But whether the ego migrates to these types of positions or the position creates or exacerbates the ego, the ego becomes problematic. Aramony trotted down the path of excessive spending, and all at the United Way's expense. Some of Aramony's less-purposeful expenditures were reported in early 1992 in *The Washington Post:*

- Aramony was paid $463,000 per year.

- Aramony flew first-class on commercial airlines.

- Aramony spent $20,000 in one year for limousines.

- Aramony used the Concorde for transatlantic flights.

- Aramony owned a $430,000 condominium in Manhattan.

- Aramony paid an $80,000 annual salary to a young woman(17) with only a high school education with whom Aramony was having an affair.

- Aramony owned a $125,000 apartment in Coral Gables, Florida.

At his trial, where he was convicted on twenty-two felony counts of fraud, conspiracy, income tax evasion, and financial-transaction fraud, the jury was treated to testimony regarding his affair with the seventeen-year-old whom he would reward with a job at the United Way (discussed earlier), other affairs, and the creation of spin-off entities that would confuse even the best of the accounting sleuths, something that was done with the help of two executives Mr. Aramony had hired. Those executives entered guilty pleas and testified at Aramony's trial. Ah, there's that principle: never trust the people you cheat with. Still, human nature and Yeehaw Cultures being what they are, Aramony had been able to use these two men in his years at the United Way as a means of keeping all the spending quiet. He did so with the mighty hook of extensive rewards, salary, and bonuses. One of Aramony's financial officers was paid $359,000 per year and as time went by, was promised other things such as a guaranteed pension.

Aramony was sentenced to eighty-four months in prison and was released in 2004. A federal court held that despite all the shenanigans, the nonprofit had no out in its contract with Aramony and required that it pay him his deferred-compensation package, a total of $4.2 million. Apparently the good folks at the United Way were not thinking diabolically enough to put a felony clause in their agreement with their CEO. They had discussed a so-called bad-boy clause, but the unseemly nature and trust found them concluding that it was best left out of the CEO agreement for the head of a national charity. The best-laid plans of mice, men, and those responsible for iconic CEOs . . . The whole Aramony era and aftermath is referred to around United Way headquarters and chapters as "the great unpleasantness."

Government CEOs: Same Pattern, Different Crimes

Those who hold political office or are appointed to political positions still carry the traits that allow the Yeehaw Culture to grow. Mike Espy's story as Secretary of Agriculture is a classic illustration of ethical collapse. A Clinton appointee, Espy was a former congressman from Mississippi, a lawyer by training, and by all accounts a rising star. The Department of Agriculture under Espy had regulations pending that would impose more rigorous processing requirements for chicken. The gist of this lovely proposal was to require less fecal matter in the whole process. Any fecal matter in one's chicken nuggets sounds quite inedible, and there were many who were holding firm with me in my views on "zero fecal tolerance." But those who know chickens and their maximum fecal levels insisted that the "zero tolerance" requirement was not necessary and that the cost, of course, of any additional requirements, let alone the cost of banishing fecal matter, is substantial for a chicken processor such as Tyson Foods.

While the regulations were so pending, Secretary Espy behaved as iconic CEOs do. He himself, at thirty-eight, was very young for cabinet-level authority and he enjoyed living the high life, despite GSA pay levels. He was also surrounded by young appointees who were not familiar with the ways of the political world, let alone the government regulations on gifts from lobbyists. As a result, Espy was able to live a jet-set lifestyle without facing any internal opposition. Espy attended the 1994 Super Bowl at government expense because he was, as he noted, there for the celebration of Smokey the Bear's years of public service. Smokey the Bear is under the Department of the Interior and a different cabinet secretary, but icons will be icons. Espy's girlfriend accepted a $1,200 scholarship from Tyson Foods, the country's largest chicken processor. There were gifts of luggage, seats in Tyson's skybox at Dallas Cowboys games, flights, lodging, and other perks. Espy's chief of staff was receiving payments from farmers seeking agricultural support programs.

All these extravagances came to light; the ensuing public pressure, along with the appointment of a special counsel, resulted in Espy's repaying $33,228 for all the gifts. Espy's chief of staff was indicted, convicted, and sent to prison, for three counts of making false statements about receiving outside income. Following the investigation by the special counsel, more than twenty individuals were indicted, fifteen were convicted, and, in toto, they paid $11 million in penalties. At his trial, where he was acquitted of all charges, witnesses such as former EPA administrator Carol Browner testified that Espy called all the rules on the conduct of government officials "a bunch of junk." Ah, there it is, that iconic notion of being above the rules. And they come as close to the legal line as they possibly can, as Espy's acquittal indicates. But their lack of an ethical compass or their inability to honor its direction contributes to the atmosphere in which the Yeehaw Culture thrives.

The Media and Their Ethical Collapses

Ethical collapses occur in ways other than financial reporting or product liability. Ethical collapses can occur in any organization and any industry. The patterns and signs are the same. Only the type of lapse changes. Two recent ethical lapses in media organizations illustrate that the iconic leader can cause more than just FASB compliance problems.

Dan Rather and the oversights and slipups in the story CBS ran on its *60 Minutes II* program on President Bush and his National Guard service show what can happen when a news organization gives too much deference to both the camera talent, Rather, and his producer, Mary Mapes, both of whom had long-standing stellar reputations in the business and had enjoyed tremendous success in the past in breaking stories. In fact, they had reached such a level of achievement that no one dared question their judgment, or even follow standard procedures for story verification and fact-checking. They were, after all, Dan Rather and Mary Mapes.

Mapes met with Bill Burkett, a man who had a history of bad blood with the Bush family in Texas. Mr. Burkett offered Mapes some memos allegedly penned by Lt. Col. Jerry B. Killian (deceased), who was Mr. Bush's squadron commander in Texas. The memo pegged Mr. Bush as a slacker. Burkett refused to disclose his source but did offer that the memos had come from someone who had been an aide to the colonel and would have had access to the files. He also indicated that the aide was unavailable for an interview. A noniconic producer or reporter would have been required to verify, document, and reverify the authenticity and source before running the story. A Journalism 101 student would have asked questions about, and conducted a more in-depth investigation into, Burkett and his motives. Instead, the story went forward, damn the torpedoes and any background checks. Mapes simply had Rather interview Burkett for the segment, it was aired within six weeks of the general presidential election, and the conclusion of the piece was that Mr. Bush had not served honorably during his time in the National Guard.

Within hours of the segment's airing on September 8, 2004, questions arose. First, Colonel Killian's son, Gary, and his stepmother (Killian's widow) went public with their statements that they had told Mapes that neither of them believed that the documents were authentic because they did not know the colonel to have kept those types of records. Then the Web bloggers weighed in with font and type checks and concluded that the documents had been created using Microsoft Word. Bill Gates was not yet there with Windows, nor were the word processing systems that would follow, in 1973, when the alleged memos were dated. Old icons die hard, and when these questions about the memos emerged, Rather and CBS News and the network dug in their heels and pointed out that the story must be true because President Bush was not reacting. Rather flew to Texas to interview Burkett once again, and in this interview Burkett confessed that he had lied about the source of the documents. After twelve days of iconic stubborness, Rather issued an on-air apology on September 20, 2004, saying he was "personally and directly" sorry. CBS News president Andrew Heyward called the report a "mistake, which we deeply regret."

The memo that was the basis of their story turned out to be questionable. They had disregarded the opinions of some experts on the authentication process, and they had also failed to conduct background interviews for purposes of establishing authenticity. One scholar referred to the network's lapses as "beyond imagination." In short, the very basics of journalism had been ignored not because those at CBS did not know them but because icons precluded the need for following them. Whether Accounting 101 or journalism at the same freshman level, the cultural issues are critical if lines are to be drawn, employees are expected to speak up, and fool's errands halted. Whether in newsrooms or boardrooms, the iconic CEOs and their sycophantic underlings wreak havoc.

The New York Times debacle with the made-up and plagiarized stories of editor Howell Raines's star, rising reporter Jayson Blair; USA Today's problems with fired iconic reporter Jack Kelley; and The New Republic's similar problems with Stephen Glass all carry parallel threads: iconic reporters, deferential managers, and an unwillingness to question the obvious errors (one of Blair's stories put tobacco fields in West Virginia, one of Kelley's stories had heads rolling down the street after a bombing, and one of Glass's stories had a source that was traced back to a nonexistent company). There is also one more parallel—among the staff members of each of these organizations, there were discussions, objections, concerns, and questions raised that were too easily dismissed (along with some of those who raised them). Yeehaw Cultures can exist in any industry and any type of organization once the icon gets a grip on the minds of those who become the icon's subjects.

The same pattern emerged yet again when Newsweek ran a story in May 2005, as penned by star investigative journalist Michael Isikoff, that the U.S. military was guilty of gross sacrilege in its treatment of suspected Islamic terrorists. Mr. Isikoff gave the example of military personnel flushing the Koran down the toilet. The story ignited demonstrations and riots that resulted in the loss of seventeen lives. The story was not true. The story was also based on one person's word (no documents) that he had seen documents that disclosed the abuses. A one-source story on an issue of this magnitude is risky business. But allowing the story to run can be explained only as blind deference to an icon. Mr. Isikoff was, after all, the reporter who had discovered the Monica Lewinsky affair. He was a reporter's reporter. But a one-source story violates the basic tenets of journalism. His status should not have allowed him a pass. Just as an iconic CEO does not get to dictate financial results, star reporters do not get to change the rules on sources. Newsweek retracted the story.

The Antidotes for Young 'Uns and a Bigger-than-Life CEO

Cultural change and cultural controls are tall orders. These elements in ethical culture are perhaps the most difficult because of deference to CEOs, particularly those iconic ones. Shortly after Jack Welch retired as GE's CEO, the company had to issue a material earnings restatement. Questions about GE's accounting had always floated about, but no one in the investment community or among analysts dared raise the issue because Mr. Welch was often touted as the greatest manager of all time. Mr. Welch would perhaps be more accurately described as the greatest earnings manager of all time. GE was possibly just quarters away from ethical collapse when Mr. Welch retired and the company reversed the financials for the years of Welch's domination of the numbers. Also, the company had to change its cultural mind-set on meeting those numbers, the pervasive fear factor, and the irrational reverence for Welch. In fact, there was much more anecdotal evidence of Mr. Welch's domineering, iconic, and Yeehaw nature that emerged following his retirement. Mr. Welch's somewhat messy divorce (a natural outcome of adultery with the editor of the *Harvard Business Review*; see the discussions of antidotes later in this chapter for more information) resulted in revelations about his retirement package that had not been properly disclosed to the shareholders. He was given an apartment, access to sporting events, and $86,000 per year for five days of consulting. That all was changed when the light of day was shone upon it, courtesy of Jane Welch in their divorce proceedings. Welch now consults for free and pays for all, from tickets to the apartment. GE settled with the SEC on charges related to the nondisclosure of the retirement benefits. The company was forced to cut the final ties to its era of the bigger-than-life CEO and the resulting concentration of power and assumed infallibility that accompanies these iconic figures. No one dares question them even as the company bears the brunt of an ego run amok. Mr. Welch's op-ed about these events that appeared on the pages of *The Wall Street Journal* was just plain embarrassing because it contained no justification, correction, or qualification. Sadly, this is a piece I now use to teach my students about the difference between rationalization of misconduct and real ethical analysis. Welch had nothing but rationalizations for an ethical misstep, excesses, and a huge lapse in judgment. But the self-perceived infallibility revealed in the piece does offer insight into the lack of accountability and distorted perspective that he had enjoyed. The effect of the editorial was to demonstrate that the emperor wore no clothes. This is a tragically flawed human being whose judgment was questionable. No CEO is perfect, and icons are best left to the computer screen, not the CEO slot. Not questioning CEOs, no matter what titles and accolades are theirs, or their decisions, regardless of how well they have done or the power they wield, takes the company on a trot down the road to ethical and other resulting forms of collapse. Ethically healthy organizations do not offer autonomy to any officers or executives. Jim Collins in his latest book, *Good to Great,* and also in a *Fortune* analysis of seventy-five good decisions, points out that good decisions come from leaders listening to dissenting views. Perhaps the lack of communication about ethical issues is simply another indication of a failing company because communication and dissent appear to be critical for effective management, not just an effective ethics programs and ethical culture.

Iconic CEOs have a tendency to surround themselves with those who are willing to let sleeping icons lie. The direct reports to the CEO and other senior officers are in awe of their famous and seemingly infallible superiors and are unwilling to raise issues or point out the elephant in the room. 'Tis best not to raise the ire of the gods.

Making sure the top tier of a company does not breed a culture of ethical collapse requires a focus on both of these structural components of the Yeehaw Culture: the iconic CEO and the young 'uns who defer. Eschewing silence and fear, we aim for a culture of openness, disclosure, and, yes, even a challenge here and there to those larger-than-life executives. Deferential treatment breeds ethical collapse.

Antidote #1 for Young 'Uns and a Bigger-than-Life CEO: Don't Hire Iconic CEOs and Get Rid of CEOs Who Become Icons or, at a Minimum, Curb Your CEO

Easier said than done, you say, but at the heart of this governance matter may be the very survival of the company. In thinking about this antidote, remember this: icons are highly overrated. In hiring a CEO, board members should think through very carefully the trade-offs in hiring that big name. There are no data that show that a big-name CEO results in higher returns for shareholders. Al Dunlap had a hit with his revamping of Scott Paper (accomplished by downsizing) and the board brought about one heck of an uptick in the value of Sunbeam stock with just the announcement that Chainsaw Al would be taking the helm. However, Chainsaw then took Sunbeam right into accounting improprieties and bankruptcy within a two-year period. Chainsaw Al was not the magic potion that solved business problems. He was the king of the hill in terms of legendary CEOs, but he destroyed the company he was hired to save. Also, the SEC was standing nearby with a whistle, ordering everyone out of the pool and right into fines and settlements, along with the restatements.

Stephen Bollenbach was a legendary CFO who was brought into Marriott to see it out of its post–tax reform slump. Brilliant minds can work wonders and Bollenbach found a creative way to spin off Marriott's debt, but the result was the beginning of a long streak of litigation by investors against the company, reputational damage, and a fundamental lack of trust between Marriott and the investors it needs in its creative construction and resort financings. Now Bollenbach heads Hilton with mixed results. He spent $3.7 billion to acquire Promus, a move that put Hilton's debt at $5.5 billion. The customer growth has come more from changes in reservations than the acquisition bet.

There is always a downside to the iconic CEO, whether hired or created. Carly Fiorina is perhaps the top case study on the drawbacks of the CEO who becomes an icon by rising through the ranks. Hewlett-Packard is back to square one, including having a new CEO. Peter Bijur rose to iconic status when he settled a discrimination suit against Texaco, largely based on some tapes furnished to *The New York Times* by a plaintiff's lawyer. Bijur settled the suit against Texaco for $176 million and a promise of all manner of programs, corrections, scholarships, etc., and on into all things EEOC-required. Instantly Bijur became a legendary CEO. Magnanimous, sensitive, iconic Bijur. Recorded conversations that damn allegedly racist investigators can turn out to be flawed, poorly transcribed, and, well, just plain wrong. Perhaps, as some noted, the settlement was premature, if not just wrong. Or perhaps the tone of the tapes justified Bijur's swift action. Bijur, iconic status ensured, went down a path of bizarre behavior that forced the board to ask for his resignation following a meeting in which the members indicated they had lost confidence in him. Son of a gun, Bijur, like Kozlowski, remodeled the company's New York City apartment at company expense. And like most everyone at Enron, Bijur had a romance with a subordinate he eventually married. Then there was the ubiquitous behavior of an icon using the company jet for personal trips. An internal audit referred to all these matters as "lapses in judgment." The icon would have to go nonetheless.

When in doubt, go with the plodder CEO, not the icon. My work on companies that have paid dividends for a hundred years concludes that the nonglitzy CEO, mostly hired from within, provides the steady hand and long-term returns for a company. In fact, when Tyco and Kozlowski acquired Ludlow, one of the hundred-year companies, they gutted it within eighteen months.

Apart from erring on the side of nonicon, boards face the ongoing task of keeping the iconic CEO from turning into a tyrant. Meg Whitman, the CEO of eBay, those Google guys, Bill Gates, Michael Dell, Oprah—icons all, and who is going to tell them they are out of line? It's tough for employees to speak up when their boss has made the executive decision to be featured on the cover of every magazine every month. Icons do well as long as the company is doing well. But when there is a downturn, the power and charisma they wield make it difficult for those around them, whether in the company or on Wall Street, to question them. The pattern is even clearer in the recent slew of media missteps cited earlier. We saw the pattern occur in spades with all the dot-coms, whose former CEOs are now sitting in Starbucks using WiFi access or else working at Starbucks in exchange for tips and WiFi access. Jeff Dachis, the former CEO of Razorfish, was once asked why his dot-com-era company that did Web designs and had a $3.6 billion market cap at one time had no outsiders on the board. He responded, "I control ten percent of the company. We've created enormous shareholder value." Well, temporarily. The key to these young 'uns' and icons' companies is selling shares in time. I described the dangers of this iconic CEO and what would bring the company back from the dead in a piece written for the *Financial Times:*

> *Jeff Dachis, the former chief executive of Razorfish, saw his company's stock debut at $56 per share in 1999. Razorfish reached its earnings peak in 1999 when it had net income of $14m. In 2000, however, the company posted a $148m revenue loss and by May 2001 its shares were trading at $1.11. Dachis was quoted as saying that he did not see the need for outside directors on his board: "Management isn't screwing up. What's good for me is good for all shareholders."*
>
> *No matter how good a digital technology company is, it still needs business expertise to run smoothly. Dachis and the Razorfish board not only lacked that experience; they did not acknowledge it as important until it was too late. Still in their thirties, the executive team's renowned expertise in product development was not matched by its experience in finance or management. They appeared unfamiliar with one of the key tenets of corporate governance: good business decisions, operations and financial probity come from companies with a diverse management team. Singular in age and background, the company lacked depth.*
>
> *This was nowhere more evident than in the company's optimistic press releases and earnings statements and projections. A company at ethical risk is one that not only boasts of double-digit earnings growth but also promises more. The pressure on employees is acute and the result is that many will cut corners, whether in the poor treatment of customers as a cost reduction measure or in the creative reporting of income.*
>
> *Razorfish was a stunning performer in the new economy. Its earnings for 1999 were 483 percent higher than its earnings for 1998. And it assured shareholders that the best was yet to come.*
>
> *Even when the market had begun its unfavourable turn in the first quarter of 2000, Razorfish released a statement in April 2000 that its net income was up 22 percent and that it was firing on all cylinders. Jeff Dachis pledged to reinvent Fortune 1000 businesses with his know-how.*
>
> *How things change in just one year. One year later, there were no percentages in any of the company's announcements, but plenty of "pro-forma losses." Dachis was replaced as chief executive. The primary goal was now a "return to profitable operations and positive cash flow." Three outsiders were immediately added to the board.*
>
> *In short, Razorfish returned to the basic principles of business: watch your costs, make and market a good product and seek guidance from those outside*

your business to help you recognize the important issues. From an ethics perspective, we could add one more: be honest and accurate in your predictions about future earnings. It is simply not possible to sustain growth in the 400 percent range. But no one at Razorfish acknowledged this—until the market did it for them.

There are certain fundamentals of business that no icon can change, and one of them is that a business can survive the loss of a CEO. Fear of losing a CEO only contributes to the self-perceived power of the iconic CEO. Scrushy, Kozlowski, Keating, Ebbers, Skilling, Lay, Dunlap, and all the others in this stable of autocrats knew no one would challenge them. That knowledge emboldened them. Further, the knowledge that they cannot be replaced breeds an environment in which their conduct, no matter how bizarre, unethical, or illegal, continues unchecked as employees and boards grapple with the legend among them. The stories earlier in this chapter demonstrate that executive power, unchecked, continues to expand. If unquestioned, it crosses over into unethical choices and from there quite nearly always into illegality. No icon can be above the law or the company code of ethics, or even be permitted to believe himself or herself to be. Deference creates bigger icons.

The process of curbing icons is the same as the one for encouraging employees to report violations of the law or the code of ethics. Employees will be the first to see the missteps of a leader who is drunk with the power and acclaim icons enjoy. If those missteps are reported and the board takes action, the cultural march to collapse, as led by the icon, is halted. And if those in charge have mastered antidote #2 coming up, things should proceed directly to confrontation with the icon. The fascinating thing about icons is they are unable to realize how far they have drifted. They reach a point where their decision making is irrational because they fancy they can beat anything since they have been, for some time, the smartest people in the room. To them, rules, laws, and ethics are for the less gifted. Enter Martha Stewart. Her total savings from unloading her ImClone stock one day before the company made the public announcement that its anti-cancer drug, Erbitux, would not get FDA approval, was about $40,000. To a billionaire such as Martha, $40,000 is like a Blockbuster rental fee to you and me. A frenzy of phone calls between Martha, on her way to Mexico, and her broker's assistant preceded the convenient sale of the stock. If she had just been candid about the conversations and her knowledge of CEO Sam Waksal's sale of his shares, the SEC might have slapped her with a civil fine and been done. Icons will be icons, and Martha began a process of trying to get stories straight among three people: her broker, her broker's assistant, and herself. There were alterations in phone logs, backdating of stop-loss orders, and all those nifty practices that will get you a conviction for obstruction of justice.

No one could keep his or her story straight, and the young broker's assistant sang like a canary. His trial testimony of Martha's autocratically rude behavior during the trial is Visa-ad priceless. Someone should have suggested to the domestic diva, "Keep the stock. You'll be better off."

But underlings let icons do as they wish, and the result was a conviction, not for selling the stock but for the attempted cover-up afterward. In hindsight the conduct looks amazingly dumb, especially given that the ImClone stock is now doing well and can only go up with its FDA approval. Icons do incredibly dumb things because those around them fail to point out their folly or even just curb their conversations about stock and resulting cover-ups. Sometimes they go to prison, but they always affect shareholders. Martha's own company stock tumbled from $70 per share to as low as $5.92 and hovers in the $20 range, with sales and revenues not yet recovering from this 2002 lapse in judgment.

Hire and keep a CEO who spends his or her time at the company with the employees, not on stage, screen, and television. Wendelin Wiedeking, the CEO of Porsche, has, over a twelve-year period, turned that company around in everything from production efficiency to vehicle design. Porsche is on a roll, as it were, with increasing sales, popularity in the marketplace, quality in production, and reduced costs in the factory. He got the company to this point by spending a great deal of time with employees on the factory floor. "I've got friends in the factory. I don't need bodyguards there, like some other CEOs." Yet if someone were to say in a business publication, "That Wendelin Wiedeking is really something," the blessed and welcome reaction would be "Who the heck is Wendelin Wiedeking?" One only hopes that the success and the path recruiters are beating to his door do not turn this successful plodder into an icon.

Antidote #2 for Young 'Uns and a Bigger-than-Life CEO: Always Question the Icon

Even icons have mundane legal rights. Companies must have grounds for their removal. Those grounds can be difficult to come by when no one asks questions. Ironically, more questions should arise the better the performance and the longer the streak runs. "How is this possible?" is the question that should be on the tip of every board member's tongue. Too often boards take a hands-off approach to CEOs who meet numbers goals. When the company continues to do well, boards almost always coast. While more is coming (in Chapter 5) on boards, this antidote applies to everyone, from shareholders to analysts. Enron, Tyco, Adelphia, HealthSouth, WorldCom, and the others described earlier all had phenomenal performance records. Rather than assuming the best in the best of times, shareholders, analysts, and the media should raise questions.

If it sounds too good to be true, it probably is. Just before GE announced that it would be issuing financial restatements, the insightful Bill Gross of Pimco sent out some thoughts on his fears about the company that were triggered by an article in *The Wall Street Journal* that quoted GE Capital's Marissa Moretti for an explanation on the company's near-record $11 billion in debt offering. Her explanation was that "absolute yields are at historic lows . . . so we think now is the right time to be doing an offering like this." Her thoughts triggered Mr. Gross's thoughts that "historic lows" was not accurate and his view that Ms. Moretti was hiding something. His thoughts on what GE was hiding?

- GE had the benefit of a Aaa rating but its commercial paper totaled three times the amount of the bank credit lines they held to back up that commercial paper

- The commercial paper market was sensitive at this time, with funds not as readily available, and, therefore, presented a risk for GE in trying to refinance all this paper

- The ordinary standard for credit line backups on commercial papers was that companies had to have at least the amount of all their commercial paper in credit lines, but GE had $50 billion of commercial paper that was *not* backed by credit lines

- Mr. Gross chided the market for its lack of oversight on such a development

- The issuance of the $11 billion was not at an opportune time. Rather, GE was trying to cover itself for the commercial paper and the heat it was beginning to feel from the market about its lack of self-discipline on meeting the usual standards for security on commercial paper.

- Mr. Gross also chided Ms. Moretti, former GE CEO Jack Welch, and current CEO Jeff Immelt for not being totally forthcoming about this issue as well as answering the question of how GE was growing earnings at a rate of 15 percent per year. Gross noted that brilliant management were not bringing those earnings. Rather, he reflected, the earnings were coming from acquisitions (a hundred in five years) and that GE was using "near hedge fund leverage of at times, what appears to be (based on its Aaa rating) non-hedge fund risk."

He was completely correct. The response from the market was that Gross had a screw loose. The market was icon-drunk. Mr. Gross was not only correct in his analysis, he was correct to question. Of course, Bill Gross, as the manager of the world's largest mutual fund, runs the risk of becoming an icon himself. And the ego is not completely in check. In 2003 he issued an annual report/letter in which he came out against the war in Iraq. The objections raised in response and the outrage offered by investors indicate that his senior management team should have issued a "No, don't do this!" and the negative attention proved to be problematic for the giant fund.

The following are simple questions that should be asked of CEOs and might have flagged problems at the companies discussed earlier:

- How is it possible to meet earnings predictions to the penny for so many quarters in a row?

- If earnings are this terrific, where's the cash?

- What's this note in the 10-K on officers' holding interests in companies we do business with?

- Could we walk through the numbers on the acquisition?

- Could we have more presentations here at the board meetings from frontline and nonofficer employees?

- If we look at accounting, regulatory, and product issues in the industry, what are our vulnerabilities? Our problems? Our evolving areas of concern? Of regulators?

- How are these double-digit returns continuing?

- Why such high officer turnover? (See Antidote #3, too.)

When in doubt, ask. Even when not in doubt, ask. Ronald Reagan handled Mikhail Gorbachev the way boards should handle CEOs: "Trust, but verify."

Antidote #3 for Young 'Uns and a Bigger-than-Life CEO: Monitor Who Is Hired and Who Is Fired and Who Replaces Them and How Much They Are Paid

A board cannot defer to the CEO in the selection of the officer team because we now know from the companies' histories that the lack of maturity and experience with business cycles in the executive ranks can contribute to an ethical collapse. If this one antidote had been applied in any of the companies cited previously, boards might have taken action sooner. Adelphia had family members for officers. HealthSouth was losing officers with experience and had high turnover, and the new recruits were barely old enough to work in post-college entry positions. Yet these inexperienced and unseasoned employees were given senior executive status. In WorldCom and Tyco, the second-in-command had been groomed for his job from the time he was in his late twenties and early thirties and was given full autonomy on financial matters. What we have are the obvious and easily discernible signals about cultural decline in the age, composition, and turnover of the executive team. Looking closely at hires, changes, and terminations is critical for the board. For example, if the boards had simply interviewed the departing CFOs at HealthSouth or followed up on the concerns of the executive who was monitoring the KELP at Tyco, they would have heard an earful and had the knowledge—perhaps put more aptly, the goods—to take action sooner. In this post-Sarbanes-Oxley world, boards must be even more vigilant. But they must be efficient in their vigilance, and following these patterns of hires, fires, promotions, and compensation plans offers critical information and signals.

For investors, this sign of ethical collapse is easy to track in publicly filed documents and even easier to control by a board watching officer slots and attrition. Watching these changes and evaluating the composition of the management team is as important as studying the numbers. Remember who puts those numbers together. It is not the auditors, but the officers. The numbers are only as sound as the management team.

Often just a look at the nature of the pay packages offers a hint at the hook the CEO may use to keeps things under control. And don't look at just the officers. Look at those employees who are close to the vest and whom the CEO wants to keep that way. For example, former NYSE chairman Dick Grasso's administrative assistant, SooJee Lee, was paid $240,000 per year. These are high-pressure times, but the motivation for the salary was perhaps more than good performance. The salary was a hook, a means of ensuring loyalty from the person who knows all the secrets (the loyal administrative assistant is the very fuel of this dysfunctional structure and sycophantic atmosphere between the top and their direct reports).

Antidote #4 for Young 'Uns and a Bigger-than-Life CEO: Conduct in Personal Lives Matters

Adultery is a room silencer. Talk about this issue in a speech about ethics and culture and people in the room avert their eyes or the BlackBerrys come out. No one wants to discuss personal lives. "Invasion of privacy," they cry. "Moralizing," they say. But intellectual honesty demands a look at the personal lives of CEOs. At the risk of joining the Larry Summers club for those who endure public ridicule and the follow-up penance for suggesting research in a controversial area, I offer my observation that the conduct of CEOs in their personal lives not only matters but may be a window into the soul of the CEO as a leader and business manager.

The companies in which these frauds occurred all had executives with peculiar spending habits. Many of them also had CEOs with peculiar personal lives. In this, the era of nonjudgmentalism, we are loathe to delve into personal lives. However, a harsh reality wants to slap us around as we try to get our arms around failed companies. Neither we nor CEOs function very well when we suffer from moral schizophrenia. Debauchery doesn't contain itself within definitive lines of personal vs. business life. CEOs are not demons in their personal lives and then magically transformed into giants of integrity once they report to the office. Behavior in personal lives is not a bad predictor of behavior in the executive suite. Dennis Kozlowski slogged through what might be called his "technically not embezzlement" trials that offered an embarrassing glimpse at yet another tragically flawed human being. If Tyco had acted on the egregious personal conduct of its then-CEO, it might not be struggling to recover now. Remember, as noted earlier, that a full two years before Tyco's real numbers and Kozlowski's sales tax evasion and spending problems came to light, partner Lewis Liman at Wilmer Cutler sent that e-mail noted earlier about the girlfriend and the payments. If only someone had confronted the issue of the affair, they might have cleaned up the lax personal loans and spending procedures as well as the weak board before Tyco shareholders suffered. Those who were aware averted their nonjudgmental eyes. They had a tool for prevention that they did not use.

Scott Sullivan's adultery via the workplace as well as his marijuana and cocaine use came out during defense lawyers' cross-examination of Sullivan during Bernie Ebbers's trial. These moral missteps occurred even as Sullivan was busily capitalizing $11 billion in ordinary expenses. Bernie divorced his wife of decades and married a WorldCom employee during the years of inflated earnings. Recall also that HealthSouth's former CEO Richard Scrushy, now in the midst of his trial for various frauds, is on wife number three, and he carries a string of nine children among the three ex-wives. Divorcing one wife of decades and marrying another younger woman, often an employee, during the years of inflated earnings, is a pattern that these CEOs, Skilling, and far too many others share.

And it's not just marriage, adultery, remarriage, affairs, and more remarriage that we should be wondering about and evaluating. There is an amoral, if not immoral, flavor of hedonism and bizarre behavior by the iconic figures. Enron's officer retreats had a Tailhook flavor. They allowed themselves to be photographed with scantily clad dancing girls for, one presumes, the retreat scrapbook? The employees were regulars at strip bars when they were celebrating a new deal. And, as we know, with three thousand off-the-book entities created and Enron deals with each of them, that's a great deal of celebrating at strip bars. Scrushy's radio show, band singing, and female rock group promotion activities also cut into his day and, apparently, his concentration on earnings and financial reports.

The scandals could go on, and they do, even when executives retire. Jack Welch's affair with the former editor of *Harvard Business Review,* Suzy Wetlaufer, got her fired for a conflict of interest because at the time the affair began she was doing an interview with Mr. Welch for the Ivy League B-school's magazine. It also landed them both in *The Wall Street Journal* because Jane Welch, wife of Jack Welch for thirteen years, ratted Ms. Wetlaufer out, reporting the conflict to her superiors at Harvard. The result was the bitter divorce battle that brought the mighty wrath of the SEC and GE's settlement with the agency for the failure to disclose the details of Welch's compensation package. Hell hath no fury, and Jane Welch bared all of Jack's personal finances and expenses.

Reaction to the Boeing board's ouster of CEO Harry Stonecipher ranged from "good for Boeing," to television analyst Bill Maher's nonchalant irritation reflected in his show's monologue, "Who cares what a sixty-eight-year-old guy does?" There has also been great murmuring from my colleagues in business ethics about Stonecipher; Boeing; and "private lives," "police state," and "moralizing."

The Boeing-Stonecipher issue brought the reemergence of the question of compartmentalization. The compartmentalization theory ran rampant during the Clinton presidency. During l'affair Lewinsky many were outraged at the investigation and intrusion into his private life. Others argued that it was not his private life that was at issue but rather perjury related to his conduct in his private life. Still others formed a third school of thought with their "Never mind the perjury, what about the adultery?"

Can we isolate the private unethical conduct of executives, political leaders, officers, and directors from our evaluations and determinations of whether they are or will behave ethically as fiduciaries, the managers of others' funds? Perhaps the question has no easy answer, and an exploration of the private lives of those who yielded our greatest corporate scandals nets some inconsistencies in concluding whether private standards and behaviors are important predictors or determinants of ethical conduct in business. The answer to the question of whether private conduct is relevant yields a definite answer only in its indefiniteness. The answer on compartmentalization and relevance of private conduct to behavior in business is "Maybe." The nature and extent of the private conduct and whether it is part of a pattern may provide a better framework and a more definitive answer than "Maybe." But, given the pattern, it's worth a look and follow-up.

Then again, how does one detect and prevent fraud? Consulting industries and audit specialists have been working at developing measures, tools, and signs for decades, if not a full century or so. Those methods clearly have their flaws. Perhaps what we need is a scale for measuring the moral development or character of those officers to whom the financial reports are entrusted. One measure of moral development is private conduct. How we treat those who are the closest to us and, at least in theory, the most important to us is telling. If they can be treated with disregard and breaches of trust, it is not a leap in logic to conclude that the same character flaw can see its way clear to be dishonest with those who are not even acquaintances. Such a theory of "morality matters" will hardly be embraced for the sake of morality. However, there are other reasons for invoking a standard of personal moral fiber as a requirement for employment at the executive level.

Sacking people for affairs is not all that bad of an HR or ethics principle because there is much more accomplished by doing so than mere moralizing. What darts through my mind and, I have discovered, from many conversations through the minds of many employees is "How on earth do these people have time for this stuff?" A factory line worker can't take time for an officer retreat or have a break long enough to spark a romance. Employees juggle demands of home, job, family, and, for some, education at night. Yet, those to whom they report and who demand private jets to maximize their efficiency somehow find the time to take on all the complexities of a new relationship while maintaining a marriage? Just the thought of the lies needed for the cover-up is exhausting to the frontline employee. One employee asked me, "How can anyone think clearly when they are dating while married and with a family?" Just the calendar and logistical problems boggle the minds of employees who must be at their desks from eight to five or in the factory from seven to four.

Adultery matters for moral reasons, but it also matters for the fundamental governance reason that an officer consumed with romance, secret meetings, and a cheating partner is not at optimum performance level, as it were. Employees understand this element of distraction and its attendant risk, irrespective of moral issues. They know they could not do their jobs as well and also know their code of ethics on affairs between those who share reporting lines, and failing to take action against an officer having an affair with an employee sends confusing signals about codes, expectations, propriety, culture, and even what is and is not appropriate conduct in the workplace. Cleaning up a culture and maintaining it requires definitive, egalitarian, and unequivocal signals when violations of codes and standards occur, regardless of who is involved.

Having worked with Boeing following its first ethical issues surrounding the use of Lockheed Martin proprietary information in a defense contractor bid and its second involving CFO Michael Sears's premature post-retirement employment discussion with Defense Department contract official Darleen Druyun, I fall in with the school that concludes there was no choice but to end the Stonecipher relationship with Boeing, either through termination or resignation. Cleaning up a culture requires definitive signals. As signals go, this was a dandy.

Adultery also matters as a workplace issue because those who seek respect from employees must earn it. The rush of forbidden lust is short-term pleasure. We like to think that those who establish and enforce the rules have progressed beyond addictions and indiscretions. We particularly like to think so when they are preaching ethics to us as employees. Those who would lead should assume the mantle of role model. The corporate disasters outlined earlier tell us that the captains of industry were busily involved in activities that not only distracted from the intense focus demanded at these high levels of business but served as a risk to the company itself when exposure inevitably came. If the review of the collapsed companies is a representative set, checking the personal lives—and in particular, the adultery of the CEO and/or CFO—may be a formula for saving the company.

Adultery matters because it is a measure of character. But it matters also because of old-fashioned risk. There's a fine line between an office romance and sexual harassment, and there seems to be somewhat of a direct line between executive adultery and executive-induced accounting fraud. The Nashville folks don't refer to adultery as "your *cheatin'* heart" without good reason. Most are loath to admit it, but sexual tomfoolery reveals a character flaw that serves those who would perpetuate corporate shenanigans. Our review of the scandals over the past five years shows that more often than not, the two go hand in hand. While we may never know which came first, wandering corporate officers' eyes, whether on the job or in retirement, do not bode well for the company. The effect on the company culture may not be measurable, and those officers may never graduate to Ponzi schemes and other forms of fraud. Not every monogamous CEO is a winner, and not every adulterer fails in business. However, when officers are dishonest with the single most important person in their lives, i.e., their spouses, it is not a stretch to conclude that they are capable of being dishonest with those with whom they do not share a day-to-day relationship: investors, suppliers, customers.

Examining this issue and its necessary infringement upon personal lives is a difficult one that finds many officers and employees rankled because of the intrusion. Those to whom officers are accountable, the boards and eventually the shareholders, should send clear signals to those officers about expectations for behavior. In so doing, they send clear signals to employees and create or preserve a culture of honor and forthrightness, whether in private lives or financial reports. How officers behave personally can be very telling, providing insight into personal values and even management style. Kozlowski was significantly different from his predecessor, John Fort, who drove a Pontiac with no air conditioning. When Fort took over as interim CEO following Kozlowski's resignation, he immediately grounded all the Tyco aircraft, eliminated the executive dining room, and prohibited employees from taking each other out on the company tab. Michael Rigas, the only Rigas not convicted, also behaved differently from his father and brother. He continued to drive his Toyota and was known throughout the company for his diligent reimbursement of the company for personal expenses, ranging from $3.45 for postage to airfares for personal trips.

Over the past few years as I have struggled to help students formulate their own ethical standards, I have come to realize that there is no such thing as "business ethics." There are personal ethics that are applied in every setting, from marriage to the executive suite. If such is the case, then the moral fiber of an individual matters if the company is to have an ethical culture.

Antidote #5 for Young 'Uns and a Bigger-than-Life CEO: Mold and Shape the Young 'Uns

An iconic CEO cannot exist when surrounded by seasoned talent. One stark difference between the executive structure of these collapsed companies and companies that last over the long term is that the board has put tremendous effort into grooming, growing, training, and nurturing an executive team with depth. Boeing has survived because it has a layer of officers who are capable of running the company. They are seasoned executives with broad experience. It's tough to pull the wool over the eyes of an executive who has experience and who has options. One antidote for an autocratic CEO is to have direct reports who have options. Those who can go elsewhere do not live in fear and just do whatever the iconic CEO asks. Their talent and experience give them backbone. A look at those who entered guilty pleas in these companies, particularly in the case of HealthSouth, shows that they knew that what they were doing was wrong. They feared for their jobs, and at their youthful ages with so little experience, there really were no jobs that could give them the same level of income. They had been promoted too quickly and given too much too soon. Ironically, they knew it and so they succumbed. Tenacity comes from options.

Some management texts would refer to this process as succession planning, a board looking out for the future. What boards may not realize is that by engaging in the process of nurturing future leaders for the company with clear skills and values, they are also creating a buffer for the iconic CEO and the havoc he or she can wreak if unchecked. One check and balance for that CEO's power is a talented senior management team with depth and experience. I don't suggest that we keep young people out of senior management. The key is for boards to train them well, give them depth, and mentor them in their climb to the top. We are now ready to address those boards.

Sign #3

Young 'Uns and a Bigger-than-Life CEO

Antidotes

1. Don't hire iconic CEOs and get rid of CEOs who become icons or, at a minimum, curb your CEO.

2. Always question the icon.

3. Monitor who is hired and who is fired and who replaces them and how much they are paid.

4. Conduct in personal lives matters.

5. Mold and shape the young 'uns.

CHAPTER FIVE

Sign

4

Weak Board

*I would like to begin by asking: What should a CEO
expect from a board? A short answer might be: "Giving a lot
of really good advice, but not too much of it."*

—Ken Lay, former Enron chairman of the board, April 1999

*Most of us made it to the chief executive position because of a particularly
high degree of responsibility.... We are offended most by the perception that
we would waste the resources of a company that is a major part of our life
and livelihood, and that we would be happy with directors who would
permit waste.... So as a CEO I want a strong, competent board.*

—Dennis Kozlowski, former Tyco CEO, circa 2001

The boards of companies at risk of ethical collapse are weak and ineffectual. Tolstoy's adage does apply here: all effective boards are alike
for the same reason, and all weak boards are weak for different reasons. Some of the boards in ethically collapsed companies were weak because
they were inexperienced. Others were weak because of the presence of friends
of management who would do whatever management wanted. Others were
weak because of conflicts of interest. Some boards simply had qualms about
reining in that autocratic and iconic CEO. Other boards were weak because
board members failed to attend meetings or because the structure of the board
meeting itself—with major proposals approved over the phone without directors being given the chance to read materials in advance and with little or no
discussion—was flawed. Some boards just deferred to that infamous iconic

CEO. Still other boards of these ethically collapsed companies had knowledgeable and independent people on them, but the result was boards composed of too-busy members who could not devote the time necessary for effective service and decision making. Many of the boards had a combination of these factors. They were not necessarily incompetent boards, but their members did not devote the necessary thinking, time, and detached input necessary for strategic oversight.

A weak board cannot step in and halt the inexorable march of the Yeehaw contingent in the company. While diverse in their causes of weakness, the boards of collapsed companies are all inevitably pitifully weak. Sarbanes-Oxley cannot guarantee a strong board. It is a beginning, but its rote and perfunctory checklists are not enough to create a board with the insight and gumption necessary to curb a culture headed for ethical collapse.

HealthSouth: A Study in Everything That Could Make a Board Weak

HealthSouth takes the prize for the board with the most negative factors. When the HealthSouth financial restatements began to emerge and emerge and emerge again, one of its directors, Joel C. Gordon, stated to the press, "We [directors] really don't know a lot about what has been occurring at the company." There's a confidence builder for corporate governance. However, the statement is not nearly as stunning as it seems when we explore the nature of this board.

Composition of the Board

Nearly all the HealthSouth directors had a Scrushy hook in them. The hook is a conflict of interest that would keep the director from defying either Scrushy or those who were operating under his iconic spell. As noted previously, anytime a company has changed CFOs five times in five years, the board may want to conclude that there is a problem and ask a few questions, conduct a little survey among employees, or even double-check the addition on the numbers. The interrelationships of the directors with Scrushy is as stunning as the statement that they really did not know what was going on at HealthSouth. The following is the list of interrelationships and the characteristics of the members of HealthSouth's board:

- One director earned $250,000 per year from a consulting contract with HealthSouth over a seven-year period.

- Another director had a joint investment venture with Mr. Scrushy on a $395,000 investment property.

- Another director's company was awarded a $5.6 million contract to install glass at a hospital being built by HealthSouth.

- MedCenterDirect, a hospital-supply company that was run online, did business with HealthSouth and was owned by Mr. Scrushy, six directors, and the wife of one of those directors.

- The same three directors had served on both the audit committee and the compensation committee since 1986.

- Two of the directors had served on the board for eighteen years.

- One director received a $425,000 donation to his favorite charity from HealthSouth just prior to his going on the board.

The board members were so conflicted that there was no incentive for candid feedback on the financials or other issues at the company and every incentive to keep quiet and let Mr. Scrushy have his way. One corporate-governance expert has noted, "There has been so much sleeping on the job at the Health-South board that it could rise to gross negligence." One Delaware judge issued an opinion on one aspect of litigation against the board: "The company, under Scrushy's managerial leadership, has been quite generous with a cause very important to Jon F. Hanson [the director who accepted a donation to his college football hall of fame] . . . compromising ties to the key officials who are suspected of malfeasance."

Conflicts

Worse, these conflicts on the HealthSouth board still existed despite the fact that the board itself was dominated by insiders. For example, in 1996 eight of the fourteen board members were also company officers. To the extent those inside:outside ratios improved in later years, the conflicts described earlier sprung up in the relationships between outside directors and both the company and Scrushy. To add to the board's conflicts, the company had an extensive loan program for its executives in order "to enhance equity ownership." The key executives owed significant amounts of money to the company for funds borrowed in order to exercise their stock options. The board approved those loans, and in some cases forgave them or did not require repayment. Scrushy had a $25.2 million loan. When Scrushy was indicted, a court ordered the loan due and payable. The company's June 2005 10Q indicates the loan has not been repaid. In 1999 there were $39 million in loans outstanding to the officers of the company. This creditor-debtor relationship between the company and its executives creates a conflict of interest in terms of management's ability to issue forthright financial statements (because the price of the stock is dependent upon those numbers, and the price of the stock fuels the value of the executives' options as well as their ability to repay the loans), which is now prohibited under Sarbanes-Oxley.

The compensation of the directors was not bad in a cash sense: $10,000 annual retainer, $3,000 per board meeting, and $1,000 per committee meeting. However, the directors also received 25,000 shares of HealthSouth common stock in January of each year. The directors were heavily invested in HealthSouth.

Missing Red Flags

Like WorldCom, HealthSouth had litigation pending that should have been a red flag to the board. The problems with reduction in earnings and questions about Medicare reimbursements in 1998, along with the allegations of Health-South officers' selling stock without disclosing material financial setbacks for the company, should have sent the board into at least a special investigation/special report mode. But Scrushy smoothed his way through the crisis and the board ambled along, content with his extraordinary explanations. HealthSouth enjoyed some recovery from the 1998 setback, with its stock climbing back from $5 to nearly $16 by May 2002. However, during this period the company was involved in a whistle-blower lawsuit that alleged Medicare fraud. Further, the company brought a defamation suit against a former employee who had accused HealthSouth of admitting Medicare patients that its facilities were not equipped to handle. Kimberly Landry, the former employee, as noted earlier, had posted her concerns on the Internet. Sometimes these employees are right, sometimes they are wrong, but then again, sometimes they are the tip of the iceberg, and their claims are always worth investigating. Boards cannot afford to assume that employees are wrong. In fact, boards should assume that they are the tip of the iceberg and follow up, question, and confront. When regulators come calling, directors should assume the worst. Like parents of teens, boards should assume officers are guilty until proven innocent. And they should hold a trial, complete with rebuttal evidence, to determine guilt or innocence. "Trial" is symbolic here for investigation, reports, confrontation, and even oversight of the litigation.

Perhaps what is most revealing in terms of deciphering what was wrong with HealthSouth's board are the guidelines it adopted in April 2003, within months of the company's collapse. Those guidelines, now posted on the company website, address everything from the conflicts of interest to the majority of the board being composed of outsiders to all the former *modus operandi* of the Scrushy board. The issues were obvious, and the practices of the Health-South board violated the most basic notions of corporate governance. Hindsight does not speak here. The shortcomings of the HealthSouth board begged for attention, but those indefatigable earnings were blinding. Perhaps a safety tip is that anytime a company meets its earnings predictions for forty-seven quarters in a row, one might want to look into everything, from the board to the auditors.

Enron: A Deceptively Impressive Board

Enron's board was a model in corporate governance if it were to be judged by the standards of those who have given us the ideal board structure for effective corporate governance. However, appearances do not translate into action. A business school dean, several CEOs from other companies, an economist, and one of Britain's foremost experts on accounting, among others, were part of Enron's board. However, the lessons on weak boards from Enron are perhaps the most instructive in terms of forcing us to examine more closely both how a board works and who board members really are in terms of their relationships with management. Kenneth Lay handpicked Enron's board, and their deference to him and the officer team of Skilling and Fastow showed in that they were not mildly curious about what has been called a "dizzying" number of off-the-books partnerships, LLPs, and LLCs, that were, oddly, named as if the company were being run out of the frat house: Raptor, JEDI, and a host of other film references. Even if one is not trained in the ways of FASB, this touch of Yeehaw should have at least piqued propriety's curiosity or pricked the conscience.

Composition of the Board

The standard for board membership at Enron was twofold: the appearance of depth, and possible political connections for the company. For example, Wendy Gramm, an economist, the former chairman of the Commodities Futures Trading Commission, wife of then-Senator Phil Gramm, and someone who has been called "the Margaret Thatcher of financial regulation" by *The Wall Street Journal,* was placed on the board for the clear inside political connections both she, as a former federal official, and her husband enjoyed. Ken Lay described the Enron board in 1999 at a conference on corporate governance at St. Thomas University in Houston, a description that hindsight finds stunning:

> In reference to the qualifications of new board members, Enron's corporate governance guidelines emphasize "the qualities of strength of character, an inquiring and independent mind, practical wisdom and mature judgment." No doubt, this list says a lot. At the same time, it does not say very much. Nevertheless, these are the qualities we look for in a board member. It

is no accident that we put "strength of character" first. Like any successful company, we must have directors who start with what is right, who do not have hidden agendas, and who strive to make judgments about what is best for the company, and not about what is best for themselves or some other constituency. Judgment becomes very complicated in cases of labor and shareholder issues. And when I say "company," I mean all of its constituencies, including employees, customers, communities, and, obviously, shareholders.

Putting it in the terms used by today's popular management consultant Steve Covey, we look first and foremost for principle-centered leaders. That includes principle-centered directors.

The second thing we look for are independent and inquiring minds. We are always thinking about the company's business and what we are trying to do. We want board members whose active participation improves the quality of our decisions.

We look for diversity as well. In my opinion, diversity is not just a varied mix of sex, race, religion, and all the other characteristics. It also extends to a variety of experiences, which is very important for any board. On the Enron board, we have a director who is the former dean of the Stanford business school, currently the Senior Professor of Accounting at Stanford. He serves as chairman of our audit committee. Another director was formerly a member of the British House of Lords and House of Commons, as well as Energy Minister. In addition, we have one of the most prominent business leaders in Hong Kong, who is in business around the world and involved very actively in all kinds of public and business issues. Yet another director is the co-founder and former president of Gulf and Western, and a very active entrepreneur and investor. Two directors are CEOs of large U.S. corporations, one high-tech and the other now in lodging, although when the latter came on the board, he was chairman of a large financial services company. Another board member is the former head of the Commodities Future Corporation. She is of Asian descent and has a Ph.D. in economics.

We also have a former professor of economics and a former head of General Electric's Power Division worldwide. At the time he retired, that division represented forty percent of G.E.'s total worldwide business. Another senior executive who runs an investment fund and has a Ph.D. in mathematics chairs my finance committee. We have the former president of Houston Natural Gas, the former head of M. D. Anderson, the former head of a major energy and petroleum company, and a former Deputy Secretary of the Treasury and Ph.D. economist on the board as well.

This board truly embodies a broad spectrum of experiences. We are also trying to recruit an African-American who heads a worldwide financial *services business and one of the largest financial institutions in South America. So the message is simple: try to get directors with the experiences and cultural insights your company will need as it becomes increasingly global. The board should be diverse in order to bring to the table a wide range of experiences not only in business but also in many other fields. Board members should be uniquely accomplished. Most importantly, they should have achieved distinction themselves in their chosen line of work. And I believe our board satisfies those criteria.*

Finally, we look for individuals who have mature judgment—individuals who are thoughtful and rigorous in what they say and decide. They should be people whom other directors and management will respect and listen to very carefully, and who can mentor CEOs and other senior managers.

Dreams turn to dust and ideology dissipates in the interest of attracting rubes. One of the ironic appointments (technically, the shareholder elections here were meaningless) to the board was that of Dr. John Mendelsohn, who also served on its audit committee. On the face of it, Mendelsohn's board membership seems impressive because he was a nationally known figure as a leading cancer researcher and he was the director of the Anderson Cancer Center at the University of Texas in Houston (the cancer center that developed Erbitux, the anti-cancer drug developed by ImClone, whose stock Martha Stewart would sell at a most opportune time). However, what few did not realize was that Mendelsohn had neither the background nor experience in finance at even rudimentary levels. This babe in the woods was hit by hedge-fund wizards such as Fastow who pulled the wool over the eyes of analysts. Fooling the likes of Mendelsohn, impressive as he was in his own field, was a cakewalk. Mixed metaphors aside, Mendelsohn was a useful idiot to the finance boys at Enron.

The other board members and their titles and affiliations were (at the time of Enron's collapse):

Kenneth L. Lay—Chair and CEO, Enron

Robert A. Belfer—CEO, Belfer Management

Norman P. Blake Jr.—Chair, president, and CEO, Comdisco

Ronnie C. Chan—Chair, Hang Lung Group

John H. Duncan—Former chair of executive committee, Gulf + Western

Robert K. Jaedicke—Professor of accounting, Stanford University

Charles A. LeMaistre—President Emeritus, University of Texas, M. D. Anderson Cancer Center

Paulo V. Ferraz Periera—Executive vice president, Group Bozano

William C. Powers Jr.—Dean, University of Texas School of Law

Frank Savage—CEO, Savage Holdings

Raymond Troubh—Financial consultant

John Wakeham—Chair, Press Complaints Commission

Herbert S. Winokur Jr.—Chair and CEO, Capricorn Holdings

Conflicts

Ken Lay and Jeffrey Skilling, prior to his abrupt August 2001 departure, were the only insiders on the board, thus providing corporate-governance gurus with the assurance that plenty of outsiders were minding the store. However, the board members had clear conflicts of interest that happened to be below the radar of both the SEC and corporate-governance standards. Perhaps the most obvious conflict for all the directors and what should have been a red flag was that they were the seventh-highest-paid directors in the United States, with a total compensation package of $380,619. There are not many who could risk losing that amount of scratch on an annual basis; walking away from it because of a showdown with management was out of the question at $100,000, let alone $400,000. Also, watching the directors' stock sales might have given investors and shareholders a hint that perhaps not all was well deep in the heart of Texas. They were collecting stock as compensation and then selling it off. Dean Jaedicke, who chaired the audit committee, sold $841,000 in Enron shares, $500,000 of it in 2001, the year when it all came unraveled. Norman P. Blake Jr. sold $1.7 million of his Enron shares in 2000. Charles A. LeMaistre, who had Dr. Mendelsohn's job and Enron board seat prior to his retirement from the cancer center, sold $842,000 of his stock in 1999 and in 2001.

Many of the specific conflicts that existed among board members were not widely known because they did not require any form of SEC disclosure. They were the perfect type of conflict to conceal fraud because no one on the outside was aware of them, but they were significant enough conflicts to make the board members beholden to management, particularly Mr. Lay. Dr. Mendelsohn, again a member of the audit committee, had received donations of $92,508 for his cancer center from Enron and $240,250 from Ken Lay and his wife, Linda, after joining the Enron board in 1999. The total amount Enron had donated to the center since 1985 was $1,564,928.

There were also directors who had business ties with the company. Herbert S. Winokur Jr., one of Enron's original directors from its founding in 1985, served on the board of Natco Company, a firm that did business with Enron subsidiaries. While the amount of $1.5 million in business seems small next to Enron's alleged numbers, a conflict must be judged from the perspective of Winokur, not just from Enron's view. This was below the SEC radar because disclosure of directorships in privately held companies is not required.

There were other conflicts among the board members. Frank Savage, a senior executive at Alliance Capital Management, was an Enron board member who saw to it that his company recommended to investors that they should be aggressively buying Enron stock. That recommendation never changed or faltered, even when board members and officers were selling off their Enron stock in droves and serious questions about the company's accounting began to percolate. Lord John Wakeham, a member of the audit committee, served as a consultant for Enron's European unit for $72,000 per year since 1996. Wendy Gramm is now the director of the Mercatus Center Regulatory Studies Program at George Mason University, to which Enron donated $50,000. Subtle, small in comparison to Enron's alleged assets and income, but real in terms of the benefits and meaning to the directors involved.

The board was really a tight-knit, connected community easily controlled by management. That the conflicts were subtle made it more difficult for investors, analysts, and shareholders to understand this inherent weakness in the board.

Missing Red Flags

Despite the conflicted interests of board members, no board could have been blindsided by the Enron collapse. There had been information and warnings, but the board, conflicted and perhaps confused, did not take action. The failure of the board to catch or act upon obvious "red flags" shows its complicity and perhaps its greatest weakness. At the Senate hearings conducted by the Permanent Subcommittee on Investigations (PSI), Exhibit 1 was a chart titled "Red Flags Known to Enron's Board." Just a few of the red flags are highlighted below.

AGGRESSIVE ACCOUNTING. At the February 1999 audit committee meeting, Andersen partner David Duncan told the members that Enron's accounting practices tended to "push limits" and were "at the edge" of generally accepted accounting principles. The minutes of that meeting show that Mr. Duncan, who was in charge of the Enron account, presented a chilling picture on Enron's accounting. In both the practice of law and accounting/auditing, there is a code language. When a lawyer issues an "aggressive opinion," it means that what the client wants to do is illegal, but the lawyer doesn't want to lose the client's business. In accounting/auditing, an "aggressive opinion" means that the company is probably not earning a dime, but the auditor is willing to go along with the fairly wild accounting practices. Duncan and other Andersen representatives provided the audit committee with a one-page summary called "Selected Observations 1998 Financial Reporting." This summary sheet qualifies as a red flag because in early 1999 the board still had the opportunity to follow up on issues, halt certain transactions, and prevent the further deterioration of the company's financial position that resulted from Mr. Fastow's continued domination of financial strategy, both within and outside the company. The format of the one-page summary was one in which Duncan highlighted the key accounting issues, including "Highly Structured Transactions," "Commodity and Equity Portfolio," "Purchase Accounting," and "Balance Sheet Issues." These issues were presented in a matrix in which Duncan evaluated three categories of risk for Enron: "Accounting Judgments," "Disclosure Judgements [sic]," and "Rule Changes." Mr. Duncan assigned one of three letters to each of the three categories: "H" for high risk, "M" for medium risk, and "L" for low risk. Each issue had at least two H's in each risk category. While the board may have been told of the risk, it apparently did not appreciate the seriousness of the problem because it seemed to rely on both management's and the external auditors' judgment and allowed the risk levels to continue. The audit committee minutes from the London meeting state "Mr. Duncan discussed the financial reporting areas that [Andersen] had determined to be high priorities due to inherent risks present. He stated that the ongoing high priority areas included structured transactions, the merchant portfolio, commodity trading activities, project development activities and intercompany and related party transactions."

Mr. Duncan and Andersen felt they were passing the buck to the board in terms of accountability for accounting. The board, on the other hand, took the presentation to be an imprimatur from Mr. Duncan and Andersen that Enron's accounting, while pushing the envelope, was within the rules. Lord Wakeham is what is known as a "chartered accountant" in Great Britain, the equivalent of a CPA, and the chair of an audit committee at another publicly held company. He is a recognized leader in financial reporting and reforms related to disclosures. He referred to Enron's structure as "relatively new" and "not done by many companies in the world" but within the bounds of accepted accounting principles. This acknowledgment that there could be perhaps some merit in the directors' claims is critical because meaningful reform (i.e., antidotes for the Yeehaw weak board) mandates that reforms be effective even in the face of a diabolical management team. In short, Enron executives may have been sufficiently taciturn in their disclosures, presumptively arrogant in their dismissal of board concerns, and confusingly sophisticated in their presentations that the board would have needed something more to wade through the claptrap.

WHAT CODE OF ETHICS? WAIVING IT, AND WAIVING IT AGAIN AND AGAIN. The board was alerted to Mr. Fastow's involvement with the off-the-books entities because it required that Enron's code of ethics be waived in order to allow an officer to hold such a position, do business with Enron, and receive compensation for doing such business. At least twice in 1999 the board voted to waive the code of ethics (although the minutes refer to it as a suspension of the code, whatever that means) so that Mr. Fastow could play this dual role. The continued laxity in waiving the conflict-of-interest policy for Mr. Fastow so that he could operate the SPEs was critical to Enron management in its ongoing byzantine operations.

The Enron code of ethics had both a general and a specific policy on conflicts of interest. The author acquired the Enron code of ethics in an eBay auction for thirty-seven dollars. Interestingly, when the code arrived, it was still sealed, untouched by human hands. The author views this purchase from a former Enron employee as a small donation to that employee's lost retirement account, held largely in Enron stock. The general Enron ethical principle on conflicts provides as follows:

Employees of Enron Corp., its subsidiaries, and its affiliated companies (collectively the "Company") are charged with conducting their business affairs in accordance with the highest ethical standards. An employee shall not conduct himself or herself in a manner which directly or indirectly would be detrimental to the best interests of the Company or in a manner which would bring to the employee financial gain separately derived as a direct consequence of his or her employment with the company.

The provisions that apply specifically to officers provide:

The employer is entitled to expect of such person complete loyalty to the best interests of the Company. . . . Therefore, it follows that no full-time officer or employee should:

. . . (c) Own an interest in or participate, directly or indirectly, in the profits of another entity which does business with or is a competitor of the Company, unless such ownership or participation has been previously disclosed in writing to the Chairman of the Board and Chief Executive Officer of Enron Corp., and such officer has determined that such interest or participation does not adversely affect the best interests of the Company.

While the CEO could approve a waiver of the policy for everyone except himself, the waiver for Fastow was nonetheless run by the board at least three times. The board relied on a technicality and indicated that it was not waiving the code but rather simply ratifying what Ken Lay had already done. Dr. Jaedicke said that the ratification was not actually a waiver but an enforcement of the code of ethics because the code permitted the waiver in the discretion of the CEO and that the effect of the board's ratification was simply to state unequivocally that the conflicts policy and the waiver policy were valid. Dr. Jaedicke somehow misses the point that the board could have said, "No way!"

IMPROBABLE EARNINGS. Throughout the period of 1999 to 2001, the board was informed that gross revenues had doubled and tripled and that these funds were being generated by the LJM off-the-books entity that Fastow was operating. The corporate minutes do not reflect that any director questioned either the odds-defying numbers or the unconventional means of achieving them.

PUBLIC NOTICES OF TROUBLED WATERS. There were more red flags that followed after 2000. However, there was little the board could have done at this point to halt Enron's march to collapse. The board's easygoing nature with the type A financiers of Enron had given the Yeehaw boys a long tether, and they made optimal use of that tether by wrapping the board up in it. The board did miss additional red flags after 2000, but by then the horse had bolted from the barn. The leverage was so high, the failure to disclose so blatant, and the officers so freewheeling that Enron was no longer salvageable. But there are some 2000 board tidbits that are instructive for future boards on what not to do if effective governance is the goal:

- Bethany McLean's "Is Enron Overpriced?" article appears in the March 5, 2001, issue of *Fortune* magazine. The minutes for the audit committee meeting refer to the article as "prominent," but there would be no follow-up or inquiry by the board or anyone else. Only the shortsellers took the cue. They would pocket a 24 percent ROI on their bets against Enron.

- The April 2001 board meeting minutes reflect a discussion of the fact that 64 percent of the company's international assets were "troubled" or "not performing." Prior meetings had characterized the situation as one in which 67 percent of the company's assets were "underperforming." That figure translated to a $2.3 billion overstatement of assets on the company's balance sheet.

- The summer of 2001 saw Enron's rapid unraveling. Despite virtual disintegration before its eyes, board members remained sullen and mute. The board was informed that Andrew Fastow had transferred his interest in one of the many off-the-books entities (LJM) to another Enron employee, Michael Kopper, because Fastow's ownership demanded greater SEC disclosure. The board was also informed of the existence of the

Jedi and Chewco partnerships. If the creation of so many entities and the waiver of the code were not red flags, then surely the continuing transfer of assets among employees in an international shell game involving SPEs with goofy names should have piqued one or two of the directors' mildest curiosity.

- Even the sudden resignation of CEO Jeffrey Skilling and the whistle-blower letter from executive vice president Sherron Watkins did not move the board to action. Indeed, the law firm it hired to investigate the allegations concluded that there was nothing there. Prescient in terms of assets, but dead wrong on misconduct by the officers.

Lax Processes

Administrative issues plagued this board as well, those pesky issues of attendance, participation, rotation, and procedures. Audit committee member Ronnie C. Chan missed more than a quarter of Enron board and committee meetings in 1996, 1997, and 2000. By remaining in his slot for over a decade, Dean Robert K. Jaedicke, professor emeritus at Stanford and its former dean, violated one of the best standards for corporate governance: rotation of audit committee members and chairs. However, Dr. Jaedike had served as chair of the Enron board's audit committee since 1985. Half of the audit committee members were from outside the United States, a goal Mr. Lay expressed as important so that Enron had input from those who worked and lived in the international community. But international directors bring along with their expertise a set of administrative problems. The first is the one of attendance. International members of boards of U.S. companies have lower attendance rates for both board and committee meetings. The second problem is that there are significant differences in financial-reporting transparency and audit standards in other countries. In all likelihood, their disclosure standards are far lower because the United States has always dragged the rest of the world, kicking and screaming, into transparent financial reporting and governance. What to us is mandatory disclosure is to many from outside the United States more information than anyone needs to know.

Even when the board was involved in approving transactions, its process was not at a level necessary for the degree of complexity involved. At the first board meeting on the LJM1 partnership, the board approved the conflicts waiver, authorized a major stock split for Enron, voted to increase the number of shares for employees in the company's stock compensation program, approved the purchase of a new corporate jet, authorized an investment in a Middle Eastern power plant, discussed a reorganization/restructuring at Enron that Mr. Lay had planned, and approved the LJM1 creation. And all before lunch! All on the phone, and all just two days before the end of the quarter! The minutes show that the meeting lasted one hour, that there was little discussion or debate, and that the directors had had access to the information on LJM for only three days prior to the meeting.

Omissions and Oversight

Enron board members remained defiantly insistent on their ignorance, right through the congressional hearings on Enron. Norman P. Blake, John H. Duncan, Herbert S. Winkour, Dr. Robert K. Jaedicke, and Dr. Charles A. LeMaistre all testified before the committee. Mr. Winkour, who chaired the Enron finance committee, said, "We cannot, I submit, be criticized for failing to address or remedy problems that have been concealed from us." Their claim runs counter to the board minutes. It is perhaps impossible to know what the directors really understood about Enron's situation. But it is clear that the board had given fairly wide latitude and carte blanche supervisory controls to a financially sophisticated team of managers.

One simple safety tip for boards, even those with a Beelzebub management team: hold the officers to the code of ethics. Had the Enron directors simply honored the company's own code of ethics, the entire byzantine empire of film-named SPEs could have been nipped in the bud. Further, another simple safety tip for directors everywhere: read the 10-K and the appendixes before you sign. All the Enron directors were required to sign 10-K filings, and in 1999 and 2000 nearly three thousand separate entities were listed, including some six hundred with the same PO box address in the Cayman Islands. That's a bit of a heads-up if one can presume that directors of public companies really do read the 10-Ks before signing them. However, yet again, if the directors were not furnished with the appendixes to the 10-K, not an uncommon practice, they might not have been aware of the increasing numbers and the Cayman concentration. A safety tip for all directors of publicly held companies: check the appendixes.

Deference

There were moments when the Enron board perhaps realized that there were issues in and among Fastow and his Jurassic SPEs. In October 1999, when Fastow, Skilling, and Lay requested additional approvals for LJM2 and more waivers, the finance committee held what was described as a "vigorous discussion." None of the members ever read the private-placement memoranda for the LJM SPE series. Therein lies another safety tip for directors: read the documents for the companies you are authorizing and then doing business with. In fact, one board member received information on the LJM2 series as a potential investor but confessed that he tossed it before even reading it. Fastow clearly understood the rubes he had under his thumb. Prior to the October board meeting in which LJM2 was approved, Fastow had already engaged Merrill Lynch to market the LJM2 partnerships. Merrill Lynch would later pay a heavy price for its involvement in these private placements.

The board continued to exact additional requirements with each additional SPE approval, but those requirements involved approval by the very executives who were responsible for coming up with the complex structure designed to conceal the company's true financial picture. The board put the foxes in charge of the henhouse. By the time the board faced a third series of LJM partnerships, it had assurances that all Enron and LJM transactions would be approved by Richard Causey, Enron's former chief accounting officer, as well as Skilling. Both were indicted on federal felony charges; Causey entered a guilty plea and Skilling's trial was ongoing in May 2006. The audit committee also mandated an annual review of all of the transactions among and, as we now know, in between the firms, but Enron collapsed before the first annual review. There's that horse-out-of-the-barn problem. Also, no director was struck then or when interviewed by the congressional staff members by the sheer magnitude of the off-the-books deals. In a 1999 report on one series of transactions, the first of the LJMs, the board learned that LJM had generated $200 million in earnings in eight days and had an internal rate of return of 18 percent. All in all, not bad work and, once again, no heavy lifting.

As noted in Chapter 3, at one point Fastow's compensation became an issue, and the way the Enron board dropped the ball on its inquiries there indicates its obsequious nature. When the onetime review of Fastow's compensation was announced as a precondition for approval of future SPEs, Dr. LeMaistre, as head of the compensation committee, requested information on Fastow's and all 16(b) officers' compensation from Mary Joyce, Enron's senior compensation officer. As noted earlier, nothing happened. Under even the most hands-off approach to corporate governance, it is tough to imagine a more satirical situation. Understanding the fearful task ahead, of actually confronting the CFO of a company on whose board they sit, these two directors asked legal counsel for Enron to draft a set of questions they could take with them to meet Mr. Fastow. Herewith, an excerpt from the script:

> We very much appreciate your willingness to visit with us. Andy, because of the current controversy surrounding LJM I and LJM II, we believe it would be helpful for the Board to have a general understanding of the amount of your investment and of your return on investment in the LJM entities. We understand that a detailed accounting of these matters will be done in connection with the response to the SEC inquiry. In responding to our questions with respect to your interest in the LJM entities, we would appreciate your including

any interest . . . that the members of your family may have had in the entities.

The directors did get some information from Mr. Fastow, including the fact that he had made $43 million from LJM Series 1 and 2, but Fastow never did respond to their request for more information on his ROI or return their follow-up phone calls. When Mr. Fastow was asked by Dr. LeMaistre and Mr. Duncan whether any other Enron employees were involved in financial relationships and transactions with the company, he responded that there were not. The Powers investigation, commissioned by the Enron board that could not get answers and after it was all too late, found that Fastow and other employees had created the Southampton partnership, a deal that landed them significant profits from the company that paid their salaries. They had pumped in $5,800 and received $1 million in immediate returns. Not bad work if you can get it in a company with fear, silence, and a scaredy-cat board.

WorldCom: Bernie's Board

WorldCom had its own brand of a Yeehaw board. While it did not fall for off-the-books partnerships, there were loans to an overextended CEO, and plenty of personal benefits and deference.

Composition of the Board

The board at WorldCom was often referred to as "Bernie's Board." Carl Aycock had been a member of the board since 1983, when the original company was founded. Max Bobbitt and Francesco Galesi, who were friends of Ebbers, joined the board in 1992. And one board member, Stiles A. Kellett Jr., an original board member and friend of Ebbers from the early motel-meeting days when the four created the company that would become WorldCom, resigned in October 2002 after revelations about his extensive use of the company jet. All of these directors went from hardscrabble backgrounds to millionaire status because of their affiliation with Bernie, and they were beholden to him. A former board member, Mike Lewis, said few board members would disagree with Ebbers: "Rule No. 1: Don't bet against Bernie. Rule No. 2: See Rule No.1." Their roots back to the company meetings at the Western Sizzlin' Steakhouse in Hattiesburg, Mississippi, created a bond of devotion, secrecy, and mutual assistance, even when it was at the company's expense.

Three of the board members, not counting Bernie, were insiders, and four had been with Ebbers from the very beginning of WorldCom. Scott Sullivan was a member of the board, the CFO, and also the secretary of the corporation. There were interlocking directors, directors who were also directors of subsidiaries, and, in effect, a tightly woven web of insiders on the board. For example, Digex was WorldCom's website company, and WorldCom owned 61.4 percent of its stock. And directors served on the boards of both.

As compensation went, WorldCom's board was not a generous benefactor. The (outside) directors were paid $35,000 per year, $750 per board or committee meeting, and $1,000 for committee meetings not held on the same day as the board meeting. The chart below shows the members of the board and their affiliation as well as their stock holdings. Many of the directors held extensive interests in WorldCom—an investment that may have clouded their judgment on decisions about the extensive loans to Bernie.

Board Member	Background	# shares held (WorldCom)
James C. Allen	Investment director, Meritage Private Equity Fund; came on the board in 1998 with WorldCom merger with Brooks Fiber Properties, where he was CEO and chairman	412,749
Judith Areen	Dean, Georgetown Law Center since 1989; professor since 1976	113,849
Carl J. Aycock	Director since 1983, officer of WorldCom until 1995; CFO of Ebbers's motel corporation until 1992	972,875
Ronald R. Beaumont	COO, WorldCom; WorldCom officer since 1996; director of Digex	2,063,798
Max E. Bobbitt	Former CEO, Asian American Telecommunications; telecom consultant	433,749
Bernard J. Ebbers	President, CEO; director of Digex; director since 1983	26,946,871
Francesco Galesi	Chair, Galesi Group; real estate, oil, telecom	1,800,393

Stiles A. Kellett Jr.	CEO Kellett Investment	6,120,361
Gordon S. Macklin	President, NASD, 1970–87; chair, Hambrecht & Quist, 1987–92; director, Franklin Templeton Funds	224,387
Bert C. Roberts Jr.	Former chair, CEO, MCI; director of Digex	1,705,968
John W. Sidgmore	Director, vice chair since 1996; COO 1996–98; CEO, UUNET Technologies until 1996; director, MicroStrategy	5,534,544
Scott D. Sullivan	CFO, treasurer, secretary; director of Digex	3,264,438
All directors and current executive officers		49,593,982 or 1.7 percent

While many governance experts argue for share ownership as a means of ensuring board accountability, such a facile rule opens another door to abuse. The share ownership may be so significant that the directors do nothing that will jeopardize the value of their shares. But the WorldCom board had other problems.

Conflicts

When Ebbers was removed as CEO and a new board took over, Dick Thornburgh, the former Pennsylvania governor and U.S. attorney general, was hired to study what went wrong at WorldCom, including with the board. The final Thornburgh report concluded that the board had abdicated its responsibilities in terms of compensation oversight in approving significant loans to Ebbers without complete documentation and, in some cases, without even signatures. By the time the board really took charge, it found that the loans to Ebbers totaled in excess of $415 million. Ebbers had used his WorldCom stock to secure loans for his many business and personal ventures. When the loans came due, he was unable to pay and either he or his creditors had to dump the WorldCom stock that had been pledged as security to repay the loans. Ebbers had also pledged a total of about $1 billion in WorldCom stock to his creditors for loans. WorldCom stock was doubly collateralized. The sale of such large blocks of stock would have sent the price of WorldCom stock plummeting. So, the board advanced or loaned Ebbers more money, taking the same shares as security for the loan, thus putting WorldCom in a secondary position to Ebbers's personal creditors. WorldCom directors had agreed to take a subordinated security interest in stock that had already been pledged, placing it well at the end of the line of creditors. The whole loan scheme presumed that World-Com's stock price would remain the same. And the scheme thereby created incentives for Ebbers and the board to keep that stock price up there, largely with inflated earnings and deflated expenses.

The assumption about Ebbers's ability to repay the loans or the stock was not a good one. By 2001, when WorldCom's stock price began to drop, Ebbers's net worth had slipped to $295 million, $286.6 of which was World-Com stock. Ebbers was not the shrewdest of souls in terms of his personal investments because their whopping worth consisted of the remaining $8.4 million. With WorldCom's share price dropping, the board had climbed into a bottomless pit, but the loans continued from 2000 through 2002. Further, as the stock ownership chart shows, the board's significant holdings in World-Com found self-preservation instincts kicking in to stabilize the stock price. This is one downside to the corporate-governance experts' recommendation that director share ownership ensures good governance. Sometimes the concept backfires with a conflict.

Missing Red Flags

A continuing theme and new safety tip for boards emerges from looking at WorldCom: when employees file suit against the company, check into the allegations they make in their suits, particularly those that center on accounting improprieties. In a class-action suit filed in 2001, WorldCom employees provided affidavits that WorldCom was "understating costs, hiding bad debt, backdating contracts to book orders earlier than accounting rules allow." Some examples included receivables that were over seven years old and significant delays in paying suppliers in order to increase net profit figures. The 113-page suit was filed in federal district court in Jackson, Mississippi. The board was aware of the suit, but when it was dismissed, so too were the allegations. The board did nothing to investigate the charges despite the fact that the complaint had attached to it a hundred interviews with former WorldCom employees, striking in their detail. In hindsight we now know that the employees were spot-on in their analysis and assertions.

Deference

The board deferred to Ebbers, who had been the company's only CEO for all nineteen years WorldCom had existed. The board could not bring itself to terminate Bernie even though the company's shares were tumbling as fast as its accounting issues were growing. Ebbers's removal came only after the value of the company's stock had declined by 82 percent in 2002, to $2.50 per share, down from the $60-plus prices in 1999. Before the bankruptcy, WorldCom would finish its run at 83 cents per share. Ebbers was reportedly stunned that Bobbitt and Kellett, two longtime friends who were on the board thanks to Bernie, delivered his termination notice over the phone as he was working at WorldCom headquarters.

Ebbers had been given full authority by the board on all matters. In 2000 the compensation committee was concerned about a talent drain to the dot-coms. That is, there was concern that key executives might be lured away by the promise of stock options in the dot-com/telecom bubble. The key executive retention program was born. The key to the key executive retention program was that the compensation committee (the board never approved the plan) turned over to Ebbers full discretion to determine who was covered and how much they were given. As it turns out, Ebbers and CFO Sullivan were the only key executives in Ebbers's mind. Each received a retention bonus of $10 million in 2000. Those bonuses now must be returned.

Even Ebbers's departure characterized his relationship with the board. His severance package included $1.5 million per year for the rest of his life, thirty hours of use per annum of the company jet (which may not be much of a perk, given the travel restrictions at Club Fed), full medical and life insurance coverage, and consulting fees.

Lax Processes

The WorldCom board was not a crackerjack one in terms of basic governance processes. The compensation committee, headed by Stiles Kellett, approved the loans to Ebbers, but the loans were not taken before the full board because legal counsel for WorldCom indicated that full board approval was not necessary. Two board meetings went by after the Ebbers loans were approved before the board was informed of them. The board then approved them without requesting any advice from WorldCom's general counsel.

In March 2002 the SEC announced that it was probing the accounting and finances of both WorldCom and Qwest, two of the country's telecommunications giants. Running parallel to the SEC investigation was an internal investigation by WorldCom's internal audit group, headed by Cynthia Cooper. Running parallel to both the SEC investigation and the internal audit review (something Cooper notified the audit committee about) was the board's discovery of the extent of the Ebbers loans and his resulting ouster as CEO.

Cooper arranged to meet with Max Bobbitt, the head of the board's audit committee, secretly at a local Hampton Inn so that there would be no repercussions for her or her staff as they completed their work. When the head of internal audit indicates that there are problems, meetings at local motels are perhaps not a best practice for an audit committee. A meeting was perhaps in order. But lax processes did not allow this board to respond to alarms.

In the summer of 2002 John Sidgmore, the interim CEO, made the rounds of the television talk shows to discuss the WorldCom board and how it could have made so many loans. When he was confronted about board approval, his legalistic and somewhat weaselly response was that the board did not approve the loans, the board ratified the loans. Small wonder such folks could not rein in Bernie or draw lines on those loans. Legalistic interpretations don't change the conflicts created by the board's laxity, deference, and conflicts.

Tyco: Acquiring Directors with Little to Say

Tyco's board is a perfect study in weakness. The clear consensus of outside evaluators is that the board members were far too "unquestioning" of Mr. Kozlowski. One expert referred to the board as "asleep at the switch" because "the stock price was up. The profits were up. No one wanted to rock the boat." The causes of no boat rocking were the same as with the other companies and boards. Round up the usual suspects on corporate-governance failures.

Composition of the Board

One business writer described the Tyco board as "an assemblage of Kozlowski associates and insiders, led by ex-CEO John Fort." In 2001 the board had the following compositional issues:

- Of the twelve board members, eight were current or former Tyco employees.

- The board's lead director, Frank Walsh, was a former Tyco employee.

- Four of the members had served at least ten years on the board, with two serving for almost twenty years.

With the exception of Wendy Lane, added in 2000, new board members came only through Tyco's acquisition of their companies. With Tyco's ethical collapse, one money manager noted that the Tyco board "poorly served the 240,000 employees and shareholders. Being a director of a corporation isn't an honorary position designed to dress up one's obituary. It is essential that we add new independent voices to the board." This board could have been called Dennis's board.

Conflicts

The Tyco board also had issues of self-dealing, disclosure, and conflicts. Tyco paid $20 million to one of its outside directors (although he was a former Tyco employee), Frank E. Walsh, and a charity he favored, for Walsh's role in brokering a deal for one of Tyco's acquisitions. The acquisition was CIT Group, and Tyco acquired it for $9.5 billion. Mr. Walsh was paid in July 2001, but the board was not told of the payment until December. Mr. Walsh was indicted and would later plead guilty to a violation of a New York statute as well as settle civil fraud charges with the SEC. He withheld information about the brokerage fee from the Tyco board. Further, he did not disclose the fee, contrary to requirements for all directors who receive compensation, on the company's SEC filings. Restitution to Tyco is part of Walsh's sentence.

Kozlowski also managed to get the board members beholden to him. Warren Musser, a director of TyCom, had borrowed $14.1 million from Mr. Kozlowski and Mr. Swartz because Musser and his wife were in financial distress. This loan was also not disclosed in the documents for either Tyco or TyCom. Michael A. Ashcroft, an international tycoon from Britain, joined the Tyco board in 1997 after the merger of his company, ADT Ltd. (an alarm and security firm). At the time he joined the board, Lord Ashcroft owned a home in Boca Raton, Florida, that he had purchased in 1990 for $2.3 million. But business acumen being what it was among the Tyco board members, Ashcroft sold the home in October 1997 to his wife for $100. Mrs. Ashcroft then sold the same home that same day for $2.5 million to Byron S. Kalogerou, a Tyco vice president at that time who was equally possessed of shrewd business qualities. When the suspicious straw-man and straw-woman transfers were first investigated by the state of New York, nothing came of it because the company explained that the house was in poor shape, purchased by Tyco, put in Kalogerou's name, fixed up at Tyco's expense, and used as an executive residence. Kalogerou was in Luxembourg on business on the day of the purchase, which leads us to the question of how Tyco was able to have its officers participate in such transactions when they were out of the country and unaware that they were taking title to houses purchased by the company. Those who live in the area indicate that Kalogerou never lived in the home and that it was paid for by Tyco. Records also reflect that ADT (another Tyco company, and since there were about three hundred acquisitions, the list was long and relatively undistinguished) paid the water bills during Lord Ashcroft's ownership and that Kozlowski paid other utility bills on the house. The investigation was reopened, following the disclosure of Kozlowski's and Tyco's difficulties. However, the board's curiosity about the housing and conflicts issues was not piqued, and it conducted no investigation of its own.

Lax Processes

Tyco subordinates did not question top executives. In turn, the board and senior executives did not challenge Kozlowski. With no contact between the board and the second-tier managers, the result was one isolated and deferential board. Mark Connolly, the director of securities regulation in New Hampshire (the former headquarters for Tyco), who conducted an investigation into Tyco's failure to disclose material financial information, noted, "How do you have a situation where hundreds of millions of dollars were taken and the board and the auditors seemingly didn't know?" Tyco settled the charges with New Hampshire through a consent decree and a settlement of $5 million. Connolly had also noted that correction required the board to resign, something that would happen eventually as the company restructured itself. Connolly referred to the board's lax supervision as "gross misconduct." Mr. Connolly also noted that "it is apparent there existed a sufficient lack of controls that, in effect, allowed such egregious activity to occur."

One investigator described his experience in looking into just the property and Kozlowski home-ownership issues as follows: "The reality is the board wasn't really functioning the way they should. They approved a lot of stuff. Now, having gone through this trauma, the company says it's conducting an internal investigation and one wonders how thorough it will be."

When the board's lack of attention to both what was happening in the company and Kozlowski's personal habits became public, shareholders rose in revolt. Before the problems with Tyco and its accounting emerged, *The New York Times* reported in June 2002 that Mr. Kozlowski was being *investigated* by the district attorney's office in Manhattan for sales-tax evasion of $1 million on $13 million in art sales over a ten-month period. Mr. Kozlowski immediately resigned from Tyco following the emergence of the report and before an indictment was handed down. The indictment was handed down the following day.

Mr. Kozlowski's indictment revealed that in order to avoid paying sales tax in New York, he shipped empty crates from New York to Tyco's headquarters in New Hampshire and then took the paintings back and forth between New York and New Hampshire so as to dupe sales-tax authorities. His indictment came just after the collapse of WorldCom, which followed on the heels of the collapse of Enron. The result was that a cloud of distrust settled over the market, with investor and shareholder perceptions that everyone was corrupt. Kozlowski's indictment affected not just Tyco's share price but the market in general. A market that was already reeling dropped 215 points in one day, and Tyco's stock fell 27 percent. One expert described the tsunami-like ripple in the market upon Kozlowski's indictment as follows: "When a CEO steps down for (alleged) tax evasion, it sends the message that all of Corporate America is crooked. It makes you think, 'Why did he do it? Is there another shoe to drop?'" The perception of corruption also hit the Tyco shareholders, who now realized that there was a bit of a problem with the company. Within two months of Mr. Kozlowski's indictment, investor groups were proposing a proxy battle to oust the board that was in place during his tenure, noting that a board that had allowed such things to occur on its watch could not be held to accountability.

Self-Dealing

As noted previously, Tyco had a key employee loan program and an infamous "relocation" program. In the case of general counsel Mark Belnick, Tyco funded his family's horrific trek from Connecticut to Manhattan despite Belnick's having been hired away from a Manhattan law firm. The executive loans moved at a fast and furious pace, with few questions asked and even fewer people certain about who signed off on what and who was responsible for signing off and who was responsible for repayment and forgiveness. Small wonder the first jury deadlocked. Tough to find embezzlement when so many people knew money was flowing—and all assumed with authorization.

In its lawsuit against Kozlowski (in which it seeks to be paid back for the spending, loans, and bonuses), the new Tyco board alleges that Kozlowski appropriated funds and that he concealed the nature of his compensation and that of the senior officers from the board and the board's compensation committee. The Tyco board also named Belnick and former CFO Mark Swartz in the suit and seeks recovery of the KELP loans from them. With two of the three now convicted and headed to prison, collection may be problematic.

Adelphia: It's All in the Family

It's not entirely clear that Adelphia really had a board of directors. Adelphia's board was a study in "we're the Rigas family and we don't care about corporate governance because we don't have to."

Composition of the Board

The Adelphia board consisted of the executive team, which, you will recall, consisted of John Rigas and his two sons. To balance things out, however, daughter Ellen Rigas's husband, Peter Venetis, was added to the board, as, one presumes, the token brother-in-law/son-in-law/outsider. There were four outsiders on the board. However, the Rigas family controlled a sufficient number of shares that they could choose those board members. So much for the theory of shareholders nominating directors in order to bolster corporate governance. Naturally, an insider and a son, Timothy Rigas, chaired the Adelphia audit committee.

Loans and Self-Dealing, Again

As one expert has explained, Adelphia was just "plain-vanilla-old-fashioned self-dealing." Wayne Carlin, the regional director for the SEC's northeast division said, "The thing that makes this case stand out is the scope and magnitude of the looting of the company on the part of the Rigas family. In terms of brazenness and the sheer amount of dollars yanked out of this public company and yanked out of the pockets of investors, it's really quite stunning. It's even stunning to someone like me who is in the business of unraveling these kinds of schemes." Another expert called it is a classic "personal piggy bank" case.

Nobody was really clear about who owned what between Adelphia and the Rigas family. Companies that were acquired by Adelphia often ended up in the hands of Rigas family members because the lines were so blurred between corporate and personal property. So blatant was the commingling of personal and corporate funds that the local tax collector provided records showing that Adelphia paid its real estate taxes and those for all of the Rigas families and their twelve homes with one check. Adelphia also paid $12.8 million for the construction of a golf course owned by the Rigas family.

And then there were the loans to the Rigas family members. The total amount for the loans climbed to $2.3 billion because the amounts were concealed ever so artfully in Enronesque fashion in off-the-books entities. Once again, the loans were necessary to cover either the personal business ventures of the family or to help them purchase a sufficient number of shares to ensure their ownership stake and control of the company. The endless and vicious cycle continued. To avoid calls on their loans and hence the stock, they had to keep lending more money, or the Rigases' sale of their stock would send the price dropping with even more grave results for the heavily leveraged company and family. This part of the story was like the WorldCom Ebbers loans, except done far more easily with family members on the board. When an analyst revealed that he had uncovered at least $1 billion in off-the-books debts for which Adelphia had exposure, the company and this ne'er-do-well board were forced to file an 8-K making disclosure about the debt (over twice the amount the analyst had spotted).

The Antidotes for a Weak Board: Making Things Better Beyond Sarbanes-Oxley Mandates and the Facile Ideas of Corporate-Governance Gurus

These boards, which should have been a line of defense against the other factors (numbers pressure, fear and silence, sycophancy), proved too weak to stand as the checks and balances for cultures that were galloping toward the slippery slope of collapse.

Antidote #1 for a Weak Board: Get Yourself a Strong Board

Ah, easier said than done! Perhaps, but surely these case studies provide guidance on what we *don't* want in board members if we expect them to have the backbone, experience, and expertise to stand up to the iconic CEO and behave proactively in getting both performance and information from officers and employees. With only a few exceptions, we should perhaps conclude that family may not offer the sort of chirping dissent we need from board members. Exceptions arise here and there, but for the most part, the family board is dysfunctional—and like Tolstoy's unhappy family, in many ways. So, herewith are some suggestions on how to be sure the company has a board with backbone.

Dig Deeper on Conflicts

The statutory restrictions on conflicts of interest and disclosure address only directors' relationships with the company (consulting and compensation) or with employees at the company (whether the company employs any relatives included under the SEC standard). However, there are other types of very real conflicts that have emerged from the study of these companies to tell us that checking more thoroughly can reveal that a director is not truly independent. The Enron officers had a friend on their board in Dr. Mendelsohn because his center was beholden to the company and the Lays for donations. Charitable-organization interrelationships are a conflict that does not emerge in the standard statutory checklist but is very real nonetheless.

Conflicts can arise from intense friendships and interrelationships of dependency among CEOs who are hoping, as they serve on one another's boards, for favorable treatment and a heap of complacency. The NYSE board was a study in unperceived conflicts, on the part of the participants as well as on the part of those in the market. CEOs whose companies were regulated by Chairman Grasso served on the committee that established his compensation. Small wonder that Grasso's compensation totaled $130 million for the period from 2000 to 2002, despite the Exchange's lackluster performance during an economic downturn from the burst dot-com bubble, the post-9/11 economic setbacks, and a series of scandals that saw investors move their funds away from the stock market. His pay surpassed even the highest-paid CEO on the board, by $55 million.

The story of Citigroup, AT&T, and Jack Grubman provides a fascinating look at how silly the reasons for the back-scratching turn out to be. Grubman, telecom's star analyst and a true cheerleader for WorldCom right down to the collapse, had another encounter with two CEOs that reveals both his willingness to do whatever it takes and the bizarre symbiosis that occurs among board members who are interconnected.

Grubman, the father of twins, wanted to see them admitted to one of Manhattan's most prestigious preschools—the 92nd Street Y. He sent the following memo to Sanford Weill, the chairman of Citigroup:

> On another matter, as I alluded to you the other day, we are going through the ridiculous but necessary process of pre-school applications in Manhattan. For someone who grew up in a household with a father making $8,000 a year and for someone who attended public schools, I do find this process a bit strange, but there are no bounds for what you do for your children.
>
> Anything, anything you could do Sandy would be greatly appreciated. As I mentioned, I will keep you posted on the progress with AT&T which I think is going well.
>
> Thank you.

Citigroup pledged $1 million to the school at about the same time Grubman's children were admitted. In exchange, Weill asked Grubman to "take a fresh look" at AT&T, a major corporate client of Citigroup and on whose board Weill served even as AT&T's CEO, C. Michael Armstrong, served on Citigroup's board. Weill was counting on Mr. Armstrong's support in ousting John Reed as co-CEO of Citigroup. Weill and Armstrong succeeded in their mutual collaboration for ouster, and Grubman, crowing, sent the following e-mail to Carol Cutler, another New York analyst, to bring the preschool admissions full circle with market analysis and battles for board control:

> I used Sandy to get my kids in the 92nd Street Y pre-school (which is harder than Harvard) and Sandy needed Armstrong's vote on our board to nuke Reed in showdown. Once the coast was clear for both of us (ie Sandy clear victor and my kids confirmed) I went back to my normal self on AT&T.

Grubman upgraded AT&T from a "hold" to a "strong buy" during the Weill preschool-favor period. After Reed was ousted, Grubman downgraded AT&T again. Grubman said that he sent the e-mail "in an effort to inflate my professional importance."

There is also the problem of directors' doing business with officers (Health-South) or even (HealthSouth again) with the CEO's wife. There may be loans between officers and directors. There may also just be a lifetime relationship that any director would find difficult to lose through disagreement or, perhaps, ouster, as was the case with Bernie Ebbers and the WorldCom board. There are no SEC mandates on disclosure for these types of more intricate relationships, so we are forced to explore further. A checklist for digging deeper on conflicts with directors follows:

- Mutual charities between directors and officers

- Mutual organizations, activities, fund-raisers

- Other boards and their service there

- Business partners, business entities that involve officers, their spouses, children, and others who are closely connected with the officers

- History of donations—to whom, to what

The search is for relationships that could spring into a back-scratching arrangement—interconnections do not always involve pure business transactions and mazes that may not always emerge under regulatory disclosure standards. When grappling with multimillion-dollar deals, regulatory materiality standards that cause statutory disclosures to kick in are bare-bones standards. Human nature is such that conflicts could arise long before the threshold levels for accountants and regulators are reached. For example, Coca-Cola is reeling from accounting questions, the Frozen Cake false marketing study, and other issues such as flat sales that perhaps led to the first two problems. Warren Buffett, the oracle of Omaha, was a member of Coke's board until 2006, and most shareholders took great comfort in Buffett's presence there. But units of Buffett's Berkshire Hathaway did $185 million in business with Coke, and the amount of business has been creeping up slowly to the "1 percent of revenues" standard that Coke uses for disclosure that a director is no longer independent. That amount of business is nothing to sneeze at for Coke or Buffett's company, but it does fly below the statutory disclosure radar. The two are intertwined, and what Coke decides to do on fountain sales and distribution affects profoundly Buffett's costs of operation. Even Buffett himself has acknowledged that the board of Coke has not performed as it should. Too many scandals, too little oversight, and a management team that was headed down a path of ethical collapse. As noted earlier, Coke has been making changes and still has time to reverse some of the trends and pull itself back. There has been progress but there remains that tall order of introspection that perhaps means a pullback from these cozy relationships that exist, but exist legally and well within nondisclosure standards. The question remains as to whether the directors can be sufficiently critical of themselves to change their own culture even as the new management team at the company implements changes and leads Coke out and away from the mires of illegal and unethical conduct. Interestingly, a new executive of Coke has invited me to speak at a company event. Takes guts and a new mind-set to have a blunt ethics professor in for her thoughts.

Don't Fall for the Governance Myths on the Ideal Director and Find the Real Thing

If we were to follow corporate-governance suggestions for the ideal director, the qualifications and limitations would be as follows:

- Must own stock in the company

- Cannot serve for longer than ten years

- Must retire at age seventy

- Must be nominated by shareholders

These tests are perfunctory and far too facile to ensure the depth and independence that make for good directors. The case studies show that most of the board members met these requirements, and it was still not enough. The in-vogue suggestion that directors be nominated by shareholders means that majority shareholders, as in the case of the Rigas family and Adelphia, would have the control of the board anyway.

Likewise, there is the business perspective on the ideal board composition, in terms of background:

- A director with political clout, that is, access to government officials for purposes of company issues. Look at the performance of mutual funds with directors such as Lynne Cheney (spouse of Vice President Dick Cheney), former senator Alan Simpson, and Wendy Gramm (wife of former Senator Phil Gramm and former Enron director). They walked away with six-figure fees in exchange for "political clout," and investors lost capital in the double-digit range.

- A director from academia for independence and credibility (Dean Jaedicke of Stanford failed miserably as an Enron director)

- A director who is a partner or of-counsel with the company's outside legal firm (the beholden nature of the relationship compromises independence)

- A director who is a principal in a company that is a major customer (conflicts)

- A director who is a principal in a company that is a major supplier (conflicts)

- A director who is affiliated with the company's financial resources (bank, underwriter, etc.) (conflicts)

The second list of an ideal board is about as likely to produce independent oversight as the standards established by corporate-governance experts. Perhaps the reason for so many fundamental failures in corporate governance is that businesses, governance experts, and regulators are not focusing on the key characteristics that produce a good director who is competent, independent, and forthright.

The ideal qualifications for a director are:

- No financial ties in terms of contracts, consulting, or business arrangements with the company, its parent, or any subsidiaries

- Competence through experience, financial knowledge, industry expertise, or work in the company's products, services, or niche

- Sufficient time to devote to being a director, beyond just the meeting attendance. The professional director always attends meetings because they are his or her livelihood. However, there is little likelihood that such a director will spend time at the company or find a way to interact with employees. Professional directors are on recruiters' lists and carry impressive credentials, but independent and competent board performance is different from the ability to run in the public-company-board circles.

- Not dependent upon board retainers and fees. The ability to walk away from the compensation paid is a critical component in director independence. It was unlikely that an Enron director would have threatened resignation if, for example, management did not cough up the information on Andrew Fastow's compensation because taking an almost $400,000 reduction in income in one fell swoop is a tough hit. And the amount paid to a director need not reach those levels to constitute a significant portion of the director's income. For example, many boards have retired community and business leaders. Walking away from that extra $35,000 per year may be tough for them to do on their limited incomes with no other earnings potential. In seeking out good board members, a financial-independence assessment becomes critical because need affects the ability of directors to challenge management.

- Unimpeachable integrity. Boards need directors who have walked away from opportunities because those opportunities either pushed the envelope in terms of legality or actually were illegal. Perhaps there is some mixture of leadership in this requirement, but the single most important qualification for any board member is the ability to question management and say no when warranted. I would offer an example of a board member who has walked away, but these events are few and far between and Walter Miller, the Marriott director who quit rather than spin off the bondholders from the assets, is the only example I can find of the level of fortitude needed. In all the stories of all these companies, word from one of the directors could have halted the continuing descent of their companies. Such ethical gumption is rare but is indeed the force upon which we are dependent and upon which all governance should hang.

When all the best practices and governance standards are drafted and all the statutory constraints put into place, we remain dependent upon individual integrity and ethical courage, an ability to say no to management. When GE completely revamped its board in 2002, just prior to the effective date for Sarbanes-Oxley reforms, it went beyond the statutory requirements and required those directors who did business with the company to step down. It stopped its practice of awarding stock options to directors. It also moved to a greater majority of outside directors. Still, an expert noted that just restructuring was unlikely to produce the change GE was looking for in terms of getting the company, reeling from its accounting issues, back on track. GE's stock price had tumbled at that time about 34 percent because of earnings restatements issued by CEO Jeff Immelt. Structural change in the board cannot, in and of itself, ensure that a company's culture will be restored or maintained. But a board lacking in members with integrity, independence, and a respect for process facilitates a culture of ethical collapse. Ultimately, the board's efficacy depends upon individual ethical courage, and the board's composition and example can set the tone for the rest of the organization. (See Chapter 2 antidotes for more details.)

Solomon Asch's work on what is now called "groupthink" offers some insights into what we should be looking for in the ideal board member. The Asch studies involved groups of ten students (the studies were originally done at Swarthmore), nine of whom were instructed in advance to make a choice regarding the length of a line that was obviously wrong, i.e., they were to state that the longest line was the shortest line. A tenth person was then brought in to participate in the exercise, with the tenth student being asked to respond after the nine so-called confederates had made their (incorrect) choice. Despite the correct answer being obvious and the answers of the first nine students being obviously wrong, 74 percent of the number ten subjects would go along with the choices of the other nine and pick the incorrect line. The subjects in the Asch experiments ignored an obviously correct answer and picked an incorrect answer despite overwhelming evidence to the contrary. They conformed to the behavior of the nine people who preceded them and made incorrect choices.

When I was working with a board of a nonprofit organization that had been forced to terminate its CEO following an ugly series of events including personal issues (affairs and divorce, again), loans, and questions about the awarding of company contracts, the board members felt they had ignored their gut as these events were laid before them. Their collective gut had told them that lending money to the CEO was a bad idea, but they all went along. When I asked why, one of them explained, "Because it's hard to sit in a room and disagree with people you respect who think it's okay." I pointed out that they had summarized effective corporate governance in one sentence: being able to sit in a room of gifted and bright people and raise questions about troubling issues that no one else sees or is willing to raise is the single most important talent a director must have. Groupthink overpowers that gut that every director, investor, and employee should trust.

The director who had made this point about the challenges and pressures of confrontation then added, "You're asking us to do something that human nature wants to avoid." Exactly. The detailed look at these companies and the list of questions for directors to ask that are presented in this antidote demonstrate that the ethical and legal lapses of these companies and their boards' complicity were not masked, nuanced, or in the infamous gray areas. However, no one on the board raised the obvious points or confronted officers with the difficult questions. Finding directors who have that ability is critical. Fortunately, the Asch studies offer guidance on how to find such a director. The bright side of the Asch studies is that 26 percent of the subjects were willing to state the obvious in a room when nine others disagreed with them. What were the 26 percent like? They exhibited independence, leadership skills, and a strong dedication to data and the discernment of facts. For example, some would postpone their answer as they asked for a ruler to collect more data. This antidote is a means of helping the 26 percent collect more data in a board setting—raise the questions and not commit to more ratifications, approvals, or actions until that data is forthcoming. Imagine if one member of the Enron board had said, "No more SPEs until Fastow comes clean with the compensation figures." The role of effective director is not so much one of confrontation as one of a detached viewer seeking objective data. Management may not have a complete set, so the effective board member and leader waits for that information. An even more effective leader insists upon it. And a great board member sets up an investigation to find it until the puzzle has all of its pieces and is framed properly for resolution. Perhaps effective directors could be obtained if we took those who meet the measurable standards listed and then trained them in the drawbacks of groupthink and the dynamics and resolutions that emerged in the Asch studies.

Among the companies studied here for having ineffectual boards, there has been some change. For example, as of the proxy filed in January 2003, all of the Tyco board members who held their positions during the Kozlowski years have left. The new Tyco board is striking in its depth, and its proxy is also an eye-catcher for its candor about past events as well as its goals and mission for the company as it goes forward. In short, there's some good folk running this company now. The board at Saks Fifth Avenue not only terminated the officers responsible for the accounting problems related to vendor chargebacks, it reopened its own investigation when word reached it that there was more to the problem than initially thought. If all boards could take their leads, we might prevent future ethical implosions.

Antidote #2 for a Weak Board: Get Information from Employees

Even with the best directors, a board cannot change a Yeehaw Culture or prevent its rise if the information about what is really going on in the company does not make its way to the directors. Because management serves as a filter for bad news, particularly in a Yeehaw Culture, the board needs access to employees and employees need access to the board, either directly or indirectly, to serve as conduits for the flow of information. Once again, the adage from the antidote to fear and silence: the collective wisdom of employees always exceeds the collective wisdom of management. And if a board is looking for truth in terms of what is really happening, it needs those employees.

In all companies that collapse ethically, and certainly in the companies that have been studied here, there were always employees who (1) saw the legal or ethical problems and (2) could not find anyone within the company who would listen to them, or if they did find someone, were then terminated, demoted, or just generally run out of the company. For example, Michael "Junior" Vines was a thirty-year-old bookkeeper at HealthSouth who was earning $39,000. Based on the knowledge he had gained in a few accounting courses at the local community college, he detected fraud in HealthSouth's financial processes and records. He raised his concerns to supervisors and others in the company. He even sent a note to Ernst & Young describing a specific example of accounting fraud. E&Y apparently reached the opposite conclusion because it continued to certify HealthSouth's financial statements. Junior then posted his concerns on a website: "What I know about the accounting at HRC will be the blow that will bring HRC to its knees. . . . What is going on at HRC . . . if discovered by the right people will bring change to the accounting department at HRC if not the entire company."

Perhaps it was the tendency to discount bloggers on the Web. Perhaps the moniker "Junior Vines" made it seem as if a Bill Cosby character was raising the flag on accounting impropriety with a resulting discount in veracity. But this employee had precise intelligence that should have given pause. What happened with the information? Either it did not make its way to the board or the board was nonresponsive; in this case, the latter seems more likely.

Even in Yeehaw Cultures, the issue is not one of training employees to spot the ethical issues. The fix lies in what the board does with the information it receives. The board must have the following steps in place to prevent a Junior Vines from slipping through the cracks or being suppressed by the operatives in the culture:

- There must be some form of anonymous reporting, from a hotline to telling employees to drop the board a line. Some boards have boxes or mail addresses that encourage employees to write directly to them. That reassurance of a management bypass is critical for employees suffering in a Yeehaw Culture.

- The board, or at least the audit committee, must review every employee concern. Most boards will find that about 90 percent of what comes through will be complaints of resentment related to evaluations, pay raises, and promotions or is information that is just plain wrong. However, the board trying to change or prevent a Yeehaw Culture lives for the 10 percent. There's gold in those anonymous tips. Too many boards rely on the management filter for the anonymous feedback. When management is the problem, such an approach means that the board can never know what is really happening. Don't give management the opportunity to screen. Further, some anonymous complaints or disclosures may seem innocuous when first reported. The board can spot patterns. For example, if management has started down the path of manipulating results, it may begin with one shipment questioned by an employee. The board can follow up on the timing of the shipment and its reporting as revenue, but it can also investigate further to see if there is a pattern. Just the fact that the board is looking into shipment timing and the booking of revenue can halt the march to fabrication that so many of these companies engaged in as they tried to meet the numbers. A tip by an employee on the first time managers cross a line can set the wheels in motion to prevent fraud.

- The board must be certain that it takes action on every legitimate employee concern. For example, in the case of ethically collapsed international giant Parmalat, for its $5 billion overstatement of assets, both union officials and managers were raising questions about the opaque nature of the company's finances for at least two years prior to its collapse. Those questions were dismissed by the board. Because the questions were raised publicly and the board took no action, either with an explanation of those finances or with an investigation into them, there was no way an employee within the company would come forward. They saw the board's unresponsiveness. Employees must see follow-through and change for a good culture to continue and a bad culture to self-correct. The allegation or complaint is investigated and, if appropriate, disciplinary action and change implemented. Likewise, taking negative action against employees who raise legitimate issues and concerns means that the Yeehaw Culture has taken hold and that many more issues will arise without the board's knowledge because employees' fear trumps their desire to disclose ethical lapses by managers and officers.

Antidote #3 for a Weak Board: Challenge Officers, Managers, and Their Claimed Results

To paraphrase Brookings Institute scholar Martin Mayer's take on astronomical numbers that defy explanation, "This would be like your child coming home one day and saying, 'Mom, I made $1 million dollars at the lemonade stand today.' " Most parents would respond, "How on earth is that possible?" and then begin a Ward and June Cleaver–like investigation into what exactly the child was doing that day. When the results claimed by managment defy all odds, the role of the board, like the role of Ward and June, is to confront Wally and the Beaver to determine exactly what happened to achieve such phenomenal results. However, the ineffectual boards highlighted here and a host of others during the bubble that then later grappled with fraud whilst claiming, "We didn't know!" responded to management's reports of logic-defying results with a detached "Bully!" Think back through the list of illogical scenarios that boards had to buy:

- HealthSouth met earnings predictions to the penny for forty-seven quarters in a row.

- Parmalat officers claimed to hold almost $5 billion in a Bank of America account that did not exist.

- New Era Philanthropy was promising investors that it could double their money.

- All were experiencing continued double-digit growth.

- No other companies in the industry were performing at the levels they were, yet there was no distinctive feature or service that could explain such performance. For example, how could Finova, with its loans in the higher-risk lending market, not have as many write-downs as those capital lenders that were in the prime markets?

- Pick a number, any number, in the financials and there were questions—how are they achieving the margins? In Parmalat's case in an industry in which the best companies had operating margins of 7 percent, Parmalat was reporting margins of 12 percent, nearly double those of the best of the best. And the shortsellers had the right question for Enron: if these are the level of earnings, where's the cash?

Many forensic auditors argue that if managers engage in fraud and there is complicity or cooperation among the management team and employees, then there is no way to detect that fraud. However, forensic auditors, external auditors, and even internal auditors (and certainly boards) often miss fraud's clear signal: phenomenal returns, results, and performance. The question for a board that finds itself with phenomenal results is "How is this possible?" One lesson that comes from three phases of ethical collapses over as many decades is that the board should be doubly diligent when performance exceeds expectations. Know thy numbers, but know how they were begotten. The question may be posed in a way that asks management to explore what, for example, Parmalat does so differently that it is able to nearly double the operating margins of the best in the industry. When logic flees and tap dances ensue, the board has its answer. Let the internal investigations begin. The beauty of challenging information is that the board is not dependent upon officers' reports. When management cannot explain its own numbers, dig deeper into what may be the valleys of the shadows of fear and silence. There's a root cause that may or may not be fraud. If it's good news, market the ability to double margins. If it's bad news, you can self-correct and avoid the severe market penalties that accompany a fallen company in which the board is surprised by its management's misdeeds. In Parmalat's case, an investigation by the board of those margins would have led it to the hedge activities and manipulating debt into equity by managers in the company's South American divisions.

More recently, Frank Zarb has come to represent the hard-core director needed for those times when an iconic CEO has brought down the wrath of regulators and the market on the company. Zarb, who joined the AIG board in 2001, was a close personal friend of former AIG CEO Hank Greenberg. Indeed, descriptions of the AIG board put most of the members into the "friend of Hank" category. Zarb and Greenberg lunched together regularly, and Zarb was Greenberg's self-appointed successor. Greenberg had designated Zarb as his step-in should the eighty-year-old Greenberg became incapacitated. When the accounting issues surrounding finite risk policies emerged and AIG was reeling from regulatory attention and postponed financials (as well as the accompanying drop in share price), Zarb took the lead in the boardroom and demanded Greenberg's resignation. Greenberg remains livid. Zarb was correct. Zarb acted in the best interests of AIG, was able to put aside loyalty, and served the best interests of the shareholders. Zarb had a heck of a confrontation, some truly awkward personal moments, and socially challenging behavior as part of this ouster. However, AIG was in desperate need of self-correction and resolution of its accounting issues. With the iconic Greenberg in place, serious reform was not possible. Zarb did what effective directors are supposed to do, even when the cost is friendship.

Antidote # 4 for a Weak Board: Pay Attention to Perks

Speaking of operating margins, one of the clues that something was terribly awry in nearly all of these companies was that they seemed to be able to provide unbelievable perks to officers and employees alike. The presence of such perks provides a board with a baseline question: How is it that we offer perks and amenities that other companies are simply unable to afford? Perhaps the officers have an HR recruitment strategy. Perhaps there are special deals. Perhaps motivation is the reason. However, the explanation was a culture in which these companies treated company money as if it were their own and spent most of the till accordingly. Finova offered employees time for workouts and an on-the-premises exercise facility. When its sister companies were cutting expenses, Finova was planning opulent headquarters in Scottsdale, Arizona, where land is more expensive than anywhere else in the Phoenix metro area, Finova's home base. Employees at Enron enjoyed services and benefits that other companies could never afford to offer. Employees had a health club, doctor's office, subsidized Starbucks coffee, concierge, massages, and car wash on site. Workout rooms, generous retirement plans—you name it, and Enron employees had it. Charles Keating gave the employees at his American Continental headquarters a clothing allowance at an upscale store near the Arizona Biltmore so that their attire would be at a certain level of quality. Those same employees enjoyed lunch brought in from one of Phoenix's finest restaurants at no charge to them. These perks were legendary and were used as recruiting tools.

Sometimes the perks are limited to just the officers, such as Kozlowski's parties, Scrushy's jet, Sullivan's commuter jet to and from WorldCom, the Rigas family golf course and opulent Christmas festival. Sometimes the personal spending of the officers reveals motivation for the numbers drive or the beholden structure of the officer team to the CEO. Recall, for example, that Sullivan at WorldCom and Fastow at Enron were building $10 million and $11 million homes, respectively, when their companies collapsed. That addiction to the trappings of success can be revealing. There's that personal life edging its nose into the company tent. But officer spending and perks matter as directors try to keep a thumb on the pulse of the company's ethical culture. Yeehaws spend like yeehaws do on a Saturday night in town. Money flows like water. Apart from the director's duty to control that spigot, there is the additional responsibility of determining what lies beneath the spending tendencies and the lavish perks.

The simple question for a director when perks beyond description are bestowed on company employees is "How is this possible?" The beauty of this inquiry is that it is not dependent upon anything except the director's powers of observation.

Antidote #5 for a Weak Board: Walk Around

Back in the eighties, one of the management consultant/guru fads was known by the acronym MBWA, or management by walking around. The theory behind this now-faded principle of effective management was that executives stayed in their offices so much that they were unaware of what was really happening in the company, had little contact with employees, and were isolated from issues and trouble spots. This theory of management went by the wayside, succumbing to "good to great" and the pilfering of cheese and whatnot. Ironically, this out-of-vogue idea may have been one of the better management catchphrases. Sometimes there is wisdom in a management fad, particularly for effective boards. If it is true that one can feel a culture of fear and silence, just as one feels the heavy humidity of a Georgia July day, then the means for taking advantage of that source of information is to get out there in the humidity. What directors will find in bringing back the MBWA is that employees can be stunningly candid in their discussions about company problems and issues because the presence of a director among them is a signal of openness. The presence of a director also sends the signal that officers report to them because this activity demonstrates a streak of independence to employees. The director is not there to micromanage. The director is there to observe and gather information.

When I served on the board of a utility, the company was experiencing great difficulty with the level of operations of its nuclear plant, i.e., the plant was not cranking out enough power (if it was cranking at all, as regulators were inclined to just shut the plant down because of its poor safety and operational cultures). We had management's assurance that all was well and that the plant was on its way to becoming a good one with a fine culture of safety. Still, the plant was shut down and the Nuclear Regulatory Commission (NRC) was not about to authorize turning it on again until we had fixed the culture. How to understand the culture?

Along with other directors, I took a tour of the plant. At one of the rooms I engaged an operator in a discussion about the plant, its problems, and why we were in a forced outage. He said, "We just want to make power. If the NRC would just get out of our faces and out of the way, we could crank this up and generate some kilowatts." I knew from his statement what was wrong. The NRC was correct: there was an attitude of defiance among our employees about just doing what the NRC wanted done. Management had painted a rosier picture than what really existed and there were serious problems with the culture at the plant, especially regarding safety issues. The result was that the board brought in culture-change experts and new managers and opened up new discussions with the NRC to work earnestly toward compliance with its standards and requirements. One employee was able to provide the information that months of arm's-length studies had not. And that information only came about from a walkabout.

This form of feedback requires that directors spend more time at a company than just board and committee meetings. Directors have to walk the floors, the halls, and the plants. Their interaction with employees over lunch and at breaks is a critical component in curbing the Yeehaw Culture. The very presence of board members sends the signal to employees who might be fearful of raising issues that there is someone outside the management loop who is in charge and will listen. When I work with companies, I always provide them with feedback I receive from employees (with names redacted). Inevitably, the ethics officers who receive this feedback tell me that they do get valuable information over their hotlines but that they never receive anything quite as candid as what employees will provide to me. The employees perceive me to be at least a quasi-outsider, someone who can objectively evaluate the concerns they raise and end the stalemate between them and management. A board member who goes on a walkabout can offer employees the same relief valve. Along the way, the director creates a powerful antidote for the Yeehaw Culture.

Sign #4

Weak Board

Antidotes

1. Get yourself a strong board.

   a. Dig deeper on conflicts.

   b. Don't fall for the governance myths on the ideal director and find the real thing.

2. Get information from employees.

3. Challenge officers, managers, and their claimed results.

4. Pay attention to perks.

5. Walk around.

CHAPTER SIX

Sign

5

Conflicts

So, is there something wrong here? Did I do something wrong?

—the ethically challenged George Costanza of *Seinfeld*

Organizations at risk of ethical collapse are family-friendly ones. Conflicts run rampant. Their officers hire relatives, contract with companies owned by relatives, and generally use nepotism to its fullest extent. And often, when confronted, they respond, "Conflict? What Conflict?" Some of the culture of conflicts reared its gratuitous head in the previous chapter when we saw how directors were put on the board because the company wanted their business or they wanted the company's business or they were doing business with the CEO. There is a distinct atmosphere of back-scratching in these companies. The culture of conflicts becomes so pervasive that the very purpose of the company is reduced to mutual benefit for the various players. Shareholders, creditors, and other stakeholders be damned, for we are making money for ourselves!

The Yeehaw Culture has consumed a company when officers begin to seek benefits for themselves, friends, and families. Self-interest controls everything from contract decisions to better judgment. The company has drifted so far toward the ethical cliff that employees are not even pointing out the least moralistic of all the forms of unethical conduct in business: the conflict of interest. We are hesitant to raise red flags about accounting judgments, personal lives, product safety, perks, and compensation, because who are we to judge? But conflicts enjoy a comfort level among the least morally developed among us because of their rote nature. Conflicts of interest are a type of math: you work for one company, you can't double your money by working for someone else who does business with your employer. You don't need Socrates or deontology to determine when a conflict exists and what to do about it. Given the simplicity of conflicts, then, when a company becomes consumed with conflicts we can conclude that everyone has pretty much surrendered to the dark side. One can hardly debate the merits of vendor chargebacks or advertising accounting when your son-in-law is the vendor or your nephew has the ad contract. What difference can it possibly make as long as everyone has two or three pieces of the pie?

The entire dot-com industry was a culture of conflicts, destined to self-destruct. When the dot-com companies went public during the Internet bubble, stock for their IPOs was doled out to suppliers, customers, family, lawyers who drafted the prospecti for the stock offerings, and anyone else the founders wanted to reward for helping them perpetuate the myth that their company was a legitimate phenomenon. The lawyers, knowing that the extent of their payment came from the success of the stock offering, touted the dot-com mightily in the prospectus. Customers assured the world that they held long-term contracts with these wunderkinds running the dot-coms. Suppliers promised discounts, and the result was that the dot-coms always created a buying frenzy when they went public. Everyone who helped create the dot-com myth profited by dumping their stock allocations onto the market during the initial sale of stock. In fact, one of the regulatory reforms relates to the way investment bankers assign share allocations for these IPOs because they could curry favor with the likes of Bernie Ebbers for WorldCom's investment-banking business if they got him in on enough initial stock allocations for these dot-com IPOs.

The specifics in a conflict of interest can vary, but the underlying theme is always the same. An individual is playing two roles, and his or her role in one regard has interests that are at odds with his or her role in another. If the dot-coms were the industry of conflicts, their stock sales produced an era of conflicts for the stock market. Consuming investment bankers, analysts, auditors, consultants, and Wall Street were webs of interrelationships that had become so sophisticated that the simple notion of conflicts was lost in all the complexities of how the conflicts arose. There was so much back-scratching that it became the presumed and preferred way of doing business. The culture of conflicts really had consumed the better judgment of too many. This sign of the Yeehaw Culture edged both companies and industries to ethical and legal collapse.

The Analysts: Conflicts Are Not Such a Big Deal, the Deal Is

The Inherent Conflicts with In-House Analysts

The research side of an investment house is always conflicted with the deal-seeking/underwriter side of the house. The infamous Chinese Wall compromise, that great and imaginary divide between functions that could affect how well the other side of the same company did, was just that, a compromise on the inherent conflict that was bound to compromise integrity. The Hells Angels' adage offers succinct insight into this management of conflicts: "Three people can keep a secret if two are dead." The assumption that the deal makers could keep a secret, and could keep it from brokers whose clients (and hence their commissions) would benefit, was flawed. However, we could perhaps be satisfied if all the investment lads and lassies did was share secrets. The secrets within the deal shops on one side of the Chinese Wall turned out to be less of a problem than the aggressive-to-the-point-of-false analyses and evaluations that those on the research side engaged in to keep the deal going or make the deal look much sweeter than it was in reality. The structure that assumed everyone could act with complete candor given the numbers pressure defied human nature. Independent analysts provide better investment advice than analysts housed within investment banks. A 2004 study comparing the performance of independent analysts with investment-bank analysts (during the 1996 to 2003 time frame) concluded that following the advice of the independent analysts yielded 8 percent more in returns. Further, independent analysts were particularly strong during bear markets. After March 2000, when the NASDAQ peaked, independent analysts were double-digit better (17–22 percent) than their in-house counterparts because they were much quicker to downgrade stocks. During a bull market, the performance is about the same because all stocks are rising.

Human nature and performance aside, virtually all the large investment bankers relied on conflicts of interest to gain business and ensure stock-value retention. And virtually all the firms have settled with the SEC or New York Attorney General Eliot Spitzer on charges related to their analysts' overly optimistic recommendations that had their roots in the desire to retain those large investment-banking clients. "Eliot Spitzer" became a dreaded phrase on the tongues of those in the financial world after his investigations discovered the infamous e-mails in which analysts contradicted the public positions they had taken on particular stocks. In their public assessments the analysts were bullish. In their private e-mails they referred to the same stocks as dogs. A culture of conflicts consumed the better judgment of the analysts, those running their firms, and even the companies themselves that were the beneficiaries of the conflicted research advice.

This description of the conflicts of interest that analysts face is terribly sterile in its generics. A specific example demonstrates how deep the conflicts ran, how improper the behavior became, and how a company sacrificed its credibility in the process. Citigroup's Salomon Smith Barney and its star telecommunications analyst of the dot-com era, Jack Grubman, continued a marketwide false impression about WorldCom that lasted for years beyond the time when WorldCom had already begun accounting fraud to maintain a false rise to the heights of the market. As noted earlier, in the month WorldCom collapsed with the admission of needing to restate $3 billion in earnings (which would later balloon to $11 billion), Jack Grubman's quote about WorldCom being world class still appeared on the company's website (as of August 7, 2002). Mr. Grubman crossed the line from analyst to cheerleader early on in the WorldCom relationship. The sycophantism of Mr. Grubman is difficult to describe because it seems almost parody, as the WorldCom ending is now known. Mr. Grubman attended WorldCom board meetings and offered advice. Mr. Grubman introduced Mr. Ebbers at analyst meetings as "the smartest guy in the industry." When WorldCom stock had lost 90 percent of its value, just six weeks before its collapse, Mr. Grubman issued his first negative recommendation on WorldCom despite having already downgraded other telecom companies.

There were conflicts fueling such logic-defying support. Salomon stood to earn $21 million in fees if the WorldCom-Sprint merger was approved in 1999. Mr. Grubman's evaluation included the following conclusion: "We do not think any other telco will be as fully integrated and growth-oriented as this combination." WorldCom did indeed give the bulk of its investment-banking business to Salomon Smith Barney, but the hook was far more personal because Mr. Grubman and others gave Mr. Ebbers (and other officers of client firms) the opportunity to be first purchasers of hot IPO stocks. The figures in congressional records indicate that Mr. Ebbers made $11 million in profits from investments in twenty-one IPOs recommended to him by Mr. Grubman. Salomon and others would later face charges of profiteering on the IPO allocations. All denied any quid pro quo arrangement, but the impression this connection left on the market and investor trust was indelible. Salomon and others would settle with the SEC for $1.4 billion on the IPO allocation and other issues. Salomon's penalty was $150 million, with another $150 million in disgorgement and $100 million for developing independent research and investor education.

Far more was at stake for Citigroup than just WorldCom's investment-banking business because the loans were tied to the value of WorldCom stock. WorldCom's biggest lender was Citigroup, which also served as personal lender for Bernie Ebbers. One expert noted, "Looking back, it looks more and more like a pyramid scheme. The deals explain why people weren't more diligent in making decisions about funding these small companies. If the money was spread all over the place and everyone who participated early was almost guaranteed a return because of the hype, they had no incentive to try and differentiate the technology. And in the end, all the technology turned out to be identical and commodity-like."

Mr. Grubman, however, had doubts about WorldCom that he expressed privately even as he continued to issue nothing but positive reports because he and his company were completely intertwined with WorldCom, Mr. Ebbers, and the success of both. In e-mails uncovered by an investigation of analysts conducted by Eliot Spitzer, Grubman had complained that he was forced to continue his "buy" ratings on stocks he considered "dogs."

Those Soft-Dollar Conflicts

Percolating beneath the conflicts within the firms and the individual use of market-moving research was the issue of soft dollars. While widely used, rationalized, justified, and touted, the practice of compensating advisers with soft dollars is a conflict of interest. The SEC describes it as follows:

> Under traditional fiduciary principles, a fiduciary cannot use assets entrusted by clients to benefit itself. As the Commission has recognized, when an adviser uses client commissions to buy research from a broker-dealer, it receives a benefit because it is relieved from the need to produce or pay for the research itself. In addition, when transactions involving soft dollars involve the adviser "paying up" or receiving executions at inferior prices, advisers using soft dollars face a conflict of interest between their need to obtain research and their clients' interest in paying the lowest commission rate available and obtaining the best possible execution.

Rather than being paid a fee for advice, the adviser was given a portion of the commission from the broker designated as the trader for the client. For example, on a pension fund, the significant trades made on the advice of the investment adviser could produce millions in compensation. The more the client trades, the more the adviser earns. Regardless of avowed integrity, a conflict exists and abuses occurred. In many cases, the allegations of self-interest in the commissions trumped the interests of the client. For example, the pension fund in Chattanooga, Tennessee, is involved in litigation with its former adviser, William Keith Phillips, and his firms, UBS Wealth Management USA (Paine Webber) and Morgan Stanley. The case is ongoing, but Morgan Stanley's position is that the pension plan was a knowledgeable investor with an understanding of markets, fees, and relationships. The issue at the heart of the litigation is conflict of interest and whether the portfolio structure and holdings advice was influenced by the potential for commissions for the investment adviser. Given the $5 trillion in pension funds in the United States, and the ongoing general questions about pension funds, accounting, and benefits, the issue is neither trivial nor remote. The SEC is conducting its own investigation of the situation. The fallout continues as other cities follow suit, as it were. San Diego is also involved in a dispute with its pension-fund adviser, and cities in Florida, Virginia, and Pennsylvania are pursuing differing levels of complaints against their advisers.

The irony is how long the percolating ethical issues that led to these collapses in firm behavior and client relationships have been with us. In 1998 the SEC released a report on its one-year sweep investigation of seventy-five broker-dealers and 280 investment advisers. Fully three years before the market drop caused intense scrutiny, the SEC had issued a wake-up call, a warning, and a proposed solution. The following excerpt from the executive summary of the SEC investigation includes the conclusions that soft dollars were being used for inappropriate expenses and that the disclosures to clients were inadequate:

> While most of the products acquired with soft dollars are research, we found that a significant number of broker-dealers (35%) and advisers (28%) provided and received non-research products and services in soft dollar arrangements. Although receipt of non-research (or non-brokerage) products for soft dollars can be lawful if adequate disclosure has been made, our sweep inspections revealed that virtually all of the advisers that obtained non-research products and services had failed to provide meaningful disclosure of such practices to their clients. Examples of products acquired included: advisers using soft dollars to pay for office rent and equipment, cellular phone services and personal expenses; advisers using soft dollars to pay an employee's salary; an adviser using soft dollars to pay for advisory client referrals and marketing expenses; an adviser using soft dollars to pay legal expenses, hotel and rental car costs and to install a phone system; and an unregistered hedge fund adviser using soft dollars to pay for personal travel, entertainment, limousine, interior design and construction expenses.
>
> We also found that, even with respect to research and brokerage products and services within the safe harbor, many advisers' disclosure of their soft dollar practices was inadequate, in that it did not appear to provide sufficient information to enable a client or potential client to understand the adviser's soft dollar policies and practices, as required under the law. Nearly all of the advisers that we examined made some form of disclosure to clients regarding their brokerage and soft dollar practices. Most advisers, however, used boilerplate language to disclose that their receipt of research products and services was a factor that they considered when selecting brokers. In our assessment, only half of the advisers that we examined described in

sufficient detail the products, research and services that they received for
soft dollars such that clients or potential clients could understand the advis-
ers' practices.

The vigorous defense offered by investment firms and their advisers/analysts in the arbitration proceedings brought by clients is that the pension plans are sophisticated parties that understand the fee arrangements and the trade-offs for independent advice and research vs. commission-compensated advice. They also remind us that there is a net savings to the client. Perhaps so, but the clients should have been given the opportunity to choose those cost savings. The SEC's findings from nearly eight years ago explain the disparate views: there is a disconnect in the resolution of the conflict in that the adviser's disclosure may not be as forthcoming as they believe it to be. One survey found that 75 percent of respondents could not accurately define a fund expense ratio and 64 percent did not understand the impact of expenses on fund returns.

The effect of all these conflicts was the ethical collapse of far too many investment houses and a loss of public trust in an industry. The rampant conflicts contributed to a Yeehaw Culture that was causing increasing compromises. A classic sign of a Yeehaw Culture is that there are conflicts galore, but no one seems concerned, the rationalizations fly, and the self-dealing continues until financial collapse occurs. With the investment houses, the collapse of the bubble coupled with the extraordinary ethical collapses of many of their most favored "buy" recommendations brought scrutiny and the revelation of longtime practices that carried inherent risks from conflicts. In an attempt to regain public trust as quickly as possible, the regulatory actions at both the state and federal levels ended in negotiated settlements. The fines paid by the industry members for the failure to disclose the conflicts were staggering:

Citigroup	$400 million
Merrill Lynch	$200 million
Credit Suisse First Boston	$200 million
Morgan Stanley	$125 million
Goldman Sachs	$110 million
Deutsche Bank	$87.5 million
Bear Stearns	$80 million
J. P. Morgan	$80 million

Lehman Brothers	$80 million
UBS Warburg	$80 million
U.S. Bancorp Piper Jaffray	$32.5 million
Thomas Weisel Partners	$12.5 million

The settlement total from a series of cases brought by Spitzer alone was $1.4 billion.

These were not difficult ethical questions, but the conflicts culture was so consuming that the firms reached a point of no return, until the regulatory cleansing. Conflicts in an organization, when not checked, grow into amazing lapses in judgment. Finding a culture of conflicts means a Yeehaw Culture is also there percolating.

The Audit Profession: Conflicts and Consulting

Even the audit profession, the watchdog for conflicts and other misdeeds that can impair the ability to provide a fair and accurate financial picture, became inherently conflicted during our last go-round of ethical collapses. Both the audit firms and the industry operated in a culture of conflicts. Like the analysts', their conflicts had become such standard industry practice that no one even acknowledged their existence. Those who did offered the same pseudo-intellectual/sophisticated arguments that the clients understood these arrangements and that the audit firms were saving their clients' money by performing dual roles: discretionary business consultant and public watchdog over financial reports. The venture into consulting activities proved problematic for audit firms in the exercise of their better judgment during audits. Retaining the consulting business became more critical than keeping the audit business, so the auditors became client pleasers, at the expense of the integrity of the audit.

Arthur Andersen, joining all the other audit firms in unified chorus at that time, assured one and all that auditing and consulting do mix and that the integrity of one is not affected by the desire to retain the other. Between 1999 and 2001, nonaudit fees for the then–Big Five accounting firms climbed from 10 percent of their total revenues to 70 percent, and the percentage of publicly traded companies using nonaudit services from their external auditors climbed from 75 percent to 96 percent. Andersen and the others offered their sincere assurance that thousands of years of human nature could be reversed just by their willing it to be so. The practice was pervasive, that of mixing consulting and audit in the same external firm. The following list of companies shows the ratio of nonaudit fees to audit fees in the pre–Sarbanes-Oxley days:

Allegheny Energy	3.1
Ameren	2.3
American Power Conversion	5.1
Apple Computer	12.6
Avon	2.9
Best Buy	4.4
Boston Properties	4.8
Constellation Energy Group	4.1
Dominion Resources	1.2
Duke Energy	3.5
Equitable Resources	3.9
First Energy	5.9
Gap	13.5
John Hancock	9.75
Johnson & Johnson	4.6
Lafarge North America	3.1
Liz Claiborne	2.2
Manpower	3.6
Marriott International	4.7
McGraw-Hill	2.2
Motorola	16.0
PG&E	3.6
Reliant	5.1
TXU	3.0
VF	5.2
Walt Disney	4.1

Following the revelations about Enron and its consulting fee/audit ratios, but prior to any regulatory mandate, some companies changed their policies.

For example, Disney dropped Price Waterhouse from its dual consulting/audit roles with the company. According to *Accountancy Magazine*, nonaudit fees earned by the Big Four in 2003 fell by 27 percent as companies corrected the conflict.

However, not all companies on the ratio list escaped the audit/consulting conflict. For some companies and their auditors, the dollars were too great and the auditors/consultants had too much to lose on the consulting side to rock the boat on the audit side. Sarbanes-Oxley would make such volatile combinations in auditor/client relationships illegal. But the cultures within the companies and the audit professions that embraced these cozy relationships led to lapses in audit judgments. In some cases, managers convinced all-too-easily-convinced auditors to go along with what was creative and/or aggressive accounting that led to postponing the inevitable disclosure of struggles that were masked by high-risk accounting and financial reporting practices. The following list shows the audit ratios and fate of companies that did not escape the inherent conflict in time:

Bristol Myers Squibb	4.5	Overstated earnings by $2.5 billion; settled charges of channel stuffing with SEC through a deferred prosecution agreement
Delphi Automotive Systems	7.7	Admitted overstating revenues; filed for bankruptcy
Halliburton	1.1	Changed its accounting voluntarily and settled with the SEC for $7.5 million over timing of disclosure of changes
Kmart	10.4	Restatements; former CEO and CFO charged by SEC with improper booking of revenues; company enters Chapter 11 bankruptcy

With the detailed restrictions on services a company's external auditor can provide, it would seem that this ratio issue is a dead one. However, the classification of audit vs. nonaudit fees and services does have discretion. The result may be that the inherent conflict is concealed because of the manner in which fees earned by the external auditor are massaged into being audit fees.

"Cozy with a client" is street jargon for describing the type of relationships that arose between audit firms and their clients during the period from post-savings-and-loan collapse until 2002 and the passage of Sarbanes-Oxley. And at the heart of many of the Yeehaw Cultures we could find a conflicted auditor as well. Enron and Arthur Andersen. Waste Management and Arthur Andersen. WorldCom and Arthur Andersen. Baptist Foundation of Arizona and Arthur Andersen. Where fraud was going, Arthur Andersen was never far away. Its presence was not coincidental, nor was it bad luck in its choice of clients. Andersen, perhaps more than any of the other Big Five (at that time) accounting firms, was the auditor/consultant conflict writ large. Quite commonly Andersen's consulting fees exceeded its audit fees, and retaining the consulting fees became the driving force for what it would and would not do in the audit. Its independence on its audits became compromised by the drive for consulting revenue.

Andersen and Enron: Cultures of Conflicts Galore for Both

As noted earlier, the Houston office of Andersen needed Enron as a client. Enron's audit and consultant fees totaled over $50 million, a figure that was, as auditors say, "material" to Andersen in Houston and audit partner David Duncan. Andersen also had the classic conflict that was a concern in the profession at the time, that consulting fees exceeded audit fees and that audits might be compromised in order to retain the consulting arrangement and its fees.

But there was more coziness to the client-auditor relationship than just the accommodations for retaining the account and the fees, particularly between Enron and Andersen. The amount of work the audit firm was doing with that one company, between consulting and audits, meant perpetual presence at the company site. The result was the loss of that bright line; the delineation of roles became muddled as the standards for auditor propriety and the audit function slipped. One of the reasons the external auditor's staff and the client's staff (Enron employees) were so inextricably intertwined was that Andersen performed and reviewed both the internal and external audit functions. Andersen was validating the internal control systems even as it was designing them. As one of my colleagues has noted, this would be like having my students grade their own papers. Human nature being what it is, the numbers were pleasing to the client but nowhere near the financial reality an independent auditor should present.

The Enron-Andersen relationship offers an illustration of how enmeshed an auditor could become with a company, the entity it was supposed to be watching as a public auditor. David Duncan was a close friend of Enron's chief accounting officer, Richard Causey, who was responsible for approving those off-the-books SPE transactions that Mr. Fastow was handling as both CFO and principal. Mr. Causey and Mr. Duncan traveled together, lunched together, and golfed together, which, apparently, opened doors for cooking the books together. As noted earlier, Mr. Causey entered a guilty plea and was sentenced to seven years. Further, the employees at Enron were not sure who the Andersen employees were and who actually worked for Enron because many Andersen staff had permanent offices at Enron, were often hired by Enron, and were a daily presence just as Enron employees were. Seven former Andersen accountants became Enron employees in 2000 alone. After Enron's collapse its employees indicated that they even celebrated the Andersen auditors' birthdays in the office because they were so uncertain who worked for Andersen and who worked for Enron and they did not want to risk offending anyone. Right down to the fraud, this was a gracious company, if nothing else. They were one big happy, albeit conflicted, family.

The result of the close personal and staff relationships between Andersen and Enron was Andersen's willingness to go along with practices its partners clearly saw as problematic. The Enron board's ratification of the off-the-books entities appears to have been a tip of the hat by the board to the very nervous David Duncan because of his concerns and because those in headquarters at Andersen had similar concerns. As noted earlier, Benjamin Neuhausen, a partner at Andersen's home base in Chicago and a member of the firm's Professional Standards Group, raised concerns in an e-mail to Mr. Duncan. He recognized the conflict of interest in the off-the-books arrangements at Enron and wondered in writing how a board could possibly approve such transactions. David Duncan agreed that the whole idea was bad, but counted on the board to take the active role of questioning and, perhaps, resistance. But our studies in Chapter 5 taught us that wasn't gonna happen.

Both men, experienced auditors, saw the problems with Enron's practices but could not bring themselves to play referee. Instead, they opted for the best of both worlds—they kept the client and passed the buck to the board. But strength is not the forte of boards in a Yeehaw Culture. Each deferred to the other, with the auditor conflicted on fees and the boards conflicted for any number of reasons, from compensation to contracts to doing business with the company. The culture of conflicts creates a hopeless circle of impropriety, with those in the circle unwilling to call the others because of mutual obligations.

Family Conflicts: A Favorite in the Yeehaw Culture

The Yeehaw Culture loves a good fiefdom. The whole clan is brought in for family fun and profit. And even nonprofit Yeehaw Cultures rope in friends, family members, and others they can count on for the sycophantic traits so critical to the continuation of the Yeehaw Culture. The United Way's William

Aramony created complex spin-offs that allowed him to hide many of his expenses. The spin-offs also served as a way to hiring family beneath the board's and the public's radar. When the board can't figure out the structure of the spin-offs, it can hardly determine who's hiring whom. One spin-off hired Aramony's son, Robert, as its president. In addition, $80,000 of United Way funds went to Aramony's girlfriend, as noted earlier, for consulting even though she did no work. Once again, not bad money for no heavy lifting. The key to the workless job is finding a Yeehaw Culture where a relative works. This same pattern of hiring family, friends, and girlfriends is the kind of thing that makes royal families dysfunctional. Something outside family blood is, all in all, a good thing when it comes to keeping a steady course and sanity, whether for the sake of the crown or for the corporation. Despite this logical admonition, the conflicts stories of our Yeehaw Culture companies are stunning in their chutzpah.

Enron: Father, Son, Sister—We Are Family

At Enron, Ken Lay's son Mark, with his father's help, created two privately held technology firms. Within just a few months after the companies were created, these fledgling oganizations managed to sign a Fortune 100 company as a customer. Enron not only signed contracts to do business with both of these Lay Jr. companies, it even invested in one of them. In addition, Enron hired Mark Lay as a consultant at a salary of $1 million for a three-year contract. Enron also tossed in twenty thousand stock options to be certain it lassoed this talent. Ah, those no-heavy-lifting jobs that come from families who run a Yeehaw Culture.

Enron used a travel agency that was co-owned by Lay's sister Sharon. Alliance Worldwide Travel booked more than $10 million in travel for Enron and its employees. Enron was pretty much the agency's only client. Fiction cannot produce conflicts this extreme.

Adelphia: Family Profit at Company Expense

Adelphia was a study in "Conflicts! What conflicts?" Nobody was really clear who owned what between Adelphia and the Rigas family. Doris Rigas, the matriarch, was paid $12.8 million for her work as a designer and decorator for Adelphia offices. The Rigas farm, thought to be selling honey for a profit, was really just a business that provided landscaping, maintenance, and snow-removal services to Adelphia—for a fee, of course, and all without that nasty competitive-bidding process that becomes a part of most organizations. Adelphia invested $3 million in *Songcatcher*, a film produced by Ellen Rigas Venetis, the wife of a board member (who was placed on the board following their marriage as the token outsider/independent director) as well as the daughter of John Rigas. The film did not go on to box-office success or even a mention at the Sundance Film Festival. It never even made it to cross-country flights.

There were also conflicts galore among officers, board members, and the Rigas family—with the officers and board members actually competing with Adelphia to purchase cable systems, and with something that takes the term *chutzpah* to a new level: the company providing the credit, collateral, and financing for family members to make the purchases for themselves. But financing the board members' purchase of competitors was not the end of the self-dealing. These Rigas-owned, Adelphia-financed companies would then contract to sell cable services to Adelphia. Not only did they breach the duty of loyalty to the corporation by acquiring properties that would be considered a corporate opportunity, the Rigas family used the company's credit to do so. They then made the company pay full retail to purchase back the capacity. Nell Minow of the Corporate Library described Adelphia as follows: "Even the existence of a credit line that allows the family to buy cable systems raises conflict-of-interest questions because the company was actually funding the family's ability to compete for properties."

Tyco: What Are Friends For?

Tyco director Frank Walsh was the wildly successful finance broker mentioned previously for his acumen in bringing Tyco together with the CIT Group and netting $20 million as a fee—a fee that was not disclosed to the board until some months later, conflicts being what they are. Mr. Walsh also owned two firms that leased aircraft to Tyco for a total of $3.5 million per year.

But Mr. Walsh was not alone in terms of friendly relations between directors and Tyco. Director Stephen Foss owned a company that was paid $751,000 by Tyco for a pilot and Cessna aircraft. There were competitive bids for the contract, but the relationship was not disclosed until the SEC investigated and mandated the disclosure of a "related party transaction." Director Joshua Berman was paid $360,000 per year between 2000 and 2002 for "legal, regulatory and other professional services." Director Richard Bodman was of-counsel for the law firm that performed most of Tyco's legal work.

Dennis Kozlowski's friends had contracts with Tyco that paid very well. Wendy Valliere was a personal friend of the Kozlowskis and earned $7.5 million as her fee for decorating the Kozlwoskis' new New York City apartment.

Kozlowski even hired his yacht expert, Michael Castania, in 1996 as a Tyco executive who was housed at Boca Raton. His executive role was pretty much limited to leading Team Tyco in corporate yacht races. He did earn Tyco a fourth-place finish in the Volvo Challenge Race in June 2002. The purpose of Team Tyco, Tyco's sponsorship of it, and the yachting races remain a mystery to the Tyco employees, its shareholders, and pretty much all the courts handling the larceny and embezzlement cases as well as the shareholder suits for fraud. And that mystery is nothing compared to the one of Kozlowski's hiring his second wife's former personal trainer for a position at Tyco, although no one is clear what that position was or even what the trainer's corporate talents were.

HealthSouth and Upseedaisees: A Family of Companies

As the list in Chapter 5 indicates, the HealthSouth board members were all intertwined in existing Alabama businesses and with Richard Scrushy. Many were also doing business with HealthSouth. But in some cases the conflicts were more nuanced as the directors did business with or were investors with Leslie Scrushy, Scrushy's third wife, in her company, known as Upseedaisees, a company specializing in postpartum clothing. The accounting related to Scrushy's personal investments, his wife's company, other companies Scrushy owned, and HealthSouth was terribly confusing. The confusion was difficult to clear up because Scrushy's personal accountant committed suicide just before HealthSouth began unraveling. Perhaps he had grown weary of saying and writing, "Upseedaisees." Ah, the drama conflicts offer. Apparently Upseedaisees had a loan from Scrushy's other holding companies, but Scrushy's accountant for those companies indicated that there was never any intention that it be paid back. It was also not immediately clear exactly who employees of Upseedaisees worked for. It could have been the Scrushys, HealthSouth, Upseedaisees, or even the accountant because the duties varied from office work to yard work. Scrushy filed a police report after the death of his accountant that accused this pitiful soul of embezzling $500,000. It is quite possible that sheer confusion over who owned what, who owed how much to whom, who was working for whom, who could be disclosed, who could not be disclosed, who reported to whom, and who was on the board of each company got so confusing that the next life, even with the embezzlement problems, looked better to the accountant.

Perhaps it will never be clear who paid for the jet trips by the rock groups that Scrushy created and performed with and the girls' band that "toured" with him. The traveling Scrushy show of guitars, drums, rock 'n' roll, and the trappings of wealth was unique, and quite expensive. No one challenged the use of the corporate jet for a health-care company for such purposes. With these autocratic personalities, awarding contracts to friends and family members seems perfectly natural because their perception is that they have grown the company, they know what's best, and they are in charge. Conflicts? What conflicts? I got all my friends and family with me.

CEOs and Personal Gain: Ahead of Company Interests

As noted, Bernie Ebbers had been granted extensive loans from the WorldCom board. But those loans had to be made if Ebbers was to meet the margin calls on the loans that were coming due for his personal investments. With the share pricing dropping, Ebbers's dumping stock into the market to raise the cash for the margin calls would have been devastating to WorldCom. Consequently, the board kept granting more loans. However, there were layers of conflicts beneath these Ebbers loans. Mr. Ebbers's personal debt relationships with the various banks were fraught with conflicts because the banks were lending money to Mr. Ebbers with the hope of gaining WorldCom business. At least one shareholder suit focuses on this interconnection. Mr. Ebbers's personal loans are reflected in the following chart:

Lender	Amount	Status
Citigroup	$552 million	$88 million repaid
WorldCom	$415 million	Collateral seized
Bank of America	$253 million	Repaid
UBS Paine Webber	$51 million	Repaid
Toronto-Dominion	$40 million	Repaid
Morgan Keegan	$11.6 million	Repaid
J. P. Morgan Chase	$10.8 million	Repaid
Bank of North Georgia	$10.8 million	Repaid

The banks that loaned Ebbers money did get results. Ebbers saw to it that his favorite banks, indeed those banks most generous with him personally, were awarded a significant amount of WorldCom's business. Citigroup is the parent company for Salomon Smith Barney, an investment banker and home to that telecommunications analyst who became Ebbers's and WorldCom's biggest cheerleader, Jack Grubman. Grubman's continuing positive reports on WorldCom, despite the slide of the company's stock and the clear signals from the market, earned him a subpoena to the congressional hearings, alongside Messrs. Ebbers and Sullivan.

Grubman's relationship with WorldCom's senior management continues to be an issue in regulatory and litigation matters. WorldCom gave the bulk of its investment-banking business to Salomon Smith Barney. Then Salomon saw to it that Mr. Ebbers and others got first crack at the hot IPO stocks. Being first in line on these IPOs was a terrific perk, as well as a huge financial conflict for Ebbers. The allocation practice is referred to as spinning. During the heyday of the dot-coms, many of the IPOs were so anticipated and the value of the shares increased so dramatically that getting in on the ground floor when the shares were first offered was a critical financial move. For example, in 1999 the average increase in IPO stock prices during the first day of trading was 60 percent. As noted earlier, Ebbers benefited greatly from IPO allocations. Ironically, his biggest gain was on Qwest shares, but by 2000 their value had dropped 95 percent, largely because of questions about its accounting. Never trust the people you cheat with. In exchange for WorldCom's continued business, Grubman issued nothing but positive reports on WorldCom as he became completely intertwined with the company, Ebbers, and the success of both. Citigroup made $21 million from handling the WorldCom-Sprint merger. Mr. Grubman was attending WorldCom board meetings and offering advice to the members, which we know was not exactly crackerjack. Grubman even attended Ebbers's wedding to his second wife. Of course, Mr. Grubman billed his employer for the trip. There's that coziness rearing its conflicted head again, with another analyst involved.

Further, Ebbers was not the sole beneficiary of the Salomon Smith Barney IPO allocations, although he was the largest. The congressional hearing list shows that other officers and directors also benefited from Salomon's preferential treatment on IPOs for its best customers. Stiles A. Kellett Jr. (director, 31,500 shares), Scott Sullivan (CFO, 32,300 shares), and James Crowe (former director) were also beneficiaries of the IPO allocations. Again, never trust the people you cheat with. It turns out that conflicted advice is often bad advice, and many who had been allocated shares of WorldCom hung on to them for too long because their man Grubman was offering overly optimistic views on telecommunications-related companies' stock. Citigroup and Salomon both continue to deny there was any quid pro quo between Ebbers and them for WorldCom's investment-banking business. Interestingly, Adelphia had analyst conflicts similar to WorldCom in that Salomon Smith Barney was its lead underwriter even as its parent, Citigroup, was a primary creditor.

The Antidotes for Conflicts

These are sordid affairs, these complex interrelationships that guaranteed personal gain at the expense of, in some situations, the company's survival. These companies' ethical cultures had deteriorated to a point where there was no well-defined line between corporate assets and personal desires. Part of creating an ethical culture rather than a culture of ethical collapse involves drawing such lines each day between what belongs to the company and what would constitute personal use of that company property. Corporate officers do not awake one day and say, "I believe that I will hire my girlfriend's trainer for the company!" And directors do not suddenly have an epiphany that prompts them to think, "I believe I will propose a $20 million brokerage fee from the company." They ease into these large conflicts with small ones, from private use of the company jet to forming a company to contract for the jet services. How is it that AIG could create a complete off-the-books company, Starr, for purposes of compensating its key employees and not recognize the conflicts inherent in their ownership of interests in that company, whose interests were then tied to the performance of AIG? These conflicts are not close calls, those discretionary areas in which what's best for the company happens to benefit someone on the board or a relative of an officer. These are conflicts cubed. Layers upon layers of conflicts, and all with self-interest at their heart, not the interests of either the business or the customers, let alone the shareholders. Once the culture of conflicts takes hold, self-interest clouds judgment. Personal interests take priority over what its best for the company. The Rigas family may have used Adelphia as a piggy bank, but Ebbers, Sullivan, Fastow, and others used sophisticated business structures to accomplish the same purpose—using the company as a means of self-enrichment. William Aramony benefited by having his girlfriend paid $80,000 per year at the United Way's expense. Conflicts finesse that nastiness in embezzlement, but they are a means of enrichment at company expense. To avoid the path to these multimillion-dollar conflicts, a path that leads right to ethical collapse, we don't quite need a twelve-step program, but there are a number of steps that can be taken and precautions implemented to prevent the organization's being consumed by a culture of conflicts.

Antidote #1 for Conflicts: Believe in Conflicts of Interest

Virginia, your little friends are wrong. Yes, conflicts of interest do exist and, yes, they can wreak enough havoc to cause ethical collapse. From analysts to audit firms to self-indulgent and self-dealing directors and CEOs, we have lived through an era in which conflicts were accepted because, well, we were all big boys and girls who would never let a conflict of interest influence us. That attitude of sophistication has cost us dearly. A conflict is a conflict is a conflict, and human nature kicks in when a conflict arises. The very definition of a conflict is that one interest we are charged with protecting must suffer when we serve the other interest we also protect. The company entered bankruptcy and the shareholders lost nearly all of their investment when the directors and officers at WorldCom served their own interests with the loans and accounting practices brought on by the pressure and incentives to meet the numbers. Markets and market trust suffered when analysts compromised their loyalty to those who rely on the integrity of their research. Shareholders, analysts, companies, and even audit firms suffered significant financial harm when auditors yielded to their own interests rather than their professional duty of candor and disclosure. The accounting profession's reputation was tarnished.

For decades the audit profession refused to recognize the potential harm that could come from the desire of an audit firm to please a client who also utilized its consulting services. The presumption was that auditors possessed a sufficient level of sophistication and ethical resilience to avoid succumbing to the pressures of placing an imprimatur on financials that were "overly aggressive" in the underlying accounting practices or, worse, just simply wrong and, ergo, fraudulent. Enron was a study in the psychology of how conflicts of interest and financial pressure, as well as the financial rewards from that conflict, can consume even the straightest of arrows. David Duncan was a respected man in the profession and in his community. He also saw the risky accounting practices of Enron, but as long as the board was willing to go along with the practices, he was prepared to offer Andersen's certification. He also understood what the loss of $50 million in revenue to the Houston Andersen office would mean. Indeed, that amount was not immaterial for Andersen as a whole. The result was that a man who hardly had a parking ticket to his name ended up entering a guilty plea to obstruction of justice and turning state's evidence against his employer. As noted earlier, Mr. Duncan withdrew his guilty plea in 2005 after the U.S. Supreme Court reversed Andersen's conviction for obstruction. The Justice Department will not retry Andersen, and Duncan's outcome looks favorable after five years of back-and-forth in the criminal justice system.

The first step in preventing a culture of conflicts is unequivocal acceptance of the foundation for prohibitions against conflicts of interest. The past five years witnessed a winking tolerance of conflicts in the name of our supposed sophistication. *The Wall Street Journal* has led the charge in its mockery of the new regulations prohibiting conflicts of interest. The *Journal* allows that someone who is good enough enjoys immunity from human nature. Such exemptions excluding the gifted from the mundane conflicts rules are misguided and unrealistic. What should be obvious from the discussion of both weak boards and the presence of conflicts in the Yeehaw Culture is how difficult and awkward it becomes to turn down, curb, rein in, or remove those to whom we are beholden. Would that all our sophistication could make the face-to-face confrontations and the answer "No!" any easier.

We are sophisticated in a technological sense. And many of the analysts, auditors, executives, and board members were among our brightest business minds. However, ethics have not changed with technology. Old-fashioned back-scratching and erudite quid pro quo still exist, even in hedge funds based in the Caymans. Leaders must embrace the philosophy of a conflict is a conflict is a conflict. Any wavering or winking tolerance ripples through an organization and allows employees latitude. They start small, with little favors, but then work their way up to first crack at IPOs and contracting with friends, family, and anyone else who can give them a break in their personal lives. The principles of conflicts of interest cannot be muddled if a culture of conflicts is to be curbed. One way to send the signal on conflicts is with a clear policy.

Antidote #2 for Conflicts: Establish Definitive Conflicts Policies and Enforce the Rules

Companies need conflicts policies on everything from contracting with relatives to accepting Christmas gifts from vendors to rebate fees from airlines and transfer agents. The easiest policies to enforce are the "nothing" policies. No Christmas gifts. No contracting with friends, relatives, or your girlfriend's former personal trainer. And on those rebates and other types of funds that come back to you via your customers, the easiest policy is "It all belongs to the customer."

Put in a $25 limit on gifts and employees engage in interpretations that will be maddening. "Is that retail or wholesale?" "Does that include tip?" "Is that face value?" "Can I just take a three-hundred-dollar Christmas gift in lieu of the twenty-five-dollar ones each month throughout the year?" The employee mind knows no limits on interpretation when the door is opened with a maximum-value policy on accepting gifts. The stretch begins to get those trinkets, tickets, and toys within the company maximum. "Nothing" is the policy employees understand most easily and follow most readily. "Nothing" also sets a clear cultural tone because employees are not second-guessing how someone was able to finagle the gift as they speculate over value. In short, no one is clear on the $25-limit policy because everyone interprets $25 differently. No one interprets "nothing" variously.

The amount of money spent on "stuff" in the name of doing business is not easily quantified, but if employees and my students are to be believed, it is a critical part of business success. Oh, the rationalizations we offer for the quid pro quo of lunches, dinners, tickets, golf, and all manner of freebies, the stuff that business relationships are made of. "You build relationships." "In some countries, it's all cultural and you have to give gifts, or you can't do business." If we dig deeply enough on the ethics of stuff, the precursors to conflicts that help us let down our guard and graduate into the more appealing levels of coziness, we find that there are again business issues to be addressed, not simply ethical prohibitions on conduct. We care whether an executive does business with a relative because the executive should be looking out for the company, not his or her relatives. And we should care about the stuff employees give and receive, for that same reason and one more. Have we ever really determined whether exchanging stuff is really the most efficient or effective way of building the relationships we say we are? If "stuff" is the stuff of business relationships, why are these gifts one of the first things to go in the event of a company budget crisis? If quid pro quo is so critical to do business, why are we so quick to axe it when a budget crisis hits?

This practice of giving and expecting gifts for doing business has been done for so long for so many that it has become accepted, in all its forms, large and small, without questioning the impact it has on the ethical culture of an organization and, more important, whether these gifts actually provide any benefit for those who own or support the organization. The gifts, trinkets, perks, and various benefits that slide across company lines, from one business to another, have created a sense of entitlement, an expectation that to do business, you must provide personal gifts to employees responsible for those decisions (and perhaps more). But accepting gifts creates a conflict of interest. Comfort with conflicts grows, as does the culture of conflicts—which creates one part of the Yeehaw Culture. It's not the $25 plate of cookies that we worry about—it is what follows, and what follows after that as those barriers are broken down and we graduate into the fictionlike atmospheres of the companies of ethical collapse.

Antidote #3 for Conflicts: Delineate What Belongs to the Company and What Belongs to the Customer and Ne'er the Twain Shall Meet in Employees

There are so many quids floating around from company to employees and back to company again that we have actually entered a bit of a twilight zone when it comes to anteing up on the quos. For example, when Pricewaterhouse-Coopers faced the issue of travel rebates that it earned from airlines based on the number of miles its employees had flown during the year (while en route to do work for clients who had paid for the employees' flights), PWC simply kept the rebates. However, those rebates arose because of PWC employees flying at their customers' expense. Those rebates were given to PWC by the airlines in order to encourage PWC to continue to book its employees on that airline. In other words, the airlines were giving PWC a gift in exchange for PWC's business. However, that gift meant that what the PWC clients were charged for travel reimbursement was not the amount of the expense because the rebates lowered the cost to PWC. Some excerpts from the PowerPoint slide show presented to the PWC management committee as it wrung its hands over what to do with the rebates demonstrate how the firm had lost sight of the fact that the funds did not belong to them. The funds were earned because of client expenditures, not theirs.

Avoid difficult questions from clients.

What do we gain from passing savings through?

Our people, not our clients, are inconvenienced by not being able to fly airline of choice.

A series of e-mails between partner Neal Roberts and the assistant travel director indicates that the issue of responsibility to the clients had been consumed in a series of rationalizations centering on logistics:

"It's hard to make an admission that we did anything wrong in the past."

"It's a question of right and wrong. And it's not our money, and we should give it back to our clients."

"I think that would be a technical nightmare."

"Well, we are the best audit firm in the world. I'm sure we can figure that out."

"Yeah, I'll let you fight that one. There's a lot of resistance to the fact that we're doing this in the midst of a year when the results aren't that great anyway."

"Because it's a lot of money, you mean?"

"Yes."

The rebates meant more revenues for PWC and bigger bonuses for its employees. However, PWC now has the incentive to make airline decisions based on rebates, not based on cost to the client, flight schedules, or other objective factors. Further, these are funds being returned for frequent flights. The customers whose routes had the highest rebates deserved the lowest cost. PWC was conflicted in its retention of those funds as well as in its policies on nondisclosure.

This same mentality consumed Citigroup recently as it kept the fees from a fund-transfer agent rather than rebate those amounts to the customers who had invested in the fund. Citigroup had received $104 million in negotiated fees from First Data. Citigroup had been advised by Deloitte that keeping those funds would not fly with the SEC. So, Citigroup arranged to have the funds go to its trust, with First Data acting as a type of subtransfer agent and Citigroup Trust as the transfer agent, thus allowing the fees because they were not directly payable to Citigroup as the fund manager. The fees from the transfer agent never belonged to Citigroup. They belonged to the investors in the mutual fund. The SEC noted, in its settlement with Citigroup for $80 million in penalties, $19 million in interest, and repayment of the funds:

> "This a very basic principle—that fiduciaries protect the financial interests of those to whom they owe an obligation. The services here were not some sort of cash cow that they were allowed to divvy up."

The process for selecting the company that would serve as transfer agent should have been a simple one: competitive bids. Rather, the contract was awarded in a manner that involved conflicts of interest between the fund manager (as a fiduciary for the investors) and the best interests of the investor. What happened was that the investors were not given the benefit of the best bid or transfer agent. Instead, they were treated to a transfer agent who promised to pay the most money to their fund manager. Customer first and only is the policy most easily understood and most readily followed.

Antidote #4 for Conflicts: Don't Waive Your Conflicts Policy

Serious cultural issues arise when awarding contracts and employing people boil down to who knows whom in the company. The result is that friends, family members, and others with personal connections to employees and officers get the contracts. Here the best and simplest rule is "No." No contracting with friends, family, and other relatives. Often companies waive these policies in the interest of a better price or closer proximity. Perceptions arise from the choice, no matter how logicial, cost-efficient, or price-based that decision may be. Before waiving any ethics policy, and especially concerning conflicts, those who are considering the waiver should not underestimate the organizational grapevine and how it can carry news, albeit mistaken news, as an officer, manager, or other employee sees the benefits of a contract awarded. These family-and-friends contracts, entered into even with the blessing of a policy waiver, introduce a coziness into the company that represents the very beginning of a gradual degradation of those absolute lines on conflicts that employees respond to so well. One exception to the policy yields three more circumstances for an exception. When the air is laden with heavy quid pro quo, an ethical culture suffers because ethical standards fall by the wayside in other areas. Waiving the contract-conflicts policy signals that we are here to help ourselves and our friends. The accountability to shareholders and clear demarcation of right and wrong are lost as ethical lapses become comfortable.

Enron has taught us much about ethical culture and the lack thereof, but the one overarching principle that emerges with great clarity is that waiving one's own conflict-of-interest policy can be the beginning of a tailspin. A company's rules on conflicts, such as one that prohibits officers from doing business with the company, are in place because without such constraints, the officers and other employees end up making deals for self-preservation or enrichment and not for the company's best interests. Having three thousand off-the-books entities was in the best interests of Andrew Fastow for preserving his job and because he was pocketing finder's fees for the transfer of Enron assets to the off-the-books entities in which he was a principle. A one-time waiver is never a one-time waiver. Once the barrier has been removed, the culture does not stop or even stagnate. It pursues a lower and lower level of behavior, and certainly not one consistent with the written anticonflict policies.

Antidote #5 for Conflicts: Review Ownership and Interrelationships

A conflicts audit would not be a bad idea. A conflicts audit means that the company checks investments of directors and officers and determines whether there are any interrelationships with vendors, suppliers, or service companies. Looking at HealthSouth, we see that contracts were entered into with companies that were joint business ventures with the CEO and the directors. Those ownership interests would not show up just with the name of the company. Another aim of the audit would be disclosure by employees (including officers) of their ownership interest in any organization that is, has been, or could be a customer or supplier/vendor of the company. Often an annual disclosure triggers an employee's realization that there has been a conflict of interest with a contract that may have been entered into without the employee's realizing the conflict at the time. Hindsight as an employee reflects on a disclosure form can be helpful in discovering conflicts that were previously put at naught.

Antidote #6 for Conflicts: Keep It Simple! Remember, There Are Only Two Ways to Manage a Conflict

In 2004 U.S. Supreme Court Justice Antonin Scalia accepted a ride on the vice president's private jet for a weekend of duck hunting while the vice president was a named party in a case that was about to be heard by the U.S. Supreme Court. The duck hunting trip came to the public eye through third-party reporting, not through Justice Scalia's disclosure. His defense was that there was no conflict because he and the vice president were never in the same duck blind together. Likewise, Justice Ruth Ginsburg became a target of conflicts discussion when a third party revealed that her name had been lent to a NOW Legal Defense Fund lecture series and that NOW was a party to several cases pending before the court. Justice Ginsburg's response to those who cried, "Conflict!" was that the lecture series was a lovely thing. Two of the greatest minds in the country had difficulty seeing the conflicts their activities were creating. The lecture series may be terrific, and keeping one's distance from the vice president's duck blind may be a good thing. However, neither response changes the fact that the justices had a conflict they neither disclosed nor discussed.

Why must conflicts be so difficult for us? And why do we continue to move the line to allow conflicted behavior? Why do we tolerate conflicts more and more? We make this all far more complicated than it needs to be.

There are two ways to manage a conflict: get rid of it or disclose it. Instead of being forthright or simply refusing to engage in the conflicted behavior, we rationalize. We waive conflicts policies. We convince ourselves that there is not too much money involved. We believe we are sophisticated enough to overcome that only-human feeling of being beholden to someone who has given us something. We are not. A culture of conflicts is a Yeehaw Culture that takes us down a path of ever more flexible ethics. Get rid of the conflicts and employees have an ongoing reminder about the role of ethics in business. Enforce absolutes on conflicts and everyone in the organization remembers that he or she works as a fiduciary for the owners, investors, and, in the case of nonprofit, donors. An absolute and consistent policy on conflicts is one that sets a remarkable tone for an organization. Conflicts are simple: don't, or disclose. What's even better is that an ethical culture becomes very simple once the conflicts policies are stated clearly and honored.

Sign #5

Conflicts

Antidotes

1. Believe in conflicts of interest.

2. Establish definitive conflicts policies and enforce the rules.

3. Delineate what belongs to the company and what belongs to the customer and ne'er the twain shall meet in employees.

4. Don't waive your conflicts policy.

5. Review ownership and interrelationships.

6. Keep it simple. Remember, there are only two ways to manage a conflict.

CHAPTER SEVEN

Sign #

6

Innovation Like No Other

You know, if we hadn't had all those expenses, we would have had earnings.

—Attributed to a dot-com CEO, circa 1999

I've never not been successful at business or work, ever.

—Jeffrey Skilling, at Enron's height of power, circa 1999

Companies barreling toward ethical collapse fancy themselves as being above the fray, below the radar, and generally not subject to the laws of either economics or gravity. These companies enjoy tremendous success initially (largely attributable to that numbers pressure), and this unsurpassed performance results from something different, some unique approach to doing business, a novel product like nothing the world has ever seen, or even being the first into a new industry. Their CEOs are often entrepreneurs who are bright, energetic, and motivated. And they have beaten the odds and enjoyed success in the rough-and-tumble world of business. A certain arrogance comes from their unique and singular achievements. They could never subscribe to the mundane Newtonian theory of what goes up, up, and up must eventually come down. Rather than acknowledge gravity's forces (as they apply to business), they pledged to find new ways of keeping things up, including fraud when circumstances warranted. These companies and those in charge saw themselves as visionaries who could reinvent business and certainly their industries. In their innovative minds, the drab rules the rest of the world follows were little more than meaningless constraints that suppressed their brilliance. However, despite their deeply held convictions that they were unique, competition followed them, as competition always does when it sees numbers going up, up, and up. But head-on competition was beneath them. These cultures of ethical collapse shunned the dull play in the center of the field, where competition slugs it out with higher quality, lower prices, and better service. Mixed metaphors aside, these folks believed themselves to be end-runners who could skirt the hard work and time-consuming nature of practice, effort, strategic thinking, and long-term rewards. Being so far above the rest of the world entitled them to ignore that world's rules. And so they did. P'shaw, they said to rules of law, corporate governance, and ethics. Out damned Stone Age constraints. They were omniscient and would do as their innovative minds guided them.

This sign of ethical collapse is not an indictment of innovation or a conclusion of an absolute link between the two. This is not a warning that innovation is bad or that innovation causes ethical collapse. Rather, this is a warning that innovation without the other tools of business, including ethics and those antidotes for this sign and the others, is a common thread in companies that experience ethical collapse. This reinvented ethos carries over into fairly straightforward areas such as accounting, something many of them truly did reinvent, in a most creative, albeit illegal, way. Their stories are remarkable, the stories of their self-perception and accolades gripping, and the fixes relatively straightforward for any organization that wants innovation, just not in ethics and/or accounting.

The Self-Acclaimed Superstar: Above the Mere Mortal with Big Heads and Innovation

The self-touted notion of "innovator like no other" among ethically collapsed companies is never spun entirely out of whole cloth. When these organizations began or enjoyed their success under iconic CEOs, there was some justification for their feelings of superiority and distinction. HealthSouth was labeled an organization whose delivery model would change the health-care industry, and its approach of one-stop surgery, physical therapy, and full treatment did attract patients and physicians. Enron truly was visionary in its recognition that a national energy market would reduce prices for everyone, if the states would just cooperate with deregulation. WorldCom's basic business model was brilliant. At the time deregulation of telecommunications was just beginning, Ebbers employed a simple economic model to grow a business: buy long distance wholesale, sell it retail, but at a cheaper price than the bulky Baby Bells. His timing was impeccable. Dennis Kozlowski took Tyco from a sleepy lab and research company to a multinational conglomerate that had synergies among the firms he acquired. As noted earlier, just the disclosure that Al Dunlap was to become CEO of Sunbeam, after his phenomenal performance at Scott Paper, sent the stock market whirling and buzzing. Shareholders could take great pleasure in gains that came from just the announcement of a change in leadership to the turnaround stylings of Dunlap. Adelphia came about because John Rigas saw the potential of cable television and began consolidating smaller companies to offer a wide range of service along with affordability. NASA, a government agency afflicted by the pressures of ethical collapse, had met a long series of goals, including on-time delivery of a man and his car to the moon. Charles Keating, with his American Continental Homes and Lincoln Savings, was a critical part of the growth and development in Arizona and a strong presence as the California housing market took off in the 1980s.

These were brilliant businesspeople with good ideas who did not begin either their companies or their expansions of them by saying, "You know what would be good? A gigantic fraud! This is the way I will make money. Perhaps a Ponzi scheme is the way to go!" Rather, they gradually slid there as hubris consumed them and they did whatever it took to maintain their unique and revered status in the marketplace. Innovators actually reach a point where they begin to believe and publicize the hype about themselves, as if repeating how innovative they are will somehow preserve the status quo, if not improve upon it.

Enron: King of the World

Jeffrey Skilling's favorite response when anyone questioned the ruthlessness or legitimacy of Enron's energy trading was "We are the good guys. . . . We are on the side of angels." When other utility executives spoke of changing their industry, they spoke of "the Enron model" as the strategic vision of the future. Enron set as a goal, with the launch of its broadband company, to become "the biggest e-commerce company in the world." The rest of the world consisted of dunces, dullards, and those who were simply too slow on the uptake for the fast pace and brilliance of Enron. Skilling had another favorite line when the poor schlubs of earthbound businesses and mundane accounting rules would ask such basic business and finance questions as "If you are making so much money, where's the cash?" He would dismiss them out of hand as "not getting it." Enron boasted that it was the "world's largest energy company," and a plaque in the lobby of its former Houston headquarters read, "The World's Leading Company." No small claim, but one that was readily believed and embraced by those within the walls of the Big E.

WorldCom: Bigger, Better, Brighter

WorldCom's attitude was that it was better, brighter, and bigger than anyone else, either before or after. Its attitude is best summarized as "the rest of the business world has never done it right before, but we know how to do it." To a large extent, WorldCom employees and management were correct, at least initially, about their innovation and ideas. As noted earlier, Ebbers's ideas about telecommunications were grounded in basic economics and, if executed properly, would have positioned WorldCom as the leader in the industry. Several quotes from Ebbers's letter to shareholders in the 1999 WorldCom annual report are revealing, indicative of the belief in his culture of innovation. Written at the height of the telecom and dot-com markets, and just after the World-Com takeover of MCI, the language is telling: "What we do better than any other name," "WorldCom has become the preeminent Internet and data company of the world," and "We continue to lead this market of virtually unlimited demand and mind-boggling speed."

WorldCom was not alone in its belief that it was bigger, better, and brighter. The WorldCom era on Wall Street has been likened by those who were competing with the company to being in a race with an athlete who is later found to be on steroids. In fact, at AT&T, Michael Keith, the head of its business services division, was replaced after just nine months on the job because he could not match WorldCom's profit margins. When Mr. Keith told C. Michael Armstrong, CEO of AT&T, that those margins were just not possible, he was removed from his position. William T. Esrey, the CEO of Sprint, said, "Our performance did not quite compare and we were blaming ourselves. We didn't understand what we were doing wrong. We were like, 'What are we missing here?'" During WorldCom's heyday, analysts would visit Sprint and tell the executive team to dump local business and follow the WorldCom model. Mr. Esrey described that era as follows: "You should have seen [it] in the '92, '95, '96 period, all of the guys from New York would come by with their suspenders—you know, the investment bankers—and would say: 'You've got to get rid of this slow-growing local business. It's a dog.'"

Tyco: Offshore Brilliance

Tyco's Dennis Kozlowski prided himself on being a market leader in a traditional business, not the newfangled dot-com industry. And his unique model, as he explained to *Business Week* when it featured him as the country's best CEO, was strength through acquisitions—building a conglomerate in an era when others believed it to be dead. Kozlowski purported to be the anti-dot-com in the era of the dot-com. In fact, Kozlowski denounced the popular stock options of the dot-com era: "Options are a free ride...a way to earn megabucks in a bull market." Like many innovators, Kozlowski was a tax dodger, and not just on his personal art collection. He took great pride in his innovation of moving the company headquarters to Bermuda for the offshore tax breaks as part of Tyco's acquisition of ADT in 1997. The deal was structured as an ADT takeover of Tyco so that the company could remain based in Bermuda. Tyco had a team of lobbyists and consultants from Accenture, a former Andersen consulting arm that became independent in 1999 and changed its name to Accenture in 2000. The team weaseled the tax-avoidance idea through the nation's legislative branch without risking congressional wrath. *Innovative* was the term used to describe Tyco's too-clever-by-half offshore tax avoidance.

AIG: Offshore Accounting, Again

And speaking of offshore businesses, AIG was another self-perceived innovator both in the general concept of insurance and in the accounting related to the sale of insurance. It was in 2001 that AIG announced the beginning of what would become the accounting scandal of 2005 that would topple its CEO and bring the SEC to the door of the AIG boardroom. In a press release related to its new insurance and reinsurance products, AIG noted that it would be selling new forms of insurance from Bermuda through Allied World Assurance Company (AWAC). The now-controversial CEO Hank Greenberg offered his take on AIG's innovations, i.e., creative insurance and reinsurance, property catastrophe treaty reinsurance, as well as certain specialty lines:

> *Commenting on the formation of AWAC, M. R. Greenberg said, "Insurance markets have experienced unprecedented demand for a number of coverages, without which businesses cannot operate prudently. AWAC will supplement existing market capabilities and capacity, providing a broad range of insurance coverages worldwide for businesses that have large and complex risks. In Michael Morrison [added as an executive and board member of AWAC because of his company's investment in the venture], we have a seasoned industry executive, with unparalleled knowledge of the global insurance marketplace. Along with his team of senior underwriters, Mike will serve AWAC's clients well."*

For those of you who feel yourself to be victims of doublespeak, fear not. The quote is pure hype and code for "we can fiddle with the accounting so that we all look a great deal better from both a risk and an accounting perspective." One analyst, commenting on AIG's troubles, said that the company had an air of superiority for so long that many wondered whether it was really that good or whether there was something going on beneath the radar. Now, he added, with the real numbers in and real accounting applied, he will have a chance to see how it really performs.

Adelphia: What Happens When Greek Gods Run Companies

Adelphia's annual reports referred to its "innovative" and "unique" marketing plans that allowed it to obtain customers in ways no other cable companies could. It also touted its "clustering strategy," something it envisioned before others understood where the cable industry was headed. No one is really sure what the clustering strategy was or if it worked, because Adelphia's numbers, on everything from subscribers to revenues, turned out to be spun out of whole cloth. It also referred to itself as "the premier business communications provider." Adelphia's clear message from its annual reports was that it was somehow positioned differently from the other cable providers and so would be able to capture more of the cable market than any other provider as its clustering strategy evolved.

Finova: The Financial Innovators

The name Finova was chosen for this company as a combination of the terms *financial* and *innovators*. However, former Finova employee folklore holds that the word *finova* actually means "pig lips." Like Finova's actual financial performance, we may never know the truth. The following excerpt offers the backdrop for Finova's growth experience and its self-perceived status of being unlike any other capital-lending firm:

> FINOVA, headquartered in Phoenix, Arizona, quickly became a Wall Street darling. Its growth was ferocious. By 1993, its loan portfolio was over $1 billion both through its own loans as well as the acquisition of U.S. Bancorp Financial, Ambassador Factors and TriCon Capital. In 1994 FINOVA had a successful $226 million stock offering. By 1995, its loan portfolio was $4.3 billion. Standard & Poor's rated the company's senior debt as "A" and Duff & Phelps upgraded its rating to "A" in 1995 when FINOVA issued $115 million in convertible preferred shares and its portfolio reached $6 billion. FINOVA's income went from $30.3 million in 1991 to $117 million by 1996 to $13.12 billion in 1999. Forbes named FINOVA to its Platinum 400 list of the fastest-growing and most profitable companies in January 2000.

Finova pledged annual growth of at least 10 percent, and having achieved that growth, its stock price was above $54 per share by 1999. However, both its overly conservative and overly aggressive accounting led to its auditor's refusal to certify the 1999 financials, a resulting delay in their release, and then the termination of the auditor. Pre-bubble auditors could be a testy lot, demanding such things as real numbers and adherence to accounting rules. As a result, Finova's newly chosen replacement auditor also refused to certify Finova's financial statements. Righteous indignation was flowing like Freon in a Phoenix summer. Finova officials complained that if the auditors had a problem with the accounting, they should have spoken up sooner and not waited until the eve of the annual report. Dear reader, use your imagination to reenact the confrontations that occurred leading up to the public dispute and delays in the release of financials.

The result of all the posturing and the postponed financials was a double whammy for this innovator. There was not just the market panic that comes from the delay and a resulting decline in Finova's share price. What followed were detailed explanations and revelations regarding Finova's accounting practices in everything from loan write-downs to the capitalization of ordinary expenses, which shook confidence so much that the share price would drop to $0.88 as Finova became the seventh-largest bankruptcy in the history of the United States. Although, once again, who can really be sure on that ranking? Those numbers remain in question, but we can conclude that the collapse was one of the nation's bigger bankruptcies as far as we knew.

HealthSouth: Creative Health Care and the Books to Go with It

HealthSouth was a self-described innovator, one whose annual report and marketing model indicated that it was changing the way health care, outpatient surgery, and patient wellness programs were delivered. That delightful and colorful model is still available on the company website today. Its service model, the four steps from diagnosis through surgery through inpatient rehabilitation to finally outpatient rehabilitation, was also its distinction from other health-care providers. Actually, the four-step model isn't bad. It is a shame that a CEO who wanted to be a rock star got in the way of its execution. It was as if that model allowed the company to lord its numbers over its competitors as evidence of its unique abilities. HealthSouth self-described itself as creating "the hospital model for the future of health care." However, the vision apparently carried over into the financial reports and gave the company license to provide the numbers of the future, not actual ones.

Those numbers were delivered for forty-seven quarters in a row, bringing the officers their compensation, bonuses, ESOPs (Employee Stock Ownership Plans), stock plans, and even the ability to repay significant loans ($39 million to the top five officers) that turned on the price of HealthSouth stock. But the HealthSouth officers, led by the indomitable Scrushy, were convinced they were beyond the bell curve. In the 2002 proxy statement the HealthSouth board's compensation committee included the following description of how well Scrushy had served the company, unlike most of the other dullards of business:

> In evaluating Mr. Scrushy's performance in 2000 and recommending Mr. Scrushy's compensation for 2001, the Committee took note of the significant improvement in HEALTHSOUTH's stock price after a period of significant depression in late 1998 and 1999. The Committee noted that, under Mr. Scrushy's leadership, HEALTHSOUTH's stock price had increased 203% from December 31, 1999 through December 31, 2000, the fourth-best performance of all S&P 500 companies for 2000.

Fannie Mae : The Most Ethical Company in America, Not Counting the Financials

Fannie Mae was named by *Business Ethics* magazine as the most ethical company in America for 2004. Its honor was announced about the same time Fannie Mae confessed its need to restate earnings (along with the related departure of its CEO), and was in the midst of a wrongful-termination allegation by Fannie Mae employee Roger Barnes, who raised questions about Fannie Mae's accounting. Before filing suit, Mr. Barnes settled with Fannie Mae. The story is the same: the accounting policies were adopted with the idea of meeting earnings goals so that executives, the innovators, could collect their bonuses. For example, if $200 million in expenses had been booked as they should have been in 1998, it would have reduced earnings to a point that would have cost then-CEO Franklin Raines $1.1 million in bonuses. This classic use of "cookie jar reserves" was the defiant act of a management team of innovators who had hubris to the third power because they had done so well with an organization so heavily regulated.

There was also a blatant deception in Fannie Mae's portfolio in that the mortgage-backed securities it kept were cherry-picked as part of a clear management philosophy that was communicated to employees in the following mantra: "Keep the best, sell the rest." In violation of GAAP rules, Fannie Mae waited to classify loans so as to give itself the best shot for backing on its portfolio. In the meantime, investors were buying into Fannie Mae based on the belief of the value of those mortgages. Information was withheld, the timing on disclosures of the true nature of the loans and Fannie Mae's portfolio were in violation of GAAP, and investors were purchasing securities believing the hype about the magnificent performance of Fannie Mae as well as its beneficent role in society. Investors were purchasing the worst of Fannie Mae's portfolio, unbeknownst to them until the accounting practices unfolded and revealed layers of "innovation" there. The restatement of earnings was at $1 billion through midyear 2005, and the restatement continues after the SEC demanded changes for the past four years of financials. One of the ironies that is consistent with the culture of innovation is that Freddie Mac, Fannie Mae's sister agency in the federal government, had already issued its earnings restatements based on similar accounting issues. The executive team at Fannie Mae would not take steps to correct its financial statements for over one year following Freddie Mac's restatements. The failure to internalize, self-correct, or learn from the mistakes of others is similarly situated in the innovator's mind. If you fancy yourself as being above the rules, you also buy into the delusion that those who falter are not doing it right or, among the more diabolical, were simply not smart enough to evade regulators.

Innovative Accounting—EBITDA: The Accounting Choice of the Innovator

All the companies discussed above were firm believers in pro forma accounting. That is, they believed in presenting numbers using the earnings before interest, taxes, depreciation, and amortization (EBITDA). This Fred Flintstone–sounding theory was a favorite of innovators for minimizing that nasty part of doing business that takes away from making money. The theory behind EBITDA, and its notion of not counting certain expenses, is that the numbers folks need an earnings figure that represents the real growth of the company to allow more meaningful comparisons. Significant variables across companies, such as the amount of depreciation, meant that real earnings comparisons were distorted because depreciation is a huge number for a contractor, but nonexistent for the dot-coms. Earnings for the contractor could have been fabulous, but the depreciation wiped them out. Lots of cash there, but nothing to show in those financials. Dot-coms, on the other hand, had little depreciation and their earnings looked fabulous compared with the mundane contractor following the accounting rules. Comparing earnings with depreciation taken out for the contractor is misleading in terms of actual cash earnings. Hence, EBITDA was born. It did have a certain sincere logic at the beginning. Unfortunately, the innovation of this already innovative group took EBITDA to new heights.

EBITDA was born, oddly and ironically, in the 1980s with Michael Milken, the junk-bond king and one of the early innovator personalities, and his fellow merry raiders. Mainstream businesses and analysts back then viewed EBITDA as a dubious financial analysis tool of a renegade band of ne'er-do-wells who tossed about the term as if it were some new discovery that the rest of the financial world had missed. Soon, however, companies began to discover that

EBITDA did not have the constraints of those testy GAAP rules. Investors and analysts came to rely on EBITDA more and more, as if it were cash flow. EBITDA is an accounting trick that flies beneath the radar and has some glaring faults, such as ignoring the expenses of a company. Depreciation for companies that use equipment heavily is a real expense because of the need to replace that equipment so often. But their EBITDA looks the same as a company that has as its only real equipment its office building, which is depreciated, and accurately so, over decades. The cash needs of the two firms are remarkably different. Such differences never plague the innovators, so EBITDA it was for all and all for EBITDA.

Perhaps WorldCom benefited the most from employing EBITDA because with its creative capitalization of $11 billion in ordinary expenses, its EBITDA looked even better because those capital expenses were not part of the computation. Not only were the innovators cooking the books, there was a double boiler going: there were no ordinary expenses, and capital expenses did not count under EBITDA. But all in this group of innovators—Enron, Adelphia, HealthSouth—relied on the magical innovation of EBITDA to report their stellar rules. All in all, EBITDA is not a bad way to report revenues, albeit revenues that are divorced from reality. Sarbanes-Oxley has fixed this issue by requiring that real numbers accompany "non-GAAP," i.e., EBITDA, numbers. You can spin any numbers yarn you want, but the real numbers must appear side by side.

The World's Accolades—Praise from All Quarters and Everyone Within Believes

All these companies enjoyed remarkable levels of praise from the business community. They were admired, respected, revered, and cited as best on just about every list that existed. It was as if these companies were seeking the accolades to validate themselves. Beneath the accolades they were crumbling, but the praise kept the wolves at bay and the doubts dismissed.

Enron: The Tops for Employees—If You Get Out in Time

Enron earned rankings of twenty-second and twenty-fourth in *Fortune*'s "100 Best Companies to Work For" in 1999 to 2001. The key to enjoying working at Enron was getting out in time, however. Enron collapsed in October 2001. So enamored was the world of this innovator from Houston that professors traveled great distances to study this company that was performing like no other. Professors Samuel Bodily and Robert Bruner were in the belly of Enron, studying it for its innovations and position as a giant in management, as the company collapsed. Innovators' reputations die hard. Even after Enron had gone south, the stock was trading for cents, and Skilling, Lay, and Fastow were hauled before Congress to take the Fifth or claim ignorance, Bodily and Bruner wrote a piece for *The Wall Street Journal* titled, "What Enron Did Right."

Fannie Mae: Corporate Citizen Extraordinaire

Franklin Raines was the consummate Washington insider, chosen to head up Fannie Mae. Iconic and revered, Raines, the son of a janitor who had built the family home from scraps of houses being torn down in the area around Seattle, rose from poverty to the pinnacle of the business world. When he took over Fannie Mae in 1999, he became the first African American to head a Fortune 500 company. There were few who did not respect Mr. Raines, and his testimony before Congress as Enron, WorldCom, Adelphia, and others were collapsing helped shape much of the new business regulation that came through the Sarbanes-Oxley reforms passed as a result of those hearings. Raines had reshaped Fannie Mae and earned it respect with a performance that defied market and government expectations. Until, of course, the earnings restatements began. He left; Fannie Mae struggles to recover as it copes with reality.

Tyco: The Moguls Return, They Saw, They Conquered

Tyco and its executives were referred to as "darlings of American investors." Kozlowski was featured on the cover of *Business Week* and was called "the most aggressive dealmaker in Corporate America." He was included in the magazine's top twenty-five managers of the year. Indeed, when Tyco's problems and accounting issues emerged, many of Wall Street's "superstar" money managers were stunned.

WorldCom: It Could Do No Wrong

Business Week referred to WorldCom as "the very model of a 21st century phone company. . . . The deal [MCI] will offer businesses one-stop shopping for all their communications needs." WorldCom was an international phenomenon from Mississippi that began with a meeting in a coffee shop as a former basketball coach huddled with some of the locals to start a long-distance company that would grow into a global telecom. Before they moved to the dark side on accounting, WorldCom had purchased sixty-five other companies, including several of the largest in the world. When Bernie used to tell his story at press conferences and analyst meetings, he would get standing ovations. "Wall Street was more than captivated by these new guys; they were eating the lotus leaves and it made companies like AT&T and Sprint look stodgy in comparison."

The Local Pride Factor That Tolerated a Little
Fudging Here and There

Perhaps more important than the world's accolades for these innovators were the hometown accolades. What may partially explain how these companies were able to go on for so long without detection of the fraud percolating beneath the awards and recognition is that they had so much local support. Parmalat had grown from a dairy farm with four or five cows into an international grocery company with 36,000 employees. Parmalat was the pride of Italy, the owner of a successful soccer team, and an example that Italy could be a major player in something beyond fashion, pasta, and Tuscan furniture. Enron put Houston on the map. Enron was a darling of Wall Street and known internationally, but it was not based in the usual power concentrations of New York, Los Angeles, Chicago, or San Francisco. Here was the energy company of the future, and it had sprung from Houston. WorldCom's Jackson and Hattiesburg, Mississippi, roots made it the pride of the state. Mississippi's hometown company was gobbling up some of the largest corporations in the world. Adelphia's Coudersport had a population of just five thousand, and it had produced the sixth-largest cable company in America. HealthSouth, a major market player and a revisionist in the health-care industry, came from Richard Scrushy, a native son of Alabama who had lived in a trailer park for a good portion of his adult life. Tyco was formed in New Hampshire and was taken to great heights by a man who had grown up in Jersey.

There were very few who were not rooting for these hometeam companies. When red flags popped up, disbelief was followed by assurances born of blind loyalty. For example, when Kozlowski was indicted for sales-tax evasion, there were still many who wanted him to stay. "Investors definitely like him and regard him highly. It's very important that he stays." Likewise, when Enron collapsed, the company was in bankruptcy, and Fastow emerged as the architect of the off-the-books entities, a Houston friend who had worked in the community with Fastow said, "The person I know bears absolutely no relation to the person who has been characterized, in some reports, within the walls of Enron."

Richard Scrushy and his wife, Leslie, remain a regular part of the flock at Guiding Light Church in Birmingham. The pastor's wife has said, "I've seen him so often in church with members of his family. I believe he is a man of integrity." Richard Scrushy's website traces his humble roots back to Selma, Alabama, and he capitalized on the home-team mentality. Some experts attribute the hung jury in his criminal trial to the fact that so many jurors (the trial was held in Scrushy's home state) were sympathetic to the small-town boy who made it to the big time. Their resentment of the government trying to bring Scrushy down a peg or two, or all the way down to prison, resulted in reasonable doubt. Mr. Scrushy was indicted four months after his acquittal on federal charges of bribery and fraud, charges he pled not guilty to. A local television station, owned by Mr. Scrushy's son-in-law, even featured two 30-minute recaps of the trial each day, complete with commentary that many find favorable to Scrushy. In fact, Scrushy was acquitted of all charges. The local support for Scrushy was stunning. Amazingly, at 10:30 P.M. and 6:30 A.M., 200,000 viewers tuned in for the trial coverage of what amounted to, for those in Alabama, the trial of the century. The analysts included a reporter who once did PR work for HealthSouth and a former member of Scrushy's defense team. And the economic impact to Birmingham of losing a company like HealthSouth was staggering. A $300 million hospital that was under construction has been sitting as a huge eyesore of a shell since HealthSouth's bankruptcy in 2003. Now the construction work is gone and the downsizing of HealthSouth from its fifty thousand employees has taken its toll on the economy. The locals have a hard time accepting the conduct or demise of their hero. If you interview either the innovators, whether convicted or walking free, or the locals, you find, despite the crumbled ruins about them, a universal attitude reflected by "if the government had just let us alone, we could have pulled it out." HealthSouth has responded to a suit by Scrushy with allegations that he "pillaged" the company. A judge has ordered Scrushy to repay his bonuses. HealthSouth agreed to a $200 million fine to settle SEC charges and has put its legal issues behind it.

Perks, Perks, Perks

Another common trait of ethically collapsed companies is that they seem to be able to afford extensive benefits that other companies simply don't have the margins to provide. These companies are awash in perks others companies, with their human margins, can only dream of.

Enron: A Concierge and Starbucks

Ken Lay spread around the Enron largesse. Employees enjoyed an on-site health club, on-site physician, and great retirement programs. Mr. Lay spared no expense on officer retreats, with race cars available for executives. Enron's annual executive meetings, held each January, kept getting more extravagant, even legendary in their opulence. The Enron excesses are legion. The January 2001 executive team meeting was held at the Hyatt Regency Hill Country Resort in San Antonio and included an open bar and fistfuls of free cigars. Local strippers indicated that they could tell when an Enron deal closed because their take on a post-work-day shift following one of those deal consummations was often $1,200.

Tyco: Jimmy Buffett and China

Tyco, like Enron, was a company whose perks were head and shoulders above the rest, with breakfasts delivered to employees on china, a masseuse available every Friday, and opulent offices in Boca Raton. Kozlowski's spending alone was legion among company CEOs. There was that infamous Sardinia birthday party for his wife that ran for days and had Jimmy Buffett playing the gig. The tab for the bash was put at $2.1 million, most of which was listed in an 8-K filed by the board after it realized what was happening within the company, an epiphany that arrived when its CEO was indicted for sales-tax evasion.

HealthSouth and the Others

HealthSouth was offering stock options to Tommy Mottola, the Sony record producer (who never exercised them), with the hope that he would promote the rock groups that had captured Scrushy's attention. Along the way Scrushy bought a jet, a boat, and cars too numerous to list, all at company expense as part of the necessary trappings of being a CEO.

None of the company founders or officers concealed the trappings of their innovation. They all spent to excess, leaving no doubt that they deserved their wealth and station because they were a cut above. *Discreet* was not a term in the vocabulary or behavior of the innovators. Whether personal or company money (and in some cases no one is sure), they spent to show.

A Culture of Wizards and Hubris: The Products of U.S. Business Schools

Mea culpa. I fear that we in business schools unleashed many of the monster innovators who masterminded these creative financing mechanisms. We must at least take credit for creating EBITDA. A list of executives directly beneath the CEOs of their companies finds the majority of them holding their MBAs. The senior officer group of Enron was a collection of well-trained MBAs who had been given the hypertechnical tools typical of financial education in MBA programs in the 1980s. In fact, Enron hired 250 new MBAs per year for its management team. The credentials for the Enron executive team were as follows: Jeffrey K. Skilling, the former CEO of Enron, held an MBA from Harvard. Andrew Fastow, the former CFO, held a Northwestern MBA. Clifford Baxter, a former vice chairman who, as described earlier, killed himself shortly after the Enron revelations became a daily media event, was a Columbia MBA. Scott Sullivan, the CFO of WorldCom, had an undergraduate degree in accounting. The Rigas boys of Adelphia had Harvard and Wharton MBAs. They all also seemed to keep score by the salaries, cars, and houses they accumulated. After being fired, Andrew Fastow and his wife, Lea, an heiress, seemed unbowed as they continued to build their 11,500-square-foot home, and his friends say that the amount of money someone made was his only measure of a person's worth and success.

The MBA curriculum since the 1980s has focused on financial models designed to smooth earnings and produce double-digit returns for interminable stretches, things history tells us are not possible. There was a mind-set on "gotcha" financing methods that found ways around the rules and raised money in opaque ways. Along the way, there was nary a discussion of values, moral absolutes, or even virtue ethics. The mandates of the accrediting body for business schools curriculum (AACSB) contain no specific references to issues such as honesty, disclosure, and fairness. To the extent ethics were a part of the curriculum in this era, it consisted of the *noblesse oblige* issues for executives and their social responsibility. The focus was on environmental, health, and safety issues and corporate philanthropy. (Greater coverage of these issues emerges in Chapter 8.)

The MBA curriculum of the 1980s and 1990s that produced these executives who went on to create the Yeehaw Culture in their companies carries a certain disdain for traditional business principles of low cost, quality, service, and real profits. These executives were trained by a curriculum that convinced its charges that they were better, smarter, and above the proletarian notion of reporting debt and expenses. Managing earnings was taught as a means of delivering shareholder value. It wasn't cooking the books, it was financial engineering. But they were never given boundaries, or lines they should not cross, as they "managed" earnings. They learned the tools for managing earnings but never discussed the ethical issues involved in manipulation of earnings, another term for the same practice but far less pretty and nonthreatening. This callous financial model took its toll on the ethos of the MBAs. Professors James Stearns of Miami University and Shaheen Borna of Ball State University interviewed three hundred incarcerated inmates at three minimum-security prisons and compared their responses with those of students at eleven MBA programs. The inmates showed just as much integrity, or more, when presented with ethical dilemmas. Inmates were more concerned about customer service while MBAs were more concerned about pleasing shareholders. Inmates were also less likely to pirate employees from other companies than were the MBAs.

Those of us in business schools unleashed, perhaps unwittingly, skilled unethical automatons into the market, amoral technicians who were capable of tapping into financial complexities that rested in the loopholes of law and accounting. Skill was everything. Values were nothing. There were no moral absolutes. We created and fueled the hubris that would consume so many of them as they found success with their well-honed talents in areas of financial application and interpreation that demanded ethical judgment. Without that judgment, they rode the Yeehaw Culture to the largest frauds and bankruptcies in our history.

The Antidotes for Innovation Like No Other

Couching themselves as somehow different and immune from the mundane rules of doing business and the general economic forces of markets allowed the Yeehaw participants their air of superiority, one that placed them above competition, rules, and self-correction for their legal and ethical drifts. "No worries" was the credible mantra of these wizards of hubris for a time because they had convinced themselves that they were unique. Then the employees who worked for these executives bought into the unique myth, as did investors, analysts, and shareholders. Those who were not innovators stood in awe of them. Their very certainty about their innovation and ability served as a cover for the developing and underlying problems at their companies.

An executive team that can dupe itself and so many others does not begin with the intention of fraud. Rather, they begin with innovation that is executed poorly or simply hits the reality of a mature market or the skills of a new innovator. To keep the momentum of double-digit earnings, innovators must resort to schemes, artifice, and rules violations undertaken with the noble intent of preservation. When former WorldCom CFO Scott Sullivan entered his guilty plea, he told the judge he knew what he had done was wrong (capitalizing $11 billion in ordinary expenses does cross a few legal, ethical, and accounting lines) but added that it was a misguided attempt to save the company. A self-perception, born of that initial innovation and initially unique market position and standing, consumes logic. Unlike those who have gone before and failed in such deceptions, these innovators in a Yeehaw Culture believe that they will be able to pull it all off and maintain the company's position. Scott Sullivan met with two accountants, Buford Yates and Betty Vinson, when they objected to the schemes, artifice, and frauds for which they were being asked to serve as accomplices. They wanted to tender their resignations. They had been asked to make entries that took from reserves (the cookie jar) to boost results so as to meet the earnings expectations of the market. Sullivan explained the need for team players to see the company through a temporary earnings, accounting crisis.

At some point, even innovators must comply with the rules of accounting and tend to the mundane aspects of business. When a company's claims of innovation and distinction purchase a self-perceived immunity from the buffetings of the market, the requirements of business operations, the principles of accounting, and even the financial laws and regulations, the executive team transforms itself from an energetic group of innovators with the best of intentions into a diabolical group hell-bent on preserving the status quo as well as their status and position. They are consumed by the company's share price, something that was the key to their own personal financial position and wealth accumulation.

The absence of scrutiny only extends and expands the cover-up period during which innovation has vanished and the executive team is buried beneath the harsh reality of business and the unrelenting demands of operations, markets, and customers. To breathe during this immersion in harsh reality, the executive teams prop open windows and doors with toothpicks of flimsy accounting and create temporary air vents. They hope that these passing fixes will last until they can undertake massive reconstruction. This factor in the culture finds the executives leading the employees down a primrose path that has them believing that ordinary rules do not apply to them. Everyone in the company drinks the Kool-Aid of "We're better. We're different. The rules either don't apply, or we don't need the rules." More important, they believe they can manage the situation until it all can turn around. They cannot, and understanding their own psychology as well as the odds, with a bit of business history and economics tossed in, serves as an antidote for the innovation factor in ethical collapse.

Antidote #1 for Innovation Like No Other: Recognize Limits on Ability and That Truth Cannot Be Managed

The work of MIT professors David Messick and Max Bazerman poses the question, applicable in ethical collapses: how do bright people make such ridiculous choices when they are running an organization? The self-perceived uniqueness of individuals who make such choices is a critical component of their inability to see the folly of their choices:

We all correctly believe that we are unique individuals. However, theories about ourselves lead us to unrealistic beliefs about ourselves that may cause us to underestimate our exposure to risk, take more than our fair share of the credit for success (or too little for failure), or be too confident that our theory of the world is the correct one. If most of the executives in an organization think that they are in the upper ten percent of the talent distribution, there is the potential for pervasive disappointment.

Further, this tendency of self-perceived uniqueness coupled with the so-called psychological illusion of control, the belief that they can manage and fix the situation, can lead executives down the path of numbers manipulation. They really do believe (and it is a firmly held belief) that they will be able to control the situation sufficiently until they have a chance to correct it and get those numbers back to where they need to be, indeed, where they used to be. For example, Scott Sullivan's reference to his employees about the company being like an aircraft carrier (see Chapter 3) that needed to land a couple of planes was classically symptomatic of the belief of a self-perceived innovator caught in a declining situation. Messick and Bazerman note:

One reason we think that we are relatively immune to common risks is that we exaggerate the extent to which we can control random events. Experiments have demonstrated the illusion of control with MBA students from some top U.S. business schools, so there is no reason to think that executives who have attended these schools will be immune to them.

When the revelations about Enron began to emerge and those in business began to realize the magnitude of the accounting misstatements in the case, *The Wall Street Journal*'s Holman Jenkins Jr. wrote a piece about Enron's officers titled, "How Could They Have Done It?" based on the work of Messick and Bazerman. Managers and executives make misguided decisions because they base those decisions on factors they deem to be reasonable at the moment but have nothing to do with either the realities or ethics of the situation:

- Erroneous confidence

- Exaggerated sense of control

- Experience with "good future events"

Messick and Bazerman explain what happens to managers and others who make such poor decisions that in hindsight cause us all to utter collectively, "Where were their minds and what were they thinking when they made these choices?" All the examples used by Messick and Bazerman show leaders who felt that they were somehow unique, different from those in the past who had confronted the inability to meet financial goals. Hubris has far more impact on financial-reporting decisions than perhaps we have acknowledged. Greed is there as well, but it cannot fully explain the level of risk taken in circumstances in which the financial gain cannot be equated with the risk taken. Erroneous confidence and exaggerated sense of control emerge as causes of poor choices in high-pressure situations—particularly in those organizations in which "innovation," "market leader," and "a cut-above" have been the bywords of the culture.

This attitude is a dangerous one for an ethical culture. There can be no violation of rules if the rules don't apply. Making the journey to "no rules" opens the door to fraud. By the time the full psychology of the self-perceived innovators kicks in, they are unable to spot the difference between their choices and the legitimate path to success. Fraud is hardly fraud if you have convinced yourself that the rules on fraud don't apply to you. The following statements collected over time, and recognitions for innovations, demonstrate the level of delusion within these Yeehaw Cultures. Those who uttered the statements or were recipients of adulations were doing just the opposite of the words they spoke and using questionable means to enjoy success. Still, they felt the now ironic words, not their conduct, captured reality:

Quote/Award Question	Answer
What company's CEO was named one of *Business Week*'s top managers for 2000 and 2001?	Dennis Kozlowski, Tyco
What companies' CFOs were named CFO of the year for 1999, 2000, and 2001?	Andrew Fastow, Scott Sullivan, and Mark Swartz, Enron
What company was ranked forty-fourth, twenty-fourth, and twenty-second by *Fortune* as one of its 100 best companies to work for?	Enron
What company was described in 2001 as having a delivery and marketing model that would change its industry?	HealthSouth
What CEO said in 2001, "We have no perks, not even parking spaces"?	Dennis Kozlowski, Tyco
What CEO said, "We are the good guys. We are on the side of angels"?	Jeffrey Skilling, Enron
What company had a sixty-four-page, award-winning code of ethics?	Enron

"People have an obligation to dissent in this company. . . . I mean, I sit up there on the 50th floor, in the library. I have no idea what's going on down there, so if you've got a problem with it, speak up. And if you don't speak up, that's not good."

Jeffrey Skilling, Enron

"It's more than just money. You've got to give back to the community that supported you."

John Rigas, Adelphia

"You'll see people who in the early days . . . took their life savings and trusted this company with their money. And I have an awesome responsibility to those people to make sure that they're done right."

Bernie Ebbers, WorldCom

"Boards should be absolutely certain that the company is run properly from a fiduciary standpoint in every degree. I am a great believer in the audit committee having full access to the auditors in every way, shape, or form."

Chainsaw Al Dunlap, Sunbeam

"It must really piss you off to hear Cendant and Tyco mentioned in the same sentence."

Said by Henry Silverman, CEO of Cendant, to Dennis Kozlowski.

"Henry, it drives me nuts." (in a conversation circa 1998, the time Cendant was openly and voluntarily grappling with accounting issues discovered in a company it acquired and Tyco's accounting was just warming up into cooking the books)

Dennis Kozlowski

"It is wholly irresponsible and unacceptable for corporate leaders to say they did not know—or suggest that it is not their duty to know—about the activities and operations of their company, particularly when it comes to risks that threaten the fundamental viability of their company."

Franklin Raines, former CEO of Fannie Mae, during his testimony in support of Sarbanes-Oxley

It turns out that the talk was just talk, and the only walk would be their perp walks when ethical collapse occurred. This element of innovation in the Yeehaw Culture, more so than the others, requires intensely training executives to remove their senior-management blinders and understand employee perceptions of their conduct. Even innovators must comply with the rules of accounting and tend to the mundane aspects of business. Antidotes must break down the egocentrism that consumes these highly successful (to date) and driven individuals who have come to believe that they can defy the odds and are above the rules, laws, regulations, and basic economies. It was fascinating to watch both Mr. Lay and Mr. Skilling testify at their criminal trial in 2006. Their testimony reflected a victim mentality. They knew what they were doing; it was the rest of the world trying to impose artifical constraints on their unique company. Mr. Lay went so far as to allege that *The Wall Street Journal*'s coverage of Enron was part of the reason for the company's failure. They attempt to defy the odds of truth coming out, but they also try to defy economic cycles and business history, two more antidotes for the innovation obsession that fuels ethical collapse.

Antidote #2 for Innovation Like No Other: Keep in Mind the Basics of Economics and Economic Cycles and Business History

One observer who watched the rise and fall of Enron noted (referring to Enron but clearly applicable to all the companies examined here), "If they had been going a slower speed, their results would not have been disastrous. It's a lot harder to keep it on the track at 200 miles per hour. You hit a bump and you're off the track." Enron's earnings from 1997 to 2001 were ultimately restated, with a resulting reduction of $568 million, or the disappearance of 20 percent of its earnings for those four years.

The special report commissioned by the Enron board following the company's collapse described its culture as follows: "a flawed idea, self-enrichment by employees, inadequately designed controls, poor implementation, inattentive oversight, simple (and not so simple) accounting mistakes, and overreaching in a culture that appears to have encouraged pushing the limits." Fastow openly touted his strategy of spinning Enron's debt off its books into SPEs. Such candor seemed refreshing. However, for Fastow it was hubris writ large. He had found an accounting loophole and was thumbing his nose at those who live by the mundane spirit of those rules and the law. He, bright innovator that he was, had proudly found a way around it all. Let the rest of the world live by the dull compliance with rules. He would soar with the loopholes. A disregard for the rules, a manipulation of the rules, and a refusal to acknowledge the basic economic rules are the characteristics of the innovators in a Yeehaw Culture.

Innovators continue to believe that they can outperform all others in what has been a relatively low-earnings industry. When all was said and done, WorldCom was a utility. And as any student of a basic microeconomics course can describe, utilities have had stable but not stellar earnings over the years. While WorldCom had revenues galore, its acquisitions also gave it debt galore; thus, its shares were overpriced from the outset because the innovators made investors believe that the company was somehow a cut above your basic utility. "The real issue isn't accounting. It is the incentive people had to use questionable accounting. The truth is that this never was an industry which made phenomenal returns. People forget this was foremost a utility business."

How soon they do forget, particularly business history and the lessons of economic cycles. The tendency to push the envelope on financial reports, inventory, and shipments is not unique to the United States or this century. A lack of foundation in business history, or even just general history, allows innovators to put on blinders in their zeal to conquer all. Worse, those who invest in the innovators' schemes also lack the historical perspective to draw parallels; perhaps if they could show the wisdom and restraint in not providing capital fuel for the fire of the innovator, they could save the innovators and themselves. Innovators are innovators, and their tactics and ploys to stay on top of a market in which they were the first movers are limitless in their creativity but certain to be carried out because invariably they think that they are unlike any other business and no one has ever seen the likes of them before. The following excerpt documents the eerily similar experience of the Holland tulip market in the 1630s:

> The story of the founding and growth of the Holland tulip market is a remarkably similar one. When the tulip was developed, people were enamored of it. They began buying tulips, fields of tulips and developing tulips. When tulips were no longer available, they began buying tulip bulbs because they would have a tulip at some time in the future. When there were no bulbs left, they created a market for tulip bulb futures. At the height of the market, one tulip bulb future cost $10,000 in present-day dollars. There was a market of air with complete dependence on the creation of bulbs in the future; these were investments in air completely dependent upon the honor of those selling these derivative tulip instruments.
>
> Eventually investors realized that those who sold the futures could not possibly deliver all that they had sold and the market collapsed. The impact on the Holland economy was centuries in length.

In these bubble economies, investors, consultants, auditors, executives, and analysts are eager to be part of what seems an unending upward swing. Fearful of disembarking too soon or causing others to do so, everyone pushes the financial-reporting envelope, from the user who strains credibility to the executive who manipulates to meet investor and analyst expectations. The pattern includes irrational expectations:

> *This* [the 1990's bubble] *was not the first speculative bubble. The broadband boom has its match in the railway boom of the late 19th century. The Internet boom resembled the radio boom of the 1920s, when one of the favorite stocks, RCA, went from $1 a share to almost $600 a share in just a few years. And, of course, investors believed there was a "new economy" in the 1920s, too. More recently, the Japanese bubble economy of the late 1980s and the euphoria that preceded the Asian financial crisis of the late 1990s offer striking analogies. In each case, it was assumed that trees would grow to heaven.*

Following the 1929 stock market crash and the revelations about the many shell corporations whose financial status was unclear or misrepresented, there was tremendous fallout in the market:

> *But the 1920s bubble burst in late October, 1929. By mid- November, 1929, the Dow plunged to 198 from its September, 1929, high of 381. By July, 1932, the Dow hit forty-one, down 89%. It would not surpass its 1929 high for twenty-five years.*

When all of the financial-reporting scandals of the 1999–2002 period emerged, there was a mass exodus of investors from the stock market into bonds and cash or cash equivalents. By October 2002 the NASDAQ had collapsed to a low of 1139 from its May 2000 peak of 5085—a fall of 77.5 percent. Perhaps the worst revelation was that so many of the companies of the so-called new economy (listed on the NASDAQ) had restated their earnings, a downward adjustment of $148 billion, and the result was, collectively speaking, they had not made a dime since 1995.

The pattern is indeed the same across decades, bubbles, and markets. And following each market crash comes intense regulation. Regardless of investors' lack of wisdom in structuring their portfolios and believing financial reports and results that defy gravity, the burst bubble means that there must be penance for the abuse of investor trust. Sarbanes-Oxley is the additional regulation that results. The regulation is complex and expensive in implementation. Even after that regulation has taken effect, there remain the same issues relating to ethical dilemmas underlying financial reporting, particularly in cycles of profound economic growth. Maintaining expected numbers creates pressures, especially when those numbers are expected on a quarterly basis. Accounting treatments that may be overly aggressive are more easily utilized when so much is on the line in terms of stock performance and the reaction of the market to earnings reports that are down by even pennies. The other factors in the Yeehaw Culture worked hand in glove with the mind-set of the innovators, who divorced themselves from history and the basics of economics and finance, in order to believe that they could somehow defy the odds and economic principles.

The significant legislative and regulatory reforms, many still ongoing, following the dot-com bubble burst and the Enron, WorldCom, Tyco, and Adelphia debacles represent that third great regulatory reform involving financial markets since the mid-1980s. Even as the reforms begin to take hold, we have new innovators upon whom even the most recent history lessons have been lost. AIG is an insurance company like no other insurance company before it. And its reinsurance techniques were reinventing the way companies carried risk, insurance, and debt. Along the way there was apparently some reinvention of accounting standards as well. AIG settled with the SEC and Eliot Spitzer for $1.64 billion. AIG CEO and president Martin J. Sullivan released the following statement in announcing the settlement: "These settlements are a major step forward in resolving the legal and regulatory issues facing AIG. We have already implemented a wide range of improvements in our accounting, financial reporting, and corporate governance, and will continue to make enhancements in these areas. AIG is committed to business practices that provide transparency and fairness in the insurance markets." Mr. Spitzer included the following in his statement on the settlement: "AIG was and is a solid company that didn't need to cheat. It finds itself in this position solely because some senior managers thought it was acceptable to deceive the investing public and regulators. However, by changing management, implementing reforms and providing restitution to injured investors, customers, and states, the company has placed itself on a path toward resurgence." Both are correct—the company is bringing itself back from ethical collapse. But the regret is the billion-dollar-level fine, the distraction from doing business, and the time and effort put into corrective and remunerative behaviors. The goal in looking at what causes ethical collapse is introspection. Do we have any of the signs? Are we doing things here that are similar to what these other companies were doing? The end result is prevention, not redemption.

One wishes AIG and its new team well, but there is that nagging question that must be asked. We all somehow see ourselves as the most ethical person in the room and, collectively, as a part of ours, the most ethical company ever to grace the American business front. Drawing the parallels and self-correcting constitute the prevention tools for ethical collapse. How can executives as bright and capable as those who were running both AIG and Warren Buffett's Berkshire Hathaway's General Re at the time of the strategies that resulted in a regulatory clamp-down not see the similarities between their accounting and risk strategies with these cooperative spin-offs and Enron's tactics, albeit much greater and riskier, behavior? Just the use of offshore entities should have raised some eyebrows if not flags. Sometimes pulling ourselves back even when we are well within legal bounds prevents regulatory fallout. There's that turn of the path, not the first step. These are neither close calls nor novel issues. They are the types of accounting and disclosure issues Sarbanes-Oxley was passed to prevent, but somehow executives in great companies still today fancy themselves different from the "other guys" and above the fray of head-to-head competition. So have all the other executives in each of the previous series of ethical collapses. Bright, capable professionals and executives find the lessons of other companies lost in translation.

The classic question, too often repeated when scandal hits, is that of federal Judge Stanley Sporkin: "Where were these professionals . . . when these clearly improper transactions were being consummated? Why didn't any of them speak up or disassociate themselves from the transactions?" Judge Sporkin referred to the lawyers and the accountants who did not fulfill their roles in reining in the innovators. In the late 1980s we lost 525 savings and loans to bankruptcy. In California alone, of the thirty-six savings and loans that went bankrupt, twenty-eight had received clean audit opinions. Auditors gave their imprimatur to questionable accounting used by the S&Ls. In this most recent cycle, many analysts proved handmaidens to the innovators and through their glowing evaluations lent their credibility to teetering dot-coms and telecoms. The cover of *Fortune* for May 14, 2001, just after the bubble burst, featured analyst Mary Meeker and the caption "Can We Ever Trust Again?" One year later the cover of *Fortune* featured Sallie Krawcheck and the caption "In Search of the Last Honest Analyst." During the junk-bond era of the 1980s, investment-banking firms and analysts sang the praises of the deals, mergers, and hostile takeovers. We even had the same behavior that the bubble witnessed: insiders dumping stock. The infamous Boesky and Milken represented the top of the prosecutorial hill during that round of innovators gone berserk.

The pattern is the same. We lose our minds, anchors, and rational thought in the exuberance of the boom. Innovators skirt statutes, accounting rules, and the laws of economics in the irrational exuberance. But even as the behaviors are the same, so are the results: prosecutions, convictions, financial collapse, and extensive regulatory reform. The savings-and-loan-collapse reforms came through the Financial Institutions Reform, Recovery and Enforcement Act of 1989 (FIRREA), 12 U.S.C. §§ 191 et seq., which required new minimum capital requirements for loans. The Boesky/Milken era resulted in the Insider Trading Sanctions Act, 15 U.S.C. § 78u-l (2002) which made it possible for the government to recover as a penalty three times the amount of profit made or loss avoided from the inside deal. (Milken was charged with insider trading, but that charge was never proven. He entered guilty pleas to lesser offenses.) There was also the Insider Trading and Securities Fraud Enforcement Act, 15 U.S.C. § 78ff (2002), which upped the penalties for insider trading to ten years and $1 million. Sarbanes-Oxley has reformed everything from corporate boards to audit practice to audit firms to the penalties for shredding documents.

To understand business history and economic cycles, innovators should be reminded that when someone raises questions about their company, its performance, and its market-defying climb, they should explore the questions, not denounce the questioner. For example, Scott Cleland, founder of Precursor Group, a Washington, D.C.–based investment research firm, not only predicted that the WorldCom-Sprint merger would fail but also that once the merger failed that WorldCom would be a "dead model walking." Innovator Bernie Ebbers called Mr. Cleland an "idiot." Mr. Cleland was the prescient one. If the questioner is mistaken, the market benefits from the response and analysis of the company. If the questioner is right, the company may still have time to self-correct. Additionally, board members should be cognizant of these questions and rein in the innovators, or at least address the issues being raised by objective observers outside the company.

Those who were able to spot the problems with Enron, WorldCom, Adelphia, and Tyco tout no special skills other than following the basics of economic and financial analysis. As noted earlier, analyst John Olson talked with former employees who described Enron as doing everything "on the edge." Olson was quoted after Enron's collapse as feeling that too many Wall Street analysts were being *schnuckels*, a Yiddish word for "dupe." His simple advice was that too few "kicked the tires" of the company. Peter Eavis of TheStreet.com also raised questions about Enron, including how Enron's profit may have been due to constant asset transfers. He also wrote about Andrew Fastow's dual roles as CFO of Enron and principal in the companies taking title to Enron assets. Not only did no mainstream media outlets or analysts pick up on his observations or questions, no board member did, either. And history was repeating itself with Enron. Middle West Utilities collapsed in the years following the 1929 stock crash precisely because it too had an astounding amount of off-the-books debt through interconnected companies and interlocking boards. Its structure was so complex that it took the Federal Trade Commission seven years to unravel its financial structure. When it did collapse, Samuel L. Insull, its CEO, was very much a Ken Lay, someone who had been generous with political donations and someone who quickly became a target for vilification. He was tried for fraud and embezzlement, left the country as lawsuits from shareholders were litigated, and died of a heart attack while waiting for a subway in Paris. He had only 85 cents in his pocket. Mr. Insull "went down with his ship." Middle West's collapse was responsible for the passage of the 1934 Securities Exchange Act (15

U.S.C. § 78), the Public Utility Holding Company Act, and the Federal Power Act, the last two being federal laws in which Enron found loopholes.

It's not the glowing media reports and analyses that help curb the activities of the culture of innovation that goes awry. It is the negative reports that force introspection and can be the impetus for self-corrective action. If someone has found an Achille's heel, innovators will deny it. Boards should explore it, and everyone should be asking more questions. The pattern is the same if the questions are ignored. Innovation continues its march to fraud. However, if the questions produce introspection, the company may survive. Like all happy families, companies that survive do so because they have responded to questions and have the time and ability for self-correction.

Antidote #3 for Innovation Like No Other: Honesty and Candor

As difficult as it is for innovators to believe (because they fancy themselves immune to the dull advice of ages past), the best policy for increasing a company's share price is honesty. Chasing the magic formula is their mind-set, but as antidote #1 shows, the magic formulas fail. The following is an excerpt from *CFO Magazine*, which appears to be doing some of its own penance for naming Fastow, Swartz, and Sullivan of Enron, Tyco, and WorldCom, respectively, as CFOs of the year:

> *Honesty is the best policy, if a company's leadership wants a better stock price.*
>
> *That's the conclusion of the Rittenhouse Rankings survey, which claims that there's a positive correlation between candid communication and superior share-price performance. Of the sample 100 Fortune 500 companies surveyed, the top-ranked ones boosted their share prices over a two-year period by 21.5 percent, while bottom-ranked companies saw only a 7.3 percent increase.*

In other words, if a company is to enjoy the market's grace, it should be forthright in its communications. This antidote inculcates a culture that teaches employees, officers, managers, and the board to face up to earnings issues and not mask them. The goal is to solve business setbacks strategically, not through manipulation of the numbers. With the business and economic-cycle backdrop, the lesson is that markets extract from companies bad quarters and bad years, no matter how good the innovators who run them. The task is not one of hiding those quarters but finding ways to recover or, in some situations, prevent them. A downward turn in one segment of the market, such as housing, does not mean that all segments are down. One of the strategic counterbalances, then, is diversification. With cushioning available during economic and market cycles, the pressure is far less on even innovators to begin their market manipulations. This antidote requires far more long-term planning and open discussions about the buffetings of the market. It requires deeper thinking and greater long-range planning, all undertaken with the confidence that the company or organization will survive temporary setbacks that come with the ups and downs of the market. Even for nonprofits, there are times during which donations decline (generally when businesses also have a downturn). If they have developed plans for adjusting, such as postponement of construction, renovations, and accessions, the pressure to raise money is less likely to consume the innovators into crossing ethical and legal lines.

The key point is that no business can survive, no matter how clever the manipulation, without facing up to its downturns and problems. If the news is bad, the question is not "How do we mask it?" The questions are, instead, "How do we solve this problem?" and "How did we get into this situation in the first place?" and "How can we prevent the same thing from happening again?" Manipulation of numbers, rules, and markets is a short-term and shortsighted fix, and innovators need to be trained to understand that it is in no one's best interest to resort to deception, not just for the sake of avoiding fraud charges but for the sake of moving the organization forward.

Antidote #4 for Innovation Like No Other: Resilience to Pressure

Professor David Woods of Ohio State University has done extensive work with engineers, most particularly those who have been with NASA and have succumbed to pressure to overlook safety issues in the name of budget constraints or to meet a launch date. His observations about engineers run parallel to those about managers of Yeehaw Cultures. He calls the training required to help them make correct decisions on safety issues "resilience engineering." He has discovered that these engineers understand right from wrong and are fully cognizant that they have crossed ethical or legal lines in their decisions and actions. However, they simply do not have the resilience to withstand the pressure placed upon them by others who are interested in meeting goals, whether it be the launch date or the quarterly earnings numbers. There is much in the literature on psychology to help apply this antidote. Every business manager, every student of business, every officer of any organization, and every board member should study some of the classic literature on the compliant nature of human beings. This human nature is part of the Yeehaw Culture. Understanding it can create opportunities for structural curbs and help us develop the moral fiber to withstand pressure. How do we create managers and employees who are resilient enough to withstand the numbers pressure that consumes the Yeehaw Culture? How do we give them the backbone to stand up to managers who have asked them to cross ethical lines? What gives them the strength to do the right thing when their job and income hang in the balance? What allows an employee to muster the strength to stand up to an innovator who is taking all of them places, and with the compensation that goes with a winner?

Herein lies the heart of ethics in any organization. We spend far too much time on codes of ethics, training employees on what is and is not a conflict, and what the rules are on price-fixing. Even innovators know when they have crossed ethical and legal lines. They have just rationalized their way around the element of conscience. Knowing right from wrong in the Yeehaw Culture is not the issue. Acting to stop the wrong is what we need. Acting to halt wrongs cannot come about unless and until we have openly discussed human nature, explored personal values, and alerted employees to the types of obstacles the Yeehaw Culture can create but which they should overcome. This deeper exploration is what is missing from nearly all ethics programs and most corporate cultures as they struggle with the primeval compliance programs that cannot conquer these elements of human nature or delve into the better part of ourselves that will work to curb innovators.

Individual Priorities and the Better Road Not Taken

There are some key pieces in the business literature that offer insight into our makeup when we are faced with pressure, difficult circumstances, and the realization of a setback. One is "The Parable of the Sadhu," by Bowen H. McCoy. The following description of this piece and its key points for managers was adapted from another article I wrote for the *Accounting Education Review* in 2004 for training students in ethics.

This article remains one of Harvard's most frequently requested reprints because it deals with introspection regarding ethical choices. Bowen McCoy was a successful Wall Street investment banker when he took a sabbatical for the purpose of climbing to the summit of one of Nepal's highest ranges. McCoy's attempts to climb the summit in the past had yielded only altitude sickness and McCoy's retreat to the villages at base camp as others went on to reach the summit.

The climb this time is going well because McCoy is not experiencing altitude sickness and the weather is cooperating. On the day he will reach the summit, he and his companion, along with their Sherpas and parties from other countries, are proceeding well during that small window of opportunity that they have before the sun melts the steps they have carved in the ice located in the narrow passageways to the summit. Anticipation for finally reaching their goal has all of the climbing parties excited.

But they encounter a religious pilgrim, a sadhu, who is not dressed appropriately, collapsed in the snow and suffering from altitude sickness. To be certain that the pilgrim survives would require them to carry him back down to the village below their base camp. To do so would mean that they could not make the climb because of the loss of daylight and proper conditions for the ascent. So, each person and climbing party offers some help. One group offers additional clothing. Another group offers food. Still another waits to be sure that the sadhu is revived enough that hand-eye coordination is restored. A final group points down the mountainside to the base camp and village below, as if offering directions to the sadhu on how to proceed. Then they all move on in their climb and all reach their goal of the summit.

Only after the climb does McCoy's companion confront him with the reality of what they have done. Stephen, McCoy's partner, notes that they all perhaps contributed to the death of another human being. Although they can never know whether the sadhu lived or died, McCoy and Stephen are left with a hollow feeling of "our goal accomplished, but at what cost?" There are several key teaching points in the piece that offer students insight into resolving ethical dilemmas, one that is life or death in this reading:

- Ethical choices can mean that a goal is not achieved or is achieved in delayed fashion.

- When there are groups responsible for making ethical decisions, each person defers to the next, with the deceptive comfort that ultimate accountability does not lie with any one individual.

- Changing one's values (in this case, respect for life) in a different setting (in this case, a grueling mountain climb) may seem justified, but ultimately achieving the goal produces a gnawing feeling of "At what cost?"

- The parallels to business found in McCoy's story offer true parabolic qualities for students: the climb is rugged with challenges, there are often limited windows of opportunity for success, ethical choices can mean temporary setbacks in achieving goals, others are always willing to go on despite ethical dilemmas confronting them in their quest for the goal.

- Defining dilemmas in the either/or conundrum (either I let the sadhu go and make the climb, or I help him and again miss my goal) produces choices that disregard ethics and values. McCoy points out that his most memorable experience is not achieving the summit but, rather, those moments he spent in the village at base camp when he had altitude sickness and the rest of his party went on. The immersion in culture, the weddings experienced, and the kindness of the villagers were the true rich experiences of his climbs, not the conquest of the summit.

- McCoy cautions about the need for values in place up front so that when we are confronted with ethical dilemmas, our values are not compromised for the goal.

- McCoy provides students with the notion of regret for ethically shallow choices such as the one that he made on the mountainside that day.

The piece forces us to think in these terms: "When all is said and done, how comfortable will I be about the decisions I have made in order to meet a goal?"

Understanding Authority and Pressure and the Need to Resist Both

There are in addition to that part of the antidote that forces managers and others to explore themselves individually a requirement that they understand the components of authority, pressure, and groupthink. Understanding the dynamics that lead good and smart people to do ethically dumb things is critical *before* the manager faces the dilemma and the pressure of the moment. Not much has changed in terms of the ability of authority to force good people into bad decisions or in the fear that makes us go along with the crowd despite what we know to be true, or even the consequences to everyone going along. Stanley Milgram's studies from the 1960s about pressure's impact on those who violate ethical standards serve as a chilling reminder to us about our potential for losing all perspective in a situation in which authority demands of us a wrongful act. In his seminal *Behavioral Study of Obedience,* Stanley Milgram documented how pressure clouds moral judgment. Forty years have passed since Milgram's experiments on obedience to authority. Often dismissed as studies that were an anomaly caused by the study of an obsequious generation, his work enjoys newfound respect as the dynamics of those companies examined here emerge. Individuals within these companies were willing to do whatever it took to keep the numbers where they needed to be, despite the inevitable losses such falsifications would cause as well as the pain to shareholders dependent on the company and its earnings and share appreciation.

Milgram wrote, "When you think of the long and gloomy history of man, you will find more hideous crimes have been committed in the names of obedience than have ever been committed in the name of rebellion." He also notes that "obedience is the psychological mechanism that links individual action to political purpose."

In studying Milgram's shock (literally and figuratively) experiments, managers and employees can learn that we are willing to inflict pain on others when the perceived pressure to follow orders and directions is great enough, even when we are distressed about doing so. Milgram's experiments involved the administration of electric shocks by his subjects to a victim when the victim gave a wrong answer. The victim was instructed to always give a wrong answer. The subjects were ordered to give increasing levels of shocks when the victim's wrong answers continued. These subjects could see their victims' pain as the shocks were administered. For the most part, the experiments ended when the victims protested and refused to continue further. Milgram documents anxiety, nervous laughter, and other signs of tension in the subjects, but still a willingness to continue to administer the shocks until the victim or the experiment administrator stepped in to stop the process. A summary of Milgram's data shows the extent of obedience by the subjects:

- None refused to administer the electric shocks.

- None stopped before the level of shock reached 300 volts.

- Only five of forty refused to obey the order to administer shock beyond 300 volts.

- Only fourteen of the forty stopped on their own.

When first exposed to Milgram's work, many are taken aback that the experiments could go on with so many for so long without objection. Ah, enter nine years of cooking the books at Parmalat, the multiyear loans at Tyco, the family operations and expenses at Adelphia, and at least two solid years of booking ordinary expenses as capitalized ones at WorldCom and we realize that individuals under the pressure of authority will not only do as told but also remain silent about what is happening. However, the subjects were paid for their participation and were paid only if they continued with the experiment. The insights on monetary motivation are instructive and chilling. Further, several telling comments from the subjects offer insight into the need for humanity and sensitivity in making monetary choices. One subject noted, "I'm gonna chicken out. I'd like to continue, but I can't do that to a man. I'll hurt his heart. You take your check. No really. I couldn't do it." Another said, "Oh, I can't go on with this; no, this isn't right. This is crazy."

The subjects who refused were a small number, but their comments offer priceless teaching moments. "This isn't right." Those words offer the very essence of Milgram's experiments. Compensation can cloud judgment, but virtue can triumph if there is a bright line of right and wrong.

The Power of Groupthink

Despite the passage of nearly fifty years, the Asch studies remain valid in their findings and instructive in human nature. His "Effects of Group Pressure on the Modification and Distortion" today still serves as a reminder about the importance of resisting group pressure in decision making. Solomon Asch undertook his studies because he was fascinated by the presence of what would come to be called "groupthink." Asch's experiments on incorrect statements made because of group pressure were inspired by the tradition in his home of filling a cup of wine at an empty place at the table for the prophet Elijah. As children, Solomon, his siblings, and cousins were taught that the prophet would visit all Jewish homes during Passover and take a sip of the wine left at the empty spot. Though the level of the wine never declined, children, including Asch, swore that it did, and each followed the other's thinking and statements in this regard. The wine level never changed, but the group pressure caused him and other children not only to say otherwise but to pass along the prevailing myth to other younger children.

In the Asch studies, you recall from earlier discussion, a tenth person, who was not part of the nine precoached confederates, was brought in and would, 74 percent of the time go along with the choices of others in the room, despite the obvious error in that choice. The vast majority conformed to the behaviors of the nine people who preceded them in assessing line length.

The Asch experiments remind us to be cautious about the need for social respect and, in the case of business, reward for performance getting in the way of truth and facts. Being aware of the tendency to conformity in a group setting and our desire for social support, even in the context of the workplace, is a critical part of developing resiliency to pressure. The insights of the study are that even the brightest of us succumb to peer pressure in situations in which we may know what we see, but others see things differently and are saying so, generally to preserve status and continue the achievement of financial goals.

However, perhaps most instructive about the Asch studies is the nature of those who did not succumb to the pressure of the nine who offered incorrect choices. The characteristics of the 26 percent are independence, leadership skills, and a commitment to data and facts. For example, a request for a ruler to measure the lines was an example of a resolution beyond simply going along with the crowd or offering perception reaction. The dissenters were the ones with true leadership skills, and those skills emerged most obviously during moments of ethical challenge when right from wrong seems obvious. Not succumbing to peer pressure without first undertaking adequate analysis and review of the facts is a key cultural factor to be developed if resiliency is to thrive. Leaders emerge from the pressure and difficulties of these situations by applying the simple test of truth.

Resiliency cannot, however, be an antidote unless the organization is applying and using the other antidotes for factors such as numbers pressure and fear and silence. The antidotes for self-perceived innovation are more personal in nature and introspective because they address the individual personalities that can affect an organization's course, rightly or wrongly. Resiliency cannot exist in organizations in which student ten is always punished for raising the question about the length of the line. There is a meeting ground for individual courage and organizational receptiveness. The two can meet only when companies apply the antidotes for all seven signs.

Sign #6

Innovation Like No Other

Antidotes

1. Recognize limits on ability and that truth cannot be managed.

2. Keep in mind the basics of economics and economic cycles and business history.

3. Use honesty and candor at all times.

4. Develop resilience to pressure.

    a. Establish individual priorities.

    b. Consider the road not usually taken.

    c. Understand the roles of pressure and the power of authority.

    d. Watch the power of Groupthink.

CHAPTER EIGHT

Sign #

7

Goodness in Some Areas
Atones for Evil in Others

*It's more than just money. You've got to give back
to the community that supported you.*

—John Rigas, former CEO of Adelphia, convicted felon, quoted
by Jerry Useem in "MatchGame," *Fortune*, Nov. 18, 2002, p. 34

On both an individual and corporate level, the fallen ones in these ethical collapses all perceived themselves—and, indeed, were perceived by others—as good citizens. Active in philanthropic giving and fund-raising, these companies and their officers used a balancing scale. As long as they were good to the environment, strong on diversity, involved in the community, and generous with charitable donations, their schemes and frauds at work were not a problem. There was an odd sort of rationalization and justification that consumed these innovators. Indeed, part of their self-perceived innovation was that they were "doing well by doing good." Their philanthropic and social goodness became the salve for a conscience grappling with cooked books, fraud, insider trading—all the usual activities of ethical collapse.

Nonprofit organizations are particularly vulnerable because they feel so noble in their work that a little embezzlement is justified. This explains William Aramony's bizarre conduct with the United Way and the Baptist Foundation of Arizona's and New Era Philanthropy's gigantic Ponzi schemes that took advantage of the good-hearted nonprofit segment of the economy. As long as I am doing good, their thought processes went, how could anything I possibly do in accounting or disclosure to achieve that good be wrong?

This psychology continues to trample across the nonprofit community as Park Avenue financier Alberto W. Vilar heads into his trial for allegedly stealing $5 million from a client. He is charged with stealing from his client allegedly to make good on his pledges to various charities. And also to allegedly fix his dishwasher in his New York City apartment. Ah, the logic of the Yeehaw Culture.

As a billionaire (although who can really say if the numbers were accurate, given EBITDA) from the tech bubble, Vilar was the premier donor to the Metropolitan Opera, among other charities, and gained the title of Manhattan patron saint of the arts. No one could touch him in his philanthropy. The world was well aware of his generosity, at his behest. Beverly Sills summed him up: "He was not, how shall I say, quiet, about his giving." It was a Robin Hood story, except Vilar was not exactly a stealthy character. He loved the limelight his generosity brought. He also loved the sycophantic attitude of the nonprofits who were at his beck and call as the money flowed their way, regardless of whose money it was.

Amazingly, Vilar was even a bit much for Donald Trump. One can safely say that when one's noblesse oblige has irritated even the Donald, trouble may be brewing. Law enforcement officials allege the embezzlement for charity by Vilar was a long-standing pattern, and their first indictment of him is the tip of the iceberg. Given that he pledged an estimated $225 million and that he has made good on only half, they could be correct. Because the SEC has removed a hundred boxes of records from his business as part of its investigation, it's doubtful the pledges will be honored. Collapse is upon his business, philanthropy and all good intentions aside.

All the ethically collapsed companies discussed so far were committed to philanthropy, community, and public service. Their philosophy was that goodness in some areas atones for evil in others. To a company, indeed, to each executive in these companies, there was a strong commitment to "giving back to the community." Their dedication to philanthropy and volunteerism was the penance and the cover for any business misdeeds. Even as the fraud grew more obvious, so also did the denials because the good deeds in a community sense were equated with ethical choices. They all talked a great corporate-citizenship game and, in all cases, tossed about the cash to back up their talk.

Enron: Big Dollars and Officer Volunteers

Enron and its officers were models of philanthropic activity. Mr. Fastow was prominent in Houston's Jewish community, became active in the art museum, and had been the lead fund-raiser for Houston's Holocaust museum. The society pages overflowed with photos of the Enron officer group. There was so much community goodness floating about from the Enronites that most in the Houston area were stunned when the stories of financial collapse and accounting mumbo jumbo emerged. How could those who were so good be engaged in so much corruption?

Many Enron officers were dedicated to Junior Achievement activities, putting in the time and money for an active program in the Houston area. Andersen auditor David Duncan was a regular attendee at and fully committed to his church. His pastor gave an interview to *The New York Times* following Enron's collapse and revealed how involved he had been in discussions with Mr. Duncan regarding his concerns about what he was doing for and with Enron. Mr. Duncan was a parishioner racked with guilt. His pastor described Mr. Duncan as a decent human being who was worried about drawing lines as Andrew Fastow pushed the envelope on the accounting rules. Mr. Duncan's hardworking-family-man image and his church involvement were the ethical penance for his hard-charging, fast-tracker efforts at Andersen. He had become one of its youngest partners following his graduation from Texas A&M. His professors from his undergraduate accounting program at A&M called him a model alum who visited the campus and interacted with the students and was involved with the recruiting process. Mr. Duncan would be the last person they would have expected to cross any lines, because he was perceived as a "straight arrow." In the Yeehaw Culture, the stunning thing about the participants is the self-perceived goodness that comes from this odd balancing act between professional misdeeds and good citizen and church deeds. Fascinatingly, the world around them also bought the goodness, assuming that so much external effort for good was the measure of goodness in all areas of life.

Enron was the quintessential corporate citizen, with universities around the country enjoying its noblesse oblige. My favorites are the poor schleps in the ivory tower who were stuck with having been the "Enron Professor of Economics" and "Enron Professor of Ethics." Sweet irony. Likewise, virtually every nonprofit organization in the Houston area was an Enron beneficiary. Even the Texas Rangers were stuck with the name "Enron" on their stadium after the collapse. Then Minute Maid jumped in and the name was changed, thus eliminating the bitter reminders of the problems with Enron and its fleeting, albeit generous, presence. Robin Williams has expressed the sweet irony of this philanthropy with a new name for Enron Field, "Fifth Amendment Field." As a supporter of the Kyoto treaty, Enron was recognized in the social-responsibility and business-ethics community for its global corporate citizenship. Enron had a fifty-four-page award-winning code of ethics. Commentary following Enron's collapse included observations on how much the company's donations would be missed. You will recall that Enron and its officers had donated generously to the Anderson Cancer Center, even as its directors served on the Enron board. One of the issues that emerged in the trial of Ken Lay and Jeffrey Skilling was the difficulty the prosecution faced in putting together a jury that did not include those who would be predisposed to be favorable to the likable Mr. Lay. Enron's largesse was widespread throughout the community, and there are many organizations and individuals who remain grateful for the support they enjoyed during the heck of a ride Enron had.

WorldCom: National and International Philanthropy

Like Enron, WorldCom and its officers were ideal corporate citizens. Mr. Ebbers served on the board of trustees for Mississippi College and raised $500 million in a fund drive there, more money than had ever been raised by the small college. The halls, cubicles, and offices of WorldCom headquarters were filled with interns and graduates of the hometown college. Active in his church right through his indictment, trial, and conviction, Bernie was the regular Sunday-school teacher there. Mr. Ebbers was beloved and revered in Mississippi, so much so that even as WorldCom collapsed, those around him refused to believe that Bernie had done anything wrong. He appeared at Easthaven Baptist Church on the Sunday immediately following the revelation of the WorldCom multibillion-dollar accounting impropriety. As usual, he was ready and prepared to teach his Sunday-school class and attend services. He stood and addressed the congregation (something the pastor would not deny him, because Ebbers was a generous contributor): "I just want you to know you aren't going to church with a crook. This has been a strange week at best. . . . On Tuesday I received a call telling me what was happening at WorldCom. I don't know what the situation is with all that has been reported. I don't know what all is going to happen or what mistakes have been made. . . . No one will find me to have knowingly committed fraud. More than anything else, I hope that my witness for Jesus Christ [will not be jeopardized]." The congregation gave Ebbers a standing ovation. What fools these mere mortals be. He teaches at 9:15 A.M. and then stays for the ninety-minute service. That was until the twenty-five-year sentence.

Clinton mayor Rosemary Aultman called WorldCom, "a wonderful corporate citizen." WorldCom's $5 million grant to "underserved" children won the following praise from Jesse Jackson, whose Rainbow/PUSH Coalition had worked closely with WorldCom: "This is an example of the type of commitment our communities need from corporate America. If we provide our children with the technology to learn, we empower a new generation to compete in our technology-driven world." WorldCom gave the grant as part of its partnership with Brown University. Brown president Gordon Gee praised the program and WorldCom: "The partnership between Brown and MCI WorldCom will provide direct and lasting benefits to communities across the country and will give colleges and universities an important opportunity to advance the public mission of higher education." WorldCom took its programs for children into the international arena when it contributed school kits to 100,000 children in Central America.

WorldCom got great press when natural disasters hit because it provided free phone calls for hurricane victims. WorldCom also gave free holiday phone calls to the members of the U.S. armed forces around the world. Its support of the arts included its sponsorship of the Monterey Jazz Festival. It tapped into support from the education community when it sponsored a program developed by President Clinton for Internet training for all teachers in the seven Delta states. Its civic responsibility emerged when it established voter registration hotlines and websites with AOL in cooperation with Congress.

WorldCom loved education-related donations and programs because of the mighty press associated with such philanthropy. WorldCom got a double hit by shunning corporate welfare when it turned over its tax credits in Colorado to a scholarship fund for ethnically diverse students. The praise for this action was exuberant and earned WorldCom its rank as a socially responsible company. The managing director of the scholarship fund, called INROADS, said of the gift, "Forward thinking organizations, such as MCI WorldCom and CU-Colorado Springs, add a new dimension of support to INROADS. Pairing a strong technology-based education with challenging work experience will help students enhance their tools for success—and finding creative ways to do so will brighten their futures."

Ebbers and WorldCom had the ear of the White House because of their support for the education efforts to close the great digital divide. On April 6, 2000, President Clinton announced that WorldCom had contributed $10 million toward his cause of "closing the digital divide." Mr. Ebbers explained WorldCom's social programs by saying, "With a shortage of high-tech skilled workers in this country and groups of Americans at risk of being left behind in the digital age, this initiative helps close the digital divide while making perfect business sense. It's a good marriage of vital corporate and social objectives." The scholarships were for Hispanic, African American, and Native American students for college and were unveiled at a press conference at the White House. There were few nonprofit or community-service areas WorldCom did not touch either with donations or with free long distance. In the minds of those who were beneficiaries of the telecom largesse (temporary though it may have been), WorldCom was a model of corporate citizenship and social responsibility. Ebbers and WorldCom were brilliant at tapping into the programs that would earn it the best reputation and the most attention for its philanthropic buck. WorldCom was diabolical in its social-responsibility stratetgy.

Tyco, Kozlowski, and University and Universal Generosity

Former Tyco CEO Dennis Kozlowski had an interesting approach to philanthropy. First, wherever there was a charitable function or need, he was there with money. However, no one is still quite sure whether he was giving the money or Tyco was. He did make sure that both he and Tyco got credit, regardless of who was actually doing the giving. Over the ten-year period from 1992 to 2002, when Mr. Kozlowski served as CEO, the company gave $35 million to charities designated by Mr. Kozlowski. However, as was the case with the company's business records, the philanthropic records also appear to have varying interpretations. There is even some confusion about who was donating how much and from which tills. Mr. Kozlowski had pledged $106 million in Tyco funds to charity, but $43 million of that was given in his own name. Add to that the $35 million pledged from Tyco and one of the two owes a great deal of money to charities.

Mr. Kozlowski served on the board of the Whitney Museum of American Art, and as a result, Tyco donated $4.5 million to the traveling museum shows that Whitney sponsored. Keeping with the conflicts theme, Mr. Kozlowski then hired the assistant registrar at the Whitney to serve as his personal adviser on the ill-fated, tax-evading personal art collection. Mr. Kozlowski was an avid fund-raiser for various philanthropic endeavors. The "avid" label comes more easily when your company starts the ball rolling with a multimillion-dollar donation. And it's always easier to swing that kind of scratch from your company if you are the CEO. Some charities do draw the line on whom they accept donations from. Mr. Kozlowski withdrew as a fund-raiser for the New York Botanical Garden when the news of his first possible indictment spread (the one for the sales-tax evasion on his artwork).

But the Tyco/Kozlowski dynamo made even more donations to education. Tyco donated $1.7 million for the construction of the Kozlowski Athletic Center (nicknamed the Koz Plex) at the private school, Berwick Academy, that one of his daughters attended and where he served as trustee. One imagines that Berwick wishes it had opted for the name of the real donor, with the resulting Tyco Athletic Complex. Another $5 million went to Seton Hall, Mr. Kozlowski's alma mater. Actually, Mr. Kozlowski had donated about $10 million since 1992 to Seton Hall, but no one there is sure from whence the donations came, from Tyco or Kozlowski. Perhaps it was the donor/employee matching program at

Tyco, wherein the company matched an employee's donations, that created confusion. However, it is unclear whether the money for the Tyco match came from Mr. Kozlowski personally or Tyco or the Key Employee Loan Program or any of the other sources of cash floating around at the discretion of the officers. It seems accounting issues affected even the donees. A Seton Hall classroom office building was named for Mr. Kozlowski when he donated $5 million during its construction. But Mr. Kozlowski was also generous with his time. In fact, he spoke to the Seton Hall business students in 2001 on the importance of integrity and professionalism in business.

Mr. Kozlowski was a national donor, seeing to charities wherever he owned a home. His donations in the Boca Raton area were made at the behest of a public relations executive he had hired to improve his image. This activity of using PR reps to maximize the splash of donations should put to rest objections about exploring this donation propensity for philanthropy as a sign of the Yeehaw Culture and ethical collapse. Perhaps the very quality of superficiality draws these Machiavellian personalities to philanthropy and social responsibility. The donations to Boca Raton charities were well placed, and the PR agent's advice there netted Mr. Kozlowski a fair amount of coverage in the *Palm Beach Post* for his contributions. Where Mr. Kozlowski's heart and donations were, Tyco wasn't far behind. Tyco gave $3 million to a hospital in Boca Raton and $500,000 to an arts center there. Mr. Kozlowski also donated to charities without public relations advice. He had donated $1.3 million to the Nantucket Conservation Foundation in his name but with the less-than-altruistic purpose of keeping the land next to his property undeveloped, a goal that the foundation shared. The 2000 annual report of the Nantucket Historical Association lists Mr. Kozlowski and Karen Lee Mayo (who was not yet Mrs. Kozlowski because the marriage to the first Mrs. Kozlowski had not yet been dissolved but who would become Mrs. Kozlowski in time for the $6,000 shower curtains and the two criminal trials) as having given between $2 million and $5 million. To top all the specifics, Mr. Kozlowski was also generous in a general way because the United Way of America gave Mr. Kozlowski its "million-dollar giver" award.

Mr. Kozlowski was not alone at Tyco in his dedication to community, the needy, and the worlds of art, science, health, education, and public relations. As he entered the courthouse to enter his not guilty plea on felony charges that he has now been convicted of, Mark Swartz, Tyco's former CFO, sported an AIDS ribbon on his lapel. Frank Walsh, the director who took the finder's fee from Tyco without the board's knowledge, has the library at Seton Hall named after him. Mark Belnick, former general counsel, had long done pro bono work for Cornell and was a longtime president of the Jewish Community Center of Harrison

(New York). Upon his conversion to Catholicism, Mr. Belnick joined the Catholic Foundation of Utah board and the board of Thomas Aquinas College.

Adelphia: Both a Quiet and a Grand Generosity

The Rigas family was personally generous with the people of the small Pennsylvania town where the company was headquartered. When CEO John Rigas read a story in the local paper about someone experiencing financial difficulties, he would send a check with a note indicating simply, "I read your story in the newspaper." One individual so helped by Mr. Rigas wrote a letter to the *Wellsvile Daily Reporter:* "Thanks for the article. I just got a check from John Rigas." Mr. Rigas offered the company jet to one employee who had cancer and needed treatment at a special hospital in Cleveland. Mr. Rigas then followed up by calling the family from one of his trips to Europe, to see how the treatment had gone. Mr. Rigas was inducted into the Cable Television Hall of Fame for his good works in Coudersport and the other communities served by Adelphia.

The reaction in Coudersport to the Adelphia collapse and all the indictments of the Rigas family was similar to the reaction of the folks in Mississippi to WorldCom's fall and those in Houston to Enron's crash and burn. One Adelphia officer said that he was in "total shock" and that he "hasn't heard Rigas utter a slur or profanity in 32 years. The whole story isn't known. That's part of the problem." One town member said, "Whatever has to be done to make it right, they'll do. People don't know the real John Rigas." Even following criminal convictions, the family had great support in the community. They knew the Rigases individually and they loved and respected them because of all they had done, often without anyone's knowing. The Rigas family did differ in that they were generous in ways other than public donations to charity. Their kindness and generosity was often out of sight, and that quiet restraint earned the family lasting goodwill. Even when John Rigas was convicted on all counts of securities fraud, mail fraud, and other charges, many in Coudersport still offered their full support of this family that was generous to a fault.

John Rigas was said to offer money without being asked, supporting the local fire department and paying $50,000 for the refurbishment of a town monument to veterans because the names had been worn away. He even paid for a McDonald's and Subway to change the outward appearance of their businesses to keep them more in line with the Coudersport Main Street USA image. Each year at Christmas, the Rigas family brought in an orchestra from one of the cities its company served to provide music for the Coudersport town Christmas party. John's wife, Doris, decorated two large Christmas trees each year with sixteen thousand lights each. John Rigas bought the only theater in Coudersport in 1951 and kept it open with low prices: Adelphia employees admitted for free; others for $4; candy for 60 cents and popcorn in a tub for $2.25.

Adelphia as a company was equally magnanimous, recognized as a terrific corporate citizen, hailed for its record on the traditional issues of environmentalism, diversity, and corporate giving. Adelphia's philanthropic program was called "Because We're Concerned," and its list of beneficiaries included the Boy Scouts and Girl Scouts of America, the March of Dimes, Ronald McDonald House, YMWC, YWCA, Habitat for Humanity, Leukemia Society of America, Lupus Foundation of America, Meals on Wheels, and Toys for Tots. The Tennessee Titans had their stadium named Adelphia Field.

HealthSouth and the Scrushy Name of Fame

From the Junior Miss Pageant of Alabama to scholarships for his community college alma mater, Richard Scrushy, like Bernie Ebbers and the Rigases, was unusually generous with the organizations and people in the small-town atmosphere in which he had experienced his stunning rise to success. The Vestavia Hills Public Library was renamed the Richard M. Scrushy Public Library because of his generous donations. There was the Richard M. Scrushy campus of Jefferson State Community College, from which he graduated with his training in physical therapy, and the Richard M. Scrushy Parkway that ran through the center of town. There was just about a weekly Scrushy charity activity, and he used his celebrity sports clients to draw attention to the events.

Like the executives at Enron and WorldCom in Houston and Mississippi, Mr. Scrushy and HealthSouth were key figures in the Birmingham philanthropic community. Sports fields and junior-college campuses held ceremonies when they took on the Scrushy name. At one event at which he was being honored for a donation, he became agitated when the spotlight was moved from him to another person on the stage. He is also a major contributor to the Guiding Light Church. Its pastor, Jim Lowe, went with Scrushy to his arraignment. Rumor has it that Scrushy has been born again. And one of his nine lives allowed him to escape conviction at a trial for eighty-plus felony counts that featured voice recordings of him referencing numbers manipulation.

Leslie Scrushy was equally involved with community projects and enjoyed at least monthly recognition for her philanthropy. She often used her company, Upseedaisees, to provide free gifts for contests and even furnished her quasi-pajama products for the gift baskets given to the Grammy nominees. A former Junior Miss contestant herself, she and Richard regularly served as judges for the local and state pageants.

AIG and Hank Greenberg

Estimates put former AIG CEO Hank Greenberg's net worth at $3 billion. Here was a man who was legendary for screaming at employees, referring to most of the world as idiots, and dressing them down for their lack of preparation. But Greenberg gave millions to charity. The Starr Foundation, ironically named after the off-the-books compensation company for AIG executives, is one of the largest private foundations in the United States, with $3 billion in assets, including ownership of 2 percent of AIG's stock. AIG may have been forced to restate its earnings, but Greenberg ran in the best of New York's philanthropic circles. Greenberg resigned from two nonprofit boards, the Asia Society and the American Museum of Natural History, when the SEC came along to investigate AIG accounting issues. Despite all of Greenberg's troubles and the fallout for AIG, you'll not hear much criticism of the man because he has always offered much to nonprofits in need. The public face of Hank's board presence is restrained, but the true believers still want to benefit from the generous Greenberg.

The Antidotes for Combating the Use of Goodness in Some Areas to Atone for Evil in Others

There's a bit of a Jekyll and Hyde phenomenon that emerges as we review these Yeehaw Culture companies and their generous nature. There are many more. Charles Keating flew Mother Teresa in his private jet. But the presence of a saint did not stop the sale of junk bonds by his Lincoln Savings and Loan. Sam Eichenfield, former CEO of Finova, was named Phoenix Man of the Year for his philanthropic activities. But Finova ended up in bankruptcy following its accounting nightmares. Ford's pledges to produce vehicles that exceeded environmental standards and to release a corporate-social-responsibility report each year earned it a place on a pedestal in corporate-social-responsibility circles. But its pledges on greenhouse gases did not translate into forthrightness in letting customers (or, for that matter, federal safety officials) know that there were problems with the Explorer and its tires in other countries. There is no requirement under federal standards for a company to disclose problems with its vehicles in foreign countries—no legal requirement, but perhaps an ethical obligation that somehow was not part of the social-responsibility strategy focused on the environment. Coca-Cola's onetime CEO Douglas Daft traveled the country speaking and professing devotion to diversity, a dedication that earned Coke recognition from social-responsibility groups. But its dedication to diversity did not keep the company from using inflated marketing numbers in the test market for value meals for Burger King with Frozen Coke or prevent it from overstating earnings related to sales to distributors. Merck has a wonderful program for getting free and discount prescription drugs to those who need them, but that goodness did not translate into candor in its financial reports. The SEC discovered that Merck had recorded $12.4 billion in co-pays as revenue, co-pays being money it would never receive.

This pattern of no correlation between philanthropy/social responsibility and integrity in business operations, products, and financials is so certain that if you bring me a company that touts loudly its goodness with a publicly professed dedication to philanthropy, social responsibility, environmentalism, and/or diversity, I am convinced that I can show you a company that is crossing ethical lines in its safety, wage and hours, financial reporting, and any other area that leaves room for interpretation of the law but also demands ethical standards of behavior. What is it about these companies and their officers that leads to this enigma? Why this fundamental disconnect between knowing right from wrong and angelic behavior in the context of social good? This connection or pattern has several probable causes.

Cause #1 of Goodness in Some Areas Atones for Evil in Others: Ego

How they do fawn over donors! One simple explanation could be that the same type of ego that fuels a fraud also craves the spotlight. Donations to charity are a sure means of gaining newspaper coverage and certainly a spot in society and all the perks and publicity that brings. Scrushy got angry when they took the spotlight away from him. Mr. Kozlowski hired a PR representative to get him into the limelight via philanthropy. The cause may be no more complex than a need for attention. Herein lies yet another a chicken-and-egg issue. Is this the sort of insecure egotist you want running the company? Or perhaps the frauds and missteps occurred because there was an insecure egotist running the company.

Cause #2 of Goodness in Some Areas Atones for Evil in Others: Brings in Business, Customers, and Publicity

The diabolical personality would not be above undertaking charity just for the sake of more business. Tyco, WorldCom, Adelphia, Enron, and Health-South all enjoyed the benefits of their name out there in the public because of these philanthropic activities. A $100,000 donation might well be millions in free advertising. Customers make choices on cable companies and long distance because a company paid for calls from soldiers or from relatives following a storm. Goodwill is a nebulous accounting concept, but its impact is fairly clear-cut in terms of drumming up new customers and retaining current ones. The philanthropy and community service generate business and preserve relationships.

All con artists network their way to success. In these cases, the networking was for a company (with individual recognition along the way). There may well be a business reason for all these voluntary acts and donations. But understanding that the motives may not be pure is a critical part of combating this factor in the Yeehaw Culture. Assuming the motives are pure sets the stage for assumptions about character in other areas. Just because a guy heads up the United Way does not mean that he is incapable of cooking the books.

Cause #3 of Goodness in Some Areas Atones for Evil in Others: Professors and Sixties Logic on the Inherent Evil of Capitalism

Another *mea culpa*. When these MBA executives who have come under indictment since 2001 came through their business schools and earned their degrees, there was a decidedly rain-forest tone to the curriculum and a negative attitude about business in general. Some years ago a former dean asked me to look into a new way of teaching students business ethics. He wanted to stop sending our students over to the philosophy department for their ethics training. His reasoning was that "they go over there, find out capitalism is a tool of the devil, and then switch majors." His theory had one more part to it. Those who did not switch majors and returned to study business came back with a guilt complex. They assumed, based on the views of their philosophy professors, that they had already sold their souls to the devil, so what possible difference could a little cooking of the books mean in their eternal damnation? So, those who remained became comfortable with crossing ethical lines.

Ethics instruction during the era in which the crop of officer felons was trained was not virtue ethics. Rather, these students were given a heavy dose of social responsibility and little or no discussion of the ethical issues in financial reporting. Their ethics instruction focused on these distinct areas:

- Environmentalism
- Diversity
- Human rights
- Philanthropy
- Giving back to the community

The ethics books and curriculum of this generation of business leaders (and regretfully, still today) define doing the right thing in these areas as ethics writ large. Moral relativists are hesitant to establish bright lines between right and wrong, except in areas they deem appropriate. These topics and guidelines for business ethics come directly from the AACSB accrediting body for business schools, which mandates the following content in the business-school curriculum if the school desires AACSB accreditation for its programs:

- Ethical and global issues
- The influence of political, social, legal and regulatory, environmental and technological issues
- The impact of demographic diversity on organizations

Those trained under this pedagogical philosophy will order, "No sweat shops," but could never bring themselves to say, "Always be honest." They can condemn lumber companies for destroying the rain forests, but they would never suggest that corporate executives should control their conduct in their personal lives. To students trained in this era of business-ethics instruction, a demented sort of logic and attitude has resulted. As long as the company had a good record on community development and contribution, a little fraud was fine. They were not trained to ask the question "Does social conscience in some areas atone for the lack of moral conscience in finances and financial reporting?" Fannie Mae was named number one by *Business Ethics* magazine in its annual list of the most ethical companies in America in the same month that Fannie Mae's multibillion-dollar accounting deception was unfolding. The CEO was forced out by his board because of questions about the firm's financial reports even as the same group that created the parameters of ethical behavior in such a facile and arbitrary manner was honoring the company. True, few organizations have done more to help individuals get affordable housing than Fannie Mae. But recognition for a job well done does not justify misrepresentation in the marketplace.

The Borna and Stearns survey data mentioned in Chapter 7 show that the result of this focus in the business schools' ethics education was a disconnect between virtue ethics and the MBA curriculum. Something was formulated in these students that made them comfortable with fraud. Seventy-five percent of MBAs said the primary role of a company is to maximize shareholder value, 71 percent said satisfying customers was the goal of a business, and only 33 percent said producing a quality product was the goal of a company. Those numbers differ from the results when the students are surveyed prior to business school—68 percent, 75 percent, and 43 percent, respectively—demonstrating that there is some change brought about by business-school training.

The officers and companies that were headed down the road to ethical collapse were putting all their eggs in the social-responsibility basket and gaining the necessary recognition and imprimatur for being "good and ethical companies." The measure of moral development in business turned out to be fairly easy to achieve, and the cunning executives in these Yeehaw Cultures learned how to manipulate the contrived system that had been established for determining whether a company was ethical. They used the checklist and did not worry about troubling notions of virtue ethics in financial reports. They had met the standards for ethical behavior in business and followed them. Indeed, they capitalized upon these facile tests for ethics and social responsibility, using them for recognition and great press.

Cause #4 of Goodness in Some Areas Atones for Evil in Others: The Perfect Balance

In addition to all the other causes of this mind-set that justifies fraud and other financial-reporting problems but is dedicated to philanthropy and social responsibility, there is another quite simple one, which builds upon the others and is perhaps in combination with them: goodness in one area atones for evil in the others. The dedication to social responsibility became the penance for any misdeeds in accounting, financial reporting, and use of corporate assets. How could those who were so good on the outside be so rotten on inside operations? In fact, the goodness on the outside was the license for the misdeeds on the inside. There is a psychology of moral relativism at work here. This trade-off is illustrated dramatically in the movie *Changing Lanes*. A young lawyer discovers that he has been a party to fraud and embezzlement and is about to engage in forgery, and all at the behest of his senior partner, who also happens to be his father-in-law. When the young junior partner finally confronts his father-in-law, he asks him how he can live with himself, given all the misdeeds of forgery, embezzlement, and fraud that he has perpetrated on his clients. His father-in-law gives him the philosophy of atonement by explaining that he has made a great deal of money through such schemes but that the money goes to scholarships for inner-city children. The money funds the youth symphony. The money has built and refurbished schools. His philosophy is that if at the end of the day he has done more good than harm, he's happy. He weighs the good that he is able to do with the money against the wrongs he committed to get it. 'Tis a dangerous philosophy that has taken too many executives down that path of fraud and other missteps, all in the name of doing good.

Antidote #1 for Goodness in Some Areas Atones for Evil in Others: Shift Attitudes on Social Responsibility in Business

For far too many years war has raged between capitalists, as represented by Nobel Prize–winning economist Milton Friedman, and stakeholders, as represented by the entire academic world. The battle shakes out as follows: Professor Friedman believes managers should not get involved in social issues because it's not their money. He also argues about the efficiency of such a system, the arrogance of a manager making decisions on social issues for shareholders, and a host of other very logical arguments about why corporations should not get involved in Boy Scouts, Planned Parenthood, and even the somewhat less controversial causes of the ballet and Little League. The stakeholder theorists, on the other side, opine that the corporation is owned by more than the shareholders and that stakeholders such as customers, employees, and the community all have an interest in the corporation and should have their interests served as well. Stakeholder theorists argue that they need a say in a corporation's environmental practices because it is their environment, too. Professor Friedman maintains that their say in the corporation's operations, decisions, and environmental practices comes through the ballot box and legislation. They can accomplish change there, a change that requires a majority of voters to at least agree on the policies touted by the officials serving in office.

But as it pertains to the Yeehaw Culture, Professor Friedman has one more point in his corner. Managers should not get involved in social issues because the ego developed through their public generosity and beneficiary obsequiousness fuel the Yeehaw attitude. Further, groveling is a poor basis for making decisions as the stewards of the shareholders' money. Whether the powerful corporate personality craves the attention and accolades of philanthropic generosity and social responsibility or the attention exacerbates an existing egotist (or creates the ego) is irrelevant.

The extensive presence of corporate managers in philanthropic activity and excessive attention to social responsibility create a vulnerability in the individual manager and, as a result, in the company. The companies that had Yeehaw Cultures teach us that the accolades from the community/social-responsibility commitments embolden managers (who may or may not already be prone to do so) to cross lines in their management of company funds. It is perhaps time to divorce the functions of social responsibility and business as dysfunctional partners. The lines of virtue become muddled as managers mix social responsibility with virtue and finances. These two distinct roles of business have supporters who want more from companies. But the detractors have an argument. It is clear that social responsibility/philanthropy and virtue in operations do not mix well together because the two socially acceptable activities become both the penance and the front for unethical or illegal activity in other parts of the company.

Within companies, then, managers and boards should revisit their donations, policies, and even those blasted volunteer programs. Yes, yes, there are a few companies that can handle both, but efficiency and the Friedman argument should trump even those efforts. My observations over three decades of felled companies with Yeehaw Cultures is that employees hammering away at the Habitat for Humanity outing are likely to use that activity to atone for a little channel stuffing at the office. Glorifying employees for community involvement seems to create an inflated sense of goodness that introduces licentiousness in accounting and business operations. Managers who are doing good and enjoying the accolades for such may feel so good about themselves that misdeeds at work seem trivial. The philanthropy of John Rigas is a perfect illustration. Embezzlement coupled with extraordinary generosity? Why not? When the end is important enough, the means can be whatever.

However, the problem of business vs. social responsibility is further-reaching than just economic theory and Friedman's inherent offense at a manager casting about company (and hence shareholder) money to causes that may run counter to shareholders' views. The managers and employees doing all this volunteer work simply may not be capable of handling both the administration of a business and the administration of dollars for charity, community, and other socially responsible programs. In short, managers and employees caught up in the good of other organizations and causes may not be thinking deeply enough about their own company's needs, goals, and strategic visions. While there is much good to be said about strategic opportunities a business can seize to resolve issues related to the environment, diversity, human rights, and sweatshops, those decisions should be made against the backdrop of doing what is best for those who own the business.

The following was taken from the introductory page of United Airlines' "About United" website. In this, the first introduction an employee or investor would have to the company, we find:

> Our commitment to corporate social investment extends around the globe. Many of these activities take advantage of our unique capabilities as a global airline and involve both our employees and our customers. Our philanthropic wing, the United Airlines Foundation, provides much of this support.
>
> While our support takes many forms, it has a single goal: to make the world a better place for our customers and employees to live, work, travel and do business. Learn more about our commitment by visiting the links below.
>
> Arts and culture
> Customer involvement
> Diversity
> Education
> Health
> Volunteerism
> United Airlines Foundation

How much lovelier it would have been to take all the effort put into these voluntary programs and apply it to running an airline or, perhaps saving the pension plans of employees. A pensionless workforce seals its fate because of the impact on morale. United is a classic example of social responsibility and the accompanying accolades trumping business strategy, operations, and success. Bankruptcy is its fate. General Motors (GM) has been reduced to junk-bond status, has announced layoffs, and is selling cars to everyone as if they had an employee discount. Still, the focus of the GM website is all on social-responsibility issues. On the opening page for GM stock investors we find corporate responsibility above investor information. The components of corporate responsibility? Earnings? Nay, nary a mention. Here are GM's corporate responsibilities:

Community

Education

Environment

Reporting

Safety

Workplace [this encompasses the ubiquitous diversity]

One additional click gets you to GM's debunking of the myths about the U.S. health-care system, including its two-line mythbuster that the United States does not have the best health care in the world. Junk bonds are not a far leap from an organization that would devote this much effort on its investor page to the politically charged issue of health care, and in such a glib fashion. Today the company struggles to survive.

Another example, and one cited endlessly in the business-ethics and social-responsibility literature, is that of Malden Mills and Aaron Feuerstein. In 1996 Aaron Feuerstein, CEO of Malden Mills in Massachusetts, rose to international fame and became something of a legend in the world of business ethics by continuing to pay his employees even after a fire had gutted his plant. He met the payroll for idle workers as the company rebuilt, and he was lionized throughout the media. Here was a CEO with a unionized plant that was strike-free, a boss who saw his workers as a key to his company's success. The national attention to Feuerstein's act brought more than the adulation of business-ethics professors—it brought increased demand for his product, Polartec, the lightweight fleece the catalog industry loves to sell. Yet Malden Mills was in bankruptcy by 2002. It has emerged from Chapter 11, but not under Feuerstein's control, although he remains on salary at the company. He is an iconic CEO, but not with a weakness for financial chicanery. He has a weakness for social responsibility, to the extreme, as in self-destructive extreme. When all was said and done, it wasn't Feuerstein's money that paid those employees. Even in a privately held company, creditors have an interest in seeing the business succeed.

While the Yeehaw Cultures had other factors that reduced them to financial shenanigans, they understood a simple principle. Indeed, they had figured out a loophole to this whole ethics expectation: goodness in social responsibility and philanthropy makes up for business shortcomings, including a little fraud just to be sure the company can devote resources to solving the nation's healthcare crisis. These egotistical and costly endeavors not only nourish the Yeehaw Culture, they distract perfectly healthy cultures from the business of just doing business.

This indictment of the wide swath businesses cut in embracing social responsibility does not mean there is not wisdom in addressing these issues. However, the parameters of business rein in rogue attention-getters and who use philanthropy to atone for internal finagling. There are issues and times when a business should address an evolving social issue, and the result can be that the business happens to reap recognition. Perhaps it is in its best interests to be certain that sweatshops are not part of international operations or even a part of a supplier's network. The backlash against Nike for its experience with the Vietnamese subcontractor sweatshops illustrates the need to address these human-rights problems for the sake of both the workers and the shareholders. L. L. Bean undertook an extensive inspection of its suppliers to determine whether sweatshops were in their networks. The program was extensive, but it was also silent. The program began before sweatshops became a hot-button issue and certainly before any public attention was being drawn to companies with human-rights violations. No one was aware of the L. L. Bean inspections, which were conducted, at great expense, to be certain that conditions were appropriate and suppliers were living up to their contractual commitments to L. L. Bean on factory conditions and worker treatment. However, L. L. Bean accomplished two things with its volunteer inspection program that happened to also address an evolving social issue. L. L. Bean was saved the public relations nightmares that Nike, Kathie Lee Gifford, and others experienced when they were caught (sometimes unawares) of sweatshops in their supply chains. Further, L. L. Bean's quiet approach netted it respect and reputational capital that benefit its owners. Bean's program is, however, a far cry from the extensive philanthropy of awards of the companies with Yeehaw Cultures.

Managing such an issue with an eye on personal or company recognition and awards sends not just a signal of personal aggrandizement to employees.

The deeper message such practices send to employees is to embolden those who would use these hot-button issues as a substitute for achievement. Further, this superficial dedication for the sake of recognition provides a means for companies to find themselves to be virtuous in business even when they doctor the numbers to conceal the lack of achievement. The widespread nature of the Yeehaw Culture and this balancing notion of atonement require a shift in business practices and attitudes generally. That can come about when we embrace those companies that are willing to weather the media storms for not offering the usual platitudes of social responsibility. Perhaps the time has come to embrace those businesses that simply go about their business. When they do reach out to the community or commit to solve a social issue, the work is done in the best interests of their companies and done in a quiet manner that befits legitimate concern and dedication about the issue, the group, or the impact of the company's behavior on others. Is it better to be known as an ideal corporate citizen for twelve years that then crashed and burned into bankruptcy, leaving employees without pensions and shareholders without investments, or as a company that survives for the long term, providing for generations of support for employees, their families, and their communities? Business talent lies in the latter, not the former, approach. In fact, the former seems to be a substitute for solid business operations and real success.

Antidote # 2 for Goodness in Some Areas Atones for Evil in Others: Investigate Your Company and Explore the Depths and Interconnections of Social Responsibility and Community Involvement

In revisiting company attitudes on social responsibility and philanthropy, the following factors are critical:

- How much does the company give to charity?

- Are there any connections among board members, officers, officers' families, and the charities?

- What are the charities? Why these charities?

- If a company foundation handles the charitable giving, who runs that foundation and what are the guidelines for its gifts?

- What relationships do officers, managers, and board members have with the charities' founders and officers? Look for webs of connections. The goal here is to put egos in check. Further, the Kozlowski self-serving model, along with the Enron board donations, demonstrates the need for understanding close interconnections in philanthropy.

- What are acceptable alternatives to the complexities of managing charitable donations, causes, controversies, and demands? Buffett's Berkshire Hathaway once let the shareholders decide by vote which charities will receive what portion of the money available for distribution. The managers were not involved with the charities or their designation, except to the extent they offer their own funds for donations. The onetime Buffett model removed the onus, the responsibility, and the fuel for Yeehaw egos from the company equation.

- How much time do employees devote to volunteer work? How are those hours weighed in performance evaluations? Is there a better way to engage customers and community? Does the program place undue pressure on employees? Does the volunteer program serve as cover for employees who may not be performing?

These are radical remedies, suggesting that perhaps companies revisit the whole notion of "doing well by doing good." Less focus on goodness and more focus on basic virtue ethics of right vs. wrong represent a radical departure from current corporate attitudes, and certainly from the training of MBA students since the 1970s. The boastings on the websites, the volunteer hours, and even the donations may need to be curbed so that employees understand that goodness is not measured by all-too-often superficial social-responsibility measures. Rather, goodness is measured by forthrightness in all aspects of business.

Antidote # 3 for Goodness in Some Areas Atones for Evil in Others: Be Skeptical—Be Very Skeptical—of Philanthropy and Social Responsibility

Beware the socially responsible company. Watch out for the big donors. There is a certain con component in the Yeehaw Culture. The con men and women of the Yeehaw Culture have figured out a formula for drawing attention away from company performance and, in many cases, its financials. Even without the Yeehaw Culture, this dedication to causes and charity seems to be a distraction from running the business. The result is not just a lack of focus, but also a diversion of funds that were needed for simple things, including, for example, the employees' pensions. That distraction comes in the form of virtuous efforts in the community, charities, and all those social goals one can now find on pretty much every company's website. Stunningly, that information will be located on the investor-information home page. As cynical as it seems, skepticism about social responsibility and philanthropy may be one of the most certain determinants of a Yeehaw Culture. If you find these present in a company, check for the other factors of ethical collapse because the generosity and service may be a cover for a troubled soul and even more troubled books.

Sign #7

Goodness in Some Areas Atones for Evil in Others

Antidotes

1. Shift attitudes on social responsibility in business.

2. Investigate your company and explore the depths and interconnections of social responsibility and community involvement.

3. Be skeptical; be very skeptical of philanthropy and social responsibility.

CHAPTER NINE

Applying the Signs for the Future

You make enough billion-dollar mistakes, and they add up.

—Enron analyst, circa 2001

O ne of the questions I am frequently asked is "If this is so good, can you use the seven signs to predict companies at risk?" Absolutely. That is the plan. These are factors to use in performing a qualitative analysis of a company. The numbers and assurances of safety or integrity are meaningless, as our sad tales in previous chapters have shown, if we are unsure about the culture of the organization. The seven signs are a form of qualitative analysis that can be applied to any company to determine the level of risk. And there are a few companies I have my eye on because I worry that they may be on the path to ethical collapse without application of the antidotes.

Apollo Group and the University of Phoenix

The Apollo Group Inc., parent company for the University of Phoenix, worries me. There are already rumblings with a negative Department of Education (DOE) report on recruiting activities, and the SEC is at its doorstep. But take a look at the company's growth. Double-digit growth, from a one-building operation in the 1980s to a multinational corporation with ninety thousand employees. And its executive team? Young, bright, and a full generation younger than the founder, Dr. John Sperling, who retired as chairman in 2004 at age eighty-three.

The findings of recruiting violations by the Department of Education, a group that controls the Apollo Group's future because of its ability to grant student loans, should be a fear-inducing event for any business executive. The DOE could shut down this private university by refusing to allow student federal loans. But the take of these executives was that they had done nothing wrong and that a bunch of bureaucrats who had interviewed just sixty recruiters and found some financial pressures on them had blown things out of proportion. The DOE report tells a far more serious story, such as recruiters indicating that they were asked to stay home on the days the government agents were there so that they could not be interviewed and possibly reveal what they knew. University of Phoenix recruiters told regulators tales of trainers telling them to skirt the regulations by saying and doing things a certain way. The numbers culture revealed in this report is astonishing, with "Monday huddles" rewarding the recruiters who had met their numbers and humiliating those who had not. "Heads will be on the chopping block" was a warning from one recruiting manager whose staff's numbers were down. Reading through the forty-five-page report gives the impression that the atmosphere was one of always meeting your numbers, no matter what. The crass recruiting flies in the face of being an institution of higher learning. The report is damning, a financial-pressure wake-up call for any organization, let alone a company subject to regulatory review and control.

The story on the DOE program review and the SEC concerns about its nondisclosure erupted at the time I had been asked to do three training sessions (on ethics, no less) for University of Phoenix management-leadership academies. I had one session left when the story was reported publicly. I talked with the manager who had recruited me, as it were, for the training. He had little power in the organization, but I discussed with him the need for the officers to be absolutely candid about what was happening. I also noted that when I came I would have to speak to the managers there about the company's difficulties because it would otherwise be the elephant in the room. He agreed with me and understood that I would discuss the issues. When I did so, several vice presidents stayed for the training. I had included the Apollo Group in my evolving slide presentation on companies that experience potential ethical collapse events. After I finished my one-hour presentation, two of the officers stood to defend themselves and the company. The disaffected response of the young executives was that they could not believe the company would be included on such a list. They offered assurances to the group that all was well, that the DOE report represented just a few bad apples and that the company was indeed ethical. I was not invited back for any future leadership academies. The CEO, Todd Nelson, referred to the problems and the report as a "hiccup." Mr. Nelson resigned abruptly in January 2006 and received a severance package of $1.8 million as analysts issued investor cautions.

There is no question that the University of Phoenix can teach all of us in business and higher education a lesson or two. It found a niche in adult education that was not being addressed and seized the moment. Its ongoing double-digit growth and international expansion have brought the perks of success to many young people who staff the management and executive ranks. Its stock went from $9 to $98 in four and a half years. But the University of Phoenix now has competition from community colleges, other private universities, and even public state universities that have changed to better accommodate the adult student. Its phenomenal growth period has ended and it must make the switch from innovative exponential growth to the slugfest of competition. It is difficult to determine whether the executives can wean themselves from the increases in the value of the company's stock and the perks that come with double-digit growth. They must also lay to rest the fantasy that they are immune from the mundane demands of government bureaucrats.

The innovator mind-set in this company is pervasive because it has rewritten the template for higher education and has enjoyed the initial success of being the first entrant in a field ripe for the financial harvest. We have already learned that its required financial reports filed during this time did not disclose to investors the DOE investigation. The results were not given until the press reported the violations. The response of the executives? Well, they relied on the classic loophole in law and accounting: the $9.8 million in fines paid to the Department of Education were not material! So immaterial that once Apollo did disclose the fines and the program review, its stock dropped 36 percent in two months. Anytime the government regulator (DOE) that controls the future revenue flow of a business (through student loan access) has determined that there are violations, there is a qualitatively material event. Indeed, the focus on recruiting numbers and the aggressive programs there that brought the wrath of the Department of Education have blinded management to the strategic issues it must face. Potential students have more opportunities now. The low-hanging fruit that Apollo once plucked so easily is gone. It must work harder for those numbers and there will be higher costs. The exponential growth is over. The issue that remains is whether the executives running the company can make the transition from innovative loner to tough competitor. However, the shortsellers are out and about in the industry. Apollo is not the only company in adult education with such issues. Think of the profile of the private education/for-profit schools: think entrepreneurs, larger-than-life founders, young executive teams, numbers pressure, weak boards, innovation, and the noble goal of education and the seven signs are there. And one more worry comes to mind. Former junk-bond king Michael Milken is heavily invested in for-profit education and sees it as the wave of the future.

Coca-Cola—A Chance to Change

Coca-Cola has been embroiled in litigation with its bottlers over questions about finances and contract provisions. And there was, of course, that very interesting marketing study, i.e., buying boys and girls to go buy Frozen Coke at Burger King during a test-market period that was highlighted in Chapter 3 (more details appear there). Matthew Whitley, who had been with Coke since

1992, was its finance director in 2000. During some routine audit work at Coke, he ran across an expense claim for $4,432.01, a claim that was labeled as expenses for the "mystery shop." Whitley didn't know what the mystery shop was, so he questioned managers and officers about it: what the funds were for and what the "mystery shop" submission label represented. Marketing manager Robert Bader responded that the methods might be "unconventional" but were "entrepreneurial."

Whitley recommended that one of the employees responsible for the fake invoices be fired because of the excessive expense and his authorization for it. Coke did not follow Whitley's recommendation, but did fire Whitley, who then filed suit for wrongful termination. Coke first told Burger King of the issues the day before Whitley filed his suit. Whitley's lawyer had contacted Coke and offered not to file the suit if Coke would pay Whitley $44.4 million within one week. Coke did the smart thing in declining the offer and allowing the truth to come out. It disclosed the Whitley and Frozen Coke issues to Burger King. The Coca-Cola board hired the law firm of Gibson, Dunn & Crutcher and auditors Deloitte & Touche to investigate Whitley's claim.

The Wall Street Journal uncovered the lawsuit in court documents when a reporter was doing some routine checking on Coke, and ran a story on August 20, 2003, describing Whitley's experience and suit. The piece was neither flattering nor complete.

The reports of the law and audit firms concluded that the employees had acted improperly during the Richmond marketing test. As a result, Coca-Cola issued an earnings restatement of $9 million in its fountain sales. Burger King's CEO, Brad Blum, was informed of the reports and called the actions of the Coke employees "unacceptable," issuing the following statement: "We are very disappointed in the actions . . . confirmed today by the Coca-Cola audit committee. We expect and demand the highest standards of conduct and integrity in all our vendor relationships, and will not tolerate any deviation from these standards."

Coke scrambled to retain Burger King's business because Burger King threatened to withdraw Coca-Cola products from its restaurants. Burger King is Coke's second-largest fountain customer. (McDonald's is its largest.) As noted in Chapter 3, Coke settled with Burger King and its franchises.

Coke continued with its litigation against Whitley, maintaining that he was "separated" from the company because of a restructuring and that his "separation" had nothing to do with his allegations. However, in October 2003 Coke settled the lawsuit for $540,000: $100,000 in cash; $140,000 in benefits, including health insurance; and $300,000 in lawyer's fees.

John Fisher, the executive who presided over fountain sales at the time of the Burger King debacle, was promoted to a top marketing position in the fountain division in 2003. However, in April 2003 Coke's internal auditors raised questions with Fisher about why he exchanged two Disney theme park tickets that had been purchased by the company for Notre Dame football tickets. Fisher resigned shortly after, but no one at Coke has offered an explanation.

Where were their minds and what were they thinking when they got involved in such a scam? Yet think how many in the organization had to know what was happening before an audit discovered the high consulting fees. Note what happened to the auditor when he raised the issue. Here was a culture not only obsessed with numbers, but with doing whatever it took to make the numbers. They were no longer focused on strategy and Coca-Cola markets and products; they had sunk to a point of making things up to meet numbers. Worse, when someone hit upon the scheme through a suspicious receipt and challenged what was going on, a dismissal was the result.

Coca-Cola has had a phenomenal run of success on a product that has known no match. But generations and demographics change, and new strategies are required. That realization could not make its way through a numbers-obsessed organization. And Coca-Cola's board, while enjoying the presence of the likes of Warren Buffett, Barry Diller, Sam Nunn, and others experienced in all aspects of business, may have been weak in the sense that it was too demanding of its CEO to hit the numbers. Following the death of Robert Goizueta, the longtime CEO during Coke's largest growth period, the company was adrift, going through several CEOs. The company's unmistakable path toward its questionable conduct began when those numbers, now restated, were so astronomically high that there was no way to continue them without some sleight of hand. In fact, if you had positioned yourself short on Coca-Cola stock at the time Douglas Daft took over as CEO, you would be wealthy today. Daft, an iconic figure of social responsibility, gained international fame and a position in the business-ethics community for his speech on the importance of diversity following Coca-Cola's settlement of discrimination claims. All the markings of the seven signs were there.

But this company that is over a century old found some checks and balances as it ended the tenure of the superficial and iconic CEO and replaced him with Neville Isdell, a returning officer, a seasoned and experienced businessperson with a solid grasp of operations and marketing. Two checks and balances were obvious as Mr. Isdell took the helm. These checks and balances became public just months ago. They demonstrate that the top officer and the board at Coke understand how close the company had come to disastrous ethical collapse.

First, Mr. Isdell issued a stunningly candid release on Coke's declining earnings and an honest assessment of its need for a change in strategy. He pledged to make the necessary strategic changes and work to rebuild the company's strength in its brand. The second change was a board coming alive and taking a hands-on approach to assisting with the strategy and making sure that another Burger King trust violation did not occur. On the company website, anyone can contact the board directly. The contact can be by phone, letter, or e-mail and can be anonymous. This is a change designed to combat the culture that had consumed the company and driven the Burger King missteps. Strong board, candor in financial reporting and disclosure, and a call for all employees to let someone known when there is a breach of ethics or law: Coke has just implemented antidotes to curb what was a mighty Yeehaw Culture.

The story of Coca-Cola is a positive one—one that shows that companies going adrift can bring themselves back from the brink if those at the helm understand how to curb the seven signs of ethical collapse. Will Coke make it? Coke has a good chance with its addition of a few more checks and balances on those younger officers, the steady and forthright leadership of Isdell, and a return to focusing on strategy, not deceptive marketing studies, to win the competitive battles Coke now faces. The story is inspirational because not only does it show that change is possible, it demonstrates that it's not the first mistake that leads you into ethical collapse. And it is the vow not to repeat the first mistake that brings a company back from the dangerous cliff that leads to ethical collapse.

The Cruise Lines—An Entire Industry I Worry About

In the year 2004 there were 7.6 million U.S. citizens who took a cruise, an increase of 51 percent from 1995 and 11 percent over the numbers of passengers in 2003. Profit margins in the industry are high, with Carnival Cruise's net profits per day averaging about $3 million. There's that double-digit growth. The cruise lines enjoy margins like those in no other resort/travel industry and they fancy themselves immune largely because they are able to occupy a legal no-man's land, with most of them registered in Liberia, thereby avoiding U.S. taxes (even though 90 percent of their passengers are from the United States), another factor that contributes to their high margins. But the loopholes and immunity don't stop there.

Employees on the cruise ships work twelve-to-fourteen-hour days and are paid $400 to $450 per month. The workers are not entitled to U.S. labor and wage protections, and the industry has been unyielding to suggestions from the International Labour Organization of the United Nations for a work-week limit of seventy hours. Some of the workers do earn about $2,000 per month in tips, and their work year is four to ten months. They are not covered by medical insurance when they are not working on the ships. Most cruise ship workers are recruited from the Philippines, where average earnings are $1,000 per year. There may be some fomenting high dudgeon here.

Cruise ships take advantage of the jurisdictional no-man's land on environmental regulation to release effluent into the ocean, thus saving them the cost of waste disposal. With three thousand passengers on each boat, the cost of that disposal can run into the hundreds of thousands per day. The U.S. Environmental Protection Agency (EPA) has brought enforcement actions against cruise lines caught dumping in U.S. waters. For example, Holland America, a division of Carnival Cruise, entered a guilty plea to waste discharge off the coast of Alaska and paid a $2 million fine.

Criminal activity, such as large numbers of thefts and sexual assaults aboard cruise ships, also falls into a legal no-man's land. Murder on the high seas courtesy of a cruise line has become continual fodder for the news/legal cable television gab fests. Discovery in a civil sexual-assault case against a cruise line disclosed that there are a high number of sexual assaults on cruise ships, but very few of them are reported to law enforcement officials because with the assaults committed at sea, no one really has criminal jurisdiction. Further, when there is an allegation of sexual assault by a crew member, ship personnel often whisk that offender off board, onto a plane, and back to his native country. The result is evasion of any type of criminal prosecution or public awareness of the issue. While the International Council of Cruise Lines (ICCL), a voluntary trade association, has agreed to report all criminal activity for safety reasons, the rule is not mandatory and not all cruise lines are members.

The cruise industry is an untapped reservoir for trial lawyers. The dancing, wall scaling, drinking, swimming, pillow fights, food on the floor from buffet lines, more drinking, contests, jogging, and a host of other activities, all on a moving ship with strangers, create premises-liability cases that the cruise lines handle by putting in contractual provisions that require customers to travel to Miami to litigate.

There is a culture of innovation at the cruise lines because they have enjoyed tremendous growth and those margins are enviable. There is tremendous pressure to continue to meet those numbers, fill the growing number of ships with passengers, and maintain the high margins. There is also a culture of fear and silence in which employees, completely dependent on the lines for jobs, will say nothing about problems during the cruises. The social-responsibility sign kicks in as the ICCL meets regularly to discuss issues regarding dumping in the ocean and even the access of disabled passengers.

The growth cannot continue at the record pace the industry has enjoyed, and the size of the revenue pot is bound to bring lawmakers, regulators, and taxmen to the front door of the cruise industry. Coming will be revelations about other problems kept quiet for purposes of preserving the image of the cruise lines. The double-digit growth will end, margins will be eaten away, other forms of destination resorts will be able to compete more effectively with cruise-line prices, share prices will tumble, and there may be financial shenanigans by the young 'uns to meet the previous numbers goals. Those in the industry cannot continue their legal immunity and the high margins and growth that come from their unique market position. Sliding gracefully into lower returns does not seem likely.

Another I Worry About: Google

The boys from Google make me nervous because, well, they are boys. I wish them well and hope that they do have long-term lessons to teach the rest of us about business. However, if my seven signs hold up as they have over three regulatory cycles and through many other young 'uns who were bound and determined to teach the rest of us how the cabbage is cut, Sergey Brin and Larry Page, Google's founders, are still just kids. They are brilliant with fresh ideas. They fancy themselves as above the fray and the mundane businesses of the world. In fact, Google's niche and the Page and Brin abilities are phenomenal. But I spot some ethical-collapse signs here that put them at risk. It's not that they could not curb them. I only worry that they are inclined not to heed the advice of antidotes for what seems to be a pattern applicable to them.

Everyone oogles over Google. Analysts love Google and its earnings and even their management, but there are qualitative risks here. In addition to the presence of a culture of innovation like no other is the fact that the boys are two socially responsible creatures who are dedicated to making the world a better place because just running a highly successful search engine is not enough. They have thoughts on everything from the Iraq war to the usual doing well by doing good. "Do no evil" is not a bad motto for any business, but sometimes one needs a little assistance in spotting the difference between good and evil. Everyone believes they are ethical. In fact, Google's decision to go into China with information restrictions on its search engine found the company at a congressional hearing answering questions as to why it would agree to such constraints. Some Google is apparently better than no Google at all, despite the sentence of limitation its search engine now imposes on information access there.

Their position of being innovators has carried with it the accompanying earnings that defy gravity. And how does one top being a steady billionaire at that young age? What happens when the lads hit the wall that so many other innovators have when there is competition in their newfound field? Yahoo and Microsoft are nipping at Google's heels. Innovators that they are, the young men have eschewed traditional corporate structure, the same phenomenon we witnessed in so many of the fallen dot-coms. Just the road to their initial offering reveals how much they believed themselves immune from the usual rules. Giving an interview to *Playboy* magazine in full view of the SEC and other financial voyeurs on the eve of a public offering is hardly the way to ensure compliance with the prospectus requirements of the 1933 Securities Act. The result was a hiccup for Google's IPO and additional filings for whatever disclosures had been given to the folks at the Hefner empire. Periods of silence do apply to both analysts and those who occupy the Playboy mansion. When the Google IPO went forth, the boys insisted on a Dutch auction so that those who bought the shares were true investors in the company, not people who would turn around and sell the shares to profit from what was supposed to be a hot IPO. However, the Dutch auction was not as brilliant as the boys imagined, and the IPO that was once through the roof in terms of expectations settled down a bit. The Dutch auction confused investors. They had to cut the price of their shares about $20 and trim back the offering because of the fizzle. But those shares have continued to climb since the time of the IPO. Google just keeps on going and googling. Perhaps this company is a breed apart. Perhaps the boys are correct that Google is no conventional company. Many people agree. For me, that's trouble!

There is a tad of that humble hubris that peeks through at me—something others see and find to be nothing more than the musings of an ivory tower isolationist who cannot recognize a unique winner when she sees one. Still, that pattern . . . The Google founders began by thinking they could teach Wall Street a thing or two about IPOs and the way to do things right. Even their presentation at the Waldorf-Astoria raised eyebrows because it was clear no one had practiced the presentation and everything seemed off the cuff. The assumption going in was that they were different, had a unique offering and company, and that what they had to offer would trump all the traditional demands of Wall Street. Perhaps this early lesson of infallability from the IPO and the SEC will help rein in the Yeehaw Culture that has affected so many like Google with similar stories and start-ups and attitudes. How soon we forget the lessons of the dot-bombs and their cultures of ethical collapse. I offer my warning not to be destructive but to encourage the Google folks to apply some antidotes.

In fact, we may be seeing the hubris producing yet another repeating pattern in these phenomenal innovators. Google hires Ph.D.s, as Apple and Xerox did, for the purpose of developing new products. Although they do develop products, they also haven't the foggiest notion about how to get the products to market. Apple was trying to sell a $6,500 computer to college students, and Xerox got beat to the market by other companies. However, the boys insist that they are a company like no other and that this Ph.D. model will work, distinguishing them from even Microsoft, with its limited research staff. They even have the classic symptom of inexplicable perks such as the free massages (remember Enron), free meals, doctor's visits at the company, and—a new one as far as my study of perks go but a perk nonetheless—Nerf guns. And one more symptom. In this first earnings release following the IPO, the Google gang reported earnings of $805.9 million for 2004, over double the earnings for 2003. To repeat one of the antidotes for the culture of numbers pressure: How is this possible? Sound economics dictate that continuing double- or triple-digit growth is not possible. Beware, those earnings are ad revenues, and there is room for accounting interpretation on booking ad revenues. Remember AOL's debacle on its methodologies related to ad revenues. The SEC settled those issues for AOL despite its continuing claims of validity through uniqueness of business. The patterns are easy to spot, and they do repeat. Even analyst Mary Meeker, the woman we followed blindly into the dot-com bubble, was out and about overvaluing Google, and amazingly, other analysts follow suit. Speaking of suits, I would bet the shareholder lawyers will be out and about sometime soon to bring claims for the overstatements.

Other Industries and Companies to Watch

Distributors and Retailers and Those Fees Sliding Back and Forth

The fees themselves are the market's way of allocating costs and risks related to food products and their promotion and potential. The fees themselves are not problematic, but when they are undisclosed and mysterious, the accounting and financial reporting on the fees trots down the same path of silence and mystery. Sysco remains the only major food distributor to have its accounting practices cleared by two different external auditors. Sysco has not had to restate its earnings based on booking revenues related to the fees that are akin to slotting fees in grocery stores. That's far too many casualties, but the confusion is used, abused, and then restated.

Under these fee systems, manufacturers pay to play, that is, they have financial arrangements with food distributors in order to get their products into cafeterias, nursing homes, schools, and other large-sale venues. The fees are a substitute for the marketing that would be needed to pull the demand for the product through from these large customers. The fees have evolved because they serve a role in the market distribution systems. However, the undisclosed nature of the fees and relationships adds a further lack of transparency in terms of accounting and financial reporting. In addition, the wide variety of arrangements and fees often do not carry specific accounting and FASB rules for how to report, when to report, and how much to report. Therein lies another problem. Discretion abounds.

As with the complexities of Saks' relationship with its vendors on chargebacks, booking the revenues that result from these relationships leaves considerable discretion in the hands of managers whose compensation is tied to the revenues they book. The pattern is the same as the revenues with Enron's mark-to-market accounting and the acquisition costs of WorldCom and Tyco. There is plenty of discretion, and where there is discretion when bonuses hang in the balance, the numbers rarely come out lower than they should be. What was once the practice of the butcher offering the hotel chef cash of $5 to $10 to buy the hotel's meat from him has evolved into a complex relationship, with revenues running $10,000 to $25,000 per year for products or lines carried by the distributor. How and when those fees are booked remains a mystery in an accounting and practical sense. Any company operating in an industry with mystery fees is one to watch: drugstores, grocery stores, and even the bookstores enjoy fees for featuring books in their windows, on the ends of the aisles, or on display tables.

Health Care, Prescriptions, and Confusing Federal and State Regulations

Filling prescriptions has become a growth service industry, and Medco is one of the largest companies in it. It has been ranked number one for customer service in three of the past four years, has been number one on *Fortune*'s list of the most-admired companies in America, and number five on *Fortune*'s customer-service satisfaction survey. Medco's 400 percent growth in net income has brought its shareholders both outstanding returns and appreciation. It has outperformed both the S&P and the Dow. If you had invested $100 in Medco in August 2003, you would have $160 as of the end of 2004. The figure for the S&P composite is $124, and for health-care companies in the S&P, it is $109. Medco's double-digit returns are remarkable, but there are cultural risk factors that could use some antidotes. Medco's revenues and growth are dependent upon its ability to reduce the cost of drugs and its expenses in filling those prescriptions. Medco also involves the highly volatile issue of Medicare. Where there is Medicare, there is always a chance of audits, fines, whistleblowers, and all manner of intentional or unintentional incorrect reimbursement for Medicare claims. Actions filed against Medco by the federal government include alleged false claims. The company is in settlement discussion with the Justice Department over the 2003 lawsuit that accused the company of fraud. Other class-action litigation is pending, and one Ohio jury concluded that Medco owed the State Teachers Retirement System of Ohio $7.8 million for overcharging its members on generic drugs. Medco is appealing the decision, which was grounded in the jury's finding that there was a breach of fiduciary duty. Medco may not have violated any laws or regulations, but it, like other companies with intense regulatory environments, operates with discretion in interpretation. That discretion, as in other examples, coupled with earnings pressures, can sometimes create an atmosphere of temptation and wide latitude. Checks and balances can help rein in that temptation, but the checks and balances have to be put into place.

But Medco is an industry innovator. In fact, its combination motto and strategic model appears on its website as "solid foundation+innovation=brand of choice." Here is an excerpt from the president's letter in the annual report that has the lovely ring of doublespeak:

Our long-term strategy is straightforward—delivering three layers of value:

- *A foundation of operational excellence and financial discipline embodied in a client-first commitment to reliability, stability, service and trust.*

- *An innovation overlay combining technology and clinical expertise into market-focused solutions to help our clients manage and maintain a sustainable, accessible and affordable pharmacy benefit.*

- *An aspiration layer that will empower clients and members with a suite of knowledge services that shape a new standard of excellence and define Medco as the PBM industry's brand of choice.*

It does things faster and better than others in the industry. Medco's generic substitutions, at an industry-high rate of 91 percent substitution within two weeks of generic availability, is a model of efficiency. It has double-digit growth in its revenues. One-third of its board is composed of inside directors, and there is a phenomenal stock option plan available to officers, directors, and certain employees.

However, increasing demands for efficiency and reduced costs may have pressured Medco employees into practices currently under scrutiny by several state attorneys general, including allegations of canceling prescriptions to avoid late-fill penalties, not providing the full number of pills for prescriptions, favoring Merck drugs over competitors' generics (despite cost and Merck's former ownership of Medco, with affiliations and interconnections carrying over into the now-independent Medco), and not verifying ambiguous prescriptions.

Since I first looked at the company in 2003, it has made significant changes. Its board went from primarily insiders and those with consulting and other relationships with the company to a board with experience (including a former Big Four audit firm partner) and independence. But it remains part of a volatile industry, with its phenomenal and continuing performance. There are more antidotes to apply here to prevent the officers, whose stock options hang in the balance, from crossing those lines into false financial reports and other ethical shortcuts.

CHAPTER TEN

The Road Ahead

It's not the first mistake that'll kill you. It's the second,
the third, and the cover-up of all three.

—Marianne M. Jennings, circa 2003

In the spring of 2004 I sat in a meeting room at the Plaza Hotel in New York City, one of a handful of academics among a group of corporate ethics officers. This session on how to create an effective ethics program was being conducted by an ethics officer from Shell Oil. Because Royal Dutch/Shell Oil, the international parent company of Shell Oil, had just revealed in February that its reserves were overstated by about 20 percent, a mere 3.9 billion barrels, and in March the Justice Department and SEC had visited the company with subpoenas in hand, members of the media were present to hear from the ethics officer.

Her presentation was wonderful; her demeanor was amazing, given the circumstances; and her sincerity about ethics in business was heartfelt. At the end of her presentation came a harsh question from the audience—not from the media, but rather from a fellow academic, who spouted, "I come to these meetings every year and hear about the wonderful things each of you is doing at his or her company. But I come here each year and at least one new scandal has emerged in one of your companies. You explain it, you isolate yourselves from the problem, and you explain how no one could have known. Aren't you always just chasing after the problem, not preventing it? It seems to me that all of you are trying to catch the tiger by its tail."

He said it better than I, except for one thing: he is a critic, I offer a solution. When all the ethics codes are in place, the training on compliance finished, and the clear lines between right and wrong established, we must ultimately deal with the layers of complexity in large, often multinational organizations. Establishing conscience throughout such a large entity is no small task. But the chances are greater if the checks and balances for ethical collapse are in place. There are seven clear signs that emerge in every ethical debacle. Each time the SEC catches the tiger, we learn more about the tiger's evasiveness and techniques for choosing the unethical route. And, to blaspheme Tolystoy, all ethical collapses are alike. It's time to incorporate what we know from the patterns so that we can hold the tiger at bay.

A few months after I listened to the Shell ethics officer's presentation, her company would pay the SEC $150 million to settle charges related to the overstatement of the reserves. *The Wall Street Journal* would run a rather unflattering story about Shell's young CFO, who had left Polaroid as its CFO just eight months before it filed for bankruptcy. Another MBA out of Chicago, one of her coworkers issued the following statement to *The Wall Street Journal* reporter: "Ms. [Judy] Boynton was more focused on pleasing her bosses than getting them to confront serious problems."

Nothing good can come from the Shell restatements for Ms. Boynton or those around her who knew of the reserves issue. But something good could come out of it for Shell, its ethics officer, and many other companies and ethics officers around the country. Take the lessons of ethical collapse. Forget Sarbanes-Oxley form-over-substance resolutions and take a long, hard look at the seven signs. Statutory reforms and regulatory requirements are the systemic response. They are but checklists, rote in application and not terribly meaningful in terms of prevention. The seven signs get at the culture of a company. They force organizations to take a look at the dynamics that produce ethical lapses. The seven signs are not the usual cleanup following ethical lapses. They are the signals that such lapses lie ahead. Opportunities present themselves and the field is ripe with potential for ethical lapses. Some awfully smart and good people have done some ethically dumb things, particularly over the past five years. One has to ask how such obvious missteps could go on for so long with no objection. And when the press reports on the ethical and legal lapses, everyone, including many within the company, shake their heads and wonder, Why? How? These types of ethical missteps don't happen without a culture that allows them to stew and fester. The seven signs show what cultures will serve as petri dishes for ethical breaches and, eventually, once things get growing, ethical collapse.

Holding the Tiger at Bay: Catching the First Mistake

Rather than just focusing on what is or is not ethical, ethics officers and managers should be looking at the seven signs. Are they present in your company? Are they in the companies in your financial portfolio? Is the tiger ready to pounce? Or are there precautions to keep it caged? And if not, are you prepared to take a short position in your company's stock?

The ethical issues that plagued the companies that collapsed were neither difficult to resolve nor subtle in their presentation. The ethical culture is more subtle and difficult to discern. But the good news is that we know what creates a poor ethical culture and what checks and balances can prevent those problems. This is a book written to keep us away from the slippery slope. The descent into ethical collapse is fast and furious once those seven signs come together. The seven signs of ethical collapse are, however, manageable and the fall off the ethical cliff avoidable. The antidotes for curbing the behaviors that create each of the signs of ethical collapse have been delineated. All together, there are thirty-two antidotes for curbing the seven signs. And included in many of them are specific directives. These are specific changes companies can make to curb the culture—not deal with ethical lapses after the fact. Rather than chasing down violations, ethics officers should be shooing away the components of the company's culture that give rise to ethical lapses. These antidotes are perhaps the first meaningful prevention tools that will work not just to prevent ethical collapse but to improve employee attitudes about ethical choices in their organization. These antidotes are the microreforms, the ones each organization can implement to effect change in the ethical culture.

It's not the first mistake an organization makes that brings it down. It's the second mistake, the cover-up, and everything that follows that brings ethical collapse. The key is to create a culture that catches the first mistake. As long as human beings run organizations, there will be mistakes and ethical lapses. The key is to have a culture that brings that lapse to the attention of the right people with the right attitude to take the necessary steps (many of them highlighted in the antidotes) to halt the follow-up mistakes. Royal Dutch didn't make a multibillion-dollar overstatement of reserves in one fell swoop. Rather, that multibillion-dollar overstatement came about through several years of smaller overstatements brought about by financial pressure to meet reserve numbers that was bolstered by bonuses and rewards tied to meeting those numbers, all nurtured by what appears to be a culture of fear and silence. Break down any one of those signs and Royal Dutch could have stopped the overstatements before they ripened into a $150 million fine and its impact on the company's share price, cost of capital, and reputation.

Our Overall Culture: Macroantidotes

So far we have the micro companywide antidotes to prevent ethical collapse. However, there is one more component that could help make the antidotes for the seven signs work more effectively. There are aspects of our overall culture that could use some work. I cannot plunk down an ethical organizational culture in a sea of amorality (or worse) and expect the organization striving to be ethical to survive. Effecting change in our overall culture is necessary if we are to make the application of the antidotes less onerous and certainly more effective.

Changing the Ethical Culture in Financial Reporting

For all of the collapses and financial restatements that have occurred and as much legislation and regulation that has been passed, I still sense a bit of teenage-like rebellion. Contrition has waned. The reforms are detailed but not substantive. Put those two together and you have the volatile combination of resentful organizations performing perfunctory tasks that are costly and perhaps not effective. Federal Reserve chairman Alan Greenspan testified before Congress that it could not "effectively legislate morality or character." I sense resistance to ethics. More to the point, I sense resistance to the need for either ethical introspection or organizational change.

Several titles from opinion pieces by experts with their warnings, root-cause analyses, and suggestions for reform offer examples of a pervasive hesitation to embrace cultural reform at the macro level. Certainly the invisible-hand theory is applicable, and companies that collapsed did so because they were less than forthright about their financial status. However, the reforms are more than just penance for excess, they are designed to restore trust.

One piece, titled "Celebrity CEOs Share the Blame for Street Scandals," offers the theory that investors, like CEOs, are less likely to question financial reports, and CEOs are thereby able to get away with more for longer periods, until there is an eruption. According to the article, the solution lies exclusively with the CEOs and shareholders' paying closer attention. The piece also faults boards for hiring manipulators who massaged the market but did little else.

Another, "The Age of Acquiescence," advances as its root-cause theory for corporate scandals the seeds planted by Nixon, Watergate, and the sixties mentality of "live and let live." Finally, "Bring Back the Hostile Takeover" suggests that because we prosecuted Michael Milken and Ivan Boesky and halted takeover activity after the 1980s, renegades had no market form of regulation and thereby became entrenched in corporations because corporate raiders, who otherwise would have taken action to remove the manipulative CEOs, waited helplessly on the sidelines in order to avoid a Milken/Boesky fate. This theory presumes that those constrained by antitakeover regulation saw the market differently from every analyst and investment house, who also relied on the financial reports. Further, staging a takeover from shareholders who are reaping at least the temporary benefits of a stock price hovering at sixty to eighty times reported earnings is a tall order.

Even the postmortem analyses of specific companies do not offer reflective insight into the ethical-culture problems that consumed these companies and tainted their financial reports. One analysis pointed out that Enron had some great ideas and how it is tragic that they have been gutted. The observation is true enough, but the analyst misses the real message of the Enron collapse, which is that even the best strategy cannot succeed with deceptive financial manipulations and reports. Tragically, the piece by Arthur Andersen's CEO, Joe Berardino, calling Enron "A Wake-Up Call," focused on the detection of fraud, an analysis that demonstrates his lack of understanding of the role his firm played and complete disregard of the ethical parameters required for financial reporting. There were those who wanted to be certain that the accounting and the EBITDA of the new economy remained, and wrote "Enron May Be Dead but the New Economy Isn't." Finally, others found fault with the regulators, blaming them for the collapses, as the piece on New York's attorney general, "The Problem with Eliot Spitzer," did. There was also the infamous "Behind the Spitzer Curtain." Perhaps the common postmortem analyses were the "few bad apple" speeches offered by former U.S. Treasury Secretary Paul O'Neill and Pfizer CEO Henry McKinnell. However, the most disheartening were those comments that rationalized the behavior and worried only that "getting caught" was the problem. "Everybody did this. The people who got in trouble are those who are most at the edge. Enron didn't get caught. Enron got so far out on the edge that it fell off." This last analysis presumes that there is nothing amiss with conduct that everyone engages in but happens to be less than forthright.

Perhaps the pieces that I found most depressing, and, dare I say, demoralizing, were the ones that opted for a legalistic interpretation of right and wrong. When Arthur Andersen's conviction for obstruction of justice was reversed by the U.S. Supreme Court on the grounds that the judge's instructions to the jury were wrong, there were shouts of vindication, mockery of prosecutors, and complaints about where Andersen could go to regain its reputation as well as its business. Andersen was in trouble long before its Enron document-shredding party. Whether such shredding was or was not criminal is irrelevant. Andersen had deteriorated into a client pleaser and had crossed many an ethical line in performing its audit functions. Its fate may have been expedited by its conviction, but its indictment was a function of its inability to draw lines, honor absolute values, and withstand client pressures. Its reputation was lost by its own conduct. The imprimatur of a criminal conviction was meaningless once its look-the-other-way work with so many ethically collapsed companies became public.

Most recently the resentment of government action on AIG's accounting and reinsurance policies has percolated into the business press, with the argument being that nothing criminal can be proved. Ah, but the ethics are a different question. Likewise, Richard Scrushy's stunning acquittal on a $2.7 billion fraud is hailed as his vindication and a blow for overly aggressive prosecutors. Charges, no charges, acquittal, dismissal, do not exonerate Scrushy or Greenberg from ethical lapses and the ethical collapse of their companies. How can trust survive in a market plagued by CEOs who shave the treetops with their legalistic interpretation of right and wrong? How can a company change its culture when such CEOs enjoy acquittals or people defending what was fraud, regardless of whether criminal intent could be established? The law is the minimum standard of behavior. Ethics demand more if we are to have trust in business relationships, investor commitments, and the markets in general.

I find myself slightly discouraged as I realize what Warren Bennis has observed about this crisis of ethics: "Where are the business leaders? Why aren't they speaking up?" We need more than a cultural change in organizations. Oddly, I find myself in the position of telling CEOs that perhaps they should exercise some leadership. I am concerned about the lack of CEOs' participation in their own fate and that of their companies. They have become spectators in the battle for ethics, and they should be leading the charge and determining their own fate in this post-Enron, post-bubble era. There are companies that have not crashed and burned in ethical collapse. No company is perfect, but a word or two from a CEO or two could help in the battle for corporate cultural change. We need cultural change at both the macro and micro levels. And changes can't come without CEO leadership. At the macro level, some are still unwilling to recognize the need for change. A departure from the legalistic, technical approach to running a business and issuing its financial reports, coupled with a commitment to forthright disclosure, could go a long way to curb the Yeehaw Cultures. From the postmortem analyses, it remains unclear whether this commitment at the macro level exists. Regulation has seen its share of opposition, and already reforms are being proposed to the new regulations adopted pursuant to Sarbanes-Oxley. Oh, the oppressive nature of Sarbanes-Oxley, they cry! An ethical vision for financial reports would not be a bad idea and could go a long way in curbing those numbers cultures. Without the parameters of ethics encasing the detailed regulatory and professional reforms in financial reporting, the reforms become rote, viewed as mere costs of compliance, regulations to be tolerated. Worse, the missing cultural change will find those in the culture simply seeking and finding ways around the new regulations. In a speech following the close of his two-year tenure as head of the SEC, Harvey Pitt indicated that there was a central key to the restoration of the markets and investor trust—ethics.

At the micro level, the antidotes suggested in each area of ethical collapse can help companies and employees embrace not just regulatory compliance but forthrightness. We may just get ethics from employees by implementing

programs that focus on culture, not violations. However, there are macroanti-
dotes, types of attitudinal issues, that must be applied universally at the micro
level to help companies as they strive to do the right thing. These universal
changes are antidotes to the rebellious teens who want to focus only on statutory interpretations and criminal indictments and convictions as the measure
of what is ethical business conduct. These antidotes represent a recommitment
to ethics in the marketplace. Without curbing the macrobehaviors and attitudes, the microantidotes cannot take hold as strongly as they could because of
the systemic resistance to the demands of being ethical.

Universal Macroantidote #1: Voluntary Changes in Financial-Reporting Practices—Clarity, Honesty, and Full Disclosure

There are so many areas of accounting in which the correct technical solution
on disclosure and reporting can vary. For example, booking options remains
an area of contention. However, Coca-Cola and Winn-Dixie made the voluntary decision to book options as expenses. Coca-Cola's announcement also
disclosed the impact on earnings per share. Long before the regulatory battle,
these companies made decisions about forthright reporting on stock options.
Interestingly, their decision to disclose meant that now that regulation exists
and companies must book options expenses, the financial impact of expensing
the options will have already been felt, disclosed, and absorbed by the market.
These forward-thinking companies look terrific next to the resistant come-
latelys.

Microsoft has gone one step further and decided that options carry more
baggage than just the decision to record them as an expense. Its decision to
shift to restricted stock as a means of compensating its officers and other employees is a tip of the hat to the potential impact that awarding and holding
options can have on the ethical culture of a company as those options affect
managers' decisions on meeting and reporting numbers. In all the companies
of ethical collapse, extensive option awards for executives were a key part of
their compensation and incentive plans. Managers stretched, extended, and
bent the numbers for personal gain from options that remained high in value
because of a share price that rose with each met financial goal.

Clarity in financial reporting has been the exception, not the rule. Warren
Buffett's Berkshire Hathaway is known not only for its financial performance
but also for its financial-reporting clarity. Mr. Buffett's annual letter to shareholders discusses the problems with financial reporting at other companies
and highlights Berkshire Hathway's differences. Mr. Buffett's company's stock
is up 250 percent since 1999. The tech stocks of the new economy, if they are
even still around, are up 127 percent. Boeing, with its government contracts,

has enormously complex accounting, yet its financial reports are clear because it explains its accounting treatments and has remained consistent over the years in those treatments and applications.

These companies have practiced the first rule of creating a culture for avoiding ethical collapse: they have acted voluntarily and made changes beyond what the law requires. While others play games with rules and work to find ways around reporting, these companies make voluntary decisions to do more than the reporting rules require. Their strategies may never be known, but their distinct approach earns them trust. Financial-reporting leadership through actions beyond what the rules require has created a positive market presence for these companies.

The FASB Business Reporting Research Project issued a final report on voluntary financial-statement disclosures, which it defines to be "disclosures, primarily outside the financial statements, that are not explicitly required by GAAP or an SEC rule." The report concludes that voluntary disclosures help both companies and investors. The benefits of voluntary financial reporting are:

- Companies can establish their own metrics that offer meaningful measures of their financial status and allow them to report to shareholders on their predefined critical-success indicators.

- Companies that make voluntary disclosures have a lower average cost of capital.

- Companies that make voluntary disclosures have enhanced credibility and improved investor relations.

- Companies that make voluntary disclosures have access to more liquid markets with narrower price changes between transactions.

- Companies that make voluntary disclosures make better investment decisions themselves because they are more scrutinizing users of others' financial statements.

- Companies that make voluntary disclosures have less litigation and better defenses when there is litigation.

The disadvantages of not using voluntary disclosures are:

- Competitive disadvantage against those who make voluntary disclosures

- Bargaining disadvantages vis-à-vis suppliers, customers, and employees

- Litigation from meritless suits attributable to minimal and technical disclosure

The macroeconomic costs of minimal and technical disclosure are:

- The additional costs of developing, presenting, understanding, and analyzing often convoluted reports

- The drag on growth from meritless suits attributable to the lack of information

One interesting observation that the report makes is that financial reporting according to the technical rules is a waste of resources because competitors and others in the market make adjustments to the financials for such gamesmanship. In other words, the report recommends, why not be forthright about the information that surfaces anyway and avoid the drag on the cost of capital for that burden of analysis?

The report offers recommendations for individual industries on suggested metrics for measurement and voluntary disclosures but also offers the following general summary of the areas in which businesses could make voluntary disclosures that would serve to offer a more forthright picture of the financial status of the company:

- Operating data and performance measures managers used to track changes and key trends

- Forward-looking information such as management's perceptions of opportunities and risks

- Background about the company and more information about management and who the company's shareholders are

- Data and related information about intangible assets that cannot be reflected in the financial statements

Some examples from industries cited in the report include the following:

- For the chemical industry, a discussion of plant capacity and plans for additions, maintenance, etc., at various plants along with an environmental, health, and safety report

- For all industries, identification of major customers by logo

- For the computer industry, information about rollout of products and disclosure of customer reaction and customer-satisfaction surveys

- For the food industry, a discussion of the historical trend in raw-material prices and a discussion of slotting fees and how they work

- For the pharmaceutical industry, discussion of the customer base and total market for specific drugs and the total number of physicians prescribing each of the drugs, as well as full disclosure of promising new compounds, drugs and R&D

• For the textiles and apparel industry, disclosure about the percentage of garments sewn offshore and breakout of sales by men's and women's clothing as well as by product class

The reassuring common theme, both generally and specifically, is that the purpose of voluntary disclosure is the opportunity to really explain the company, the industry, and the present and future conditions investors can expect. The technical approach to financial reporting has resulted from the game-playing of each company and industry against one another as they try to codify exceptions that place them at a competitive disadvantage because of the numbers in their financial reports. And that contributes to the numbers pressure. The voluntary-disclosure system allows financial reports to better explain those numbers, the company's current status, and its potential. Voluntary disclosure is not just a competitive advantage, it is the non-rules-based resolution to concerns about the disparate impact of one-size-fits-all financial-reporting rules. And its flexibility often removes the pressure from managers and employees who feel that they are caught in an impossible either/or conundrum about how to reflect financial performance.

Fortune magazine offered a road map for restoring investor confidence, the first part of which is "Earnings—trust but verify." Sir David Tweedie, head of the International Accounting Standards Board, has referred to the bottom line of many companies as "haggis," the Scottish dish of minced entrails, and added, "If you knew what was in it, you wouldn't touch it." These pithy insights offer a sad commentary on the ethical status of financial reporting. And companies that continue to rely on the technical and legalistic "gotcha" techniques of financial reporting have not assumed a leadership position and are left with wary and doubtful investors, a result that takes its toll on stock price and the cost of capital.

Universal Macroantidote #2: Value-Based Decision Making

Value-based decision making means that circumstances, pressure, and expediency do not guide the decision, preestablished values do. For example, suppose that an employee working at a company division outside the United States is faced with a demand from a government official there for a payment in order to secure the information-systems contract his company has been trying to sell the central government.

In many companies, the decision would be just to make the payment because pressure for both the cash flow and sales goals so dictates. Everyone rationalizes the payment because it gets the job done. But the company has just trotted down the path to ethical collapse, a path on which progress is made with each ethically questionable decision. There will be a next time, and the payment will be higher. Now the employees have to cover up two payments, and the payments are increasing, thereby making the cover-up more difficult. The downward spiral begins with the flawed initial decision that seemed so justified in the pressure of the moment. By contrast, an employee in a principles-based company approaches the dilemma very differently. When faced with such a situation, even under circumstances in which the payment is arguably legal as a facilitation payment or a commission, an employee making a value-based decision does not dwell on the cash-flow issues his unit is facing or on the problem of not meeting sales quotas if this sale does not go through. Rather, the employee honors his company's preestablished principle that it does not pay bribes or facilitation payments or commissions in this context. His focus is on how to secure the contract without resorting to the breach of law or ethics, not doing whatever it takes to secure the contract. Perhaps his focus turns to an even better ethical question: why are we trying to do business in a country that is this corrupt and carries the additional costs of bribery or facilitation payments?

Pressure makes good people do ethically dumb things as they respond to cultural signals. A survey by the Institute of Internal Auditors indicates that 48 percent of auditors feel that "meeting overly aggressive financial or business objectives" is the primary cause of compromised ethical standards. The second-most-common cause is meeting schedule pressures.

One of the difficulties of restoring value-based decision making is that there has been so much drift to technical compliance that rationalization often interferes with honoring the principles. Employees far prefer sticking with the "gotcha" mentality of compliance, with form over substance. This technical approach manifests itself when personal honesty is contrasted with perceptions about business honesty. For example, among CEOs, dishonesty is pervasive on the golf course, with 82 percent confessing that they cheat at the game. Yet 99 percent of the same group believe that they are honest in business.

Universal Macroantidote #3: Restoration of Virtue Standards

Virtue standards incorporate absolutes. Virtue ethics "can be traced back to Aristotle . . . where traits such as compassion, fairness, loyalty and openness shape a person's and an organization's vision." The virtue standards are inviolate; they do not vary with circumstances. With virtue standards, the resolution of an ethical dilemma is not found in weighing the consequences of choosing one course of action over another, a form of moral relativism. Rather, virtue standards require the resolution of a dilemma according to a predetermined set of absolute values. Virtue standards require definitive lines for what will and will not be acceptable choices and actions. A virtue is a virtue and cannot be compromised, regardless of the level of pressure.

The virtue standards have been defined to include the following:

Virtue Standard	Definition
Ability	Being dependent and competent
Acceptance	Making the best of a bad situation
Amiability	Fostering agreeable social contexts
Articulateness	Being able to make and defend one's case
Attentiveness	Listening and understanding
Autonomy	Having a personal identity
Caring	Worrying about the well-being of others despite power
Charisma	Inspiring others
Compassion	Being sympathetic
Coolheadedeness	Retaining control and reasonableness in heated situations
Courage	Doing the right thing despite the cost
Determination	Seeing it through
Fairness	Giving others their due, creating harmony
Generosity	Sharing, enhancing others' well-being
Graciousness	Establishing a congenial environment
Gratitude	Giving proper credit
Heroism	Doing the right thing despite the consequences
Honesty	Telling the truth, not lying
Humility	Giving proper credit
Humor	Bringing relief, making the world better

Independence	Getting things done despite bureaucracy
Integrity	Being a model of trustworthiness
Justice	Treating others fairly
Loyalty	Working for the well-being of an organization
Pride	Being admired by others
Prudence	Minimizing company and personal losses
Responsibility	Doing what it takes to do the right thing
Saintliness	Approaching the ideal in behavior
Shame (capable of)	Regaining acceptance after wrong behavior
Spirit	Appreciating a larger picture in situations
Toughness	Maintaining one's position
Trust	Being dependable
Trustworthiness	Fulfilling one's responsibilities
Wittiness	Lightening the conversation when warranted
Zeal	Getting the job done right, being enthusiastic

One list of virtue standards applied to business organizations includes the following unvirtuous behaviors:

Saying things you know are not true

Giving or allowing a false impression

Buying influence or engaging in a conflict of interest

Hiding information

Divulging private information

Violating rules

Condoning unethical action

Taking unfair advantage

Virtue standards are the application of absolute values, not codified standards.

These very general concepts often provide the bright lines in the accounting-treatment discussions. Simplistic in description and application, they are so in order to encourage maximum transparency rather than minimal behavior. Virtue standards were touted by President George W. Bush in 2002 as he addressed the near-daily financial-reporting scandals that emerged during his presidency: "Corporate America has got to understand there's a higher calling than trying to fudge the numbers." Virtue ethics restore simplicity to resolving dilemmas and focus decision making on a few simple standards rather than on a complex series of codified and technical rules. Business ethicist Laura Nash, a proponent of virtue ethics and simpler standards, explained the role of simplicity in restoring ethics to business:

> The situations for testing business morality remain complex. But by avoiding theoretical inquiry and limiting the expectations of corporate goodness to a few rules for social behavior that are based on common sense, we can develop an ethic that is appropriate to the language, ideology, and institutional dynamics of business decision making and consensus. This ethic can also offer managers a practical way of exploring those occasions when their corporate brains are getting warning flashes from their noncorporate brains.

Rather than seeking a justification for a desired outcome, the decision maker determines the outcome by honoring the values first, not the outcome. Studying the ethical collapses demonstrates that those making decisions in these companies were not applying virtue standards in a value-based decision-making model. They were looking to produce the results they wanted and made the decisions accordingly.

Those who do not operate using virtue standards see business as a zero-sum game. Business is not a zero-sum game. There are direct and very real positive and negative impacts from the decisions officers and employees make. As noted in Chapter 3, Parmalat would have survived a bad quarter in South America. What it could not survive was concealing that bad quarter and the others that followed for nine years. A bad quarter would not mean that Parmalat would be gone, with another company stepping in to fill the void. Reporting a bad quarter would have meant that Parmalat would change its strategies and its employees would work harder. Parmalat's candid report on its less-than-optimal performance in South America would have meant that it had recognized a problem to be solved. However, Parmalat employees opted for concealment through a series of rationalizations under pressure. Ironically, rationalizations and expediency get in the way of good business decisions because the blinders of the zero-sum game offer only limited or no perspective on where the company is headed and what will come of the decision.

The lack of virtue ethics has not been limited to the innovators and the so-called new economy companies. Numbers pressure has made companies abandon virtue in the name of reaching goals. Warren Buffett wrote in 1999 that companies that cannot achieve earnings legitimately "resort to unadmirable accounting stratagems" to "manufacture desired 'earnings.' "

The list of companies affected by an SEC investigation and/or the need for restatement of financial reports was not limited to companies of the new economy. A partial list of companies with pending or resolved questionable accounting includes: AOL Time Warner (settled an SEC investigation for accounting on its advertising revenues and restated); Aura Systems (booking $27 million from 1996 to 1999 in artificial sales; settled with the SEC in 2002 with no admission; emerged from Chapter 11 bankruptcy in 2006); Computer Associates International (overstating results to inflate revenues; former CEO has entered a guilty plea to federal fraud charges); Dollar General Merchandise (overstating profits by about $100 million during 1998–2000 and restated in 2002); Dynegy Energy (Project Alpha sham transaction; SEC probe of power trades; indictment and conviction of Jamie Olis, former employee who was charged with masterminding Project Alpha; settled with shareholders in 2005 for $468 million; sham trades to inflate revenues); Elan Pharmaceuticals (restating numbers on fifty-five joint ventures and settled with shareholders); Global Crossing (inflating revenues through network-capacity swaps; settled with shareholders for $325 million); Halliburton Oil (overstating revenue and understating expenses; changed certain accounting practices and settled with SEC for $7.5 million); HPL Technologies (acquired by Synopsys in 2003) (CEO Yervant David Lepejian fabricated 80 percent of its sales revenues through forged purchase orders and overstated revenue by 328 percent in 2002. The board fired him, restated financials, and Lepejian entered a guilty plea to wire fraud); I&J (inflating worth with false sales receipts); Kmart (required to restate revenues for several years); Kroger (padding sales by managers in order to meet sales quotas; Kroger restated earnings for 2001, 2002, and 2003); Nesco (overstating earnings); Network Associates (overstating earnings); Peregrine Systems (overstating revenue by about $100 million); Qwest (overstating revenues and swap issues and a $40.8 billion restatement); Reliant Energy (overstating earnings with sham energy trades); Rite-Aid (restating earnings for 1997–99 of about $1.6 billion); Safety-Kleen (overstating earnings of $534 million); and Xerox (restating $6.4 billion in revenue over five years).

Note how the patterns repeat themselves. The reasons for the financial ethical collapses are overstatements, sham trades, understatement of expenses, and swaps. Creativity is limited, but the number of times companies engage in similar behavior in an attempt to beat the system is not.

Hope and the Road Ahead

The patterns of ethical collapse are obvious and consistent. As a professor of business ethics, I often feel the same way I feel as the mother of four children. I warn them again and again about dangers, often hidden dangers, that they have neither the experience nor the will to see. They hear me, but they ignore my advice and repeat the behavior. Generally, this pattern continues until the danger I have warned them about comes to pass. They have a near-miss with a car as they ride their bike into the street without looking. They spill a drink when it's placed too close to the end of the table. They slip and fall because they were running around the pool. I can see it coming. I know the dangers. I know that history teaches the same results and outcomes. Somehow, however, I cannot obtain the credibility I need to have my children trust my admonitions and advice unless and until the injury comes. Even worse, they have the nerve to act surprised when the inevitable occurs.

The patterns of ethical collapse, both within individual companies and in economic cycles, are the same. When there is an ethical collapse, I can demonstrate that the seven signs were there working without the antidotes. When the seven signs are present, the inevitable collapse is coming. The only variable is time. And the only thing I cannot figure out, as I cannot with my children, is why anyone is surprised when the inevitable does occur.

However, as the saying goes, the third time is the charm. Having witnessed three cycles of ethical collapse, I see that the patterns are clearly defined, the signs universal, and the outcomes similar in their disastrous impact. But with this third round of observations, I have also discovered that there are antidotes. If organizations can just work at applying them, the inevitable need not occur. Ethical collapse is not a natural market adjustment—it represents utter defiance of the principles of fairness and morality that markets and capitalism demand. If we are to continue to enjoy the magnificent benefits of the free market, we must be prepared to self-govern through ethical choices. We must also be willing to put into place the checks and balances that ensure such self-government via the free market works. Virtue ethics coupled with a healthy dose of antidotes are the key to preventing ethical collapse.

The Road Ahead

Macroantidotes: Fixing the Culture

Changing our views on financial reporting:

> Recognize our mistakes.

> Commit to forthright disclosure.

1. Employ clarity, honesty, and full disclosure.

2. Use value-based decision making.

3. Find a way for restoration of virtue standards.

Notes

Preface

xii. The number of earnings restatements   Stephen Labaton, "Earnings Restated? Don't Blame a Lawsuit for It," *New York Times*, Feb. 3, 2006, p. B1.

Chapter One: What Are the Seven Signs? Where Did They Come From?
Why Should Anyone Care?

1. *redesign of the Malibu*   Milo Geyelin, "How an Internal Memo Written 26 Years Ago Is Costing GM Dearly," *Wall Street Journal*, Sept. 29, 1999, pp. A1, A6.
2. *explosions in the Ford Crown Victoria*   Grimshaw v. Ford Motor Co., 174 Cal. Rptr. 378 (1981).
2. *Martha Stewart*   Constance L. Hays, "Prosecutor Says Martha Stewart Spun Web of Lies About Shares," *New York Times*, Jan. 28, 2004, pp. C1, C11; Greg Farrell, "Faneuil Describes ImClone Stock Sales," *USA Today*, Feb. 4, 2004, p. 1B.
3. *Maurice "Hank" Greenberg*   Jenny Anderson, "AIG and Greenberg Sever Ties," *New York Times*, Mar. 29, 2005, pp. C1, C4.
5. *"It takes FASB two years"*   Mark P. Holtzman, Elizabeth Venuti, and Robert Fonfeder, "Enron and the Raptors: SPEs that Flourish in Loopholes," *The CPA Journal*, June 8, 2003, p. 7.
6. *My presentation there*   Marianne M. Jennings, "Restoring Ethical Gumption in the Corporation: A Federalist Paper on Corporate Governance—Restoration of Active Virtue in the Corporate Structure to Curb the 'Yeehaw Culture' in Organizations," 3 *Wyoming Law Review* 389 (2003).
8. *Krispy Kreme*   Floyd Norris, "Krispy Kreme Earnings Slide; Change in Strategy Is Planned," *New York Times*, Aug. 27, 2004, p. C3.
8. *"We hit a low-carb wall"*   Floyd Norris, "Krispy Kreme Reduces 2004 Reported Profit," *New York Times*, Jan. 5, 2005, p. C1.
8. *The channel-stuffing charges*   Betsy McKay and Chad Terhune, "Coca-Cola Settles Regulatory Probe," *Wall Street Journal*, Apr. 19, 2005, p. A3.
8. *hyped marketing studies*   Chad Terhune, "How Coke Officials Beefed Up Results of Marketing Test," *Wall Street Journal*, Aug. 20, 2003, pp. A1, A6.
9. *the Merck and Vioxx situation*   Barbara Martinez and Anna Wilde Mathews, "Merck Documents Show Vioxx Tension," *Wall Street Journal*, Feb. 7, 2005, pp. A1, A3.
9. *Merck would hope for the best*   Barry Meier, "Merck Canceled an Early Study of Vioxx," *New York Times*, Feb. 8, 2005, pp. C1, C5.
9. *"DODGE!"*   Anna Wilde Mathews and Barbara Martinez, "E-Mails Suggest Merck Knew Vioxx's Danger at Early Stage," *Wall Street Journal*, Nov. 11, 2004, pp. A1, A10.
11. *very little influence on . . . choices*   Avshalom M. Adam and Dalia Rachman-Moore, "The Methods Used to Implement an Ethical Code of Conduct and Employee Attitudes," 54 *Journal of Business Ethics* 223 (2004).
12. *"The story is true"*   Hugh Aynsworth, "Bush Guard Papers Forged," *Washington Times*, Sept. 12, 2004, at www.washingtontimes.com/national/20040912-125608-4609r.htm.

12. *incredulous headline*   Maureen Balleza and Kate Zernike, "The National Campaign 2004: Memos on Bush Are Fake, but Accurate, Typist Says," *New York Times*, Sept. 15, 2004, p. A1.

12. *Jayson Blair*   Dan Barry, David Barstow, Jonathan D. Glater, Adam Liptak, Jacques Steinberg, with reporting by Alain Delaquérière and Carolyn Wilder, "Times Reporter Who Resigned Leaves Long Trail of Deception," *New York Times*, May 11, 2003, pp. A1, A20.

12. *"rich supply of scandals"*   Katharine Q. Seelye, "Journalist, Cover Thyself," *New York Times*, Nov. 21, 2005, pp. C1, C4.

12. *stories in* USA Today   James R. Healey and Sara Nathan, "Officials Have Known SUV Tire Suspicions for Decade," *USA Today*, Aug. 2, 2000, p. 1B; *In re Bridgestone/Firestone, Inc., Tires Products Liability Litigation*, 287 F. Supp.2d 943 (S.D. Ind. 2002).

12. *price-fixing at ADM*   Kurt Eichenwald, "Former Archer Daniels Executives Are Found Guilty of Price-Fixing," *New York Times*, Sept. 18, 1998, p. C1.

Chapter Two: Sign #1: Pressure to Maintain Those Numbers

17. *"The weak, the meek"*   Jerry Kammer, "Keating on the Attack," *Arizona Republic*, May 6, 1990, p. C3.

17. *17 percent of all CFOs*   Jim Hopkins, "CFOs Join Their Bosses on the Hot Seat," *USA Today*, July 16, 2002, p. 3B.

18. *most common form of numbers manipulation*   "Report Pursuant to Section 704 of the Sarbanes-Oxley Act of 2002," at www.sec.gov/news/studies/sox704report.

18. *MicroStrategy . . . restating its earnings*   James Niccoli, "Microstrategy to Restate Earnings; Stock Plummets," *Computer World*, Mar. 21, 2000, at www.computerworld.com.

18. *officers had settled charges*   www.sec.gov.

19. *with Q. T. Wiles leading it*   "ITT Qume Chief Named President at MiniScribe," *Electronic News*, Nov. 5, 1984, pp. 20–21.

19. *only criterion for performance evaluations*   Michelle Schneider, "Firm's Execs 'Perpetrated Mass Fraud,' Report Finds," *Rocky Mountain News*, Dec. 12, 1989, pp. 1-B, 2-B; Stuart Zipper, "Filings Reveal MiniScribe Struggle," *Electronic News*, Jan. 15, 1990, pp. 38, 40.

19. *Wiles was relentless*   Peter Sleeth, "Audit Compounded MiniScribe's Troubles," *Denver Post*, Aug. 6, 1989, pp. 1-H–7-H.

19. *"dash meetings"*   Andy Zipser, "Recipe for Sales Led to Cooked Books," *Denver Post*, Aug. 14, 1989, pp. 2B–3B.

19. *managers began smoothing the books*   Peter Sleeth, "MiniScribe Details 'Massive Fraud,'" *Denver Post*, Sept. 12, 1989, pp. 1C, 4C.

19. *managers shipped twice as many*   Michelle Schneider, "Miniscribe Execs Rigged Huge Fraud, Audit Says," *Rocky Mountain News*, Sept. 12, 1989, pp. 1B–2B.

19. *wrapped bricks*   Schneider, "Firm's Execs," op. cit., pp. 1-B, 2-B.

20. *Finova's . . . performance recap*   From a copy of the 1997 annual report furnished to the author by the company in 1998.

20. *Compensation . . . tied to . . . share price*   From interviews with former employees and officers of Finova.

21. *"All of Arkansas"*   Interview with Jeff Dangemond, former Finova employee and finance/portfolio manager for the company.

21. *Ernst & Young refused to certify*   Dawn Gilbertson, "Surprises at Finova," *Arizona Republic*, Mar. 28, 2000, pp. B1, B9.

21. *write-down was postponed*   Interviews with former employees and officers of Finova.

21. *not to do anything "stupid"*   Mark Maremont, "Blind Ambition," *Business Week*, Oct. 23, 1995, pp. 78–92.

21. *meet those numbers in any way*   Mark Maremont, "Judgment Day at Bausch & Lomb," *Business Week,* Dec. 25, 1995, p. 39.

21. *"That's precisely the point"*   Floyd Norris, "Bausch & Lomb and SEC Settle on '93 Profits," *New York Times,* Nov. 18, 1997, p. C2.

22. *Bausch & Lomb would settle*   Zina Moukheiber, "Eye Strain," *Forbes,* Oct. 4, 1999, pp. 58–60; Erile Norton, "CEO Gill to Retire from Bausch & Lomb; Carpenter Is Seen as Possible Successor," *Wall Street Journal,* Dec. 14, 1995, p. B3.

22. *In 2005, Bausch & Lomb announced*   "Bausch & Lomb Hurt by Internal Investigations," cfo.com, Dec. 27, 2005.

22. *Dunlap took over*   John Byrne, *Chainsaw: The Notorious Career of Al Dunlap in the Era of Profit-at-Any-Price* (New York: HarperCollins, 1999).

22. *"agreements to agree"*   Speech of Lynn Turner, chief accountant, Securities Exchange Commission, "A Menu of Soup du Jour Topics," May 31, 2001, USC, Leventhal School of Accounting, at www.sec.gov/news/speech/spch498.htm.

23. *So many write-downs had been taken*   Ibid.

23. *Channel stuffing*   Jonathan Weil, "Five Sunbeam Ex-Executives Sued by SEC," *Wall Street Journal,* May 16, 2001, pp. A3, A4.

23. *Our goal is not to capture*   Barnaby J. Feder, "An Abrupt Departure Is Seen as a Harbinger," *New York Times,* May 1, 2002, pp. C1, C2.

23. *WorldCom's revenues*   These numbers were all computed using the company's annual reports found under "Investor Relations" at www.worldcom.com. The numbers were computed using "Selected Financial Data" as called out in each of the annual reports.

23. *bigger and better mergers*   Andy Kessler, "Bernie Bites the Dust," *Wall Street Journal,* May 1, 2002, p. A18.

23. *merger/accounting drive*   Shawn Tully, "Don't Get Burned," *Fortune,* Feb. 18, 2002, p. 90.

23. *"The boost from post-acquisition accounting"*   Kurt Eichenfeld and Simon Romero, "Inquiry Finds Effort at Delay at WorldCom," *New York Times,* July 4, 2002, p. C1.

24. *analysts had trouble keeping up*   David Rynecki, "Articles of Faith: How Investors Got Taken In by the False Profits," *Fortune,* Apr. 2, 2001, p. 76.

24. *Analysts were often at a loss*   " 'Going Concerns': Did Accountants Fail to Flag Problems at Dot-Com Casualties?" *Wall Street Journal,* Feb. 8, 2001, pp. C1, C2.

24. *application of real accounting*   Robin Sidel, "Some Untimely Analyst Advice on WorldCom Raises Eyebrows," *Wall Street Journal,* June 27, 2002, p. A12.

24. *fancy merger accounting*   Lee Clifford, "Is Your Stock Addicted to Write-Offs?" *Fortune,* Apr. 2, 2001, p. 166.

24. *restructuring charge*   "Firms' Stress on 'Operating Earnings' Muddies Efforts to Value Stocks," *Wall Street Journal,* Aug. 21, 2001, p. A8.

24. *actual costs of the restructuring*   More details on WorldCom's accounting processes can be found at Jennings, "Restoring Ethical Gumption in the Corporation," op. cit.

24. *cookie jar into which management can dip*   Carol J. Loomis, "Lies, Damned Lies and Managed Earnings: The Crackdown Is Here," *Fortune,* Aug. 2, 1999, p. 84.

24. *reserves can then be used*   Louis Uchitelle, "Corporate Profits Are Tasty, but Artificially Flavored," *New York Times,* Mar. 28, 1999, p. BU4.

24. *Scott Sullivan*   Geoffrey Colvin, "Scandal Outrage, Part III," *Fortune,* Oct. 28, 2002, p. 56.

25. *income . . . rose 132 percent*   WorldCom annual report, 1998, at www.worldcom.com.

25. *revenues increased over 30 percent*   WorldCom annual report, 1997, at www.worldcom.com.

25. *Internet business . . . was up 57 percent*   WorldCom annual report, 1999, Bernard Ebbers's letter to shareholders, at www.worldcom.com.

26. *"strong, solid performance"*   WorldCom annual e-report, 2000, Bernard Ebbers's letter to shareholders, at www.worldcom.com.

26. *"Sullivan and Myers decided"* Kurt Eichenwald, "For WorldCom, Acquisitions Were Behind Its Rise and Fall," *New York Times,* Aug. 8, 2002, p. A1; Seth Schiesel and Simon Romero, "WorldCom: Out of Obscurity to Under Inquiry," *New York Times,* Mar. 13, 2002, p. C1; Kurt Eichenwald, "Audacious Climb to Success Ended in Dizzying Lunge," *New York Times,* Jan. 13, 2002, p. A20.

26. *keep line costs at 42 percent* Jared Sandberg, Deborah Solomon, and Rebecca Blumenstein, "Inside WorldCom's Unearthing of a Vast Accounting Scandal," *Wall Street Journal,* June 27, 2002, p. A8.

27. *interpretation in booking revenues* The full gory details on Enron's accounting (complete with diagrams) can be found at Marianne M. Jennings, "A Primer on Enron: Lessons from *A Perfect Storm* of Financial Reporting, Corporate Governance and Ethical Culture Failures," 39 *California Western Law Review* 163 (2003).

27. *posting noncash earnings* Matt Krantz, "Accounting Rule Eyed," *USA Today,* Dec. 3, 2001, p. 4B.

27. *energy companies disclosed what percentage* Jonathan Weil, "After Enron, 'Mark to Market' Accounting Gets Scrutiny," *Wall Street Journal,* Dec. 4, 2001, p. C1, C2.

27. *That flexibility in accounting* Floyd Norris and Kurt Eichenwald, "Fuzzy Rules of Accounting and Enron," *New York Times,* Jan. 30, 2002, pp. C1, C6.

27. *Paul Patterson* Weil, "After Enron," op. cit., p. C1.

27. *Enron's stock price tripled* "The Role of the Board of Directors in Enron's Collapse," Report of the Permanent Subcommittee on Investigation, 107th Congress, July 8, 2002, at p. 12.

27. *$100 billion in annual revenues* Rebecca Smith, "Enron Faces Collapse as Credit, Stock Dive and Dynegy Bolts," *Wall Street Journal,* Nov. 29, 2001, pp. A1, A10; www.forbes.com/finance/lists/38/2001/LIR.jhtml?passListId=38&passYear=2001&passListType=Company&datatype=Company&uniqueId=4FL0.

27. *Enron's stock would climb* Wendy Zellner and Stephanie Anderson, et al., "The Fall of Enron," *Business Week,* Dec. 17, 2001, at www.businessweek.com/magazine/content/01_51/b3762001.htm.

27. *"We've been doubling revenue"* www.sec.gov/news/press/2004-94.htm.

27. *The goal of Enron's senior management* This information is available in the SEC's complaint against Richard Causey, Enron's former chief accounting officer, and can be found at www.findlaw.com. The complaint was filed in Houston federal district court in January 2004, #H-04-0284. The information is also verified in the findings of the Powers Report, the special report commissioned by the Enron board. That report is also available at www.findlaw.com.

28. *FASB 125* More details on all of Enron's accounting processes can be found in Jennings, "A Primer on Enron," op. cit.

29. *Andersen's biggest hits* Dennis K. Berman and Deborah Solomon, "Analysts Fault the Accounting at Global Crossing," *Wall Street Journal,* Jan. 30, 2002, p. A8.

29. *Andersen was paid $25 million* Deborah Solomon, "After Enron, a Push to Limit Accountants to . . . Accounting," *Wall Street Journal,* Jan. 25, 2002, p. C1.

29. *Some companies halted the practice* Gary Strauss, "Companies Take Action to Regain Investor Trust," *USA Today,* July 17, 2002, p. 1B.

29. *David Duncan* Anita Raghavan, "How a Bright Star at Andersen Fell Along with Enron," *Wall Street Journal,* May 15, 2002, pp. A1, A8.

30. *"brutally competitive atmosphere"* Barbara Ley Toffler, *Final Accounting: Ambition, Greed, and the Fall of Arthur Andersen* (New York: Broadway Books, 2003), p. 114.

30. *"Billing Our Brains Out"* Ibid., p. 115.

30. *Joe Berardino* Ibid., pp. 117–18.

30. *so-called partner purge* The full structure of the relationships with clients and internal Andersen pressures is detailed in Susan E. Squires, et al., *Inside Arthur Andersen: Shifting Values, Unexpected Consequences* (Upper Saddle River, NJ: Prentice Hall, 2003).

30. *"Setting aside the accounting" The Role of the Board of Directors in Enron's Collapse,* Report of the Permanent Subcommittee on Investigations of the Senate Government Affairs Committee, Report 107-70, July 8, 2002 (hereinafter called PSI Report), p. 26.

31. *HealthSouth issued press releases* Press release of December 12, 2002, at www.health south.com.

31. *Its model for new hospitals* Reed Abelson and Milt Freudenheim, "The Scrushy Mix: Strict and So Lenient," *New York Times,* Apr. 20, 2003, pp. BU1, BU12.

31. *selling off their shares* These trades are now under investigation by the FBI. Milt Freudenheim, "FBI Investigating HealthSouth Trades," *New York Times,* Feb. 7, 2003, pp. C1, C3.

31. *reduction in forecasted earnings* Abelson and Freudenheim, "Scrushy Mix," op. cit., p. BU12.

31. *another restatement* Ibid., pp. BU1, BU12.

32. *"I have spent the past twenty years"* Press release of September 25, 2002, at www.health south.com.

33. *Scrushy announced with great fanfare* Abelson and Freudenheim, "Scrushy Mix," op. cit., pp. BU1, 12.

33. *"you'll get killed"* "Secret Recording Is Played at a HealthSouth Hearing," *New York Times,* Apr. 11, 2003, p. C2.

33. *"We just need to get those numbers"* Greg Farrell, "Tape of Ex-HealthSouth CEP Revealed," *USA Today,* Apr. 11, 2003, p. 1B.

33. *"What are you talking about, Bill?"* Carrick Mollenkamp and Chad Terhune, "Scrushy Lawyers Dispute U.S. Case," *Wall Street Journal,* Apr. 15, 2003, p. A6.

33. *Ernst & Young . . . was duped* Jonathan Weil, "Did Ernst Miss Key Fraud Risks at Health-South?" *Wall Street Journal,* Apr. 10, 2003, pp. C1, C3.

33. *"The level of fraud"* Ibid.

33. *"when individuals are determined"* Ibid., p. C1.

33. *"Look at how profitable"* "Secret Recording Is Played at a HealthSouth Hearing," op. cit., p. C2.

33. *"Go figure it out"* John Heylar, "King Richard," *Fortune,* July 7, 2003, p. 84.

34. *overstated revenues by $2.5 billion* Ibid.

34. *"The corporate culture created the fraud"* Ibid.

34. *"Shine a light on someone"* Abelson and Freudenheim, "Scrushy Mix," op. cit., pp. BU1, BU12.

34. *"I want each one"* Heylar, "King Richard," op. cit., p. 78.

34. *"Damn, you guys are good"* Dan Morse, "HealthSouth Ex-Finance Chief Says Scrushy Knew of Fraud," *Wall Street Journal,* Mar. 1, 2005, p. C5.

34. *"Eat s——and die"* Dan Morse, "For Former HealthSouth Chief, An Appeal to a Higher Authority," *Wall Street Journal,* May 13, 2005, pp. A1, A10.

34. *revenues have dropped 70 percent* Ian McDonald, "Marsh Post 70% Drop in Earnings," *Wall Street Journal,* May 4, 2005, p. C3.

34. *43,000 employees* Monica Langley and Ianthe Jeanne Dugan, "How a Top Marsh Employee Turned the Tables on Insurers," *Wall Street Journal,* Oct. 23, 2004, pp. A1, A9. Some put the number of employees at 60,000. Gretchen Morgenson, "Who Loses the Most at Marsh? Its Workers," *New York Times,* Oct. 24, 2004, pp. 3-1 (Sunday Business 1), 9.

34. *revenues were $2 billion more* Monica Langley and Theo Francis, "Insurers Reel from Bust of a 'Cartel,' " *Wall Street Journal,* Oct. 18, 2004, pp. A1, A14.

35. *charged with showing favoritism* Marica Vickers, "The Secret World of Marsh Mac," *Fortune,* Nov. 1, 2004, pp. 78, 80; Monica Langley and Ian McDonald, "Marsh Directors Consider Having CEO Step Aside," *Wall Street Journal,* Oct. 23, 2004, pp. A1, A11.

35. *Mercer . . . was hit . . . with an SEC request* Monica Langley and Ian McDonald, "Marsh's Chief Is Expected to Step Down," *Wall Street Journal,* Oct. 25, 2004, pp. C1, C4.

35. *Mercer settled with Eliot Spitzer* Aaron Lucchetti and Ian McDonald, "Spitzer's Targets Use His Tactics," *Wall Street Journal,* Jan. 24, 2006, p. C1.

35. *"cartel"* Alex Berenson, "To Survive the Dance, Marsh Must Follow Spitzer's Lead," *New York Times,* Oct. 25, 2004, pp. C1, C8.

35. *"Original quote $990,000"* Thor Valdmanis, Adam Shell, and Elliot Blair Smith, "Marsh & McLennan Accused of Price Fixing, Collusion," *USA Today,* Oct. 15, 2004, pp. 1B, 2B.

36. *67.1 percent of its revenue* Langley and Dugan, "How a Top Marsh Employee," op. cit., pp. A1, A9.

36. *half of MMC's 2003 income* Ibid.

36. *94 percent drop* Thor Valdmanis, "Marsh & McLennan Lops Off 3,000 Jobs," *USA Today,* Nov. 10, 2004, p. 1B.

36. *"This month's recipient"* Alex Berenson, "Once Again, Spitzer Follows E-Mail Trail," *New York Times,* Oct. 18, 2004, pp. C1, C2.

36. *"WE DON'T HAVE THE STAFF"* Ibid., p. C1.

36. *"I am not some Goody Two Shoes"* Ibid., p. C2.

37. *"We had to do our very best"* Ibid., p. C2.

37. *"Each time I see Jeff"* Langley and Dugan, "How a Top Marsh Employee," op. cit., pp. A1, A9.

37. *Kozlowski took Tyco* Daniel Eisenberg, "Dennis the Menace," *Time,* June 17, 2002, p. 47.

37. *Tyco's share price* Mark Maremont, John Hechinger, Jerry Markon, and Gregory Zuckerman, "Kozlowski Quits Under a Cloud, Worsening Worries About Tyco," *Wall Street Journal,* June 4, 2002, p. A10.

37. *Tyco became the parent company* This information was gathered from www.tyco.com; see "Investor Relations," "Tyco History."

37. *stock price had jumped fifteenfold* Alex Berenson, "Ex-Tyco Chief, a Big Risk Taker, Now Confronts the Legal System," *NewYork Times,* June 10, 2002, p. B1.

37. *Kozlowski vows* Business Week Online, Jan. 14, 2002, at www.businessweek.com.

37. *"Tyco is so big"* "Rock Hill" refers to an AMP factory in South Carolina. Tyco acquired AMP in 1999. Julie Flaherty, "Tyco Workers Say Faith in Company Is in Shambles," *New York Times,* July 6, 2002, p. B2.

37. *"If we don't hit these numbers"* Ibid.

38. *Tyco's financials were odd* Mark Maremont, "Tyco Made $8 Billion of Acquisitions over 3 Years but Didn't Disclose Them," *Wall Street Journal,* Feb. 4, 2002, p. A3.

38. *$30 billion on acquisitions* Berenson, "Ex-Tyco Chief," op. cit., p. B1.

38. *The bump to earnings* Ibid., p. B1.

38. *a $2.5 billion charge* Kevin McCoy, "Tyco Cuts Outlook, Plans $2.5B Charge," *USA Today,* Sept. 26, 2002, p. 3B.

38. *decrying as problematic* Arthur Levitt, chairman, Securities and Exchange Commission, "The 'Numbers Game,'" speech at the New York University Center for Law & Business, New York, New York (Sept. 28, 1998), available at www.sec.gov/news/speech/speecharchive/1998/spch220.txt

38. *spring-loading* McCoy, "Tyco cuts outlook," op. cit., p. 3B.

38. *"At Tyco's request"* Herb Greenberg, "Does Tyco Play Accounting Games?" *Fortune,* Apr. 1, 2002, p. 86.

39. *"The purpose of this effort"* Ibid., p. 83.

39. *"How high can we get these things?"* Ibid., p. 86.

39. *both incentives and pressure* Kurt Eichenwald, "Pushing Accounting Rules to the Edge of the Envelope," *NewYork Times,* Dec. 31, 2002, p. C2.

39. *"Tyco pursued a pattern"* Ibid.

39. *memoranda between Tyco financial executives* Laurie P. Cohen and Mark Maremont, "Secret Payment by Tyco Is Target of Investigation," *Wall Street Journal,* Sept. 30, 2002, p. A2; Laurie P. Cohen, "SEC Asks Tyco if It Withheld Data in Earlier Inquiry," *Wall Street Journal,* Nov. 25, 2002, p. C1.

39. *"financial engineering"*   Go to "Investor Relations" at www.tyco.com and click on the 8-K filed on December 30, 2002. The document is also available in the Edgar database at www.sec.gov.

39. *"Aggressive accounting"*   Ibid., p. 7.

39. *"scummiest neighborhoods"*   Daniel Golden, Mark Maremont, and David Armstrong, "How Tyco Pushed ADT Dealers into Poor Areas to Boost Growth," *Wall Street Journal,* Nov. 15, 2002, p. A1.

40. *20 percent of the contracts*   Ibid., p. A7.

40. *"The Lord will protect me"*   Ibid.

40. *cancellation rates*   Ibid.

40. *"We have found issues"*   Laurie P. Cohen and Mark Maremont, "E-Mails Show Tyco's Lawyers Had Concerns," *Wall Street Journal,* Dec. 27, 2002, p. C1.

40. *"something funny"*   Ibid.

40. *his bonus was $13 million*   Ibid.

40. *"tremendous pressure on charities"*   William M. Bulkeley, "Charities Coffers Easily Become Crooks' Booty," *Wall Street Journal,* June 5, 1995, pp. B1, B3.

41. *"Book of Reports"*   This information can be found in the criminal information, cease and desist order, and the bankruptcy filings located at the Arizona Corporation Commission website at www.ccsd.cc.state.az.us.

43. *"past decisions of national leaders"*   Columbia Accident Investigation Board, August 2003. The full report is available at www.caib.us. These excerpts are from pp. 22–24.

44. *"I don't know what Congress"*   Ibid., pp. 124–27.

44. *"And I have to think"*   Ibid.

45. *he spun debt off the books*   David Barboza and John Schwartz, "The Finance Wizard Behind Enron's Deals," *New York Times,* Feb. 6, 2002, pp. A1, C9.

46. *"One can violate SEC laws"*   Steve Liesman, "SEC Accounting Cop's Warning: Playing by Rules May Not Ward Off Fraud Issues," *Wall Street Journal,* Feb. 12, 2002, pp. C1, C8.

46. *story from Hank Greenberg's life*   Daniel Kadlec, "Down . . . But Not Out," *Time,* June 20, 2005, p. 51.

46. *"I firmly believe"*   Andrew Ross Sorkin, "Tyco Ex-Chief Is Humbled, but Unbowed," *New York Times,* Jan. 16, 2005, p. A21.

47. *jury . . . didn't buy the theory*   Andrew Ross Sorkin, "Ex-Chief and Aide Guilty of Looting Millions at Tyco," *New York Times,* June 18, 2005, pp. A1, B4.

47. *Belnick . . . found not guilty*   Chad Bray and Colleen DeBaise, "Tyco Ex-Lawyer Is Acquitted in Bonuses Trial," *Wall Street Journal,* July 16, 2004, p. C1.

47. *Marriott Corporation*   Lynnley Browning, "Marriott's Baroque Financings Draw Complaints," *New York Times,* Oct. 13, 2002, p. BU4.

48. *Xerox settled with the SEC*   Claudia Deutsch, "Accounting at Xerox Is Under Inquiry," *New York Times,* Sept. 25, 2002, p. C11.

48. *Xerox would restate $1.4 billion*   Floyd Norris, "6 from Xerox to Pay S.E.C. $22 Million," *New York Times,* June 6, 2003, pp. C1, C6.

50. *there were FBI criminal investigations*   Gary Strauss, "FBI Turns Wary Eye on Kmart's Accounting," *USA Today,* May 17, 2002, p. 1B.

50. *Saks Fifth Avenue recently announced*   Ellen Byron and Teri Agins, "Probing Price Tags," *Wall Street Journal,* May 13, 2005, p. B1.

50. *$20 million*   Information taken from 8-K of Saks & Co. filed on May 6, 2005.

50. *the SEC and U.S. Attorney's Office*   Tracie Rozhon, "Wider Net Cast in Saks Inquiry," *New York Times,* May 11, 2005, p. C1.

51. *These murky systems*   Robert Aalberts and Marianne Jennings, "The Ethics of Slotting: Is This Bribery, Facilitation or Just Plain Competition?" 20 *Journal of Business Ethics* (1999), pp. 207–15.

51. *publicly critical of senior managers*   This information is in the 8-K of May 6, 2005.

51. *improper conduct by these officers*   Tracie Rozhon, "Saks Fires Three Executives over Problems Found in Audit," *New York Times,* May 10, 2005, p. C1.

56. *perceptions about candor*   Steven Taub, "Link Found Between Candor, Share Prices," *CFO Magazine,* June 15, 2004.

57. *"time-out cards"*   www.caib.us, p. 217.

Chapter Three: Sign #2: Fear and Silence

59. *"an obligation to dissent"*   John Schwartz, "Man Who Doubted Enron Enjoys New Recognition," *New York Times,* Jan. 21, 2002, p. C8.

61. *only 66 percent would say something*   SHRM/Ethics Resource Center Joint Ethics Survey, at www.ethics.org or www.shrm.org.

61. *17 percent of CFOs report pressure*   Jim Hopkins, "CFOs Join Their Bosses on the Hot Seat," *USA Today,* July 16, 2002, p. 3B.

62. *vice president of corporate development*   Jodie Morse and Amanda Bower, "The Party Crasher," *Time,* Jan. 6, 2003, pp. 54–55.

62. *"fuzzy" accounting*   Ibid.

63. *"I am incredibly nervous"*   Michael Duffy, "What Did They Know and When Did They Know It?" *Time,* Jan. 28, 2002, pp. 16–27.

63. *"There it is!"*   Tom Hamburger, "Enron Official Tells of 'Arrogant' Culture," *Wall Street Journal,* Jan. 17, 2002, pp. A3–A4.

63. *"it sure looks to the layman"*   Ibid.

63. *Ms. Watkins confessed*   Ibid.

63. *"a job-terminating move"*   Rebecca Smith, "Fastow Memo Defends Enron Partnerships and Sees Criticism as Ploy to Get His Job," *Wall Street Journal,* Feb. 20, 2002, p. A3.

63. *he felt she was after his job*   Ibid.

63. *Fastow was the soulless heart*   McLean and Elkind, *Smartest Guys,* op. cit., p. 140.

63. *top ten list*   Matt Krantz, "Peeling Back the Layers of Enron's Breakdown," *USA Today,* Jan. 22, 2002, p. 2B.

64. *farewell dinner and roast*   Speech of Bob Wright, president of NBC, at the Wharton School, "After the Scandal: Passion, Integrity, and a Seat on the Bus," Jan. 23, 2003, at www.ge.com/en/commitment/governance/news&views/bob_wright_remarks.htm.

64. *James Chanos*   Cassell Bryan-Low and Suzanne McGee, "Enron Short Seller Detected Red Flags in Regulatory Filings," *Wall Street Journal,* Nov. 5, 2001, pp. C1, C2.

64. *Margaret Ceconi*   Julie Mason, "Concerned Ex-Worker Was Sent to Human Resources," *Houston Chronicle,* Jan. 30, 2002, at www.chron.com.

64. *"Some would say"*   Ibid.

64. *Clayton Vernon was fired*   Alex Berenson, "Enron Fired Workers for Complaining Online," *New York Times,* Jan. 21, 2002, pp. C1, C8.

64. *"Mr. Vernon acknowledges"*   Ibid.

65. *James Alexander*   John Schwartz, "An Enron Unit Chief Warned, and Was Rebuffed," *New York Times,* Feb. 20, 2002, pp. C1, C4.

65. *"dead canary in the coal mine"*   Ibid.

65. *"overanxious"*   Ibid.

65. *"thorn" in . . . Skilling's side*   Ibid.

66. *16(b) officers*   "16(b)" refers to that level of officers in a company to whom Section 16 of the 1934 Securities Exchange Act applies. These are the officers subject to the six-month, in effect, holding period on their company shares, a timing prohibition to curb acting on inside information.

67. *"That's just to show everyone"* Andy Zipser, "Recipe for Sales Led to Cooked Books," *Denver Post,* Aug. 14, 1989, pp. 2B–3B.

67. *not-so-fancy accounting strategy* Jonathan D. Glater with Kurt Eichenwald, "Big Lapse in Auditing Is Puzzling Some Accountants and Other Experts," *New York Times,* June 28, 2002, p. C4.

67. *take ordinary expenses and book them* Jared Sandberg, Deborah Solomon, and Rebecca Blumenstein, "Inside WorldCom's Unearthing of a Vast Accounting Scandal," *Wall Street Journal,* June 27, 2002, p. A1.

67. *$500 million in computer expenses* Susan Pulliam and Deborah Solomon, "How Three Unlikely Sleuths Discovered Fraud at WorldCom," *Wall Street Journal,* Oct. 30, 2002, p. A1.

68. *$33.6 million in line costs* Kurt Eichenwald, "Auditing Woes at WorldCom Were Noted Two Years Ago," *New York Times,* July 15, 2002, p. C9.

68. *perhaps Arthur Andersen should be consulted* Ibid., p. C9.

68. *no more Andersen involvement* Ibid.

68. *he established an entity* Ibid.

68. *"Scott Sullivan directive"* Ibid.

68. *as far back as July 2000* Ibid.

68. *a "cheerleader"* Hopkins, "CFOs Join Their Bosses," op. cit.

68. *"The bottomline is"* Jayne O'Donnell and Andrew Backover, "WorldCom's Bad Math May Date Back to 1999," *USA Today,* July 16, 2002, p. 1B.

68. *"not have any more meetings"* Jessica Sommar, "E-Mail Blackmail—WorldCom Memo Threatened Conscience-Stricken Exec," *New York Post,* Aug. 27, 2002, p. 27.

68. *"I might be narrow-minded"* Kevin Maney, Andrew Backover, and Paul Davidson, "Prosecutors Target WorldCom's Ex-CFO," *USA Today,* Aug. 29, 2002, p. 2B.

68. *"David and I have reviewed"* Ibid.

68. *The change . . . went forward* Ibid. See also Simon Romero and Jonathan D. Glater, "Wider WorldCom Case Is Called Likely," *New York Times,* Sept. 5, 2002, p. C9, for background and titles of employees.

69. *company as an aircraft carrier* Susan Pulliam, "A Staffer Ordered to Commit Fraud Balked, Then Caved," *Wall Street Journal,* June 23, 2003, p. A6.

69. *None . . . consulted with Andersen* Eichenwald, "Auditing Woes," op. cit., p. C5.

69. *Mark Abide* Pulliam and Solomon, "Three Unlikely Sleuths," op. cit., pp. A1, A6.

69. *"WorldRon"* Bethany McLean and Peter Elkind, "EndCom, Worldron, EnWorld," *Fortune,* July 22, 2002, p. 30.

69. *fear of discovery was so great* Amanda Ripley, "The Night Detective," *Time,* Jan. 6, 2003, p. 47.

70. *working on "international capital expenditures"* Pulliam and Solomon, "Three Unlikely Sleuths," op. cit., p. A6.

70. *Andersen auditors reported any questions* Ibid.

70. *annual banquet* Anthony Bianco, William Symonds, Nanette Byrnes, and David Poleck, "The Rise and Fall of Dennis Kozlowski," *Business Week Online,* Dec. 23, 2002, at www.business week.com.

70. *KELP* This information was obtained from the SEC's press release when it filed suit against Mark Swartz, Dennis Kozlowski, and Mark Belnick for the return of the loan amounts. See www.sec.gove/releases/litigation.

70. *loan program was available* This information comes from the Tyco 8-K filed on September 17, 2002, following revelations about both the company and its accounting and Mr. Kozlowski's questionable personal financial activities. The 8-K is found at www.sec.gov/edgar.

71. *Belnick was acquitted* Andrew Ross Sorkin, "Ex-Chief and Aide Guilty of Looting Millions at Tyco," *New York Times,* June 18, 2005, pp. A1, B4.

71. *6.24 percent relocation loans* The rate was disclosed in the 2002 proxy.

71. *he was uncomfortable*   Joanthan D. Glater, "A Star Lawyer Finds Himself the Target of a Peer," *NewYork Times,* Sept. 24, 2002, p. C8.

71. *"I don't understand"*   Ibid.

71. *more lucrative compensation*   Glater, "A Star Lawyer," op. cit., p. C8.

71. *"payments to a woman"*   Laurie P. Cohen and Mark Maremont, "E-Mails Show Tyco's Lawyers Had Concerns," *Wall Street Journal,* Dec. 27, 2002, p. C1.

72. *$72 million for personal investments*   www.sec.gov/releases/litigation.

72. *$32 million in interest-free relocation loans*   Ibid.

72. *prosecution . . . for embezzlement difficult*   Joanthan D. Glater, "Tyco Case Shows Difficulty of Deciding Criminal Intent," *New York Times,* Apr. 8, 2004, pp. C1, C4.

72. *Belnick . . . was acquitted*   Chad Bray and Colleen DeBaise, "Tyco Ex-Lawyer Is Acquitted in Bonuses Trial," *Wall Street Journal,* July 16, 2004, pp. C1, C2.

72. *compensation package for Belnick*   Andrew Ross Sorkin and Jonathan D. Glater, "Some Tyco Board Members Knew of Pay Packages, Records Show," *New York Times,* Sept. 23, 2002, p. A1.

72. *pressured by . . . Joshua Berman*   Ibid., p. A22.

73. *"I was recently pressured"*   Ibid., p. A22. Both sides acknowledge the authenticity of the memo from Ms. Prue.

73. *"stupidest thing I ever heard"*   John Heylar, "King Richard," *Fortune,* July 7, 2003, p. 78.

73. *"Interviews with associates"*   Ibid.

73. *"survivors of an abusive relationship"*   Greg Farrell, "From Emperor to Outcast," *USA Today,* May 29, 2003, pp. 1B, 2B.

73. *employees began posting notices*   John Helyar, "Insatiable King Richard," *Fortune,* July 7, 2002, p. 82.

73. *"the king"*   Jay Reeves, "Witness Says Scrushy 'Made Every Decision,'" *USA Today,* Mar. 22, 2005, p. 3C.

73. *trappings of an aloof ruler*   Dan Morse and Evelina Shmukler, "HealthSouth Ex-Treasurer Says He Found Fraud, Told Scrushy," *Wall Street Journal,* Feb. 17, 2005, p. C4.

73. *ubiquitous security force*   Helyar, "Insatiable King Richard," op. cit., p. 82.

74. *told Murphy to change the numbers*   "Witness Tells of Scrushy Yelling at Him," *New York Times,* Feb. 18, 2005, p. C3.

74. *"You have made it clear"*   "Witness Says She Was Punished by HealthSouth for Her Qualms," *New York Times,* Feb. 23, 2005, p. C11.

74. *"leave no stone unturned"*   Stephen Labaton and Heather Timmons, "Discord at Top Seen as Factor in Shell's Woes," *New York Times,* Apr. 20, 2004, pp. A1, C7.

74. *Van de Vijver first raised the issue*   Chip Cummins, "Former Chairman of Shell Was Told of Reserves Issues," *Wall Street Journal,* Mar. 8, 2004, p. A1.

75. *"I am becoming sick and tired"*   Labaton and Timmons, "Discord at Top," op. cit., p. C7.

75. *Judy Boynton*   Laurie P. Cohen and James Bandler, "Shell Finance Chief Has Faced Critics Before," *Wall Street Journal,* Mar. 26, 2004, p. C1.

75. *motivational skits*   Chip Cummins and Almar Latour, "How Shell's Move to Revamp Culture Ended in Scandal," *Wall Street Journal,* Nov. 2, 2004, p. A1.

75. *fines of $150 million*   Heather Timmons, "Shell to Pay $150 Million in Settlements on Reserves," *New York Times,* July 30, 2004, pp. C1, C7.

76. *investors in New Era*   Steve Secklow, "A New Era Consultant Lured Rich Donors over Pancakes, Prayer," *Wall Street Journal,* June 2, 1995, pp. A1, A4.

76. *Albert Meyer*   Barbara Carton, "Unlikely Hero: A Persistent Accountant Brought New Era's Problems to Light," *Wall Street Journal,* May 19, 1995, pp. B1, B10.

77. *untenured faculty member*   Ibid.

77. *Bennett was sentenced*   Steve Secklow, "A New Era Consultant" op. cit. Secklow, "New Era's Bennett Gets 12-Year Sentence," *Wall Street Journal,* Sept. 23, 1997, p. B13; Joseph Slobodz-

ian, "New Era Founder Says: God Made Him Do It," *National Law Journal*, March 17, 1997, p. A9.

78. *culture at NASA*   J. Lynn Lunsford and Ann Marie Squeo, "Shuttle Probe Faults NASA Culture," *Wall Street Journal*, Aug. 27, 2003, p. A3.

78. *"organizational structure and hierarchy"*   Columbia Accident Investigation Report, Aug. 28, 2003, pp. 199–201, at www.caib.us.

78. *"When do you want me to launch?"*   Ibid., p. 200.

78. *Those who raised safety issues*   Ibid., p. 199.

79. *bad quarter in South America*   Alessandra Galloni, "Playing Mr. Nice Guy," *Wall Street Journal*, Dec. 27, 2004, p. A1.

79. *sixty-four people have been indicted*   Elisabetta Povoledo, "A Hearing Begins, and the Aggrieved Line Up," *New York Times*, Oct. 6, 2004, p. W1.

82. *set of questions*   www.ethicsrussia.org/makingchoice.html.

84. *sold . . . under a private label*   Peter Aronson, "A Rogue to Catch a Rogue," *National Law Journal*, August 18–25, 2003, p. A1.

84. *despite his misgivings*   Ibid.

85. *Some of the invoices*   Steven Greenhouse, "Union Seeks Wal-Mart Files about Payments," *New York Times*, Apr. 9, 2005, pp. B1, B10.

86. *union activities*   Ann Zimmerman and James Bandler, "Ex Wal-Mart Exec Accused in Spending Scandal," *USA Today*, July 18, 2005, p. 3B.

86. *Coughlin entered a guilty plea*   "A Guilty Plea in the Wal-Mart Case," *New York Times*, Feb. 1, 2006, p.C1.

86. *Indeed, he resigned*   Ann Zimmerman, "Wal-Mart Pulls Retirement Pact Given to Ex-Executive Coughlin," *Wall Street Journal*, June 13, 2005, p. B8.

86. *federal judge dismissed* "Judge Dismisses Much of Wal-Mart Lawsuit," *USA Today*, Nov. 2, 2005, p. 1B.

86. *"loss of confidence in associate"*   Zimmerman and Bandler, op. cit.

86. *Bowen has asked federal officials*   Ann Zimmerman and James Bandler, "Federal Officials Asked to Probe Wal-Mart Firing," *Wall Street Journal* Apr. 28, 2005, pp. A3, A12.

86. *"If someone asks you"*   Colin Barr, "The Five Dumbest Things on Wall Street This Week," thestreet.com, Apr. 15, 2005.

87. *"10 percent gone formula"*   Del Jones, "Study: Thinning Herd from Bottom Helps," *USA Today*, Mar. 14, 2005, p. 1B.

89. *"I got back my P&L"*   Monica Langley and Ianthe Jeanne Dugan, "How a Top Marsh Employee Turned the Tables on Insurers," *Wall Street Journal*, Oct. 23, 2004, pp. A1, A9.

89. *"Employees learn very quickly"*   Thomas White, "Ethics Incorporated: How America's Corporations Are Institutionalizing Moral Values" (1990), at www.ethicsandbusiness.org/corpeth.htm.

89. *"Fink of the Month"*   Ibid.

89. *Only 60 percent of U.S. companies*   "Rediscovering a Strategic Resource: Your Employees," at www.tccgrp.com.

91. *account that did not exist*   Henny Sender, "Parmalat Unit May Offer Accounting Clues," *Wall Street Journal*, Jan. 29, 2004, p. C5; Daniel Wakin, "There Were Earlier Signs of Trouble at Parmalat," *New York Times*, Jan. 14, 2004, pp. C1, C4.

92. *Companies that put their current positions*   Stephen Taub, "Link Between Candor, Share Price" (June 15, 2004), at www.cfo.com/article.cfm/3014591/c_3042593?f=TodayInFinance_Inside; Stephen H. Penman and Xiao-Jun Zhang, "Accounting Conservatism, the Quality of Earnings, and Stock Returns," *Accounting Review*, Apr. 2002, p. 1.

93. *large expenses with odd explanations*   Chad Terhune, "How Coke Officials Beefed Up Results of Marketing Test," *Wall Street Journal*, Aug. 20, 2003, pp. A1, A6.

93. *"These actions were wrong"* Chad Terhune, "Coke Employees Acted Improperly in Marketing Test," *Wall Street Journal,* June 18, 2003, pp. A3, A6.

93. *"my relationship with Coca-Cola"* Sherri Day, "Coca-Cola Settles Whistle-Blower Suit for $540,000," *New York Times,* Oct. 8, 2003, p. C1.

94. *"Mr. Whitley was a diligent employee"* Ibid.

94. *investigation of . . . Frozen Coke* Kenneth N. Gilpin, "Prosecutors Investigating Suit's Claims Against Coke," *New York Times,* July 13, 2003, pp. B1, B4; Chad Terhune, "Coca-Cola Says U.S. Is Probing Fraud Allegations," *Wall Street Journal,* July 14, 2003, p. B3.

96. *"foot faults"* Daniel Kadlec, "Down, but Not Out," *Time,* June 20, 2005, p. 51.

Chapter Four: Sign #3: Young 'Uns and a Bigger-than-Life CEO

98. *"I hire them just like me"* William C. Symonds and Pamela L. Moore, "The Most Aggressive CEO," *Business Week Online,* May 28, 2001, at www.businessweek.com.

99. *"You got a bunch of know-nothings"* James Sterngold, "Keating: Crook or Scapegoat?" *Mesa Tribune,* Oct. 13, 1996, p. H1.

99. *regulators as "scum"* Jerry Kammer, "Keating on the Attack," *Arizona Republic,* May 6, 1990, pp. C1, C3.

99. *"Finaciopath of obscene proportions"* Ibid., *U.S. v. Keating,* 147 F.3d 895 (9th Cir. 1997).

99. *pattern of family icons* Kurt Eichenwald, "Two Executives Step Down at Archer Daniels," *New York Times,* Oct. 18, 1996, pp. C1, C4.

100. *older than his direct reports* Jerry Kammer, "Keating on the Attack," op. cit.

100. *Spitzer has filed a civil suit* Ian McDonald and Theo Francis, "AIG Probes Bring First Charges," *Wall Street Journal,* May 27, 2005, pp. C1, C3.

100. *sham transaction* Joseph B. Treaster, "U.S. Regulator Threatens Action Against A.I.G. on Press Releases," *New York Times,* Oct. 5, 2004, pp. C1, C12; Monica Langley and Ian McDonald, "Marsh's Chief Is Expected to Step Down," *Wall Street Journal,* Oct. 25, 2004, pp. C1, C4; Theo Francis and Michael Schroeder, "Did AIG Hold Back on Its News?" *Wall Street Journal,* Oct. 5, 2004, pp. C1, C3.

100. *Howard Smith* Elliot Blair Smith, "Scrutiny Tarnishes Legacy of Greenberg," *USA Today,* May 31, 2005, p. 1B.

100. *Evan Greenberg left AIG* Joseph B. Treaster and Eric Dash, "For Executive, Insurance Is Family Business," *New York Times,* Oct. 15, 2004, pp. C1, C2.

100. *legendary short fuse* Daniel Kadlec, "Down . . . But Not Out," *Time,* June 20, 2005, p. 51.

101. *$1.7 billion downward restatement* Jenny Anderson, "Insurer Admits Bad Accounting in Several Deals," *New York Times,* Mar. 31, 2005, p. A1.

101. *another $1 billion* Jenny Anderson and Kurt Eichenwald, "Big Insurer Finds More Accounting Problems," *New York Times,* Apr. 26, 2005, pp. C1, C17.

101. *accounting results using questionable policies* Ian McDonald, Theo Francis, and Deborah Solomon, "AIG Admits 'Improper' Accounting," *Wall Street Journal,* Mar. 31, 2005, pp. A1, A6.

101. *Mr. Buffett cooperated* Susan Pulliam, "How Buffett Gave a Tip That Led to Greenberg's Fall," *Wall Street Journal,* Apr. 8, 2005, p. A1.

101. *changes in accounting practices* McDonald, et al., "AIG Admits," op. cit., p. A6.

101. *"imperial"* Jenny Anderson and Kurt Eichenwald, "How a Titan of Insurance Ran Afoul of the Government," *New York Times,* Apr. 4, 2005, p. C1.

101. *"Take me anywhere"* Kadlec, "Down . . . But Not Out," op. cit., p. 51.

101. *"permeated with illegality"* Monica Langley, Ian McDonald, and Theo Francis, "AIG Received Warning in '92 on Accounting," *Wall Street Journal,* Apr. 27, 2005, p. C1.

101. *Milgram's work* Stanley Milgram, "Behavioral Study of Obedience," 67 *Journal of Abnormal and Social Psychology* 371 (1963).

102. *Greenberg ran the company*   Carol Loomis, "Aggressive. Inscrutable. Greenberg," *Fortune*, May 1999, at www.fortune.com/fortune/articles/0,15114,379097,00.html.

102. *without internal controls*   Julia Jenson, "Report Shows AIG Exes Ran Company Without Accounting Controls," *FinanceGates.com*, Apr. 26, 2005, at www.financegates.com/news/insurance/2005-04-26/aig_04262005.html.

102. *off-the-books, offshore bonus plan*   Glenn R. Simpson and Ianthe Jeanne Dugan, "Murphy Built AIG Tax Plan," *Wall Street Journal*, Apr. 4, 2005, p. C1.

102. *"The program motivated people"*   Theo Francis and Ian McDonald," AIG May Cut Starr Pay Plan," *Wall Street Journal*, Apr. 4, 2005, p. C1.

102. *executives . . . would travel to New York*   Ianthe Jeanne Dugan and George Anders, "At AIG, Exclusive 'Club' Gave Greenberg Powerful Influence," *Wall Street Journal*, Apr. 11, 2005, pp. A1, A10.

102. *"golden handcuffs"*   Ibid.

103. *"John Olson has been wrong"*   John Schwartz, "Man Who Doubted Enron Enjoys New Recognition," *New York Times*, Jan. 21, 2002, p. C8.

103. *story appeared and then vanished*   Felicity Barringer, "10 Months Ago, Questions on Enron Came and Went with Little Notice," *New York Times*, Jan. 28, 2002, p. A11.

103. *"prescient"*   Ibid.

103. *Skilling was a pick*   John Schwartz, "Darth Vader. Machiavelli. Skilling Set Intense Pace," *New York Times*, Feb. 7, 2002, pp. C1, C7.

103. *11,500-square-foot house*   David Barboza and John Schwartz, "The Finance Wizard Behind Enron's Deals," *New York Times*, Feb. 6, 2002, pp. A1, C9.

103. *Fastow was only twenty-nine*   David Barboza and John Schwartz, "The Finance Wizard Behind Enron's Deals," *New York Times*, Feb. 6, 2002, pp. A1, C9.

104. *"In an interview with CFO"*   Ronald Fink, "What Andrew Fastow Knew," *CFO Magazine*, Jan. 1, 2002, at www.cfo.com/article.cfm/3002806?f=search.

104. *"arrogance" and "intimidating"*   Kurt Eichenwald and Diana B. Henriques, "Enron Buffed Image to a Shine Even as It Rotted from Within," *New York Times*, Feb. 10, 2002, p. A1; Anita Raghavan, Kathryn Kranhold, and Alexei Barrionuevo, "How Enron Created a Culture of Pushing Limits," *Wall Street Journal*, Aug. 26, 2002, pp. A1, A7.

105. *investment community is enamored*   Daniel Henninger, "Bye-Bye Bernie Drops the Curtain on the 1990s," *Wall Street Journal*, May 3, 2002, p. A10.

105. *Even as the company was crumbling*   Kelly Greene and Rick Brooks, "WorldCom Staff Now Are Saying 'Just Like Enron,'" *Wall Street Journal*, June 27, 2002, p. A9; Jayne O'Donnell, "Ebbers Acts as if Nothing Is Amiss," *USA Today*, Sept. 19, 2002, p. 2B.

105. *"If one were to find"*   Taken from www.worldcom.com in September 2002.

105. *All color, charm*   Chris Woodyard, "Pressure to Perform Felt as Problems Hit," *USA Today*, July 1, 2002, p. 3A.

105. *He used his reputation*   Henninger, "Bye-Bye Bernie," op. cit., p. A10.

105. *net worth of $1.4 billion*   Susan Pulliam, Deborah Solomon, and Carrick Mollenkamp, "Former WorldCom CEO Built an Empire on Mountain of Debt," *Wall Street Journal*, Dec. 31, 2002, p. A1.

105. *ranches, hockey teams*   Ibid.

105. *Ebbers divorced*   O'Donnell, "Ebbers acts," op. cit., pp. 1B and 2B.

105. *ripe old age of thirty-two*   Shawn Young and Evan Perez, "Wall Street Thought Highly of WorldCom's Finance Chief," *Wall Street Journal*, June 27, 2002, pp. B1, B3.

105. *By thirty-four*   March 12, 1996 press release, "WorldCom, Inc. appoints new board member," at www.worldcom.com.

105. *"barely shaving"*   Ibid.

106. *"the whiz kid"*   Barnaby J. Feder and David Leonhardt, "From Low Profile to No Profile," *New York Times*, June 27, 2002, p. C1.

106. *Bernie's benevolence*   Proxy statements, 14-A at www.sec.gov under WorldCom for 1997–2001.

106. *he had used cocaine*   Shawn Young, Almar Latour, and Susan Pulliam, "Ebbers Lawyer Paints Sullivan as a Chronic Liar," *Wall Street Journal,* Feb. 17, 2005, pp. C1 and C4.

106. *$10 million home*   Feder and Leonhardt, "From Low Profile to No Profile," op. cit., p. C1.

106. *sole discretion in setting their salaries*   Jayne O'Donnell and Andrew Backover, "WorldCom's Bad Math May Date Back to 1999," *USA Today,* July 16, 2002, p. 1B.

106. *no internal challenges*   Susan Pulliam and Deborah Solomon, "How Three Unlikely Sleuths Discovered Fraud at WorldCom," *Wall Street Journal,* Oct. 30, 2002, pp. A1, A6.

106. *"intimidating and brusque"*   Feder and Leonhardt, "From Low Profile to No Profile," op. cit., p. C6.

107. *personally loaned the $650,000*   Shawn Young and Jared Sandberg, "WorldCom Can Pay Full Severance," *Wall Street Journal,* Oct. 2, 2002, p. B4.

107. *wanted to be the next Jack Welch*   "Spin Decoder," *Business Week Online,* Dec. 23, 2002, at www.businessweek.com.

107. *world's greatest business executive*   Anthony Bianco, William Symonds, Nanette Byrnes, and David Polek, "The Rise and Fall of Dennis Kozlowski," *Business Week Online,* Dec. 23, 2002, at www.businessweek.com.

107. *8 percent drop in Tyco's stock*   Alex Berenson, "Tyco Cleared to Sell Unit to the Public," *New York Times,* June 13, 2002, pp. C1, C12.

107. *Kozlowski's derring-do*   Mark Maremont and Laurie P. Cohen, "How Tyco's CEO Enriched Himself," *Wall Street Journal,* Aug. 7, 2002, pp. A1, A6; Alex Berenson, "Investigation Is Said to Focus on Tyco Chief over Sales Tax," *New York Times,* June 3, 2002, p. B1; Bianco, Symonds, et al., "The Rise and Fall of Dennis Kozlowski," op. cit.

107. *his humble beginnings*   Ibid.

107. *"Koz," as he was known*   Ibid.

107. *self-described risk-taker*   Alex Berenson, "Ex-Tyco Chief, a Big Risk Taker, Now Confronts the Legal System," *New York Times,* June 10, 2002, pp. B1, B6; Bianco, Symonds, et al., "The Rise and Fall of Dennis Kozlowski," op. cit.

107. *trappings of wealth were important*   Gary Strauss, "CEO Paychecks: Fair or Foul?" *USA Today,* Apr. 6, 2001, pp. 1B, 3B; Gary Strauss, "Pay Remains Robust Even as Shares Languish," *USA Today,* Mar. 25, 2002, pp. 1B, 3B.

107. *raking in $411 million*   Ibid.

107. *Kozlowski had the lifestyle*   "Spin Decoder," op. cit.

107. *$11 million on furnishings*   The information comes from a report done by David Boies for the company. Andrew Ross Sorkin, "Tyco Details Lavish Lives of Executives," *New York Times,* Sept. 19, 2002, p. C1.

107. *"We've been made out to be"*   "Spin Decoder," op. cit.

108. *remarried in 2001*   Maremont and Cohen, "How Tyco's CEO Enriched Himself," op. cit.; Bianco, Symonds, et al., "The Rise and Fall of Dennis Kozlowski," op. cit.

108. *days-long celebration*   Don Halasy, "Why Tyco Boss Fell," *New York Post,* June 9, 2002, at www.nypost.com; Laurie P. Cohen, "Ex-Tyco CEO's Ex to Post $10 Million for His Bail Bond," *Wall Street Journal,* Sept. 20, 2002, p. A5; Maremont and Cohen, "How Tyco's CEO Enriched Himself," op. cit., p. A1.

108. *internal memo on the party*   8-K, Sept. 17, 2002, at www.sec.gov/edgar.

108. *"us[ed] only about $29 million"*   www.sec.gov/releases/litigation; Kevin McCoy, "Directors' Firms on Payroll at Tyco," *USA Today,* Sept. 18, 2002, p. 1B; Theresa Howard, "Tyco Puts Kozlowski's $16.8M NYC Digs on Market," *USA Today,* Sept. 19, 2002, p. 3B. These numbers appear in the civil complaint filed by the company against Mr. Kozlowski, and the

complaint is incorporated as an exhibit to the company's 8-K filed on September 17, 2002. See www.sec.gov/edgar.

108. *"We don't believe in perks"* Bianco, Symonds, et al., "The Rise and Fall of Dennis Kozlowski," op. cit.

108. *plastic coat hangers* Mark Maremont and Laurie P. Cohen, "Tyco's Internal Inquiry Concludes Questionable Accounting Was Used," *Wall Street Journal*, Dec. 31, 2002, pp. A1, A4.

108. *$52,334 for wine* These numbers appear in the civil complaint filed by the company against Mr. Kozlowski, and the complaint is incorporated as an exhibit to the company's 8-K filed on September 17, 2002. See www.sec.gov/edgar.

108. *outraged at the press coverage* Andrew Ross Sorkin, "Tyco Ex-Boss Is Humbled, but Unbowed," *New York Times*, Jan. 16, 2005, p. A1.

109. *"general public perception of me"* Ibid.

109. *$56 million in bonuses* Andrew Ross Sorkin, "Tyco Details Lavish Lives of Executives," *New York Times*, Sept. 18, 2002, p. C1; Kevin McCoy, "Tyco Spent Millions on Exec Perks, Records Say," *USA Today*, Sept. 17, 2002, p. 1B.

109 *Kozlowski's bail* Cohen, "Ex-Tyco CEO's Ex," op. cit., p. A5.

109. *contact with investors* Berenson, "Ex-Tyco Chief, a Big Risk Taker," op. cit., p. B1.

110. *interacted with only a few* Bianco, Symonds, et al., "The Rise and Fall of Dennis Kozlowski," op. cit.

110. *Swartz served as trustee* Alex Berenson, "From Dream Team at Tyco to a Refrain of Dennis Who?" *New York Times*, June 6, 2002, p. C1.

110. *loophole in securities law* Ibid.

110. *indictment on thirty-eight counts* Nicholas Varchaver, "Fall from Grace," *Fortune*, Oct. 28, 2002, p. 114; Andrew Ross Sorkin, "2 Top Tyco Executives Charged with $600 Million Fraud Scheme," *New York Times*, Sept. 13, 2002, pp. A1, C3.

110. *CFO award* Ibid.

110. *"very, very confident of our accounting"* Stephen Barr, "Not Even Investor Scrutiny or an SEC Investigation Could Slow Tyco's Frenetic Deal Making," *CFO Magazine*, Oct. 1, 2002, at www.cfo.com.

110. *She was given bonuses* Sorkin, "Tyco Details Lavish Lives," op. cit., p. C6, and "Helping Fatcats Dodge the Taxman," *Business Week Online*, June 20, 2002, at www.businessweek.com.

110. *the "gross-up"* Ibid.

111. *"A decision has been made"* Kevin McCoy, "Kozlowski's Statement in Question," *USA Today*, Jan. 9, 2002, p. 1B.

111. *criminal complaint against . . . Rigas family* Jerry Markon and Robert Frank, "Five Adelphia Officials Arrested on Fraud Charges," *Wall Street Journal*, July 25, 2002, pp. A3, A6.

111. *one of the first cable franchises* Ibid.; Eric Dash, "Sorrow Mixed with Disbelief for Patrons of a Community," *New York Times*, July 9, 2004, pp. A1, A5.

112. *"borrow" more than $3 billion* Robert Frank and Deborah Solomon, "Adelphia and Rigas Family Had a Vast Network of Business Ties," *Wall Street Journal*, May 24, 2002, pp. A1, A5.

112. *"We've never seen anything like this"* Ibid.

112. *all $3 billion or so was concealed* Christine Nuzum, "Adelphia's 'Accounting Magic' Fooled Auditors, Witness Says," *Wall Street Journal*, May 5, 2004, p. C5.

112. *Rigases owned only 20 percent* This information was taken from the 2001 proxy for Adelphia.

112. *outside board members were astonished* Nuzum, "Adelphia's 'Accounting Magic,'" op. cit.

112. *paid his employees well* Ibid.; David Lieberman, "Adelphia's Woes 'A Total Shock' to Many," *USA Today*, Apr. 5, 2002, p. 3B.

112. *take him an hour to walk one block* Deborah Solomon and Robert Frank, "Adelphia Story: Founding Family Retreats in Crisis," *Wall Street Journal,* Apr. 5, 2002, pp. B1, B4.

113. *big spenders* D. Leonard, "Adelphia," *Fortune,* Aug. 12, 2002, p. 137.

113. *As many as twenty employees* Geraldine Fabrikant, "Adelphia Said to Inflate Customers and Cash Flow," *New York Times,* June 8, 2002, pp. B1, B3.

113. *"That woman is costing you"* Leonard, "Adelphia," op. cit., p. 146.

113. *only officers listed* The information was taken from the company's annual reports and proxies for the year 2001, found at www.adelphia.com and www.sec.gov/edgar (14 Definitive Proxy filing).

113. *chair of the . . . audit committee* Leonard, "Adelphia," op. cit., note 91 at p. 144; Deborah Solomon, "Adelphia Plans to Dismiss Deloitte," *Wall Street Journal,* June 10, 2002, p. A3.

113. *Timothy Werth* "Former Adelphia Executive Enters a Guilty Plea," *New York Times,* Nov. 3, 2003, p. B3.

113. *Brown's lack of training* Peter Grant, "Lying Was Easy for Star Witness in Adelphia Case," *Wall Street Journal,* May 19, 2004, pp. C1, C2.

113. *earnings were manipulated* Fabrikant, "Adelphia Said to Inflate," op. cit.

114. *"Jim Brown numbers"* Ibid.

14. *LeMoyne Zacherl* Karla Scannell, "Ex-Adelphia Official Testifies That He Warned Rigases on Expenses," *Wall Street Journal,* Mar. 23, 2004, pp. C1, C3.

114. *best if they "part ways"* Ibid., p. C3.

114. *"we're not telling you"* Leonard, "Adelphia," op. cit., note 91 at p. 147; www.sec.gov/edgar, March 27, 2002, 8-K filing; Geraldine Fabrikant, "Adelphia Fails to Make Note Payment," *New York Times,* May 17, 2002, p. C1.

114. *$2.3 billion in Rigas family debt* www.sec.gov/edgar, March 27, 2002, 8-K filing; Fabrikant, "Adelphia Fails to Make Note Payment," op. cit.

114. *"We did nothing wrong"* Leonard, "Adelphia," op. cit., p. 137.

114. *"a big P.R. effort"* Andrew Ross Sorkin, "Fallen Founder of Adelphia Tries to Explain," *New York Times,* Apr. 7, 2003, p. C1.

114. *acquitted of conspiracy* Barry Meier, "Michael Rigas Is Free for Now after Mistrial Declared," *New York Times,* July 16, 2004, p. B1.

114. *Michael Mulcahey* Peter Grant and Christine Nuzum, "Adelphia Founder and One Son Found Guilty," *Wall Street Journal,* July 9, 2004, pp. A1, A6.

115. *"I know the man"* Dash, "Sorrow Mixed with Disbelief," op. cit.

115. *officers in HealthSouth* The information about the officers and their ages was gathered from HealthSouth's public filings (proxy statements) for years 1994 to 2001.

115. *William T. Owens* This information was gleaned from a review of HealthSouth's 10-Ks from 1994 through the present. Its 10-K for 2002 has been delayed. See www.sec.gov/edgar for these documents.

115. *continuity in the officer team* This information was also gleaned from HealthSouth's 10-Ks.

115. *photo . . . in the* New York Times Reed Abelson, "4 of 5 HealthSouth Executives Spared Prison Terms," *New York Times,* Dec. 11, 2004, pp. C1, C2.

115. *no one to whom they could turn* John Heylar, "King Richard," *Fortune,* July 7, 2003, p. 78.

115. *"The imperial master is gone"* Reed Abelson and Milt Freudenheim, "HealthSouth's 9th Executive Is Charged," Apr. 9, 2003, pp. C1, C13.

116. *"incredibly intelligent and gifted man"* Dan Morse, "HealthSouth Ex-Finance Chief Says Scrushy Knew of Fraud," *Wall Street Journal,* Mar. 1, 2005, p. C5.

116. *wanted to be a rock star* Heylar, "King Richard," op. cit., p. 78.

116. *$233,000 per month* Greg Farrell, "From Emperor to Outcast," *USA Today,* May 29, 2003, pp. 1B, 2B.

116. *mansion in Palm Beach*   Heylar, "King Richard," op. cit., p. 78.

116. *three dozen cars*   The information on his assets comes from Reed Abelson and Milt Freudenheim, "The Scrushy Mix: Strict and So Lenient," *New York Times,* Apr. 20, 2003, p. BU1, and "Ousted Chief of HealthSouth Resists Questions on His Assets," *New York Times,* Apr. 10, 2003, p. C4.

116. *eleven businesses*   Greg Farrell, "Scrushy 'Was Set Up,' Says Lawyer," *USA Today,* Apr. 15, 2003, p. 3B.

116. *personal staff*   Ibid.

117. *3rd Faze*   Heylar, "King Richard," op. cit., p. 78.

117. *active and respected member*   Dan Morse, "For Former HealthSouth Chief, an Appeal to a Higher Authority," *Wall Street Journal,* May 13, 2005, pp. A1, A10.

117. *less-purposeful expenditures*   "Ex-Executives of United Way Indicted," *Arizona Republic,* Sept. 14, 1994, p. A6.

117. *twenty-two felony counts of fraud*   Felicity Barringer, "Former United Chief Guilty of Theft," *New York Times,* Apr. 4, 1995, p. A1.

118. *deferred-compensation package*   David Cay Johnston, "Ex-United Way Chief Owed $4.2 Million," *New York Times,* Jan. 5, 2000, p. C4.

119. *There were gifts of luggage*   David Cay Johnston, "Agriculture Chief Quits as Scrutiny of Conduct Grows," *New York Times,* Oct. 4, 1994, pp. A1, A11.

119. *appointment of a special counsel*   Bruce Ingersoll, "Espy Inquiry Focuses on Mystery Memo to Learn if Cover-up Occurred over Industry Favoritism," *Wall Street Journal,* Jan. 16, 1995, p. A14.

119. *"a bunch of junk"*   Phil Kuntz and Elizabeth Crowley, "Espy Acquitted on All Acounts," *Wall Street Journal,* Dec. 3, 1998, p. A24.

119. *oversights and slipups*   Jim Rutenberg and Kate Zernike, "CBS Apologizes for Report on Bush Guard Service," *New York Times,* Sept. 21, 2004, pp. A1, A22.

120. *Mapes met with Bill Burkett*   Ibid.

120. *questions arose*   Ibid., p. A22.

120. *dug in their heels*   Joe Flint and Greg Hitt, "Rather Retreats, Calling Report 'A Mistake,'" *Wall Street Journal,* Sept. 21, 2004, pp. B1, B4.

120. *lied about the source*   Dave Moniz, Kevin Johnson, and Jim Drinkard, "CBS Backs Off Guard Story," *USA Today,* Sept. 21, 2004, pp.1A, 2A.

120. *"personally and directly" sorry*   Flint and Hitt, "Rather Retreats," op. cit.

120. *a "mistake, which we deeply regret"*   Moniz, Johnson, and Drinkard, "CBS Backs Off Guard Story," op. cit.

120. *"beyond imagination"*   Flint and Hitt, "Rather Retreats," op. cit., p. B4.

121. *once the icon gets a grip on the minds*   Marianne M. Jennings, "Where Are Our Minds and What Are We Thinking? Virtue Ethics for a 'Perfidious' Media," 19 *Notre Dame Journal of Law, Ethics, and Public Policy* 637 (2005).

121. *story was not true*   Katherine Q. Seelye and Neil A. Lewis, "Newsweek Says It Is Retracting Koran Report," *New York Times,* May 17, 2005, p. A1.

121. Newsweek *retracted the story*   Katherine Q. Seelye and Eric Schmitt, "Newsweek Apologizes for Report of Koran Insult," *New York Times,* May 16, 2005, p. A1.

121. *material earnings restatement*   GE issued an 8-K in September 2002 clarifying its multibillion-dollar restatement. See www.sec.gov.

121. *Questions about GE's accounting*   Diane Brady, "The Immelt Revolution," *BusinessWeek,* Mar. 28, 2005, p. 64.

122. *revelations about his retirement package*   Matt Murray, "SEC Investigates Jack Welch's Retirement Deal with GE," *Wall Street Journal,* Sept. 17, 2002, p. B1.

122. *GE settled with the SEC*   Geraldine Fabrikant, "G.E. Settles S.E.C. Case on Welch Retirement Perks," *New York Times*, Sept. 20, 2004, p. C2.

122. *Mr. Welch's op-ed*   Jack Welch, "My Dilemma—and How I Resolved It," *Wall Street Journal*, Sept. 17, 2002, p. A14.

123. *the SEC was standing nearby*   Kelly Greene, "Dunlap Agrees to Settle Suit over Sunbeam," *Wall Street Journal*, Jan. 15, 2002, p. A3.

123. *long streak of litigation*   Alex Berenson, "Marriott Company in Settlement of Lawsuit Brought by Investors," *New York Times*, Feb. 25, 2000, pp. C1, C9.

123. *Now Bollenbach heads Hilton*   Christopher Palmeri and Catherine Yang, "The Light Is on at Hilton," *Business Week*, June 28, 2004, p. 66.

124. *"lapses in judgment"*   Thaddeus Herrick and Nikhil Deogun, "Insiders Assert Behavior an Issue with Texaco CEO," *Wall Street Journal*, Mar. 16, 2001, pp. B1, B4.

124. *the nonglitzy CEO*   Louis Grossman and Marianne Jennings, *Building a Business Through Good Times and Bad: The Story of Fifteen Companies, Each with a Century of Dividends* (Westport, Conn.: Greenwood, Quarum Book, 2002).

124. *Razorfish*   Marianne M. Jennings, "The Dot-Coms: Basic Values Forgotten" (2001), *Financial Times*, at www.ftmastering.com/mmo/mmo06_1.htm.

126. *unloading her ImClone stock*   Andrew Pollack and David Cay Johnston, "Former Chief of ImClone Systems Is Charged with Insider Trading," *New York Times*, June 13, 2002, pp. B1, B6; Jerry Markon, "Active Inquiry Is Underway on Ms. Stewart," *Wall Street Journal*, June 14, 2002, pp. C1, C10.

126. *If she had just been candid*   Constance L., and Patrick McGeehan, "A Closer Look at Martha Stewart's Trade," *New York Times*, July 15, 2002, pp. C1, C9.

127. *"I've got friends in the factory"*   Alex Taylor III, "Porsche's Risky Recipe," *Fortune*, Feb. 17, 2003, p. 91.

129. *negative attention proved to be problematic*   Gregory Zuckerman, "Pimco's Chief Says His Controversial Peace," *Wall Street Journal*, Mar. 4, 2003, pp. C1, C15.

130. *SooJee Lee*   Susanne Craig and Ianthe Jeanne Dugan, "At the Big Board, Grasso's Secretary Made Big Bucks, Too," *Wall Street Journal*, Feb. 4, 2005, pp. A1, A5.

131. *Behavior in personal lives is not a bad predictor*   This material in this section was adapted from Marianne M. Jennings, "Does CEO, CFO Personal Conduct Matter When It Comes to Company Ethics?" *Corporate Finance Review* 10 (1): 43–46 (2005).

131. *Liman . . . sent that e-mail*   Laurie P. Cohen and Mark Maremont, "E-Mails Show Tyco's Lawyers Had Concerns," *Wall Street Journal*, Dec. 27, 2002, p. C1.

131. *defense lawyers' cross-examination*   Ken Belson, "Key Witness on WorldCom Says He Frequently Lied," *New York Times*, Feb. 11, 2005, p. C14, and "Can a Cool-Headed Star Witness Take the Heat from the Ebbers Defense Team?" *New York Times*, Feb. 14. 2005, p. C2.

131. *Bernie divorced his wife*   Jayne O'Donnell, "Ebbers Acts as if Nothing Is Amiss," *USA Today*, Sept. 18, 2002, pp.1B, 2B.

131. *Enron's officer retreats*   Bethany McLean and Peter Elkind, *The Smartest Guys in the Room: The Amazing Rise and Scandalous Fall of Enron* (2003). This book gives the full detail and flavor of the lying, cheating, partying nature of the Enron culture.

131. *wife number three*   Greg Farrell, "From Emperor to Outcast," *USA Today*, May 29, 2003, p. 2B.

132. *Scrushy's radio show*   Helyar, "King Richard," op. cit., p. 77.

132. *landed them both in* The Wall Street Journal   James Bandler, "Harvard Editor Faces Revolt over Welch Story," *Wall Street Journal*, Mar. 4, 2002, pp. B1, B4.

132. *bitter divorce battle*   Del Jones, "Jane Welch Seeks Half of Couple's $1 Billion Fortune," *USA Today*, Mar. 19, 2002, p. 3B; Jack Welch, "My Dilemma and How I Resolved It," *Wall Street Journal*, Sept. 16, 2002, p. A14; Matt Mobray, "SEC Investigates GE's Retirement Deal with

Jack Welch," *Wall Street Journal,* Apr. 14, 2002, p. B1; Gretchen Morgenson, "Wait a Second: What Devils Lurk in Details?" *New York Times,* Sept. 17, 2002, p. 3-1 (Business Section, p. 1).

135. *When Fort took over*   Mark Maremont and Laurie P. Cohen, "How Tyco's CEO Enriched Himself," *Wall Street Journal,* Aug. 7, 2002, pp. A1, A6.

135. *Michael Rigas*   Peter Grant and Christine Nuzum, "Adelphia Founder and One Son Found Guilty," op. cit.

Chapter Five: Sign #4: Weak Board

137. *"I would like to begin"*   From an address given at a conference on corporate governance and business ethics at St. Thomas University in Houston, Texas.

137. *"Most of us made it"*   *Fortune,* Nov. 18, 2002, p. 34.

138. *"We [directors] really don't know"*   Joann S. Lublin and Ann Carrns, "Directors Had Lucrative Links at HealthSouth," *Wall Street Journal,* Apr. 11, 2003, pp. B1, B3; Greg Farrell, "Scrushy 'Was Set Up,' Says Lawyer," *USA Today,* Apr. 15, 2003, p. 3B.

139. *"so much sleeping on the job"*   Ibid.

139. *Delaware judge issued an opinion*   Ibid.

139. *eight of the fourteen board members*   This information was taken from the company's proxy statements, available on the EDGAR database under Section 14 (proxy) filings at www.sec.gov.

139. *"enhance equity ownership"*   See disclosures in proxy statements for 1995–2002, at www.sec.gov/edgar.

139. *a court ordered the loan due*   "Scrushy Ordered to Repay Loan," *New York Times,* Nov. 27, 2003, p. C2.

141. *a model in corporate governance*   David Hechler, "Report Criticizes V & E's Enron Work," *National Law Journal,* Feb. 11, 2002, pp. A1, A10.

141. *appearances do not translate*   Ibid.

141. *Wendy Gramm*   Reed Abelson, "Enron Board Comes Under a Storm of Criticism," *NewYork Times,* Dec. 16, 2001, p. BU4.

141. *"qualifications of new board members"*   From remarks delivered at an April 1999 conference on corporate governance and business ethics at St. Thomas University in Houston. The author participated in the conference and took umbrage at Mr. Lay's glib remarks on governance. Positioning herself short on Enron stock would have netted her a fortune.

143. *Dr. John Mendelsohn*   Abelson, "Enron Board," op. cit., p. BU4.

143. *sell at a most opportune time*   Ibid. Information on ImClone and Ms. Stewart: Andrew Pollack and David Cay Johnston, "Former Chief of ImClone Systems Is Charged with Insider Trading," *NewYork Times,* June 13, 2002, pp. B1, B6; Jerry Markon, "Active Inquiry Is Underway on Ms. Stewart," *Wall Street Journal,* June 14, 2002, pp. C1, C10; "The ImClone Patients," *Wall Street Journal,* June 18, 2002, p. A16.

144. *seventh-highest-paid directors*   The top six were (at that time) Oracle, Cisco Systems, United Health Group, Sun Microsystems, Dell Computer, and GE. Abelson, "Enron Board," op. cit., p. BU4.

144. *directors' stock sales*   Ibid.

144. *donations of $92,508*   Jo Thomas and Reed Abelson, "How a Top Medical Researcher Became Entangled with Enron," *NewYork Times,* Jan. 28, 2002, pp. C1, C2.

144. *total amount Enron had donated*   Ibid.

144. *directors who had business ties*   Abelson, "Enron Board," op. cit., p. BU4.

145. *other conflicts among the board*   Reed Abelson and Kenneth N. Gilpin, "2 Enron Roles Raise Questions of Allegiance," *New York Times,* Dec. 7, 2001, pp. C1, C4.

145. *Lord John Wakeham*   Joann S. Lublin, "Inside, Outside Enron, Audit Panel Is Scrutinized," *Wall Street Journal,* Feb. 1, 2002, pp. C1, C8.

145. *Mercatus Center*   Ibid.

145. *"Red Flags Known to Enron's Board"*   PSI Report, p. 12.

145. *"push limits"*   Ibid.

146. *board still had the opportunity*   Hearing Exhibit 2a, as cited in PSI Report, p. 16 at note 30.

146. *three categories of risk*   Ibid.

146. *allowed the risk levels to continue*   PSI Report, p. 18, citing Hearing Exhibit 7c, the audit committee minutes of May 1, 2000, at p. 2.

146. *"Mr. Duncan discussed"*   PSI Report, p 18.

146. *Duncan and Andersen felt*   From interviews conducted by the staff of the PSI, as reported in the PSI Report, p. 20.

147. *board was alerted to Mr. Fastow's involvement*   Lublin, "Inside, Outside Enron," op. cit., p. C8.

147. *general Enron ethical principle*   *Code of Ethics, Executive and Management* (July 2000), p. 12.

147. *provisions that apply specifically to officers*   Ibid., p. 57.

147 *run by the board at least three times*   PSI Report, pp. 25, 26.

148. *gross revenues had doubled*   Ibid., p. 12.

148. *shortsellers took the cue*   "Why John Olson Wasn't Bullish on Enron" (Feb. 2, 2002), at www.knowledge.wharton.upenn.edu; "Houston's New Celebrity," *New York Times,* Jan. 21, 2002, p. C8.

148. *April 2001 board meeting*   PSI, p. 12.

149. *whistle-blower letter*   Watkins letter to Enron chairman Kenneth Lay, Aug. 15, 2001, p. 1, as cited in PSI, p. 12.

149. *Administrative issues plagued this board*   This information is available in the SEC filings for Enron at www.sec.gov.

149. *board meeting on the LJM1 partnership*   PSI Report, p. 27.

150. *insistent on their ignorance*   Ibid., pp. 1–2.

150. *"We cannot . . . be criticized"*   Ibid.

150. *nearly three thousand separate entities*   See Enron 10-Ks for 1999 and 2000 at Edgar at www.sec.gov.

150. *"vigorous discussion"*   PSI Report, p. 28, citing the Hearing Record at p. 157.

150. *tossed it before even reading it*   Ibid., p. 28.

151. *pay a heavy price*   Thor Valdmanis, "Merrill Faces $605M Suit Alleging Sham Energy Trades," *USA Today,* Sept. 26, 2002, p. 3B.

151. *annual review of all the transactions*   PSI Report, p. 30.

151. *no director was struck*   ibid., p. 33.

151. *16(b) officers*   "16(b)" refers to those levels of officers in a company to whom Section 16 of the 1934 Securities Exchange Act applies. These are the officers subject to the six-month, in effect, holding period on their company shares, a timing prohibition to curb acting on inside information. 15 U.S.C. § 78p (2002).

151. *"We very much appreciate"*   PSI Report, p. 36, citing internal Enron documents.

152. *directors did get some information*   Ibid., p. 37. The estimated total return to Fastow and fellow employees who invested was $43 million.

152. *They had pumped in $5,800*   PSI Report at p. 37.

152. *"Bernie's Board"*   Jared Sandberg and Joann S. Lublin, "An Already Tarnished Board Also Faces Tough Questions over Accounting Fiasco," *Wall Street Journal,* June 28, 2002, p. A3; Jared Sandberg, "Six Directors Quit as WorldCom Breaks with Past," *Wall Street Journal,* Dec. 18, 2002, p. A3; WorldCom proxy for 2001, p. 6, at www.sec.gov.

152. *Carl Aycock*   Seth Schiebel, "Most of Board at WorldCom Resign Post," *New York Times,* Dec. 18, 2002, p. C7.

152. *Max Bobbitt and Francesco Galesi* Ibid.

152. *Stiles A. Kellett Jr.* Susan Pulliam, Jared Sandberg, and Deborah Solomon, "WorldCom Board Will Consider Rescinding Ebbers's Severance," *Wall Street Journal,* Sept. 10, 2002, p. A1.

152. *"Rule No.1"* Sandberg, "Six Directors Quit," op. cit., p. A3.

152. *Three of the board members* This information came from the proxies filed for the company. See www.sec.gov.

153. *As compensation went* WorldCom proxy for 2001, p. 6, at www.sec.gov.

153. *# shares held* The directors also owed MCI shares that are listed in the proxy but not included here.

153. *Background* The background on the directors was found at www.sec.gov in the proxy materials for WorldCom.

153. *Ronald R. Beaumont* www.digex.com. See Digex 8-K dated July 15, 2002, and filed July 18, 2002; Shawn Young and Jared Sandberg, "WorldCom Can Pay Full Severance," *Wall Street Journal,* Oct. 2, 2002, p. B4.

154. *final Thornburgh report* Jared Sandberg and Susan Pulliam, "Report by WorldCom Examiner Finds New Fraudulent Activities," *Wall Street Journal,* Nov. 5, 2002, pp. A1, A11.

154. *WorldCom stock to secure loans* Deborah Solomon and Jared Sandberg, "WorldCom's False Profits Climb," *Wall Street Journal,* Nov. 6, 2002, pp. A3, A18.

154. *pledged a total of about $1 billion* Sandberg and Pulliam, "WorldCom Examiner," op. cit.

155. *secondary position to Ebbers's personal creditors* Ibid., p. A18.

155. *WorldCom directors had agreed* Solomon and Sandberg, "WorldCom's False Profits," p. A18; Kurt Eichenwald, "Corporate Loans Used Personally, Report Discloses," *New York Times,* Nov. 5, 2002, p. C1.

155. *Ebbers's net worth* Ibid.

155. *the loans continued* Ibid.

155. *"understating costs, hiding bad debt"* Neil Weinberg, "Asleep at the Switch," *Forbes,* July 22, 2002, p. 38.

155. *receivables that were over seven years old* Ibid.

156. *stock had declined by 82 percent* www.worldcom.com. Go to "Investor Relations" and then to "Stock Price History."

156. *Ebbers was reportedly stunned* P. J. Huffstutter, "WorldCom's Woes Spill Over," *The Tribune,* June 27, 2002, p. B1.

156. *executives might be lured away* Barnaby J. Feder, "Bonuses Meant to Retain Talent Now Risk Anger," *New York Times,* June 28, 2002, p. C1, C6.

156. *full discretion to determine who was covered* Ibid.

156. *retention bonus of $10 million* Ibid.

156. *severance package* Ibid.

156. *loans were not taken before the full board* Ibid.

156. *Two board meetings went by* Andrew Backover, "Questions on Ebbers Loans May Aid Probes," *USA Today,* Nov. 6, 2002, p. 3B.

156. *probing the accounting and finances* Andrew Backover, "WorldCom, Qwest Face SEC Scrutiny," *USA Today,* Mar. 12, 2002, p. 1B.

156. *parallel to the SEC investigation* Susan Pulliam and Deborah Solomon, "How Three Unlikely Sleuths Discovered Fraud at WorldCom," *Wall Street Journal,* Oct. 30, 2002, p. A1.

156. *board's discovery* Ibid.; Rebecca Blumenstein and Jared Sandberg, "WorldCom CEO Quits amid Probe of Firm's Finances," *Wall Street Journal,* Apr. 30, 2002, p. A1.

157. *"unquestioning" of Mr. Kozlowski* Joann S. Lublin and Jerry Guidera, "Tyco Board Criticized on Kozlowski," *Wall Street Journal,* June 7, 2002, p. A5.

157. *"asleep at the switch"* Ibid.

157. *"an assemblage of Kozlowski associates"* William C. Symonds, "Tyco's CEO: Time to Walk the Plank," *Business Week Online,* May 13, 2002, at www.businessweek.com.

157. *new board members came only through . . . acquisition* All of this information was mined from the company's Section 14 filing for 2001. See www.sec.gov/edgar.

157. *"poorly served the 240,000 employees and shareholders"* Gregory Zuckerman, "Heralded Investors Suffer Huge Losses with Tyco Meltdown," *Wall Street Journal,* June 10, 2002, pp. C1, C12.

158. *Tyco paid $20 million* Kate Kelly and Gregory Zuckerman, "Tyco Worries Send Stock Prices Lower Again," *Wall Street Journal,* Feb. 5, 2002, p. C1.

158. *acquisition was CIT Group* Laurie P. Cohen and Mark Maremont, "Tyco Ex-Director Pleads Guilty," *Wall Street Journal,* Dec. 18, 2002, p. C1.

158. *Restitution to Tyco* Andrew Ross Sorkin, "Tyco Figure Pays $22.5 Million in Guilty Plea," *New York Times,* Dec. 18, 2002, pp. C1, C2.

158. *Warren Musser* Alex Berenson, "Board Member of Tyco Unit Owed Millions to 2 Executives," *New York Times,* Mar. 29, 2002, p. C1.

158. *Michael A. Ashcrof* Laurie P. Cohen and Mark Maremont, "Tyco Relocations to Florida Are Probed," *Wall Street Journal,* June 10, 2002, p. A3.

158. *Ashcroft sold the home* Ibid.; William K. Rashbaum and Alex Berenson, "Sale of Home of Tyco Figure Gets 2nd Look, Prosecutors Say," *New York Times,* June 8, 2002, pp. B1, B3.

158. *suspicious . . . transfers* Jerry Guidera and Marc Champion, "Tyco Probe Ensnares a Peer," *Wall Street Journal,* June 13, 2002, p. B11.

158. *Kalogerou was in Luxembourg* Ibid.

159. *isolated and deferential board* Louis Lavelle, "Rebuilding Trust in Tyco," *Business Week Online,* Nov. 25, 2002, at www.businessweek.com.

159. *"How do you have a situation"* Kevin McCoy, "Regulators Press Tyco to Settle," *USA Today,* Oct. 17, 2002, p. 2B; Mark Maremont and Laurie P. Cohen, "Tyco Nears Pact with Regulators in New Hampshire," *Wall Street Journal,* Oct. 21, 2002, p. A3.

159. *Tyco settled the charges* Kevin McCoy, "Tyco Settles Suit for $5M Without Admitting Guilt," *USA Today,* Oct. 24, 2002, p. 1B.

159. *"gross misconduct"* McCoy, "Regulators press Tyco," op. cit., p. 2B; Maremont and Cohen, "Tyco Nears Pact," op. cit., p. A3.

159 *"egregious activity"* Ibid.

159. *"board wasn't really functioning"* Alex Berenson and William K. Rashbaum, "Tyco Ex-Chief Is Said to Face Wider Inquiry into Finances," *New York Times,* June 7, 2002, p. C1.

159. *Kozlowski was being* investigated Alex Berenson, "Investigation Is Said to Focus on Tyco Chief over Sales Tax," *New York Times,* June 3, 2002, p. C1; Nanette Byrnes, "Online Extra: The Hunch That Led to Tyco's Tumble," *Business Week, Online,* Dec. 23, 2002, at www.businessweek.com.

159 *Kozlowski immediately resigned* Mark Maremont, John Hechinger, Jerry Markon, and Gregory Zuckerman, "Kozlowski Quits under a Cloud, Worsening Worries about Tyco," *Wall Street Journal,* June 4, 2002, p. A1.

159. *The indictment was handed down* Thor Valdmanis, "Art Purchases Put Ex-Tyco Chief in Hot Water," *USA Today,* June 5, 2002, p. 1B; Mark Maremont and Jerry Markon, "Former Tyco Chief Is Indicted for Avoiding Sales Tax on Art," *Wall Street Journal,* June 5, 2002, p. A1; Alex Berenson and Carol Vogel, "Ex-Tyco Chief Is Indicted in Tax Case," *New York Times,* June 5, 2002, p. C1.

159. *to avoid paying sales tax* Berenson and Vogel, "Ex-Tyco Chief Is Indicted," op. cit., p. C1.

160. *Tyco's stock fell 27 percent* Adam Shell, "Markets Fall as Tyco CEO's Resignation Adds to Woes," *USA Today,* June 4, 2002, p. 1B.

160. *"When a CEO steps down"* Ibid.

160. *proxy battle to oust the board*   Joann S. Lublin, "Tyco Shareholders Plan Proxy Fight to Oust Directors," *Wall Street Journal,* Aug. 21, 2002, p. A3.

160. *Tyco had a key employee loan program*   Information taken from Tyco's proxy statements for 2001 and 2002. See www.sec.gov/edgar.

160. *its lawsuit against Kozlowski*   The suit was filed on the same day that Mr. Belnick and Mr. Swartz were indicted and arraigned. Andrew Ross Sorkin, "2 Top Tyco Executives Charged with $600 Million Fraud Scheme," *New York. Times,* Sept. 13, 2002, pp. A1, C3.

160. *recovery of the KELP loans*   Thor Valdmanis, "Tyco Sues Former Counsel, Director," *USA Today,* June 18, 2002, p. 1B.

160. *Adelphia board consisted of*   This information was taken from the proxy for Adelphia for 2001.

161. *chaired the Adelphia audit committee*   Ibid.

161. *"plain-vanilla-old-fashioned self-dealing"*   Geraldine Fabrikant, "New Questions on Auditors for Adelphia," *New York Times,* May 25, 2002, p. B4.

161. *"The thing that makes this case stand out"*   Jerry Markon and Robert Frank, "Five Adelphia Officials Arrested on Fraud Charges," *Wall Street Journal,* July 25, 2002, p. A3.

161. *"personal piggy bank"*   Ibid.

161. *So blatant was the commingling*   D. Leonard, "Adelphia," *Fortune,* Aug. 12, 2002, p. 146.

161. *Adelphia also paid $12.8 million*   Markon and Frank, "Five Adelphia Officials Arrested," op. cit., p. A3.

161. *loans climbed to $2.3 billion*   March 27, 2002, 8-K filing. See www.sec.gov/edgar.

161. *To avoid calls on their loans*   Geraldine Fabrikant, "Adelphia Fails to Make Note Payment," *New York Times,* May 17, 2002, p. C1.

162. *Grasso's compensation totaled $130 million*   Justin Lahart, "Grasso's Pay Topped Most Peers, Drained Profits," *Wall Street Journal,* June 2, 2004, p. C3.

163. *On another matter*   Charles Gasparino, "Ghosts of E-Mails Continue to Haunt Wall Street," *Wall Street Journal,* Nov. 18, 2002, pp. C1, C13.

164. *$185 million in business with Coke*   Jessi Hempel, "Is Buffett Too Cozy with Coke?" *Business Week,* Apr. 18, 2005, p. 10.

165. *director with political clout*   Neil Weinberg and Daniel Kruger, "Mutual Back-Scratching," *Forbes,* Sept. 16, 2002, p. 128.

167. *the change GE was looking for*   Rachel Emma Silverman, "GE Makes Changes in Board," *Wall Street Journal,* Nov. 8, 2002, p. A5.

167. *Asch's work on . . . "groupthink"*   Solomon Asch, "Effects of Group Pressure on the Modification and Distortion," in E. E. Maccoby, T. M. Newcomb, and E. L. Hartley, eds., *Readings in Social Psychology* (New York: Holt, Rinehart, & Winston, 1958).

169. *reopened its own investigation*   Tracie Rozhon, "Saks Reopens an Inquiry of Deductions," *New York Times,* June 4, 2005, p. B3.

170. *"What I know about the accounting"*   Carrick Mollenkamp, "Accountant Tried in Vain to Expose HealthSouth Fraud," *Wall Street Journal,* May 20, 2003, p. A1.

171. *raising questions about the opaque nature*   Daniel K. Wakin, "There Were Earlier Signs of Trouble at Parmalat," *New York Times,* Jan. 14, 2004, p. C1.

172. *Parmalat was reporting margins of 12 percent*   Gail Edmundson, David Fairlamb, and Nanette Burns, "The Year It All Went Sour for Parmalat," *Business Week,* Jan. 26, 2004, p. 57.

173. *hedge activities and manipulating debt*   Henry Sender, "Parmalat Unit May Offer Accounting Clues," *Wall Street Journal,* Jan. 29, 2004, p. C5.

173. *Frank Zarb*   Monica Langley, "Among Casualties of AIG Mess: Two Financiers' Long Alliance," *Wall Street Journal,* May 20, 2005, p. A1.

173. *you name it, and Enron employees had it*   Alexei Barrionuevo, "Jobless in a Flash," *Wall Street Journal,* Dec. 11, 2001, p. B1.

173. *Charles Keating gave . . . employees*   From interviews with former American Continental employees.

Chapter Six: Sign #5: Conflicts

178. *research side of an investment house*   This material on analysts is adapted from a presentation made for the Institute of Certified Financial Analysts that was subsequently put in article form in the May/June 2005 issue of the *CFA Journal.*

179. *2004 study comparing the performance*   Brad M. Barber, Reuven Lehavy, and Brett Trueman, "Comparing the Stock Recommendation Performance of Investment Banks and Independent Research Firms," paper presented at the 15th Annual Conference on Financial Economics and Accounting, Nov. 2004. A summary of the paper can be found at http://papers.ssrn.com/sol3/papers.cfm?abstract_id=572301.

180. *Grubman's quote about WorldCom*   Neil Weinberg, "Wal-Mart Could Sue for Libel," *Forbes,* Aug. 12, 2002, p. 56.

180. *The sycophantism of Mr. Grubman*   Marianne M. Jennings, *Business Ethics: Case Studies and Selected Readings,* 5th ed. (St. Paul, Minn.: West Publishing, 2005), p. 298.

180. *Grubman attended WorldCom board meetings*   Randall Smith and Deborah Solomon, "Ebbers's Exit Hurts WorldCom's Biggest Fan," *Wall Street Journal,* May 3, 2002, p. C1.

180. *"the smartest guy in the industry"*   Ibid.

180. *Grubman issued his first negative recommendation*   Ibid.

180. *"We do not think any other telco"*   Ibid., p. C3.

180. *opportunity to be first purchasers*   Gretchen Morgenson, "Ebbers Made $11 Million on 21 Stock Offerings," *New York Times,* Aug. 31, 2002, p. B1; Gretchen Morgenson, "Ebbers Got Million Shares in Hot Deals," *New York Times,* Aug. 28, 2002, p. C1; Gretchen Morgenson, "Deals Within Telecom Deals," *New York Times,* Aug. 28, 2002, pp. BU1, BU10.

180. *$11 million in profits*   Ibid.; Thor Valdmanis and Andrew Backover, "Lawsuit Targets Telecom Execs' Stock Windfalls," *USA Today,* Oct. 1, 2002, p. 1B.

180. *charges of profiteering*   Valdmanis and Backover, "Lawsuit Targets Telecom," op. cit., p. 1B.

180. *Salomon and others would settle*   Final judgment, *SEC v. Citigroup Global Markets,* F/K/A Salomon Smith Barney, Inc.

180. *loans were tied to the value of WorldCom stock*   Susan Pulliam, Deborah Solomon, and Carrick Mollenkamp, "Former WorldCom CEO Built an Empire on Mountain of Debt," *Wall Street Journal,* Dec. 31, 2002, p. A1.

180. *"like a pyramid scheme"*   Andrew Backover, "WorldCom, Qwest Face SEC Scrutiny," *USA Today,* Mar. 12, 2002, p. 1B; Valdmanis and Backover, "Lawsuit Targets Telecom," op. cit., p. 1B.

182. *Grubman . . . had doubts*   Smith and Solomon, "Ebbers's Exit," op. cit., p. C1; Andrew Backover and Jayne O'Donnell, "WorldCom Scrutiny Touches on E-Mail," *USA Today,* July 8, 2002, p. 1B.

182. *stocks he considered "dogs"*   Charles Gasparino, "Ghosts of E-Mails Continue to Haunt Wall Street," *Wall Street Journal,* Nov. 18, 2002, pp. C1, C13.

182. *issue of soft dollars*   *Inspection Report on the Soft Dollar Practices of Broker-Dealers, Investment Advisers and Mutual Funds,* Sept. 22, 1998 at www.sec.gov/news/studies/softdolr.htm#exec.

182. *"Under traditional fiduciary principles"*   Ibid.

182. *pension fund in Chattanooga*   Gretchen Morgenson and Mary Williams Walsh, "How Consultants Can Retire on Your Pension," *New York Times,* Dec. 12, 2004, pp. 3-1, 3-13.

182. *one-year sweep investigation*   *Inspection Report on the Soft Dollar Practices,* op. cit.

182. *Fully three years before the market drop*   The soft dollar phenomenon came into effect in May 1975, when the practice of fixed commissions was abandoned.

182. *Inspection Report on the Soft Dollar Practices,* op. cit.

183. *disconnect in the resolution*   See "Investors Need to Bone Up on Bonds and Costs, According to Vanguard/MONEY Investor Literacy Test," press release, Business Wire, Sept. 25, 2002.

183. *75 percent of respondents*   Ibid.

183. *fines paid by the industry members*   Thor Valdmanis, "Final 2 Banks Settle for $100 Million," *USA Today*, Aug. 27, 2004, p. 1B.

185. *audit/consulting [chart]*   Ibid.

186. *nonaudit fees*   Richard M. Frankel, Marilyn F. Johnson, and Karen K. Nelson, Working Paper 4330-02, MIT Sloan School of Management, January 2002.

187. *Andersen performed . . . both the internal and external audit*   Burton Malkiel, "Watchdogs and Lapdogs," *Wall Street Journal*, Jan. 16, 2002, p. A16.

187. *Enron-Andersen relationship*   Solomon, "After Enron, a Push," op. cit., p. C1.

187. *Mr. Causey and Mr. Duncan*   Cathy Booth Thomas and Deborah Fowler, "Will Enron's Auditor Sing?" *Time*, May 20, 2002, p. 44.

188. *Seven former Andersen accountants*   John Schwartz and Reed Abelson, "Auditor Struck Many as Smart and Upright," *New York Times*, Jan. 17, 2002, p. C11.

188. *celebrated the Andersen auditors' birthdays*   Anita Raghavan, "How a Bright Star at Andersen Fell along with Enron," *Wall Street Journal*, May 15, 2002, pp. A1, A8; Thomas and Fowler, "Will Enron's Auditor Sing?" May 20, op. cit., p. 44.

189. *even though she did no work*   Desda Moss, "Former United Way Chief Charged with Looting Funds," *USA Today*, Sept. 14, 1994, p. 1A.

189. *Enron not only signed contracts*   David Barboza and Kurt Eichenwald, "Son and Sister of Enron Chief Secured Deals," *New York Times*, Feb. 2, 2002, p. A1.

189. *twenty thousand stock options*   Ibid.

189. *Alliance Worldwide Travel*   Ibid.

189. *Nobody was really clear who owned what*   Susan Pulliam and Deborah Solomon, "Adelphia Faces Irate Shareholders," *Wall Street Journal*, Apr. 4, 2002, pp. C1, C2; Geraldine Fabrikant, "A Family Affair at Adelphia Communications," *NewYork Times*, Apr. 4, 2002, p. C1.

189. *Adelphia invested $3 million*   Fabrikant, "A Family Affair," op. cit., p. C1; Geraldine Fabrikant, "New Questions on Auditors for Adelphia," *New York Times*, May 25, 2002, p. B4.

190. *board members actually competing with Adelphia*   Fabrikant, "New Questions," op. cit., p. B4.

190. *"Even the existence of a credit line"*   Ibid.

190. *a company that was paid $751,000*   Kevin McCoy, "Directors; Firms on Payroll at Tyco," *USA Today*, Sept. 18, 2002, p. 1B.

190. *Kozlowski's friends had contracts*   Mark Maremont and Laurie P. Cohen, "How Tyco's CEO Enriched Himself," *Wall Street Journal*, Aug. 7, 2002, p. A6.

191. *HealthSouth board members were all intertwined*   JoAnn S. Lublin and Ann Carrns, "Directors Had Lucrative Links at HealthSouth," *Wall Street Journal*, Apr. 11, 2003, pp. B1, B3.

191. *Upseedaisees*   Chad Terhune and Carrick Mollenkamp, "Outside Court, Leslie Scrushy Sells Pajamas," *Wall Street Journal*, Apr. 17, 2003, p. B1.

191. *Scrushy's personal accountant committed suicide*   John Helyar, "The Insatiable King Richard," *Fortune*, July, 7, 2003, p. 76.

192. *the hope of gaining WorldCom business*   Andrew Backover, "Suit Links Loans, WorldCom Stock," *USA Today*, Oct. 15, 2002, p. 3B.

192. *Ebbers's personal loans [chart]*   Pulliam, Solomon, and Mollenkamp, "Former WorldCom CEO," op. cit., p. A1; Backover, "Suit Links Loans," op. cit., p. 3B.

192. *his favorite banks*   Backover, "Suit Links Loans," op. cit., p. 3B.

192. *WorldCom's biggest cheerleader*   Weinberg, "Wal-Mart Could Sue," op. cit., p. 56.

193. *subpoena to the congressional hearings*   Susan Pulliam, Deborah Solomon, and Randall Smith, "WorldCom Is Denounced at Hearing," *Wall Street Journal*, July 9, 2002, p. A3;

Gretchen Morgenson, "Salomon Under Inquiry on WorldCom Options," *New York Times,* Mar. 13, 2002, p. C9; Gretchen Morgenson, "Outrage Is Rising as Options Turn to Dust," *New York Times,* Mar. 11, 2002, p. BU1.

193. *Grubman's relationship with WorldCom's senior management*   Charles Gasparino, Tom Hamburger, and Deborah Solomon, "Salomon Made IPO Allocations Available to Ebbers, Others," *Wall Street Journal,* Aug. 28, 2002, p. A1.

193. *first crack at the hot IPO stocks*   Morgenson, "Ebbers Made $11 Million," op. cit., p. B1.

193. *increase in IPO stock prices*   Morgenson, "Ebbers Got Million Shares," op. cit., p. C1.

193. *Qwest shares . . . dropped 95 percent*   Backover, "WorldCom, Qwest Face SEC scrutiny," op. cit., p. 1B; Valdmanis and Backover, "Lawsuit Targets Telecom," op. cit., p. 1B.

193. *nothing but positive reports*   Smith and Solomon, "Ebbers's Exit," op. cit., p. C1; Backover and O'Donnell, "WorldCom Scrutiny," op. cit., p. 1B.

193. *Grubman billed his employer*   Jessica Sommar, "Here Comes the Bribe: Grubman Expensed Trip to Ebbers' Wedding," *NewYork Post,* Aug. 30, 2002, p. 39.

193. *Salomon Smith Barney IPO allocations*   Gasparino, Hamburger, and Solomon, "Salomon Made IPO Allocations," op. cit., p. A1.

193. *other officers and directors also benefited*   Morgenson, "Ebbers Got Million Shares," op. cit., p. C15; Morgenson, "Deals Within Telecom Deals," op. cit., p. BU10.

193. *overly optimistic views*   Ibid.; Valdmanis and Backover, "Lawsuit Targets Telecom," op. cit., p. 1B.

193. *deny there was any quid pro quo*   Morgenson, "Ebbers Got Million Shares," op. cit., p. C15.

193. *Adelphia had analyst conflicts*   Deborah Solomon, "Salomon Draws Focus by SEC over Adelphia," *Wall Street Journal,* June 5, 2002, p. C1.

198. *"Avoid difficult questions"*   From a January 1999 slide show on what to do about the rebates.

199. *"This is a very basic principle"*   Gretchen Morgenson, "What's Good for Business," *New York Times,* June 5, 2005, p. BU1.

Chapter Seven: Sign#6: Innovation Like No other

205. *"We are the good guys"*   Kurt Eichenwald and Diana B. Henriques, "Enron Buffed Image to a Shine Even as It Rotted from Within," *New York Times,* Feb. 10, 2002, p. A1; "Blackout," *Frontline,* July 2001.

205. *"the Enron model"*   Kurt Eichenwald, "Audacious Climb to Success Ended in Dizzying Lunge," *New York Times,* Jan. 13, 2002, p. A20.

205. *"the biggest e-commerce company"*   Ibid.

205. *"not getting it"*   Ibid.

205. *"world's largest energy company"*   Bethany McLean, "Why Enron Went Bust," *Fortune,* Dec. 24, 2001, pp. 59, 60.

206. *"What we do better"*   1999 annual report, at www.worldcom.com.

206. *Michael Keith*   Seth Schiesel, "Trying to Catch WorldCom's Mirage," *NewYork Times,* June 30, 2002, p. BU1.

206. *"Our performance did not quite compare"*   Ibid.

206. *"You should have seen [it]"*   Ibid.

207. *"Options are a free ride"*   Mark Maremont and Laurie P. Cohen, "How Tyco's CEO Enriched Himself," *Wall Street Journal,* Aug. 7, 2002, p. A6.

207. *ADT takeover of Tyco*   Ibid.; Kevin McCoy, "Tyco Paid Big Bucks to Lobby for Offshore Tax Havens," *USA Today,* Nov. 5, 2002, p. 3B.

207. *Commenting on the formation of AWAC*   AIG press release, Nov. 21, 2001, at http://ir.aig-corporate.com/phoenix.zhtml?c=76115&p=irol-newsArticle&ID=230847&highlight.

207. *had an air of superiority*   Elliot Blair Smith, "Scrutiny Tarnishes Legacy of Greenberg," *USA Today,* May 31, 2005, p. 1B.

208. *"innovative" and "unique" marketing plans*   www.adelphia.com/investors relations.

208. *"clustering strategy"*   www.adelphia.com/relations/1999.

208. *"premier business communications provider"*   Ibid.

208. *capture more of the cable market*   Ibid.

208. *FINOVA . . . became a Wall Street darling*   Marianne M. Jennings, *Business Ethics: Case Studies and Selected Readings,* 5th ed. (St. Paul, Minn.: West Publishing), p. 276.

209. *result of all the posturing*   Dawn Gilbertson, "Surprises at Finova," *Arizona Republic,* Mar. 28, 2000, pp. B1, B9. For full details on Finova, see Jennings, *Business Ethics,* op. cit.

209. *"hospital model for the future"*   Annual reports at www.healthsouth.com.

210. *In evaluating Mr. Scrushy's performance*   Form 14 filing, HealthSouth 1999, at Edgar database, www.sec.gov.

210. *questions about Fannie Mae's accounting*   Greg Farrell, "Report Accuses Fannie Mae of Deception," *USA Today,* Sept. 23, 2004, p. 1B.

210. *"Keep the best, sell the rest"*   James R. Hagerty and Gregory Zuckerman, "Fannie Mae Accused of Rulebreaking," *Wall Street Journal,* Apr. 7, 2004, p. A4.

210. *restatement of earnings was at $1 billion*   Jonathan Glater, "Fannie Mae Corrects Mistakes in Results," *New York Times,* Oct. 30, 2003, p. A1; James R. Hagerty, John R. Wilke, John McKinnon, and JoAnn S. Lublin, "After Fannie Shake-Up, Critics Focus on Pay Pacts," *Wall Street Journal,* Dec. 23, 2004, pp. A1, A7.

212. *Enron earned rankings*   Shelly Branch, "The 100 Best Companies to Work for in America," *Fortune,* Jan. 11, 1999, p. 118. Enron appeared for the first time in the top 100 in 1999. In 2000 it was ranked as number 24, and in 2001 it was number 22. Robert Levering and Milton Moskowitz, "The 100 Best Companies to Work For in America," *Fortune,* Jan. 8, 2001, p. 149.

212. *Even after Enron had gone south*   Samuel Bodily and Robert Bruner, "What Enron Did Right," *Wall Street Journal,* Nov. 19, 2001, p. A20.

213. *his testimony before Congress*   Stephen Labaton, "Control That Was Maybe Too Remote," *New York Times,* Sept. 29, 2004, pp. C1, C9.

213. *"darlings of American investors"*   Jonathan D. Glater, "A Star Lawyer Finds Himself the Target of a Peer," *New York Times,* Sept. 24, 2002, p. C1, C8.

213. *"the most aggressive dealmaker"*   *Business Week Online,* Jan. 14, 2002, at www.businessweek .com.

213. *"superstar" money managers were stunned*   Gregory Zuckerman, "Heralded Investors Suffer Huge Losses with Tyco Meltdown," *Wall Street Journal,* June 10, 2002, p. C1.

213. *"the very model of a 21st century phone company"*   Annual report cover 1997, at www .worldcom.com.

213. *"Wall Street was more than captivated"*   Schiesel, "Trying to Catch," op. cit., pp. BU1, BU14.

214. *"Investors definitely like him"*   Alex Berenson, "From Dream Team at Tyco to a Refrain of Dennis Who?" *New York Times,* June 6, 2002, p. C5.

214. *"The person I know"*   David Barboza and John Schwartz, "The Finance Wizard Behind Enron's Deals," *New York Times,* Feb. 6, 2002, p. C9.

214. *"I've seen him so often"*   Simon Romero, "Will the Real Richard Scrushy Please Step Forward?" *New York Times,* Feb. 17, 2005, p. C4.

215. *resentment of the government*   Chad Terhune and Evelina Shmukler, " 'Scrushy Trial' on Local TV Is a Family Affair," *Wall Street Journal,* Feb. 15, 2005, p. B1.

215. *Mr. Scrushy was indicted*   "Scrushy Pleads Not Guilty to Bribery and Mail Fraud," *New York Times,* Oct. 29, 2005, p. B3.

215. *two 30-minute recaps of the trial*   Ibid.

213. *$300 million hospital* Simon Romero and Alex Berenson, "HealthSouth's Legal Problems Ripple Across Its Hometown," *New York Times,* Apr. 2, 2003, p. C1.

215. *HealthSouth has responded* "HealthSouth: Scrushy Trial to 'Pillage' Firm," *USA Today,* Dec. 29, 2005, p. 1B.

215. *A judge has ordered Scrushy* Corey Dade, "Scrushy Is Told to Repay Bonuses," *Wall Street Journal,* Jan. 5, 2006, p. C3.

215. *Lay spread around the Enron largesse* Eichenwald and Henriques, "Enron Buffed Image," op. cit., p. A1. At least three executives in the top officer group drove Ferraris. Anita Raghavan, Kathryn Kranhold, and Alexei Barrionuevo, "How Enron Created a Culture of Pushing Limits," *Wall Street Journal,* Aug. 26, 2002, pp. A1, A7.

215. *January 2001 executive team meeting* Eichenwald and Henriques, "Enron Buffed Image," op. cit., p. A1.

216. *Local strippers indicated* Ibid.

216. *head and shoulders above the rest* Zuckerman, "Heralded Investors," op. cit., p. C1.

216. *Kozlowski's spending* Don Halasy, "Why Tyco Boss Fell," *New York Post,* June 9, 2002, at www.nypost.com; Maremont and Cohen, "How Tyco's CEO," op. cit., p. A1.

216. *tab . . . was put at $2.1 million* 8-K, September 17, 2002, at www.sec.gov/edgar.

216. *offering stock options to Tommy Mottola* Jonathan Weil and Carrick Mollenkamp, "Health-South Options Award Is off the Charts," *Wall Street Journal,* Aug. 6, 2003, p. C1.

216. *MBA from Harvard* John Schwartz, "Darth Vader. Machiavelli. Skilling Set Intense Pace," *New York Times,* Feb. 7, 2002, pp. C1, C7.

217. *Northwestern MBA* Ibid.; Barboza and Schwartz, "The Finance Wizard," op. cit., pp. A1, C9.

217. *Columbia MBA* Jim Yardley and Sheila K. Dewan, "Despite His Qualms, Scandal Engulfed Executive," *New York Times,* Jan. 27, 2002, p. YNE 27.

217. *his only measure of a person's worth* Ibid.

217. *The MBA curriculum of the 1980s* www.chronicle.com, Feb. 9, 1999. J. M. Stearns and S. Borna, 1998. "A Comparison of the Ethics of Convicted Felons and Graduate Business Students: Implications for Business Practice and Business Ethics Education," *Teaching Business Ethics* 1 (1998), pp.175–95.

219. *work of . . . David Messick and Max Bazerman* "Ethical Leadership and the Psychology of Decision-Making," 37 *Sloan Mgt. Rev.* 9 (1996).

219. *We all correctly believe* Ibid., p. 10.

220. *One reason we think* Messick and Bazerman, citing R. M. Kramer, E. Newton, and P. L. Pommerenke, "Self-Enhancement Biases and Negotiator Judgment: Effects of Self-Esteem and Mood," 56 *Organizational Behavior & Human Decision Processes* 110 (1993).

222. *Rigas, Ebbers, Dunlap quotes* The last three quotes are from *Fortune,* Nov. 18, 2002, p. 54. The other materials and quotes were collected by the author from various sources, including interviews, company materials, and speeches.

222. *"Henry, it drives me nuts"* Scott Wooley, "The Conglomerator Wants a Little Respect," *Forbes,* Oct. 16, 2000, at www.forbes.com.

222. *"It is wholly irresponsible"* Labaton, "Control That Was Maybe Too Remote," op. cit., pp. C1, C9.

223. *"If they had been going a slower speed"* John Schwartz and Richard A. Oppel Jr., "Risk Maker Awaits Fall of Company Built on Risk," *New York Times,* Nov. 29, 2001, p. C1, quoting Bob McNair, a Houston entrepreneur who sold his company to Enron in 1998.

223. *reduction of $568 million* John R. Emshwiller, Rebecca Smith, Robin Sidel, and Jonathan Weil, "Enron Cuts Profit Data of 4 Years by 20%," *Wall Street Journal,* Nov. 9, 2001, p. A3.

223. *"a flawed idea"* Kurt Eichenwald, "Enron Panel Finds Inflated Profits and Few Controls," *New York Times,* Feb. 3, 2002, p. A1.

224. *"The real issue isn't accounting"* Henny Sender, "WorldCom Discovers It Has Few Friends," *Wall Street Journal,* June 28, 2002, pp. C1, C3.

224. *Holland tulip market* Marianne M. Jennings, "A Contrarian's View: New Wine in Old Bottles: New Economy and Old Ethics, Can It Work?" in Linda L. Brennan and Victoria E. Johsnon, *Social, Ethical and Policy Implications of Information Technology* (Hershey, Penn.: Information Science Publishing, 2004), as retold from Mike Dash, *Tulipomania: The Story of the World's Most Coveted Flower & the Extraordinary Passions It Arose* (New York: Three Rivers Press, 1999), p. 159.

224. *not the first speculative bubble* Daniel Yergin, "Herd on the Street: A Quarterly Stampede," *Washington Post,* June 30, 2002, p. B1.

224. *But the 1920s bubble burst* William S. Lerach, "Plundering America: How American Investors Got Taken for Trillions by Corporate Insiders: The Rise of the New Corporate Kleptocracy," 8 *Stan. J.L. Bus. & Fin.* 69 (2002), p. 71.

224. *a fall of 77.5 percent* Ibid.

224. *downward adjustment of $148 billion* Steve Liesman, "Heard on the Street, Nasdaq Companies' Losses Erase 5 Years of Profit," *Wall Street Journal,* Aug. 16, 2001, p. C1; see also David Leonhardt, "The Boom Was Real. But So Were Its Mirages," *New York Times,* June 9, 2002, p. 4.

226. *"These settlements are"* www.wsj.com, Feb. 9, 2006, and www.aig.com. Press releases.

226. *"AIG was and is"* Ibid.

227. *"Where were these professionals"* *Lincoln Savings & Loan Ass'n* v. *Wall,* 743 F. Supp. 901, at 920 (D.D.C. 1990).

227. *525 savings and loans* Kathleen Kerwin, "For Charlie Keating, The Best Defense Is a Lawsuit," *Business Week,* May 1, 1989; Richard W. Stevenson, "The Justice Department's S. & L. Learning Curve," *New York Times,* Dec. 15, 1991, p. E4; Eric Schine, "Charlie Keating Gets a Taste of L.A. Law," *Business Week,* Oct. 8, 1990, p. 46.

227. *"In Search of the Lost Honest Analyst"* *Fortune,* June 10, 2002, and beneath the caption was the stinging phrase "Her analysts are paid for research, not deals."

227. *sang the praises of the deals* Thomas A. Smith, "Institutions and Entrepreneurs in American Corporate Finance," 85 *California Law Review* 1 (1997); James B. Stewart, *Den of Thieves* (New York: Touchstone, 1991).

228. *Scott Cleland* Charles Gasparino, "Ghosts of E-Mails Continue to Haunt Wall Street," *Wall Street Journal,* Nov. 18, 2002, pp. C1, C13.

228. *"on the edge"* "Why John Olson Wasn't Bullish on Enron," at www.wharton.edu, Feb. 21, 2002, p. 3.

228. *schnuckels* Ibid.

228. *Middle West Utilities* Rebecca Smith, "Enron's Rise and Fall Gives Some Scholars a Sense of Déjà Vu," *Wall Street Journal,* Feb. 4, 2002, p. A1.

229. *Honesty is the best policy* Stephen Taub, "Link Found Between Candor and Share Price," *CFO Magazine,* June 15, 2004, at www.cfo.com.

231. *"Parable of the Sadhu"* 61 *Harvard Business Review* (Sept./Oct. 1983).

233. *Stanley Milgram* 67 *Journal of Abnormal and Social Psychology* (1963).

233. *"When you think of the long"* Ibid., p. 371.

234. *Asch studies remain valid* Solomon Asch in E. E. Maccoby, T. M. Newcomb, and E. L. Hartley, eds., *Readings in Social Psychology* (New York: Holt, Rinehart, & Winston, 1958).

Chapter Eight: Sign #7: Goodness in Some Areas Atones for Evil in Others

238. *"He was not . . . quiet"* Kurt Eicehnwald and Daniel J. Wakin, "The Double Ups and Downs of a Philanthropist," *New York Times,* May 30, 2005, pp. A1, A10.

238. *"long-standing pattern"* Ibid.

238. *pledged an estimated $225 million*   Daniel J. Wakin, "Jail on Fraud Charge for Legendary Opera Patron," *New York Times,* May 28, 2005, pp. A1, A10.

239. *Junior Achievement activities*   Jim Yardley and Sheila K. Dewan, "Despite His Qualms, Scandal Engulfed Executive," *New York Times,* Jan. 27, 2002, p. YNE 27.

239. *His pastor described Mr. Duncan*   Anita Raghavan, "How a Bright Star at Andersen Fell along with Enron," *Wall Street Journal,* May 15, 2002, pp. A1, A8.

239. *"straight arrow"*   From discussions with accounting and finance faculty at Texas A&M.

240. *ideal corporate citizens*   Chris Woodyard, "Pressure to Perform Felt as Problems Hit," *USA Today,* July 1, 2002, p. 3A.

240. *$500 million in a fund drive*   Ibid.

240. *prepared to teach his Sunday-school*   Jayne O'Donnell, "Ebbers Acts as if Nothing Is Amiss," *USA Today,* Sept. 19, 2002, pp. 1B, 2B.

240. *"I just want you to know"*   Jared Sandberg, Deborah Solomon, and Nicole Harris, "World-Com Investigations Shift Focus to Ousted CEO Ebbers," *Wall Street Journal,* July 1, 2002, p. A1.

240. *He teaches at 9:15*   Ibid.

240. *"a wonderful corporate citizen"*   Woodyard, "Pressure to Perform," op. cit., p. 3A.

240. *"This is an example"*   "$5 Million Plan Will Enhance Learning in Underserved Communities," press release, Sept. 21, 1999, at www.worldcom.com.

241. *"The partnership between Brown and MCI WorldCom"*   Ibid.

241. *contributed school kits*   Press release, Sept. 4, 1999, at www.worldcom.com.

241. *great press when natural disasters hit*   Press release, Oct. 1, 1999 (for Hurricane Floyd victims), at www.worldcom.com. This was an ongoing program. See press release, Oct. 23, 1998 (for victims of Central American hurricane), at www.worldcom.

241. *free holiday phone calls*   Press release, Dec. 21, 2001, at www.worldcom.com.

241. *Monterey Jazz Festival*   Press release, Sept. 17, 1999, at www.worldcom.com.

241. *Internet training for all teachers*   Press release, Sept. 19, 1999, at www.worldcom.com. The training, called the Marco Polo program, was free and was praised by both President Clinton and Secretary of Education Richard Riley for the opportunities it opened up to both teachers and students.

241. *voter registration hotlines*   Press release, Mar. 16, 2000, at www.worldcom.com.

239. *turned over its tax credits in Colorado*   Press release, Oct. 23, 1998, at www.worldcom.com.

241. *"Forward thinking organizations"*   Ibid.

241. *"closing the digital divide"*   Ibid.

241. *scholarships*   Press release, Apr. 6, 2000, at www.worldcom.com.

242. *the company gave $35 million*   Mark Maremont and Laurie P. Cohen, "How Tyco's CEO Enriched Himself," *Wall Street Journal,* Aug. 7, 2002, p. A1.

242. *pledged $106 million in Tyco funds*   KevinMcCoy and Gary Strauss, "Kozlowski, Others Accused of Using Tyco as 'Piggy Bank,' " *USA Today,* Sept. 13, 2002, pp. 1B, 2B.

242. *Tyco donated $4.5 million*   Don Halasy, "Why Tyco Boss Fell," *New York Post,* June 9, 2002, at www.nypost.com.

242. *hired the assistant registrar*   Carol Vogel, "Kozlowski's Quest for Entrée into the Art World," *New York Times,* June 6, 2002, pp. C1, C5.

242. *fund-raiser for the New York Botanical Garden*   Ibid.

242. *Kozlowski Athletic Center*   Maremont and Cohen, "How Tyco's CEO Enriched Himself," op. cit., p. A1.

242. *$5 million went to Seton Hall*   Maremont and Cohen, "How Tyco's CEO Enriched Himself," op. cit., p. A1; John Byrne, "Seton Hall of Shame," *Business Week Online,* Sept. 20, 2002, at www.businessweek.com.

243. *Mr. Kozlowski was also generous with his time*   Byrne, "Seton Hall of Shame," op. cit.

243. *coverage in the* Palm Beach Post   Maremont and Cohen, "How Tyco's CEO Enriched Himself," op. cit., p. A6.

243. *donated $1.3 to the Nantucket Conservation Foundation*   McCoy and Strauss, "Kozlowski, Others Accused," op. cit., pp. 1B, 2B; Maremont and Cohen, "How Tyco's CEO Enriched Himself," op. cit., p. A6.

243. *Nantucket Historical Association*   Ibid.

243. *"million-dollar giver" award*   Maremont and Cohen, "How Tyco's CEO Enriched Himself," op. cit., p. A6.

243. *AIDs ribbon on his lapel*   McCoy and Strauss, "Kozlowski, Others Accused," op. cit., p. 2B.

243. *library at Seton Hall*   Byrne, "Seton Hall of Shame," op. cit.

243. *pro bono work for Cornell*   Nicholas Varchaver, "Fall from Grace," *Fortune,* Oct. 28, 2002, p. 118.

244. *Upon his conversion*   Ibid.

244. *"I read your story"*   D. Leonard, "Adelphia," *Fortune,* Aug. 12, 2002, p. 146.

244. *"Thanks for the article"*   Ibid.

244. *one employee who had cancer*   John Schwartz, "In Hometown of Adelphia, Pride, but Worry About the Future, Too," *New York Times,* May 28, 2002, p. C6.

244. *Cable Television Hall of Fame*   Ibid.

244. *"total shock"*   David Lieberman, "Adelphia's Woes 'a Total Shock' to Many," *USA Today,* Apr. 5, 2002, p. 3B.

244. *"Whatever has to be done"*   Ibid.

244. *supporting the local fire department*   Schwartz, "In Hometown of Adelphia," op. cit., p. C1.

244. *decorated two large Christmas trees*   Leonard, "Adelphia," op. cit., p. 138.

245. *theater in Coudersport*   Schwartz, "In Hometown of Adelphia," op. cit., p. C1.

245. *"Because We're Concerned"*   See annual reports for 1999 and 2000, at www.adelphia.com/investors.

245. *Richard M. Scrushy Public Library*   John Helyar, "Insatiable King Richard," *Fortune,* July 7, 2002, p. 80.

245. *weekly Scrushy charity activity*   Ibid.

245. *became agitated when the spotlight was moved*   Reed Abelson and Milt Freudenheim, "The Scrushy Mix: Strict and So Lenient," *New York Times,* Apr. 20, 2003, p. BU12.

245. *Scrushy has been born again*   John Helyar, "Reborn Free?" *Fortune,* Nov. 24, 2003, p. 46.

245. *Leslie Scrushy was equally involved*   Chad Terhune and Carrick Mollenkamp, "Outside Court, Leslie Scrushy Sells Pajamas," *New York Times,* Apr. 17, 2003, p. B1.

246. *Greenberg gave millions to charity*   Elliot Blair Smith, "Scrutiny Tarnishes Legacy of Greenberg," *USA Today,* May 31, 2005, p. 1B.

246. *ran in the best of . . . philanthropic circles*   Daniel Kadlec, "Down . . . But Not Out," *Time,* June 20, 2005, p. 61.

246. *resigned from two nonprofit boards*   Monica Langley and Elizabeth Bernstein, "Greenberg Resigns from Two Nonprofits," *Wall Street Journal,* Apr. 11, 2005, p. B1.

247. *$12.4 billion in co-pays*   Barbara Martinez, "Merck Booked $12.4 Billion It Never Collected," *Wall Street Journal,* July 8, 2002, p. A1.

249. *Seventy-five percent of MBAs*   Mica Schneider, "How an MBA Can Bend Your Mind," *Business Week,* Apr. 1, 2002, p. 12.

Chapter Nine: Applying the Signs for the Future

259. *"Heads will be on the chopping block"*   Program review report, University of Phoenix, PRCN 2003340922254, site visit, Aug. 18, 2003–Aug. 22, 2003.

259. *a "hiccup"*   Williams Symonds, "Back to Earth for Apollo Group?" *Business Week,* Jan. 31, 2005, p. 53.

260. *the $9.8 million in fines*   Eryn Brown, "Can For-Profit Schools Pass an Ethics Test?" *New York Times,* Dec. 12, 2004, p. BU5.

260. *Milken is heavily invested in for-profit education*   Riva D. Atlas, "Milken Sees the Classroom as Profit Center," *New York Times,* Dec. 18, 2004, p. B1.

261. *The Coca-Cola board hired*   Chad Terhune, "How Coke Officials Beefed Up Results of Marketing Test," *Wall Street Journal,* Aug. 20, 2003, pp. B1, B10.

261. The Wall Street Journal *uncovered*   Ibid.

261. *"We are very disappointed"*   Chad Terhune, "Coke Employees Acted Improperly in Marketing Test," *Wall Street Journal,* June 18, 2003, pp. A3, A6.

261. *The settlement requires Coke*   Theresa Howard, "Frozen Coke Deback Settled," *USA Today,* Aug. 4, 2003, p. 4B.

263. *7.6 million U.S. citizens*   U.S. Department of Transportation, 2003 annual report on cruise industry, at www.dot.gov.

263. *Carnival Cruise's net profits*   Douglas Frantz, "For Cruise Ships' Workers, Much Toil, Little Protection," *New York Times,* Dec. 24, 1999, pp. A1, A16.

264. *sexual assaults on cruise ships*   Michael D. Goldhaber, "Ticket to Paradise or a Trip from Hell?" *National Law Journal* 22 (March 1999).

266. *When the Google IPO went forth*   Gary Rivlin, "After Months of Hoopla, Google Debut Fits the Norm," *New York Times,* Aug. 20, 2004, p. C1.

266. *teach* Wall Street *a thing or two*   Kevin Delaney and Robin Sidel, "How Miscalculations and Hubris Hobbled Celebrated Google IPO," *Wall Street Journal,* Aug. 19, 2004, p. A1.

266. *this Ph.D. model will work*   Randall Stross, "What Is Google's Secret Weapon? An Army of Ph.D.s," *New York Times,* June 6, 2004, p. BU3.

267. *earnings of $805.9 million*   Jefferson Graham, "Google Wows Investors with First Results Since IPO," *USA Today,* Oct. 22, 2004, p. 1B.

267. *overvaluing Google*   Saul Hansell, "Rah-Rah, Sis-Boom-Bah for Google! Or Not," *New York Times,* Oct. 23, 2004, p. B1.

267. *Sysco has not had to*   Constance Hays, " Rules Are Loosely Defined in the Food Service Industry," *New York Times,* Mar. 5, 2003, p. C1.

267. *financial arrangements with food distributors*   Constance Hays, "At a Food Distributor, Vendors Often Pay to Play," *New York Times,* Mar. 30, 2003, p. C1.

268. *There is plenty of discretion*   Ken Bowen and Jesse Eisinger, "Sysco Is Pulled into the Shadow over Food Firms," *Wall Street Journal,* Mar. 6, 2003, pp. C1, C3.

268. *Actions filed against Medco*   Form 10-K filed December 25, 2004. See www.sec.gov.

268. *The company is in settlement discussion*   Barbara Martinez, "Medco May Begin Settlement Talks Over U.S. Lawsuits," *Wall Street Journal,* Dec. 6, 2005, p. D6.

268. *Other class-action litigation*   Barbara Martinez, "Medco Is Ordered to Pay $7.8 Million in Ohio Pension Case," *Wall Street Journal,* Dec. 20, 2005, p. B2.

269. *Our long-term strategy*   From the president's letter, 2005 Medco annual report.

269. *double-digit growth in its revenues*   Form 8-K filed April 26, 2005. See www.sec.gov.

271. *"Ms. Boynton was more focused"* Laurie P. Cohen and James Bandler, "Shell Finance Chief Has Faced Critics Before," *Wall Street Journal*, Mar. 26, 2004, pp. C1, C3.

273. *"effectively legislate morality"* George Hager, "Fed Chief Expresses Guarded Optimism," *USA Today*, July 17, 2002, p. 1A.

273. *investors . . . are less likely to question* Robert J. Shiller, "Celebrity CEOs Share the Blame for Street Scandals," *Wall Street Journal*, June 27, 2002, p. A20.

273. *the seeds planted by Nixon* Maureen Dowd, "The Age of Acquiescence," *New York Times*, June 26, 2002, p. A23.

273. *renegades had no market form of regulation* Henry G. Manne, "Bring Back the Hostile Takeover," *Wall Street Journal*, June 26, 2002, p. A18.

274. *Enron had some great ideas* Samuel Bodily and Robert Bruner, "What Enron Did Right," *Wall Street Journal*, Nov. 19, 2001, p. A20.

274. *the piece by Arthur Anderson's CEO* Joe Berardino, "Enron: A Wake-Up Call," *Wall Street Journal*, Dec. 4, 2001, p. A18.

274. *those who wanted to be certain* Don Tapscott, "Enron May Be Dead but the New Economy Isn't," *Wall Street Journal*, Dec. 3, 2001, p. A18.

274. *others found fault with the regulators* Rob Norton, "The Problem with Eliot Spitzer," *Fortune*, July 8, 2002, p. 44.

274. *"Behind the Spitzer Curtain"* Kimberley A. Strassel, *Wall Street Journal*, June 14, 2005, p. A14.

274. *"few bad apple" speeches* David Wessel, "Why the Bad Guys of the Boardroom Emerged en Masse," *Wall Street Journal*, June 20, 2002, pp. A1, A6.

274. *"Everybody did this"* Ibid., p. A6.

274. *Andersen's conviction . . . reversed* Joseph A. Grundfest, "Over Before It Started," *New York Times*, June 14, 2005, p. A21.

275. *"Where are the business leaders?"* Jerry Useem, "From Heroes to Goats and Back Again?" *Fortune*, Nov. 3, 2002, p. 41.

275. *Harvey Pitt indicated . . . a central key* Amy Higgins, "Ethics Called Key to Survival," *Cincinnati Enquirer*, July 18, 2003, from a speech given at the Corporate Responsibility Institute, at www.enquirer.com/editions/2003/07/18/biz_pitt18.html.

276. *Buffet's company stock is up 250 percent* "Was Buffett Right?" *Business Week Online*, Jan. 13, 2003, at www.businessweek.com/o3/02.

277. *Financial-reporting leadership* Richard A. Oppel Jr., "Buffet Deplores Trend of Manipulated Earnings," *New York Times*, Mar. 15, 1999, p. C1.

277. *report on voluntary financial-statement disclosures* *Improving Business Reporting: Insights into Enhancing Voluntary Disclosures* (2001). The report can be accessed at www.fasb.org/brrp/BRRP2.PDF.

277. *benefits of voluntary financial reporting* Ibid., p. 17.

277. *disadvantages of not using voluntary disclosures* Ibid., pp. 17–18.

278. *reporting according to the technical rules* Ibid., p. 19.

278. *disclosures that . . . offer a more forthright picture* Ibid., p. 29.

278. *chemical industry* Ibid., pp. 47, 50.

278. *identification of major customers by logo* Ibid., p. 50.

278. *computer industry* Ibid., p. 52.

278. *food industry* Ibid., p. 56.

278. *pharmaceutical industry* Ibid., pp. 66–68.

279. *textiles and apparel industry* Ibid., p. 77.

279. *"Earnings—trust but verify"*   Joseph Nocera, "System Failure," *Fortune,* June 24, 2002, pp. 62–74.

279. *"If you knew what was in it"*   Suzanne Kapner, "An Auditor (and Target) in Chief," *New York Times,* Mar. 2, 2003, p. BU2.

279. *toll on stock price and the cost of capital*   Christine A. Botosan, "Disclosure Level on the Cost of Equity Capital," 72 *Accounting Review* 323 (1997).

280. *primary cause of compromised ethical standards*   *Preventing Business Fraud* (IOMA, 1999), available at www.iia.org.

280. *second-most-common cause*   Ibid.

280. *dishonesty is pervasive on the golf course*   Del Jones, "Many CEOs Bend the Rules (of Golf)," *USA Today,* June 22, 2002, pp. 1A, 2A.

280. *"can be traced back to Aristotle"*   O. F. Williams and Patrick E. Murphy, "The Ethics of Virtue: A Moral Theory for Marketing," 10 *Journal of Macromarketing* 19 (1990).

282. *virtue standards [table]*   Robert C. Solomon, *A Better Way to Think about Business* (New York: Oxford University Press, 1999), p. 18. See also Kevin J. Shanahan and Michael R. Hyman, "The Development of a Virtue Ethics Scale," 42 *Journal of Business Ethics* 197, 200 (2003).

282. *virtue standards applied to business organizations*   J. Owen Cherrington and David J. Cherrington, "Ethics: A Major Business Problem," *Exchange,* Fall 1989, p. 30.

283. *"Corporate America has got to understand"*   "Bush Scolds Newspapers," Tribune Wire Services, as reported in The *Chicago Tribune,* June 29, 2002, pp. A1, A24.

283. *"situations for testing business morality"*   Laura Nash, "Ethics Without the Sermon," 59 *Harvard Business Review* 79 (Nov./Dec. 1981), p. 88.

284. *"resort to unadmirable accounting stratagems"*   Louis Uchtelle, "Corporate Profits Are Tasty, but Artificially Flavored," *New York Times,* Mar. 28, 1999, p. BU4.

284. *AOL Time Warner*   Geraldine Fabrikant, "Time Warner Settles 2 Cases Over AOL Unit," *New York Times,* Dec. 16, 2004, p. C1. Carol Loomis, "Why AOL's Accounting Problems Keep Popping Up," *Fortune,* Apr. 28, 2003, pp. 85–89.

284. *Aura Systems*   www.sec.gov; EDGAR database; company 10-Ks.

284. *Computer Associates International*   Steve Hamm, "Computer Associates: Clearing a Cloud," *BusinessWeek,* Nov. 21, 2005, pp. 70–71.

284. *Dollar General Merchandise*   www.sec.gov; EDGAR database; company 10-K.

284. *Dynegy Energy*   Rebecca Smith, "Dynegy to Pay $468 Million to Settle Shareholder Lawsuit," *Wall Street Journal,* Apr. 18, 2005, p. C1.

284. *Elan Pharmaceuticals*   In re Elan Securities Litigation, 385 F. Supp.2d 363 (S.D.N.Y. 2005).

284. *Global Crossing*   Gretchen Morgenson, "Global Crossing Settles for $325 Million," *New York Times,* Mar. 20, 2004, p. B1.

284. *Halliburton*   Floyd Norris, "Halliburton Settles S.E.C. Accusations," *New York Times,* Aug. 4, 2004, p. C1.

284. *HPL Technologies*   SEC Complaint, filed against former CEO for fraud, 2002.

284. *Kmart*   Constance L. Hays, "Kmart Reveals the Discovery of New Errors in Its Accounts," *New York Times,* Dec. 10, 2002, p. C11.

284. *Nesco*   GAO Report "Financial Statement Restatements: Trends, Market Impacts, Regulatory Response, and Remaining Challenges," GAO-03-138 (2003).

284. *Qwest*   Andrew Backover, "Write-down by Qwest Grows to $40.8 Billion," *USA Today,* Oct. 29, 2002, p. 1B.

284. *Reliant Energy*   GAO Report "Financial Statement Restatements: Trends, Market Impacts, Regulatory Response, and Remaining Challenges," GAO-03-138 (2003).

284. *Xerox*   Gary Stoller, "Funny Numbers," *USA Today,* Oct. 21, 2002, p. 3B.

Index

decision making, 232–33, 279–82
    virtue standards and, 280–81
deference
    toward CEOs, 123, 126, 155–56
    toward iconic reporters, 121
Department of Education (DOE), Apollo
    Group and, 258–60
disclosure, 81, 104
    Adelphia's 8-k, 161
    companies engaging in full, 276–77
    for director independence, 164
    financial reporting, 275
    loan, lack of, 158
    SEC fines, conflict of interest and, 144,
        183–84
    voluntary, 276–79
dissent, 59, 78–79, 140, 162, 169–71, 235–36
    importance of, 79, 122
diversification, 229
DOE. See Department of Education
Dollar General Merchandise, 284
dot-com era, 124, 178, 179, 211
dummy bids, 99–100
Duncan, David, 29–30, 188, 195, 239
Dunlap, Al, 22
Dutch auction, Google's, 266

earnings. See also financial engineering;
        financial reporting
    managing, 24, 113
    overstatements of, 2, 21–22, 23, 26, 34, 42,
        48, 121, 210–11, 223
    predictions for, 141
    restatements of, xii, 2, 21–22, 23, 26, 31–32,
        48, 121, 210–11, 284
earnings per share (EPS), working backward
        from, 28
Ebbers, Bernard J., 206
    board members and, 152–54
    IPO/Smith Barney and, 192–93
    personal loans of, 192
    termination/severance of, 156
EBITDA (earnings before interest, taxes,
        depreciation, and amortization), 111,
        113, 211–12
    birth of, 211–12
    new economy and, 274
economy
    EBITDA in new, 274
    Holland's, 224

ego
    charity and, 247
    social issues and, 251
Elan Pharmaceuticals, 284
electric utility industry, EMF/cancer issue of,
    80
electromagnetic field (EMF), utility's
    handling of, 80
emails, 34, 35
embezzlement
    deadlocked jury on Tyco's, 160
    rationalization for, 72, 237–38
EMF. See electromagnetic field
employee(s)
    on adultery, 133
    affidavits of, 155
    anonymity of, 81, 84
    board access of, 169–71, 174–75, 263
    conflict policies and, 199–200
    ethics training/recognition of, 89–90, 94
    fear/silence of, 7, 54–55, 59–70, 78–79,
        95
    feedback/reporting, 81–82, 83–84, 96, 109,
        140, 169–71, 263
    filing suit, 155
    flatlining of, 87
    iconic CEOs and, 98, 100
    management and, 170, 174
    questions to be asked by, determining
        ethical culture, 82–83
    rewarding, 89–90
    seven signs and, 7
    termination of, 64, 69, 85–86, 87, 93, 210,
        261
    time-out for, 57–58
    transfer of, silence and, 87–88
    wisdom of, 95
enforcement, 51, 52–53
    of conflict of interest policies, 196–97,
        199–200
engineering
    financial, 39
    resilience, 230
Enron, 26–29, 103–4, 212–13
    analysts and, 228
    board of, 141–52
    code of ethics, waiving, 147–48
    conflict of interest in, 189
    employee silence/fear at, 61–66
    NPOs and, 239

reporting
crank, 83
by employees, 81–82, 263
financial, 26, 42, 43, 208–9, 273–76
reserves, overstatements of, 3, 11, 49, 74–75
resilience engineering, 230
restructuring charge, Worldcom's use of, 24
results v. values, 283
return on equity (ROE), 5, 148
return on investment (ROI), 41
revenue
compensation tied to, 268
numbers pressure and, 18
overstatement of, 186, 247, 284
revenue recognition, fraud and, 18
revenue target, working backwards from, 26, 43
Rigas, John, 111–15
sentence of, 114
spending/personal assets of, 161
Rittenhouse Rankings survey, 229
ROE. *See* return on equity
ROI. *See* return on investment
role models, 134
Royal Dutch/Shell Group, 3, 11, 74–75, 271

Saks Fifth Avenue
chargebacks of, 50, 51
new board of, 169
sales, false, 22–23, 42, 159
Salomon Smith Barney (SSB), 179
SEC settlement of, 180
Worldcom and, 192–93
Sarbanes-Oxley Act (SOX), xi, 4, 228
on auditing/consulting, 29, 184–86
boards and, 138
conflict of interest/stock price and, 140
EBITDA and, 212
Wal-Mart and, 86
Scalia, Antonin, 200–201
Scott, Lee, 86
Scrushy, Richard M., 31–34, 191–92, 214–15
autocracy of, 73–74
management team of, 115
personal assets of, 116
philanthropy of, 245
trial/acquittal of, 215
SEC. *See* Securities Exchange Commission
Securities Exchange Commission (SEC)
1997–2002 investigations by, 18

acts of, 228–29
AIG settlement with, 226
AOL and, 267
Apollo/DOE and, 258–60
CIT group and, 158
Citigroup rebates and, 199
Coke and, 8–9
conflict of interest fines of, 144, 183–84
HealthSouth and, 215
Kmart and, 50
Merck and, 247
MMC and, 35
Shell's settlement with, 271
on soft dollars, 182–83
SSB and, 180
Tyco and, 71, 109, 158
Worldcom and, 156
Xerox and, 48
self image, 53, 205, 206–7, 208, 209, 220
self-dealing, of iconic CEOs, 160, 161
settlement
ADT/SEC/Tyco, 158
AIG/SEC, 226
Apollo/SEC, 260
Citigroup/SEC, 199
Coke/SEC, 8–9
HealthSouth/SEC, 215
Shell/SEC, 271
SSB/SEC, 180
Tyco's New Hampshire securities, 159
Xerox/SEC, 48
share ownership, 154–55
shareholders
revolt of, over Tyco, 159–60
takeover by, 273
share-price performance, 229
Shell Group/Royal Dutch, 3, 74–75, 271
shock experiments, 233–35
shortsellers, 148
Sidgmore, John, 157
silence, 70–74, 87–89, 99, 118, 122–23, 264
antidotes for fear and, 80–96, *97*
Enron employees' fear and, 61–66
60 Minutes II
Rather/Mapes story on, 119–21
Skilling, Jeffrey, 103, 205
social issues, 248–49
ego and, 251
focus on/numbers and, 264
GM focus on, 253

Acknowledgments

There is a devilish part of me that wants to thank the scoundrels and the companies they ran. And so the infamous Oscar line, "Without them, I would be nothing." When yet another business scandal emerges, now a full five years out from Enron, I am sad. But as my father says, "Yes, but it's good for your business."

The better part of me has a heart that aches for the young children whose once high-flying executive fathers will spend a decade away from them. Too many children will go for years without their corporate mothers' kisses at bedtime. My heart even aches for these fathers and mothers who committed, in all, just about every white-collar federal felony out there (and some new ones thanks to misconduct post–Sarbanes-Oxley). There was no one around to save them from themselves. My hope is that the history and insights I offer here can curb rogues or halt bad judgment by good people under pressure. I'd settle for companies adopting just some of my antidotes to rein in the mothers and fathers before they turn into amoral technicians.

Those antidotes are not mine. They have come from years of the privilege of interacting with companies and the executives and employees in them who care about capitalism. They know that at the heart of capitalism is trust and at the heart of trust is ethics. So many decent and good people in business work tirelessly each day to create cultures that reward good and jettison evil. I have learned much from the executives at Boeing and Coca-Cola as they have worked to recover from ethical setbacks. I have had the opportunity to learn as professional organizations such as the Institute of Internal Auditors, CFA Institute, AICPA, and the Institute for Professionals in Taxation have taken unacceptable behavior among their members and insisted upon ethical rebirth. I am also grateful for the many companies and organizations with the courage to have me in to talk with their employees and members in my usual frank and unrestrained manner: AES, the Association of Government Accountants, AstraZeneca, Auditors General in California and Arizona, Arizona Society of CPAs, Banking Associations around the country, Bell Helicopter, Blue Cross Blue Shield, Cendant, the Defense Contract Audit Industry, DuPont, Edward Jones, the Food Marketing Institute, Glacier Bancorp, the Health Care Compliance Association, Hy-Vee, the Institute for Manufacturers' Representatives, the Institute for Nuclear Power Operators, the Manufacturers' Alliance, Maricopa

County Community College, Mattel, the National League of Cities, Pacific Steel and Recycling, Pima Community College, PRG Schultz, Raytheon, Steptoe and Johnson, VIAD, Wells Fargo, Yellow Transportation, and many city, county, and state governments and municipal leagues including those in Maine, Colorado, Minnesota, South Dakota, Tallahassee, Tennessee, Texas, Utah, and so many others. No company or organization is perfect, but half the battle in creating an ethical culture is a willingness to embrace candor. And I am candid. I've said to many of these companies and organizations, "You got guts to have me in." These companies and organizations have given me direct interaction at the front line. Their openness and efforts to be better at this ethics stuff inspired my writing and antidotes.

I have written many books, but this was my most challenging. I needed help. I got it. Ethan Friedman was my original editor at St. Martin's who had faith in this book's potential and great patience with its rebellious author. Ethan never would have laid eyes on the manuscript had it not been for the work of my agency, Venture Literary. I have the privilege of being guided through and touted in the publishing world by a former student, Greg Dinkin. It is a professor's dream come true to be taught by a student. Ethan and Greg showed wisdom beyond their years in dealing with me. I hate it when the young 'uns know more and are right. Ellis Levine provided an insightful and patient review of the manuscript. I would say I want to be like Ellis when I grow up, but I believe I am his elder. He is the consummate professional.

I had great technical support from Jenness Crawford in New York and Terry Jennings, my husband, in Mesa, Arizona. Jenness handled manuscript deliveries and questions. Terry kept the technology working at home. From printers to laptops, he is the go-to guy. And he was the guy who married me when all I had was a couple of degrees and two thousand dollars in student loans. He has been there with me during bar exams, childbirth, and books. The first two were easier on us both.

My four children know books and my "little ethics class," as they refer to it, as an integral part of life. They are patient with deadlines and a too-often distracted mother. They are willing to have our interactions on ethics shared with a world hungry for drawing lines and an understanding of the difference between right and wrong. Sarah, Claire, Sam, and John are inspirational and instructional, on a daily basis.

Finally, I am indebted to my parents, who taught me right from wrong. My degrees were superficial knowledge compared to their instruction and example. My mother passed away just as this book went into production. I miss her, but her legacy lives. She gave me that bright line between right and wrong, a line that was once so clear in our lives and in business. Too many forgot. But, Mom, I didn't. I hope I can help others as much as you and Dad helped me. This one's for you.